Lecture Notes in Computer Science 10815

Commenced Publication in 1973
Founding and Former Series Editors:
Gerhard Goos, Juris Hartmanis, and Jan van Leeuwen

T0226211

More information about this series at http://www.springer.com/series/7410

Junfeng Fan · Benedikt Gierlichs (Eds.)

Constructive Side-Channel Analysis and Secure Design

9th International Workshop, COSADE 2018
Singapore, April 23–24, 2018
Proceedings

 Springer

Editors
Junfeng Fan
Open Security Research
Shenzhen
China

Benedikt Gierlichs ⓘ
KU Leuven
Leuven
Belgium

ISSN 0302-9743   ISSN 1611-3349 (electronic)
Lecture Notes in Computer Science
ISBN 978-3-319-89640-3   ISBN 978-3-319-89641-0   (eBook)
https://doi.org/10.1007/978-3-319-89641-0

Library of Congress Control Number: 2018939449

LNCS Sublibrary: SL4 – Security and Cryptology

Printed on acid-free paper

This Springer imprint is published by the registered company Springer International Publishing AG
part of Springer Nature
The registered company address is: Gewerbestrasse 11, 6330 Cham, Switzerland

Preface

The 9th International Workshop on Constructive Side-Channel Analysis and Secure Design (COSADE) was held at Nanyang Technological University in Singapore during April 23–24, 2018. The workshop was held in cooperation with the International Association for Cryptologic Research (IACR). COSADE brings together researchers from academia, industry, and government who share a common interest in the design and secure implementation of cryptographic primitives. COSADE 2018 received 31 submissions. Each paper was anonymously reviewed by at least four Program Committee members in a double-blind peer review process. The review process relied on the EasyChair system. From the pool of submissions, 14 high-quality papers were selected carefully after deliberations by the 30 Program Committee members who were supported by 45 additional reviewers. The composition of the Program Committee was representative of the good mix between academic and industrial researchers, the geographic spread of researchers across the globe, and their expertise. We would like to express our sincere gratitude to both the Program Committee members and the reviewers for their hard work. We would also like to thank the invited speakers Jeroen Delvaux and Emmanuel Prouff for joining us in Singapore and for delivering inspiring talks. Finally, we would like to thank the local organizers Shivam Bhasin, Michael Kasper, and Marc Stöttinger for their support and for making this great event possible. On behalf of the COSADE community we are very grateful to our sponsors Alpha-NOV, Continental, eshard, NewAE, Riscure, Secure-IC, Cryptography Research, Nanyang Technological University, for their financial support. And most importantly, we would like to thank the authors for their excellent contributions. Without them this workshop would not exist.

April 2018   Junfeng Fan
                                                                 Benedikt Gierlichs

Organization

Program Committee

Zhimin Chen	Apple, USA
Christophe Clavier	Université de Limoges, France
Elke De Mulder	Cryptography Research, Inc., USA
Hermann Drexler	G+D Mobile Security, Germany
Junfeng Fan	Open Security Research (OSR), China
Benoit Feix	Eshard, France
Wieland Fischer	Infineon Technologies, Germany
Benedikt Gierlichs	KU Leuven imec-COSIC, Belgium
Christophe Giraud	IDEMIA, France
Xu Guo	Qualcomm, USA
Naofumi Homma	Tohoku University, Japan
Michael Hutter	Cryptography Research, USA
Markus Kuhn	University of Cambridge, UK
Kerstin Lemke-Rust	Bonn-Rhein-Sieg University of Applied Sciences, Germany
Tancrède Lepoint	SRI International, USA
Yang Li	Nanjing University of Aeronautics and Astronautics, China
Roel Maes	Intrinsic-ID, The Netherlands
Stefan Mangard	TU Graz, Austria
Marcel Medwed	NXP Semiconductors Austria GmbH, Austria
Amir Moradi	Ruhr University Bochum, Germany
Debdeep Mukhopadhyay	IIT Kharagpur, India
Elisabeth Oswald	University of Bristol, UK
Thomas Peyrin	Nanyang Technological University, Singapore
Axel Y. Poschmann	DarkMatter, Abu Dhabi, UAE
Emmanuel Prouff	ANSSI, France
Francesco Regazzoni	ALaRI – USI, Switzerland
Oscar Reparaz	KU Leuven imec-COSIC, Belgium and Square Inc., USA
Matt Robshaw	Impinj, USA
Kazuo Sakiyama	The University of Electro-Communications, Japan
Patrick Schaumont	Virginia Tech, USA
Alexander Schlösser	NXP Semiconductors, Germany
Brecht Wyseur	Kudelski Group, Switzerland

Additional Reviewers

Manaar Alam
Anubhab Baksi
Subhadeep Banik
Guillaume Barbu
Debapriya Basu Roy
Alberto Battistello
Begül Bilgin
Manuel Bluhm
Martin Butkus
Nicolas Debande
Santos Merino Del Pozo
Christoph Dobraunig
Dahmun Goudarzi
Hannes Gross
Max Hoffmann
Mustafa Kairallah
Elif Bilge Kavun
Bodhisatwa Mazumdar
Florian Mendel
Xiaohan Meng
Oliver Mischke
Nicolas Moro
Ventzi Nikov

Sikhar Patranabis
Peter Pessl
Léo Reynaud
Bastian Richter
Sayandeep Saha
Hermann Seuschek
Rémi Strullu
Takeshi Sugawara
Atsushi Takayasu
Adrian Thillard
Michael Tunstall
Rei Ueno
Thomas Unterluggauer
Vincent Verneuil
Karine Villegas
Ruyang Wang
Shuang Wang
Felix Wegener
Antoine Wurcker
Mo Yang
Yuan Yao
Ville Yli-Mäyry

Contents

Countermeasures Against Side-Channel Attacks (2)

Countermeasures Against Side-Channel Attacks (1)

Secure Multiplication for Bitslice Higher-Order Masking: Optimisation and Comparison

Dahmun Goudarzi[1,2]($\boxtimes$), Anthony Journault[3]($\boxtimes$), Matthieu Rivain[1], and François-Xavier Standaert[3]

[1] CryptoExperts, Paris, France
{dahmun.goudarzi,matthieu.rivain}@cryptoexperts.com
[2] ENS, CNRS, INRIA and PSL Research University, Paris, France
[3] ICTEAM/ELEN/Crypto Group, Université catholique de Louvain, Louvain-la-Neuve, Belgium
{anthony.journault,fstandae}@uclouvain.be

Abstract. In this paper, we optimize the performances and compare several recent masking schemes in bitslice on 32-bit arm devices, with a focus on multiplication. Our main conclusion is that efficiency (or randomness) gains always come at a cost, either in terms of composability or in terms of resistance against horizontal attacks. Our evaluations should therefore allow a designer to select a masking scheme based on implementation constraints and security requirements. They also highlight the increasing feasibility of (very) high-order masking that are offered by increasingly powerful embedded devices, with new opportunities of high-security devices in various contexts.

1 Introduction

Nowadays, higher-order masking is one of the soundest approaches to protect the implementation of a block cipher against side-channel attacks. Recent studies have shown that the bitslice implementation strategy can provide the best performances in software [DPV01, BGRV15, GR17, JS17]. This strategy allows to perform parallel evaluations of a Boolean circuit where the logical gates are replaced by instructions working on registers of several bits. Then, higher-order masking is applied at the Boolean level, where the linear gates become linear instructions working on registers and non-linear gates become calls to secure bitwise non-linear operations.

Since secure non-linear operations are quadratic in the masking order d (whereas for linear operation the cost is in $O(d)$), their evaluation is the main bottleneck for implementers. In the past couple of years, several multiplication schemes have been proposed in the literature offering different tradeoffs between security (*e.g.*, in terms of composability or resistance against so-called horizontal attacks) and performances (timings, randomness requirements).

© Springer International Publishing AG, part of Springer Nature 2018
J. Fan and B. Gierlichs (Eds.): COSADE 2018, LNCS 10815, pp. 3–22, 2018.
https://doi.org/10.1007/978-3-319-89641-0_1

One of the most popular algorithms is the so-called ISW multiplication scheme introduced in the seminal work of Ishai, Sahai and Wagner at Crypto 2003 [ISW03]. It provides composable security captured by the notion of *Strong Non Interference* (SNI). Based on this construction, Belaïd *et al.* proposed at Eurocrypt 2016 [BBP+16] a variant with randomness savings at the cost of only satisfying the (weaker) *Non Interference* (NI) notion. At CHES 2016, Battistello *et al.* [BCPZ16] went the other way by proposing not only SNI security but also improved resistance against horizontal attacks, at the cost of increased randomness requirements. Eventually, at Eurocrypt 2017, Barthe *et al.* introduced an alternative approach to the ISW-based multiplications. This approach is optimized for parallel implementations such as bitslicing and handles registers that hold all the shares of a given bit. It also comes with different security risks in terms of assumptions. Namely, storing the shares of a single bit potentially allows better resistance against shares re-combinations due to transitions [CGP+12, BGG+14], while leading to higher risks of re-combinations due to couplings [CBG+17]. Journault and Standaert [JS17] compared this new approach with the ISW approach for the AES S-box implemented by Goudarzi and Rivain [GR17], showing that for the optimal case, *i.e.* the masking order is equal to the size of the register, Barthe *et al.*'s approach slightly outperforms ISW multiplication. However, no comparison has been made with other masking orders.

In this paper, we aim to optimize and compare these different masking schemes, in order to better understand the performance gains and overheads that correspond to their different security guarantees. For this purpose, we first try to increase the efficiency of these four schemes, not only at the algorithmic level, but also by taking into account the implementation perspective and possible implementation tricks. We also propose an efficient way to evaluate the Barthe *et al.* multiplication when the masking order is lower than the architecture's size. Subsequently, we propose a comparison regarding different aspects such as timing cost, memory overhead, randomness usage and the given security level for each of these multiplications. Ultimately, the goal of this paper is therefore to provide insight to designers and developers who wish to protect efficiently a block cipher with higher-order masking (*i.e.*, which multiplication scheme to use depending on their needs, depending on their hardware limitations or security requirements).

This paper is organized as follows. Section 2 gives some preliminaries on bitslice higher-order masking and security notions. We then introduce in Sect. 3 the four multiplications studied and discuss the proposed optimization either at the algorithmic level or for the implementation prospective. Section 4 presents the two refresh mask algorithms (ISW and Barthe *et al.* based) that are needed when implementing a block cipher. Finally, Sect. 5 describes our implementations and the obtained performances to compare the multiplications as well as the refreshing procedures.

The code source of all our implementations is available on Github [GJRS18] under the GPL licence (v3).

2 Preliminaries

2.1 Bitsliced Higher-Order Masking

One of the most studied countermeasure against said-channel attacks is *masking*, a.k.a. *secret sharing*. It consists in splitting a secret value x into d shares $x_1, x_2, \ldots, x_d$ satisfying

$$x = x_1 \oplus x_2 \oplus \cdots \oplus x_d$$

where $x_2, \cdots, x_d$ are randomly distributed and x_1 is computed accordingly. The parameter d is then called the *masking order*.

Recently, bitslicing has been shown to give excellent performances for block cipher implementations protected with masking in software [GR17, JS17]. The bitslice implementation strategy is to perform parallel evaluations of a Boolean circuit where the logic gates are replaced by instructions working on registers of several bits. In the context of masked implementations of block ciphers, this strategy is applied to speed up the evaluations of S-boxes, which are then computed in parallel. Each XOR gate in the underlying Boolean circuit gives rise to d bitwise XOR instructions and each AND gate is replaced by a secure bitwise AND operation based on a secure multiplication scheme such as the ones studied in this paper.

2.2 Security Notions

In the following we informally recall the different security models usually considered in the side-channel community, starting from the abstract probing model (NI/SNI security), then the intermediate bounded moment model and finally the practical noisy leakage model.

At Crypto 2003, Ishai, Sahai and Wagner introduced in their seminal paper [ISW03] the so-called *probing model*. In this model, the adversary is allowed to probe a limited number of wires in a target (protected) circuit. If no adversary is able to recover secret information using up to t probes, the circuit is said to be *t-probing secure*. In their paper, the authors show how to achieve t-probing security using masking of order $d = 2t + 1$. It was later shown that a t-probing secure multiplication can be obtained with $d = t + 1$ shares [RP10] but this approach might result in some security flaws while composing several masked operations without proper mask refreshing [CPRR14]. The stronger notion of SNI has then been introduced in [BBD+16]: it allows to prove t-probing security with only $d = t + 1$ shares for the composition of several gadgets. In particular, any masked circuit composed of t-SNI secure gadgets is also t-SNI secure (and therefore t-probing secure).

Next, the bounded moment model was introduced in [BDF+17] as a relaxation of the probing model in order to capture parallel implementations of masking schemes where all the shares might be contained in a single register and processed in a single cycle (which is hardly captured with the probing model). The idea of the bounded moment model is to look at the higher-order moments to get a security parameter (since the security of a masked implementation usually comes from the need to evaluate higher-order statistical moments).

Eventually, the noisy leakage model was introduced by Prouff and Rivain in [PR13] and reflects concrete adversaries who obtain an intermediate value perturbed by a noisy leakage function. This is a more realistic side-channel model as this is typically what an attacker can recover from a side-channel analysis. Masking can be formally shown to be a sound countermeasure in such a model since the information revealed on a variable x by noisy leakages on the shares x_1, ..., x_d decreases exponentially with the masking order d [CJRR99, PR13]. The latter model is in general more tricky to manipulate, but is strictly needed to evaluate security against so-called horizontal attacks, where the repeated manipulation of the shares enable to get rid of a part of the noise as the masking order d grows. Under the condition of sufficient noise and independence, security in the noisy leakage model is implied by probing security [DDF14].

2.3   ARMv7 Architectures

We made our implementation in the generic ARM v7 assembly language. Most of the ARM processors are composed of 16 registers of 32 bits, ranging from $R0$ to $R15$: registers $R0$ to $R12$ are known as variable registers and are available for computation. The three last registers are usually reserved for special purposes: $R13$ is used as the stack pointer (SP), $R14$ is the link register (LR) storing the return address during a function call, and $R15$ is the program counter (PC).

The ARM instruction set is essentially composed of three classes (summarized in Table 1): the data instructions which performs arithmetic operations on the register, the memory instructions which allows to load and store data and the branching instructions which are used for loops, conditional statements and function calls. One important feature of the ARM assembly is the *barrel shifter* allowing any data instruction to shift one of its operands at no extra cost in terms of clock cycles. However to fully benefit from its efficiency, the rotation offset for the barrel shifter needs to be defined with immediate values instead of registers.

Table 1. ARM instructions.

Class	Examples	Clock cycles
Data instructions	EOR, ADD, SUB, AND, MOV	1
Memory instructions	LDR, STR / LDM, STM	3 or $n + 2$
Branching instructions	B, BX, BL	3 or 4

Eventually, we assume that our target architecture include a True Random Number Generator (TRNG), that frequently fills a register with a fresh 32-bit random string. We consider two different settings for this TRNG: the setting of [GR17] where one needs to wait 10 clock cycles to get a new random string;

and the one of [JS17] where one needs to wait 80 clock cycles to get a new random string. The TRNG register can then be read at the cost of a single load instruction.

3 Secure Multiplications

In this section we describe optimized low-level implementations of the four following secure multiplications:

ISW (Ishai-Sahai-Wagner, Crypto'03): probing secure multiplication,
BDF$^+$ (Barthe *et al.*, Eurocrypt'17): bounded-moment secure multiplication,
BBP$^+$ (Belaïd *et al.*, Eurocrypt'16): ISW gadget with randomness saving,
BCPZ (Battistello *et al.*, CHES'16): ISW gadget with additional refreshing.

Each multiplication is described at the algorithmic level and at the implementation level (with possible implementation tricks). We further give implementation results (clock cycles and code size) in the first TRNG setting. The four schemes are then compared in terms of performances, randomness consumption, and security guarantees in Sect. 5 in both TRNG settings.

3.1 ISW: the Standard Probing-Secure Multiplication

At Crypto 2003, Ishai, Sahai and Wagner [ISW03] proposed an algorithm to securely compute an AND gate for any number of shares d, the so-called ISW multiplication is described in Algorithm 1. They also introduced the probing model and proved that their multiplication has a security order $t = \lfloor (d-1)/2 \rfloor$ in this model. The security proof was extended to the order $t = d - 1$ in [RP10] and to the stronger t-SNI property in [BBD+16], both extensions assuming independent input sharings.

Algorithm 1. ISW (Ishai-Sahai-Wagner, Crypto'03)

Input: sharings $(a_1, \ldots, a_d) \in \{0,1\}^{32 \times d}$ and $(b_1, \ldots, b_d) \in \{0,1\}^{32 \times d}$
Output: sharing $(c_1, \ldots, c_d) \in \{0,1\}^{32 \times d}$ such that $\bigoplus_i c_i = (\bigoplus_i a_i) \wedge (\bigoplus_j b_j)$

1. **for** $i = 1$ to d **do**
2. $c_i \leftarrow a_i \wedge b_i$
3. **end for**
4. **for** $i = 1$ to d **do**
5.   **for** $j = i + 1$ to d **do**
6. $s \leftarrow \{0,1\}^{32}$
7. $s' \leftarrow (s \oplus (a_i \wedge b_j)) \oplus (a_j \wedge b_i)$
8. $c_i \leftarrow c_i \oplus s$
9. $c_j \leftarrow c_j \oplus s'$
10.   **end for**
11. **end for**
12. **return** $(c_1, \ldots, c_d)$

From two sharings $(a_1, \ldots, a_d)$ and $(b_1, \ldots, b_d)$, the ISW multiplication simply computes all the d^2 crossed products $a_i \cdot b_j$ which are then summed in d new shares c_i with new random elements $r_{i,j}$. Each new random element is involved twice in the new shares implying $\bigoplus_i c_i = \bigoplus_{i,j} a_i \cdot b_j = (\bigoplus_i a_i) \cdot (\bigoplus_j b_j)$. The ISW scheme is pictured in Algorithm 1 for the bitwise setting, where $\wedge$ and $\oplus$ denote the (32-bit) bitwise AND and XOR.

From the implementation viewpoint, we follow the work of [GR17] and implement the scheme without any particular implementation trick for any masking order d. In order to push forward the optimization, we also propose a version of the code where the nested loops are unrolled for specific values of d, namely when d is a power of 2. The performances of our low-levels implementations are summarized in Table 2. We observe that unrolling the loops allows us to save 15% to 23% clock cycles with an overhead factor from 3 to 200 for the code size. The only case where the unrolling fully benefits in both time and memory is for $d = 2$.

Table 2. Implementation results for the ISW multiplication

	Clock cycles					Code size (bytes)					Register usage	Random usage
d	2	4	8	16	32	2	4	8	16	32		
Straight ISW	75	291	1155	4611	18435	164	164	164	164	164	10	$d(d-1)/2$
Unrolled ISW	58	231	949	3876	15682	132	464	1848	7500	30324	8	$d(d-1)/2$

3.2 BDF$^+$: a Bounded-Moment Secure Multiplication

At Eurocrypt 2017, Barthe *et al.* introduced a new way to compute a secure multiplication specifically tailored for the bitwise context (*i.e.* for bitslice implementations) [BDF+17]. Their scheme handles registers holding all the shares of a given bit whereas in traditional ISW-based scheme, the shares of a variable are stored in different registers for security reasons. Nevertheless, Barthe *et al.* show that their multiplication is secure in the relaxed bounded moment model, which is argued to be sound in practice.

Intuitively the BDF$^+$ multiplication can be decomposed in different steps: the loading of the input shares a and b; the computation of the partial products between a and b; the loading of fresh randomness r; and the compression phase where these partial products are XORed all together and separated by the fresh randomness.

Its implementation is especially efficient when the number of shares d is equal to the size of the registers in the target architecture. This has been shown in [JS17] for the case $d = 32$. However, a question left open in the latter work is the scenario where the number of shares mismatches the register size. This issue is addressed hereafter.

For this purpose, we generalize the BDF$^+$ algorithm to a scenario where d can be lower than the register size. We propose a parallel version of this algorithm in which several sharings are stored in a register (*e.g.* 4 sharings of order $d = 8$

in one 32-bit register) and we describe an efficient way to perform sharing-wise rotations to keep good performances in such a non-optimal scenario. The main restriction is that our generalization only works for masking order that are power of 2 (so that the sharing size divides the register size), including the case $d = 2$ which was not taken into account in the original publication. The optimized BDF$^+$ multiplication is described in Algorithm 2.

Algorithm 2. BDF$^+$ (Barthe *et al.*, Eurocrypt'17)

Input: shares $a = (a_1, \cdots, a_d) \in \{0,1\}^{32}$, shares $b = (b_1, \cdots, b_d) \in \{0,1\}^{32}$
Output: shares $c = (c_1, \cdots, c_d) \in \{0,1\}^{32}$

1. $x_1 \leftarrow a \wedge b$
2. $r \leftarrow \{0,1\}^{32}$
3. $y_1 \leftarrow x_1 \oplus r$
4. **if** $d = 2$ **then**
5. $x_2 \leftarrow a \wedge \mathsf{ROT}(b, 1)$
6. $y_2 \leftarrow y_1 \oplus x_2$
7. $c \leftarrow y_2 \oplus \mathsf{ROT}(r, 1)$
8. **else**
9.   **for** $i = 1$ **to** $d/2 - 1$ **do**
10.   **if** $i \mod 2 = 0$ **then**
11. $r \leftarrow \{0,1\}^{32}$
12.   **end if**
13. $x_{2i} \leftarrow a \wedge \mathsf{ROT}(b, i)$
14. $x_{2i+1} \leftarrow \mathsf{ROT}(a, i) \wedge b$
15. $y_{3i-1} \leftarrow y_{3i-2} \oplus x_{2i}$
16. $y_{3i} \leftarrow y_{3i-1} \oplus x_{2i+1}$
17. $y_{3i+1} \leftarrow y_{3i} \oplus \mathsf{ROT}(r, i \mod 2)$
18.   **end for**
19. $x_d \leftarrow a \wedge \mathsf{ROT}(b, d/2)$
20. $c \leftarrow y_{3\lfloor(d-1)/2\rfloor+1} \oplus x_d$
21. **end if**
22. **return** c

Encoding. In order to make full use of the register when d is less than 32 (*i.e.* d is not equal to the architecture size), but d is a power of 2, we fill the input registers with $k = 32/d$ words of d shares. We thus process k secure multiplications in parallel. More specifically, let us denote $w_0, \ldots, w_{31}$ the bits of a 32-bit register w (from MSB to LSB). For $d = 16$, w encodes 2 secret bits z_0 and z_1 such that $\bigoplus_{i=0}^{15} w_i = z_0$ and $\bigoplus_{i=16}^{31} w_i = z_1$. For $d = 8$, w encodes 4 secret bits z_0, z_1, z_2 and z_3 such that $\bigoplus_{i=0}^{7} w_i = z_0$ and $\bigoplus_{i=8}^{15} w_i = z_1$ and $\bigoplus_{i=16}^{23} w_i = z_2$ and $\bigoplus_{i=24}^{31} w_i = z_3$, and so on.

Efficient Sharing-Wise Rotation. Algorithm 2 can directly be applied on multi-sharing input registers. The only operation which needs to be modified accordingly is the rotation $\mathsf{ROT}(w, i)$. We propose an efficient low-level implementation for such a sharing-wise rotation. Our method relies on the observation that applying an i-bit rotation to every d-bit chunck in a word w can be obtained by the following equation:

$$\mathsf{ROT}(w, i) = \big((w \ll i) \wedge \mathsf{mask}_{d,i}\big) \oplus \big((w \gg d - i) \wedge \overline{\mathsf{mask}}_{d,i}\big) \tag{1}$$

where $\mathsf{mask}_{d,i}$ is a selection mask defined as

$$\mathsf{mask}_{d,i} = \underbrace{11\ldots1}_{d-i}\underbrace{00\ldots0}_{i} \| \cdots \| \underbrace{11\ldots1}_{d-i}\underbrace{00\ldots0}_{i},$$

and $\overline{\mathsf{mask}}_{d,i}$ denotes its complement. From this equation we can directly compute the sharing-wise rotation. The main trick in the implementation is to efficiently deal with the generation of $\mathsf{mask}_{d,i}$ and the sharing-wise rotation.

The mask generation is decomposed into two steps. The first step allows to setup the mask correctly: $\mathsf{mask}_{d,0}$ is initialized with the value 0xFFFFFFFF. We then need a `correction` value which will be used to update the mask correctly. `correction` is initialized with values given in Table 3. Note that these operations are performed only once at the beginning of the multiplication. The second step will update the mask for the rotation according to the offset of the rotation given by the following formula:

$$\mathsf{mask}_{d,i} = \mathsf{mask}_{d,0} \oplus (\texttt{correction} \ll i)$$

In practice, we only store $\mathsf{mask}_{d,0}$ and `correction` in two registers and we update them accordingly in each iteration of the loop. The cost of the update is 2 cycles.

```
;;mask update
EOR      $mask, $mask, $correction
LSL      $correction, $correction, #1
```

Note that we make use of another register in order to store $\mathsf{mask}_{d,1}$ (*i.e.* the rotation by 1) which is always needed to compute the rotations of the random values (instead of computing it again each time).

Table 3. Possible values for correction

d	2	4	8	16
correction	0x5555555	0x11111111	0x01010101	0x00010001

The rotation $\mathsf{ROT}(w, i)$ is then quite straightforward to implement as describes hereafter:

```
;; rotation of $w by $i
    AND     $tmp, $mask, $w, LSL $i
    LSR     $w, $w, $(d-i)
    BIC     $w, $w, $mask
    EOR     $w, $tmp, $w
```

Since the offsets of the shift lie in a register, we cannot benefit from the *barrel shifter*. Hence the overall cost of one rotation is 5 cycles.

In Table 4, we report results of our implementation of the BDF$^+$ multiplication for d ranging from 2 to 32 for the generic version and an unrolled version (where the main advantage is to be able to hardcode the masks and values for the shifts). We observe that the unrolled version for $d = 32$ is faster and has less code size than for $d = 16$. This is easily explained by the fact that we can make full use of the *barrel shifter* in the case $d = 32$. Moreover, we observe that the unrolled version is 40% to 80% faster than the regular version. This is due to the fact that we can hardcode the masks, which makes the *barrel shifter* work again. The code size of the unrolled version ranges from 0.3 to 3 times the generic one. Note also that the code size of the generic version is decreasing as d grows because we compute the `correction` value iteratively (*i.e.* it needs $\log(32/d)$ iterations).

Table 4. Performance results for BDF$^+$ (generic and unrolled)

	Clock cycles					Code size (bytes)					Registers	Random usage
d	2	4	8	16	32	2	4	8	16	32		
BDF$^+$ generic	n/a	77	146	285	n/a	n/a	248	244	240	n/a	13	$\lceil(d-1)/4\rceil$
BDF$^+$ unrolled	34	47	81	149	120	280	356	504	808	748	13	$\lceil(d-1)/4\rceil$

3.3   BBP$^+$: Towards Optimal Randomness Consumption

Belaïd *et al.* at Eurocrypt 2016 [BBP+16] tackled the problem of minimizing the amount of randomness required in a secure multiplication. They described a generic algorithm which makes use of less randomness than ISW, reducing the former randomness requirement from $\frac{d(d-1)}{2}$ to $\frac{d^2}{4} + d$. As opposed to the ISW multiplication (which achieves $(d-1)$-SNI security), this algorithm is only proven $(d-1)$-NI secure. The original description of this secure multiplication (see [BBP+16]) is generic for any masking order $d \geq 4$ (specific algorithms for the case where $d = 2$ and 3 are given in their paper). However, it makes use of several conditional branches to process additional operations depending on the parity of the order d and/or of the loop index i.

We rewrote the algorithm such that all the conditional branches are removed, without affecting the correctness (see Algorithm 3). These changes lead to several improvements in practice: first replacing if/else statement with loops allows avoiding several conditional branches treatment that are quit expensive in ARM assembly. Moreover, by rewriting the algorithm in such a way, we can compute all the randomness on-the-fly and avoid multiple load and store instructions for the correction step. Such improvements come at the cost of a less generic algorithm (it only works for even orders d). For the sake of comparison, we have implemented both algorithms to show the performance gained in clock cycles and code size (see Table 5). We can see that our improvements allow a gain in timing ranging from 18% to 20% with an overhead of only 80 bytes of memory. Furthermore, we also unrolled the nested loops in order to get better results in timings. The timing gain ranges from 17% to 60% with an overhead factor between 3.5 and 50 for the code size for $d \geq 8$ only. For smaller d's, the unrolled version is better for both timing and code size.

Algorithm 3. BBP$^+$ (Belaïd *et al.*, Eurocrypt'16) w/o conditional branches

---

Input: sharings $(a_1, \ldots, a_d) \in \{0,1\}^{32 \times d}$ and $(b_1, \ldots, b_d) \in \{0,1\}^{32 \times d}$
Output: sharing $(c_1, \ldots, c_d) \in \{0,1\}^{32 \times d}$ such that $\bigoplus_i c_i = (\bigoplus_i a_i) \wedge (\bigoplus_j b_j)$

1. $c_1 \leftarrow a_1 \wedge b_1$
2. $c_2 \leftarrow a_2 \wedge b_2$
3. **for** $i = 3$ to $d-1$ **by** 2 **do**
4. $c_i \leftarrow a_i \wedge b_i$
5. $c_{i+1} \leftarrow a_{i+1} \wedge b_{i+1}$
6. $s_i \leftarrow \{0,1\}^{32}$
7. **end for**
8. **for** $i = 1$ to $d-1$ **by** 2 **do**
9. $r_{i,i+1} \leftarrow \{0,1\}^{32}$
10.   LoopRow$(i, i+3)$
11. $c_i \leftarrow c_i \oplus (r_{i,i+1} \oplus a_i \wedge b_{i+1} \oplus a_{i+1} \wedge b_i)$
12.   LoopRow$(i+1, i+3)$
13. $c_{i+1} \leftarrow c_{i+1} \oplus r$
14. **end for**

Algorithm 4. LoopRow Procedure

Input: indexes i, t randoms $(s_j)_{j \in \{3, \ldots, d-1\}}$
1. **for** $j = d$ down to t **by** 2 **do**
2. $r_{i,j} \leftarrow \{0,1\}^{32}$
3. $c_i \leftarrow c_i \oplus \big(r \oplus (a_i \wedge b_j \oplus a_j \wedge b_i) \oplus s_{j-1} \oplus (a_i \wedge b_{j-1} \oplus a_{j-1} \wedge b_i)\big)$
4. $c_j \leftarrow c_j \oplus r_{i,j}$
5. **end for**

3.4   BPCZ: Towards Security Against Horizontal Attacks

At CHES 2016, Battistello *et al.* described a horizontal side-channel attack on the standard ISW multiplication [BCPZ16]. This attack essentially consists in

Table 5. Implementation results for the BBP$^+$ multiplication

	Clock cycles					Code size (bytes)					Register usage	Random usage
d	2	4	8	16	32	2	4	8	16	32		
Original BBP$^+$	n/a	334	1204	4552	17680	n/a	344	344	344	344	12	$d + d^2/4$
Optimized BBP$^+$	88	274	970	3658	14218	428	428	428	428	428	12	$d + d^2/4$
Unrolled BBP$^+$	36	161	775	3018	11920	100	344	1544	5996	23732	11	$d + d^2/4$

reducing the noise in the targeted values by averaging them. More precisely, during the computation of Algorithm 1, each share a_i (resp. b_i) is manipulated d times. Hence one can *average* the noise and reduce it by a factor $\sqrt{d}$ (in a standard deviation metric). Such an attack is inherent to the ISW scheme and implies that despite the probing-security, increasing the masking order d implies increasingly high noise requirements for the masking countermeasure to bring security improvements (i.e., for the noise to be large enough after averaging, it has to increase before averaging).

Battistello *et al.* also proposed a mitigation of such a horizontal attack. Their multiplication, given in Algorithm 5, is similar to the standard ISW multiplication but the matrix of the crossed products $a_i \cdot b_j$ is computed differently (see Algorithm 6): refreshings are regularly inserted to avoid the multiple apparition of each share a_i (resp. b_i). The RefreshMasks operation is a simple ISW-based refreshing as described later in Sect. 4. The authors also proved that their multiplication is $(d-1)$-SNI secure.

Algorithm 5. BCPZ (Battistello *et al.*, CHES'16)

Input: shares a_i such that $\sum_i a_i = a$, shares b_i such that $\sum_i b_i = b$
Output: shares c_i such that $\sum_i c_i = a \cdot b$
1. $M_{i,j} \leftarrow \text{MatMult}((x_1, \ldots, x_d), (y_1, \ldots, y_d))$
2. **for** $i = 1$ to d **do**
3. $c_i \leftarrow M_{i,i}$
4. **end for**
5. **for** $i = 1$ to d **do**
6.   **for** $j = i + 1$ to d **do**
7. $s \leftarrow \mathbb{F}$
8. $s' \leftarrow (s + M_{i,j}) + M_{j,i}$
9. $c_i \leftarrow c_i + s$
10. $c_j \leftarrow c_j + s'$
11.   **end for**
12. **end for**
13. **return** $c_1, \ldots, c_d$

The implementation of Algorithm 5 is straightforward (same as ISW). The main challenge is to efficiently implement Algorithm 6 in a recursive way. In fact, due to the restrictive amount of registers available, using functions to perform the recursion in ARM assembly becomes very costly. Each recursive call needs

---

Algorithm 6. MatMult

Input: the n-sharings $(x_i)_{i \in [1..n]}$ and $(y_i)_{i \in [1..n]}$ of x^* and y^* respectively

Output: the n^2-sharing $(M_{i,j})_{i \in [1..n], j \in [1..n]}$ of $x^* \cdot y^*$

1. **if** $n = 1$ **then**
2. $\quad M \leftarrow [x_1 \cdot y_1]$
3. **else**
4. $\quad \boldsymbol{X}^{(1)} \leftarrow (x_1, \ldots, x_{n/2}),\ \boldsymbol{X}^{(1)} \leftarrow (x_{n/2+1}, \ldots, x_n)$
5. $\quad \boldsymbol{Y}^{(1)} \leftarrow (y_1, \ldots, y_{n/2}),\ \boldsymbol{Y}^{(1)} \leftarrow (y_{n/2+1}, \ldots, y_n)$
6. $\quad \boldsymbol{M}^{(1,1)} \leftarrow \text{MatMult}(\boldsymbol{X}^{(1)}, \boldsymbol{Y}^{(1)})$
7. $\quad \boldsymbol{X}^{(1)} \leftarrow \text{RefreshMasks}(\boldsymbol{X}^{(1)}),\ \boldsymbol{Y}^{(1)} \leftarrow \text{RefreshMasks}(\boldsymbol{Y}^{(1)})$
8. $\quad \boldsymbol{M}^{(1,2)} \leftarrow \text{MatMult}(\boldsymbol{X}^{(1)}, \boldsymbol{Y}^{(2)})$
9. $\quad \boldsymbol{M}^{(2,1)} \leftarrow \text{MatMult}(\boldsymbol{X}^{(2)}, \boldsymbol{Y}^{(1)})$
10. $\quad \boldsymbol{X}^{(2)} \leftarrow \text{RefreshMasks}(\boldsymbol{X}^{(2)}),\ \boldsymbol{Y}^{(2)} \leftarrow \text{RefreshMasks}(\boldsymbol{Y}^{(2)})$
11. $\quad \boldsymbol{M}^{(2,2)} \leftarrow \text{MatMult}(\boldsymbol{X}^{(2)}, \boldsymbol{Y}^{(2)})$
12. $\quad M \leftarrow \begin{pmatrix} \boldsymbol{M}^{(1,1)} & \boldsymbol{M}^{(1,2)} \\ \boldsymbol{M}^{(2,1)} & \boldsymbol{M}^{(2,2)} \end{pmatrix}$
13. **end if**
14. **return** M

---

to have access to several informations: the correct set of input sharings, namely the start of $\boldsymbol{X}_1$, $\boldsymbol{X}_2$, $\boldsymbol{Y}_1$ and $\boldsymbol{Y}_2$ as well as the correct addresses for the output sharings. This means that several registers containing those information needs to be pushed to the stack prior to each call to a recursive function and poped before the computation. As push and pop are basically load and store in ARM assembly the total cost of managing the inputs and outputs of a recursive function is approximately equal to a dozen of clock cycles for each recursive calls. This costs, on top of the associated jumps for each recursive function, is equivalent to the computation of a complete ISW multiplication. Therefore and since we restrict ourselves in this study to $d \leq 32$, we developed the MatMult procedure with macros. Specifically, for each masking order d that is a power of 2, we simply implements Algorithm 6 using macros for each possible input sharing size $n \in \{2, 4, \ldots, 32\}$, which allows us to save several clock cycles. However the main drawback of implementing the MatMult procedure in such way is that the code size exponentially grows. To lower down the explosion of the code size, we have also implemented a version of the code where the terminal case macro (for $n = 2$) is implemented as a function. This allows us to divide by up to 5 the code size while having a performance decrease of around 20%. Both timing and code size for the BPCZ multiplication with the two versions of the MatMult procedure are given in Table 6.

4   Refresh Masks

Most of the multiplication gadgets rely on the condition that their two inputs have to be independently shared in order to guaranty full security (and avoid doubling the number of shares instead). But in complex circuit involving many

Table 6. Implementation results for the BCPZ multiplication

	Clock cycles					Code size (bytes)					Register	Random usage
d	2	4	8	16	32	2	4	8	16	32		
BCPZ (macros)	108	498	2106	8698	35386	240	648	2324	9368	38168	13	$(\log(d)-1)d^2/2-(d/2-1)d$
BCPZ (functions)	134	593	2529	10473	42649	400	476	780	1996	6860	13	$(\log(d)-1)d^2/2-(d/2-1)d$

multiplications and other linear operations, this condition might not always be fulfilled (*e.g.* the two inputs of a multiplication might be linearly related) leading to security flaws as pointed out by Coron *et al.* [CPRR14]. Refreshing gadgets (in particular SNI ones) allow avoiding such kind of behavior if used systematically on one of the input of the multiplication. In this section, we describe and compare the refresh gadgets associated to their multiplication, *i.e.* the ISW refresh and the BDF$^+$ refresh.

4.1   ISW

A sound refresh can be performed by using the ISW multiplication: it simply consist in multiplying the shares a_i by the vector $(1, 0, \cdots, 0)$ and has been proven $(d-1)$-SNI secure. The ISW refresh needs $d(d-1)/2$ random bits and performs $d(d-1)$ additions. The overall algorithm is described in Algorithm 7.

Algorithm 7. ISW Refresh

Input: shares $a_1, a_2, \ldots, a_d$
Output: shares $c_1, c_2, \ldots, c_d$ such that $\sum_{i=1}^{d} c_i = \sum_{i=1}^{d} a_i$
1. **for** $i = 1$ to d **do**
2. $c_i \leftarrow a_i$
3. **end for**
4. **for** $i = 1$ to d **do**
5.   **for** $j = i + 1$ to d **do**
6. $r \leftarrow \{0, 1\}^{32}$
7. $c_i \leftarrow c_i \oplus r$
8. $c_j \leftarrow c_j \oplus r$
9.   **end for**
10. **end for**
11. **return** $c_1, c_2, \ldots, c_d$

As shown by Goudarzi and Rivain [GR17], this refreshing procedure can be optimized by partially unrolling the nested loops by taking advantages of available registers. This allows to load multiple shares at once and perform the sound operations on all of them, instead of doing it one by one. Namely, for masking orders equal to power of 2, this allows to load the a_i's four by four, namely loading $a_i, a_{i+1}, a_{i+2}, a_{i+3}$ and have the number of operations in the nested loop divided by 4. As in ARM assembly, the multiple load instruction is

Table 7. Implementation results for the ISW refresh

	Clock cycles					Code size (bytes)					Register usage	Random usage
d	2	4	8	16	32	2	4	8	16	32		
ISW Refresh	51	72	239	933	3761	224	224	224	224	224	10	$d(d-1)/2$

more efficient that several single loads, this improvement yields a very efficient ISW-based refresh implementation. The performance results of the ISW refresh can be found in Table 7.

4.2 BDF$^+$ Refresh

Barthe *et al.* in [BDF+17], along with their multiplication gadget, also provide a refreshing gadget described in Algorithm 8. It simply consists in XORing the share to refresh by a random value and a rotation of it. The iteration of the BDF$^+$ refresh $\lceil(d-1)/3\rceil$ times makes it SNI secure. The overall BDF$^+$ refresh needs $d\lceil(d-1)/3\rceil$ random bits and performs $2\lceil(d-1)/3\rceil$ additions and $\lceil(d-1)/3\rceil$ ROT. There is no particular implementations tricks except we use the same ROT algorithm introduced in Sect. 3.2 in order to keep the correctness with the specific encoding. Implementations results can be found in Table 8.

Algorithm 8. BDF$^+$ Refresh

Input: shares a
Output: shares c
1. $r \leftarrow \{0,1\}^{32}$
2. $c \leftarrow a \oplus r \oplus \mathsf{ROT}(r,1)$
3. **return** c

Table 8. Implementation results for the BDF$^+$ refresh

	Clock cycles					Code size (bytes)					Register usage	Random usage
d	2	4	8	16	32	2	4	8	16	32		
BDF$^+$ Refresh	25	25	25	25	16	116	116	116	116	110	10	d

5   Comparisons and Discussion

We conclude the paper by comparing the different implementations and discussing their pros and cons regarding both the security properties they guarantee and the performances they allow.

5.1 High Level Comparison

In Table 9 we gather the four multiplications we studied in this paper and we compare them at an algorithmic level. Namely, we give the operation counts (in terms of 32-bit XOR, 32-bit AND, and sharing-wise ROT) to perform a secure 32-bit AND between two sharings. The NI/SNI row specifies if the considered multiplication is SNI- or NI-secure. The row "max use of shares" represents (informally) the level of protection against horizontal side-channels attacks: $O(d)$ means that each shares is processed a linear number in d times (*i.e.* no protection) and $O(1)$ means that each shares is processed a constant number of times (*i.e.* protection).

We differentiate two cases for the BDF$^+$ multiplication. A first case where we consider the multiplication alone, which is SNI until $d = 3$ and only NI secure afterwards. A second case where we consider the composition of the multiplication with one iteration of the BDF$^+$ refresh (described in Sect. 4), which is SNI secure up to $d = 8$ and only NI secure afterwards (see [BDF+17]). The cost difference between these two versions is simply the cost of an elementary refresh (i.e., the addition of a share of zero). Finding the number of such refreshes that are required to be SNI at any order is an open problem. Note that for BDF$^+$, the results are given for d calls to the multiplication (since each call allows to compute $32/d$ elements).

We note that we did not perform the same addition for the BBP$^+$ multiplication since it would imply the need of a more expensive SNI refresh on the output, which would contradict the goal of [BBP+16] to minimize randomness by mixing NI and SNI multiplications instead of solely SNI multiplications (and in particular, if an SNI multiplication is then required, one could use the ISW one, or the BDF$^+$ up to order 8).

Table 9. Comparison of the multiplications at the algorithmic level.

Algorithm:	ISW	BDF$^+$ (BM model)	BDF$^+$ w. refresh (BM model)	BBP$^+$	BCPZ
NI/SNI:	SNI	SNI (up to $d = 3$)	SNI (up to $d = 8$)	NI	SNI
Max use of shares:	$O(d)$	$O(d)$	$O(d)$	$O(d)$	$O(1)$
XOR-32 count:	$2d(d-1)$	$d(3d/2 - 1)$	$d(3d/2 + 1)$	$(7d^2 - 6d)/4$	$d^2 \log(d) + 2d$
AND-32 count:	d^2	d^2	d^2	d^2	d^2
ROT count:	0	$d(5d/4 - 1)$	$5d^2/4$	0	0
Random bits:	$16d(d-1)$	$32d\lceil (d-1)/4 \rceil$	$32d\lceil (d-1)/4 \rceil + 32$	$8d^2 + 16d - 1$	$16d^2 \log(d) + d$

We also recall that this table does not mention the different risks of unsatisfied (independence) assumption mentioned in introduction. Namely the fact that the BDF$^+$ multiplication can suffer from a reduced security order due to couplings while for the other algorithms, the main risk of security order reduction comes from transition-based leakages.

5.2 Implementation-Based Comparison

Based on the results in the previous sections, we can compare the performances of our implementations of the multiplications for bitsliced inputs with higher-order masking in ARM v7. We make the comparison for five masking orders, namely 2, 4, 8, 16 and 32. Moreover, we also give the performance results for two sets of TRNG. For the first one (called the TRNG-1 settings in the following), we make the same assumption as in [GR17] that we need to wait 10 clock cycles to get a fresh 32-bit random word. For the second one (called the TRNG-2 settings in the following), we make the same assumption as in [JS17] that we need to wait 80 clock cycles to get a fresh 32-bit random word. Finally, in order to have a fair comparison between the four algorithms the implementation results are given for the computation of a multiplication between two shared 32-bit operands. This means that for the 3 ISW-based multiplication (ISW, BCPZ, BBP$^+$) the results are given for a single call to their respective functions, whereas for the BDF$^+$ multiplication the results are given for d calls to the function (since each calls allows to compute $32/d$ elements). The overall results are given in Tables 10 and 11 for respectively the TRNG-1 and the TRNG-2 settings. As illustration, we also plot the performances in clock cycles (log scale) for both TRNG-1 and TRNG-2 settings in Figs. 1 and 2 respectively.

Table 10. Multiplication performances for TRNG-1.

| | TRNG-1 | | | | | | | | | |
| | Clock cycles | | | | | Code size (bytes) | | | | |
d	2	4	8	16	32	2	4	8	16	32
ISW	75	291	1155	4611	18435	164	164	164	164	164
ISW unrolled	58	231	949	3876	15682	132	464	1848	7500	30324
BDF$^+$ bcdmacros + functions	n/a	308	1168	4560	n/a	n/a	248	244	240	n/a
BDF$^+$ unrolled	68	188	648	2384	3840	280	356	504	808	748
BDF$^+$ (+ refresh)	n/a	408	1568	5360	n/a	n/a	360	356	352	n/a
BDF$^+$ unrolled (+ refresh)	118	288	1048	3184	5440	392	468	616	920	960
BBP$^+$	88	274	970	3658	14218	428	428	428	428	428
BBP$^+$ unrolled	36	161	775	3018	11910	100	344	1544	5996	23732
BCPZ (macros)	108	498	2106	8698	35386	240	648	2334	9368	38168
BCPZ (macros + functions)	134	593	2529	10473	42649	400	476	780	1996	6860
ISW refresh	51	72	239	933	3761	236	236	236	236	236
BDF$^+$ refresh	50	50	50	50	50	128	128	128	128	128

As expected the BCPZ offers the worst performances because of the many refreshings which intend to provide resistance to horizontal side-channel attacks, for both of the TRNG settings.

Table 11. Multiplication performances for TRNG-2.

	TRNG-2									
	Clock cycles					Code size (bytes)				
d	2	4	8	16	32	2	4	8	16	32
ISW	166	837	3703	15531	63571	500	500	500	500	500
ISW unrolled	149	777	3497	14796	60818	480	872	2508	9264	36600
BDF$^+$ bcdmacros + functions	n/a	672	2624	10384	n/a	n/a	596	592	588	n/a
BDF$^+$ unrolled	250	552	2104	8208	27136	448	500	876	1204	1192
BDF$^+$ (+ refresh)	n/a	1136	3552	12240	n/a	n/a	1016	1012	1008	n/a
BDF$^+$ unrolled (+ refresh)	482	1016	3032	10064	30848	868	920	1296	1624	1612
BBP$^+$	270	820	2790	10210	38970	800	800	800	800	800
BBP$^+$ unrolled	127	525	2504	9479	36581	436	716	2096	7172	27776
BCPZ (macros)	199	1408	7202	32358	136942	576	1032	2988	11372	45932
BCPZ (macros + functions)	225	1503	7625	34133	144205	760	836	1128	2344	7208
ISW refresh	142	345	2241	10761	46713	412	412	412	412	412
BDF$^+$ refresh	116	116	116	116	116	420	420	420	420	420

The BBP$^+$ multiplication outperforms the ISW multiplication (up to 25% faster) even in the case where the randomness is cheap. The difference becomes more significant in the TRNG-2 context (up to 40% faster), since BBP$^+$ have reduced randomness requirements.

For the TRNG-2 settings, we can also observe that unrolling the loops does not offer an interesting tradeoff as the gain in timing is not very significant compared to the code size overhead.

As shown in Table 2 of [BDF+17], the iteration of the BDF$^+$ refresh requires a bit less randomness than ISW one but is more computationally involved. This is well reflected in Tables 10: the ISW refresh has better performances than the BDF$^+$ refresh for the TRNG-1 setting while it is the opposite for the TRNG-2 setting.

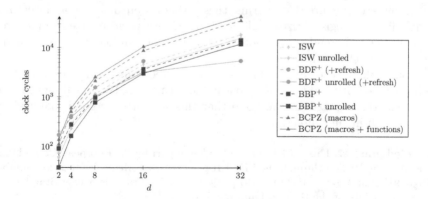

Fig. 1. Multiplication performances for TRNG-1 in clock cycles

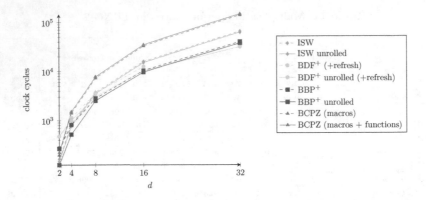

Fig. 2. Multiplication performances for TRNG-2 in clock cycles

Overall, BDF$^+$ and BBP$^+$ multiplications provide the best performances in both TRNG settings thanks to their lower randomness requirements (compared to the classical ISW). Of course these two multiplications also have weaker security guaranties (in terms of composability and resistance against horizontal attacks). On the other hand, ISW and BCPZ offer better security guaranties and hence are more involved in terms of randomness requirements, making these differences more visible in the TRNG-2 setting.

Conclusion and Future Work. One interesting consequence of this observation is that it raises interesting optimization problems on how to best exploit different multiplications in order to obtain the best security vs. performance tradeoff for full implementations (e.g., of block ciphers), which is a nice scope for further research.

Our implementations heavily relies on the use of the barrel shifter of the ARM 32-bit architecture. Comparing these schemes on different architectures and with different register sizes could lead to different performance results (even though the general trend should not differ due to the randomness requirements of the different schemes).

Of course these schemes should also be evaluated considering their practical side-channel security and not only software performances. By providing the code on an open source platform, we hope that this will provide good material for future research in that direction.

Acknowledgments. This work has been funded in part by the European Commission and the Walloon Region through the FEDER project USERMedia (convention number 501907-379156) and by the INNOVIRIS project SCAUT. François-Xavier Standaert is a research associate of the Belgian Fund for Scientific Research.

References

[BBD+16] Barthe, G., Belaïd, S., Dupressoir, F., Fouque, P.-A., Grégoire, B., Strub, P.-Y., Zucchini, R.: Strong non-interference and type-directed higher-order masking. In: Weippl, E.R., Katzenbeisser, S., Kruegel, C., Myers, A.C., Halevi, S. (eds.) ACM CCS 16: 23rd Conference on Computer and Communications Security, Vienna, Austria, pp. 116–129. ACM Press, 24–28 October 2016

[BBP+16] Belaïd, S., Benhamouda, F., Passelègue, A., Prouff, E., Thillard, A., Vergnaud, D.: Randomness complexity of private circuits for multiplication. In: Fischlin, M., Coron, J.-S. (eds.) EUROCRYPT 2016. LNCS, vol. 9666, pp. 616–648. Springer, Heidelberg (2016). https://doi.org/10.1007/978-3-662-49896-5_22

[BCPZ16] Battistello, A., Coron, J.-S., Prouff, E., Zeitoun, R.: Horizontal side-channel attacks and countermeasures on the ISW masking scheme. In: Gierlichs, B., Poschmann, A.Y. (eds.) CHES 2016. LNCS, vol. 9813, pp. 23–39. Springer, Heidelberg (2016). https://doi.org/10.1007/978-3-662-53140-2_2

[BDF+17] Barthe, G., Dupressoir, F., Faust, S., Grégoire, B., Standaert, F.-X., Strub, P.-Y.: Parallel implementations of masking schemes and the bounded moment leakage model. In: Coron, J.-S., Nielsen, J.B. (eds.) EUROCRYPT 2017. LNCS, vol. 10210, pp. 535–566. Springer, Cham (2017). https://doi.org/10.1007/978-3-319-56620-7_19

[BGG+14] Balasch, J., Gierlichs, B., Grosso, V., Reparaz, O., Standaert, F.-X.: On the cost of lazy engineering for masked software implementations. In: Joye, M., Moradi, A. (eds.) CARDIS 2014. LNCS, vol. 8968, pp. 64–81. Springer, Cham (2015). https://doi.org/10.1007/978-3-319-16763-3_5

[BGRV15] Balasch, J., Gierlichs, B., Reparaz, O., Verbauwhede, I.: DPA, bitslicing and masking at 1 GHz. In: Güneysu, T., Handschuh, H. (eds.) CHES 2015. LNCS, vol. 9293, pp. 599–619. Springer, Heidelberg (2015). https://doi.org/10.1007/978-3-662-48324-4_30

[CBG+17] De Cnudde, T., Bilgin, B., Gierlichs, B., Nikov, V., Nikova, S., Rijmen, V.: Does coupling affect the security of masked implementations? In: Guilley, S. (ed.) COSADE 2017. LNCS, vol. 10348, pp. 1–18. Springer, Cham (2017). https://doi.org/10.1007/978-3-319-64647-3_1

[CGP+12] Coron, J.-S., Giraud, C., Prouff, E., Renner, S., Rivain, M., Vadnala, P.K.: Conversion of security proofs from one leakage model to another: a new issue. In: Schindler, W., Huss, S.A. (eds.) COSADE 2012. LNCS, vol. 7275, pp. 69–81. Springer, Heidelberg (2012). https://doi.org/10.1007/978-3-642-29912-4_6

[CJRR99] Chari, S., Jutla, C.S., Rao, J.R., Rohatgi, P.: Towards sound approaches to counteract power-analysis attacks. In: Wiener, M. (ed.) CRYPTO 1999. LNCS, vol. 1666, pp. 398–412. Springer, Heidelberg (1999). https://doi.org/10.1007/3-540-48405-1_26

[CPRR14] Coron, J.-S., Prouff, E., Rivain, M., Roche, T.: Higher-order side channel security and mask refreshing. In: Moriai, S. (ed.) FSE 2013. LNCS, vol. 8424, pp. 410–424. Springer, Heidelberg (2014). https://doi.org/10.1007/978-3-662-43933-3_21

[DDF14] Duc, A., Dziembowski, S., Faust, S.: Unifying leakage models: from probing attacks to noisy leakage. In: Nguyen, P.Q., Oswald, E. (eds.) EUROCRYPT 2014. LNCS, vol. 8441, pp. 423–440. Springer, Heidelberg (2014). https://doi.org/10.1007/978-3-642-55220-5_24

[DPV01] Daemen, J., Peeters, M., Van Assche, G.: Bitslice ciphers and power analysis attacks. In: Goos, G., Hartmanis, J., van Leeuwen, J., Schneier, B. (eds.) FSE 2000. LNCS, vol. 1978, pp. 134–149. Springer, Heidelberg (2001). https://doi.org/10.1007/3-540-44706-7_10

[GJRS18] Goudarzi, D., Journault, A., Rivain, M., Standaert, F.-X.: Source code (2018). https://github.com/CryptoExperts/bitslice-masking-multiplication

[GR17] Goudarzi, D., Rivain, M.: How fast can higher-order masking be in software? In: Coron, J.-S., Nielsen, J.B. (eds.) EUROCRYPT 2017. LNCS, vol. 10210, pp. 567–597. Springer, Cham (2017). https://doi.org/10.1007/978-3-319-56620-7_20

[ISW03] Ishai, Y., Sahai, A., Wagner, D.: Private circuits: securing hardware against probing attacks. In: Boneh, D. (ed.) CRYPTO 2003. LNCS, vol. 2729, pp. 463–481. Springer, Heidelberg (2003). https://doi.org/10.1007/978-3-540-45146-4_27

[JS17] Journault, A., Standaert, F.-X.: Very high order masking: efficient implementation and security evaluation. In: Fischer, W., Homma, N. (eds.) CHES 2017. LNCS, vol. 10529, pp. 623–643. Springer, Cham (2017). https://doi.org/10.1007/978-3-319-66787-4_30

[PR13] Prouff, E., Rivain, M.: Masking against side-channel attacks: a formal security proof. In: Johansson, T., Nguyen, P.Q. (eds.) EUROCRYPT 2013. LNCS, vol. 7881, pp. 142–159. Springer, Heidelberg (2013). https://doi.org/10.1007/978-3-642-38348-9_9

[RP10] Rivain, M., Prouff, E.: Provably secure higher-order masking of AES. In: Mangard, S., Standaert, F.-X. (eds.) CHES 2010. LNCS, vol. 6225, pp. 413–427. Springer, Heidelberg (2010). https://doi.org/10.1007/978-3-642-15031-9_28

Vectorizing Higher-Order Masking

Benjamin Grégoire[1], Kostas Papagiannopoulos[2],
Peter Schwabe[2], and Ko Stoffelen[2(✉)]

[1] Inria Sophia Antipolis, Biot, France
benjamin.gregoire@inria.fr
[2] Digital Security Group, Radboud University, Nijmegen, The Netherlands
{k.papagiannopoulos,k.stoffelen}@cs.ru.nl, peter@cryptojedi.org

Abstract. The cost of higher-order masking as a countermeasure against side-channel attacks is often considered too high for practical scenarios, as protected implementations become very slow. At Eurocrypt 2017, the bounded moment leakage model was proposed to study the (theoretical) security of parallel implementations of masking schemes [5]. Work at CHES 2017 then brought this to practice by considering an implementation of AES with 32 shares [26], bitsliced inside 32-bit registers of ARM Cortex-M processors. In this paper we show how the NEON vector instructions of larger ARM Cortex-A processors can be exploited to build much faster masked implementations of AES. Specifically, we present AES with 4 and 8 shares, which in theory provide security against 3rd and 7th-order attacks, respectively. The software is publicly available and optimized for the ARM Cortex-A8. We use refreshing and multiplication algorithms that are proven to be secure in the bounded moment leakage model and to be strongly non-interfering. Additionally, we perform a concrete side-channel evaluation on a BeagleBone Black, using a combination of test vector leakage assessment (TVLA), leakage certification tools and information-theoretic bounds.

Keywords: Higher-order masking · Side-channel analysis · AES
ARM Cortex-A8

1 Introduction

There is a long history of protecting AES [15] implementations against side-channel analysis (SCA) attacks. Side-channel attacks exploit physical information, such as power consumption or electromagnetic radiation of devices running some cryptographic primitive, to learn information about secret data, typically cryptographic keys. Higher-order masking is a well-studied countermeasure against such attacks [11,22]; unfortunately, it comes at a rather high cost in terms of performance. This is a reason why in practice, well-protected implementations are not as ubiquitous as one would hope. In software, higher-order masked implementations are typically orders of magnitude slower compared to unprotected implementations, as was explored at Eurocrypt 2017 by Goudarzi and Rivain [23].

© Springer International Publishing AG, part of Springer Nature 2018
J. Fan and B. Gierlichs (Eds.): COSADE 2018, LNCS 10815, pp. 23–43, 2018.
https://doi.org/10.1007/978-3-319-89641-0_2

Simultaneously at Eurocrypt 2017, a theoretical model was proposed to study the security of *parallel implementations* of masking schemes, called the bounded moment leakage model [5]. As parallelization is a very powerful tool to increase performance, this model gives the foundation for faster protected implementations. One common way to parallelize software implementations is through vectorization. In a vectorized implementation, a single instruction operates on multiple data elements inside one vector register at the same time. For vectorization to be useful, data parallelism is required, which in the case of higher-order masking is trivially provided by the availability of multiple shares.

Precisely this approach of vectorization with data-level parallelism coming from multiple shares was used in a CHES 2017 paper by Journault and Standaert [26]. That paper studies a parallel bitsliced (i.e., vectorized with 1-bit vector elements) implementation using 32 shares on the ARM Cortex-M4. The reason for using 32 shares was the fact that the Cortex-M4 has 32-bit registers and bitslicing thus needs 32× data-level parallelism. Empirical tests in this paper confirmed that the bounded moment model is useful also in practice. Specifically, these tests showed that a 4-share version of their implementation yielded no leakage of order less than 4. It is of course still possible that the actual security order is lower, but it can at least be viewed as an optimistic result. They conclude their evaluation by performing an information-theoretic analysis of the leakage in order to bound the attack complexity for the 32-share implementation.

In this paper we study how the powerful NEON vector unit on larger ARM Cortex-A processors can be used to obtain efficient masked AES implementations. Straight-forwardly adapting the approach from [26] to obtain data-level parallelism would result in implementations with 64 or 128 shares (for 64-bit or 128-bit vector registers), which would be a security overkill and result in terrible performance. Instead we follow the approach of the bitsliced AES implementations presented in [27,30], which exploit the data-level parallelism of 16 independent S-Box computations. As a result, we present implementations using 4 and 8 shares, which in theory offer security at the 3rd and 7th order. We use refreshing and multiplication algorithms that are based on the algorithms in [5] and even slightly improve on some of them by requiring less randomness. They are proven secure in the bounded moment model and also proven to be strongly non-interfering [4]. We provide a concrete evaluation of our implementations on a BeagleBone Black, which has been used successfully before to perform differential electromagnetic analysis at 1 GHz [2]. Using nearly the same setup, we employ the popular TVLA methodology [13] in conjunction with leakage certification [18] and we show that there is actually some leakage in the 3rd order of our 4-share implementation, but not in the 2nd order. We then continue to bound the measurement complexity of the 8-share implementation using an information-theoretic approach [17].

To summarize, the contributions of this paper are that

– we provide the first vectorized instantiation of the bounded moment leakage model published at Eurocrypt 2017 [5] with strong non-interference [4];

- we provide the fastest publicly available higher-order masked AES implementations with 4 and 8 shares for the ARM Cortex-A8; and that
- we perform a practical side-channel evaluation of the 4-share AES implementation and derive security bounds for the 8-share implementation.

Source Code. The source code of our implementations is available in the public domain. It can be downloaded at https://github.com/Ko-/aes-masked-neon.

2   Preliminaries

2.1   Higher-Order Masking of AES

Implementations of cryptographic primitives such as block ciphers are typically vulnerable to attacks that use side-channel analysis (SCA). Information about physical characteristics, such as the electromagnetic radiation, of a device that executes a block cipher can be used to recover the secret key [21, 29].

A well-studied countermeasure against this class of attacks is (higher-order) masking. It works by splitting each secret variable x into d shares x_i that satisfy $x_0 \oplus x_1 \oplus x_2 \oplus \cdots \oplus x_{d-1} = x$. When $\oplus$ denotes the Boolean XOR operation, this is called Boolean masking. Any $d - 1$ of these shares should be statistically independent of x and should be uniformly randomly distributed. If this is the case, then this masking scheme provides privacy in the $(d - 1)$-probing model, as put forward by Ishai, Sahai, and Wagner [25]. The idea is that an attacker applying $d - 1$ probes to learn intermediate values of the computation will not be able to learn anything about the secret value. We call the value $d - 1$ the *order* of the masking scheme.

When masking is applied, operations on x are to be performed on its shares. For linear operations f, those that satisfy $f(x + y) = f(x) + f(y)$ and $f(ax) = af(x)$, it holds that they can trivially be computed on the shares of x individually. For nonlinear operations, several algorithms have been suggested to retrieve the correct result. In [25] it was shown how to compute a masked AND gate and, together with the linear NOT, this is functionally complete.

AES [15] in particular has received a lot of attention when it comes to protected implementations. The round function of AES consists of AddRoundKey, SubBytes, ShiftRows, and MixColums. AddRoundKey, ShiftRows, and Mix-Columns are all linear. SubBytes is not. Much research has therefore been aimed at finding efficient representations of a masked variant of the AES S-box [10, 23, 28, 33].

2.2   Strong Non-interference

Strong non-interference (SNI) is a security notion, formalized in [4], that is slightly stronger than probing security. It currently seems to be the right security notion when considering practical security. The problem with probing security is that, given two algorithms that are secure at order $d - 1$ in the probing model, the composition of these algorithms is not necessarily secure at order $d-1$. SNI, on the other hand, means that an algorithm is *composable*, guaranteeing that one can verify the security of the composition of multiple secure algorithms.

As an example to see why SNI is desirable, consider the provably secure masking scheme by Rivain and Prouff from CHES 2010 [33]. Three years later, an attack was found against the composition of the refreshing of masks and the masked multiplication [14]. The scheme was fixed subsequently. It was shown in [4] that the main difference between the original and the fixed algorithms is exactly this notion of strong non-interference.

Automated verification tools exist to formally prove strong non-interference. This gives stronger guarantees on the theoretical security of a masking scheme.

2.3   Bounded Moment Leakage Model

The probing model and its variants are not always straightforward to interpret. The fact that $d-1$ shares should be statistically independent is based on the idea that an attacker can inspect the leakage of intermediate computations on the shares separately. In software, it therefore applies better to serial implementations. When computations are performed on multiple shares in parallel, it is not immediately clear what the relation with the probing security model is.

To handle this, the bounded moment model has been proposed in [5]. It is more targeted towards parallel implementations and can deal with the concept that multiple shares are manipulated simultaneously. Barthe, Dupressoir, Faust, Grégoire, Standaert, and Strub proved that probing security of a serial implementation implies bounded moment security for its parallel counterpart. It is a weaker security notion than the noisy leakage model [11,32].

Security in the bounded moment model is defined using *leakage vectors* and *mixed moments*. For every clock cycle c, there is a leakage vector L_c. The leakage vector is a random variable that is computed as the sum of a deterministic part that depends on the shares that are manipulated, and on the noise R_c. The mixed moment of a set $\{Y_1, \ldots, Y_r\}$ of r random variables at orders $o_1, \ldots, o_r$ can be defined as $\mathrm{E}\left[\prod_{i=1}^{r} Y_i\right]$, where E denotes the expected value. Now, consider an N-cycle cryptographic implementation that manipulates a secret variable x. This results in a set $\{L_1, \ldots, L_N\}$ of N leakage vectors. The implementation is said to be secure at order o in the bounded moment model if all the mixed moments of order $\leq o$ of $\{L_1, \ldots, L_N\}$ are statistically independent of x.

2.4   Vectorization with NEON

The ARM Cortex-A8 is a 32-bit processor that implements the ARMv7-A microarchitecture. It is used in smartphones, digital TVs, and printers, among others. It was first introduced in 2005 and is currently widely deployed. Its main core can run at 1 GHz and implements features such as superscalar execution, an advanced branch prediction unit, and a 13-stage pipeline. There are 16 32-bit r registers, of which 14 are generally available to the programmer.

The Cortex-A8 comes with the so-called Advanced SIMD extension, better known as NEON, that add another 16 128-bit q registers. These vector registers can also be viewed as 32 64-bit d registers. For example, q0 consists of d0 and d1, q1 consists of d2 and d3, et cetera. Operations can typically be performed on 8-, 16-, or 32-bit elements in a SIMD fashion. While 128-bit registers are supported, the data path of the Cortex-A8 is actually only 64 bits wide, which means that operations on 128-bit registers will be performed in two steps. NEON has a separate 10-stage pipeline. In particular, it has a load/store unit that runs next to an arithmetic unit. This means that an aligned load and an arithmetic instruction can be executed in the same cycle.

NEON has been used successfully in the past to vectorize and optimize implementations of cryptographic primitives [8], but its power has to the best of our knowledge not yet been exploited for higher-order masking in the way that we propose here.

3 Vectorizing Masking of AES

3.1 Representing the Masked State

The AES state [15] is usually pictured as a square matrix of 4 by 4 byte elements. This representation leads to efficient software implementations when SubBytes is implemented using lookup tables. However, such implementations are also prone to cache-timing attacks [7], as the memory location of the value that is looked up depends on some secret intermediate value. An alternative bitsliced representation avoids these attacks. In this bitsliced representation, all the first bits of every byte are put in one register, all the second bits in the next register, etc. For SubBytes, one can now compute the S-box on the individual bits and do that for all 16 bytes in parallel. The S-box parallelism of AES for bitslicing was first exploited by Könighofer in [30] and it was also used in the speed-record-setting AES implementation targeting Intel Core 2 processors by Käsper and Schwabe [27]. At a small cost, the other (linear) operations of AES are modified to operate on this bitsliced representation as well.

However, on most devices registers are longer than 16 bits, so it would be a waste to not utilize this. AES implementations without side-channel protections choose to process multiple blocks in parallel, by simply concatenating multiple 16-bit chunks from independent blocks in one register. For example, the AES implementation of [27] processes 8 blocks in parallel in a 128-bit XMM register. When the vector registers become larger, this trivially leads to higher throughputs for parallel modes of operation.

In this section we present three implementations that, instead of multiple blocks, process multiple shares in parallel (Fig. 1). The first implementation fills a 64-bit d register with 4 shares. The second has 8 shares, that are used to fill a 128-bit q register. The third combines 2 blocks with each 4 shares, and also utilizes the 128-bit q registers. It interleaves the shares of the 2 blocks for efficiency reasons. Note that this third implementation requires a parallel mode of operation.

share 0																share $d-1$
row 0				row 1				row 2				row 3				
col 0	col 1	col 2	col 3	col 0	col 1	col 2	col 3	col 0	col 1	col 2	col 3	col 0	col 1	col 2	col 3	

Fig. 1. Register lay-out for the single-block implementations. There are 8 of these $16d$-bit vector registers. The cells on the bottom row represent individual bits.

3.2   Parallel Multiplication and Refreshing

In [5], new algorithms for parallel multiplication (including the AND operation) and parallel refreshing were proposed. They are proven to be secure in the bounded moment model and proven to be strongly non-interfering using techniques from automated program verification [3]. Correct implementations of these algorithms are critical for the security of our implementations. We suggest slightly improved algorithms for $d = 4$ and $d = 8$ that require less randomness, but we could not generalize them to an improvement for all orders. As with the original algorithms, they are proven secure using the same automatic verification tools. NEON code that implements these algorithms can be found in Appendix A.

Refreshing. Refreshing can be necessary to make sure that values in registers are again statistically independent. The refreshing algorithm in [5] requires $2d$ bytes of fresh uniform randomness. Let x (in boldface) denote a vector register that contains $[x_0, \ldots, x_{d-1}]$, where $\bigoplus_{i=0}^{d-1} x_i = x$, and let r be a vector of the same length that contains uniformly random values. In the case of AES, a single share would be 16 bits long, so a randomness vector r will be $2d$ bytes.

Then $x' = r \oplus \mathrm{rot}(r, 1) \oplus x$ is a secure way to refresh x, where $\mathrm{rot}(a, n)$ rotates a to either left or right by n shares. Note that in the case of AES, this is equal to applying a rotation by $2n$ bytes.

For 4 shares, this algorithm additionally achieves SNI. However, to reach this with 8 shares, in [5] it turned out to be necessary to iterate the refreshing algorithm 3 times. In other words, one would need to compute

$$r \oplus \mathrm{rot}(r, 1) \oplus r' \oplus \mathrm{rot}(r', 1) \oplus r'' \oplus \mathrm{rot}(r'', 1) \oplus x$$

to achieve SNI at order 7. This requires 3 vectors of uniform randomness, or 48 bytes with AES. We improve this algorithm by computing:

$$r \oplus \mathrm{rot}(r, 1) \oplus r' \oplus \mathrm{rot}(r', 2) \oplus x.$$

We verified with the current version of the tool of [3] that this also achieves SNI at order 7. Moreover, it requires one less randomness vector. In the case of AES, we now require 32 bytes of uniform randomness.

Multiplication. Multiplication in a finite field, or an AND gate in the case of $\mathbb{F}_2$, is trickier to perform in a secure way. Consider the case where one wants to compute $z = x \cdot y$. Let r and r' be uniformly random vectors. Then, with 4 shares, the algorithm suggested in [5] computes the following to achieve SNI at order 3:

$$z = x \cdot y \oplus r \oplus x \cdot \mathrm{rot}(y, 1) \oplus \mathrm{rot}(x, 1) \cdot y \oplus \mathrm{rot}(r, 1)$$
$$\oplus\, x \cdot \mathrm{rot}(y, 2) \oplus r' \oplus \mathrm{rot}(r', 1).$$

However, we can again improve this slightly such that less randomness will be necessary. Let r_4 be a uniformly random value. Then we proved using the tool of [3] that the following is also 3rd-order SNI-secure. For AES, this requires 10 fresh uniformly random bytes (8 for r and 2 for r_4) instead of 16:

$$z = x \cdot y \oplus r \oplus x \cdot \mathrm{rot}(y, 1) \oplus \mathrm{rot}(x, 1) \cdot y \oplus \mathrm{rot}(r, 1)$$
$$\oplus\, x \cdot \mathrm{rot}(y, 2) \oplus [r_4, r_4, r_4, r_4].$$

With 8 shares, we use the original algorithm of [5] that is SNI at order 7. This requires 3 randomness vectors, which in the case of AES amounts to 48 bytes:

$$z = x \cdot y \oplus r \oplus x \cdot \mathrm{rot}(y, 1) \oplus \mathrm{rot}(x, 1) \cdot y \oplus \mathrm{rot}(r, 1)$$
$$\oplus\, x \cdot \mathrm{rot}(y, 2) \oplus \mathrm{rot}(x, 2) \cdot y \oplus r'$$
$$\oplus\, x \cdot \mathrm{rot}(y, 3) \oplus \mathrm{rot}(x, 3) \cdot y \oplus \mathrm{rot}(r', 1)$$
$$\oplus\, x \cdot \mathrm{rot}(y, 4) \oplus r'' \oplus \mathrm{rot}(r'', 1).$$

We attempted to reduce this by replacing the last randomness vector by a vector with a single random value, as in the algorithm for 4 shares, but we found that this does not achieve SNI at order 7.

Randomness. Implementations that are protected using higher-order masking require a lot of randomness. To be able to prove statistical independence, this randomness should be fresh and uniformly distributed. For resisting attacks in practice, it is not so clear whether the exact requirements are this strict. For instance, it might also be fine to expand a random seed using a pseudo-random number generator, or even to re-use randomness [1]. We consider this discussion to be out of scope of this work. However, because the impact on the performance can be very significant, we consider various approaches that occur in the literature. The first is to read all the randomness that we require from /dev/urandom using `fread`, like in [2]. This is the most conservative approach, but it is rather slow. Second, we also consider the case where all required randomness is already in a file that needs to be read into memory. The third approach assumes that there exists a fast true random-number generator and only considers the cost of a normal load instruction (`vld1`), like in [23].

The AES implementation with 4 shares requires 8 bytes per refresh and 10 bytes per masked AND. In the next section we will see that this amounts to $10 \cdot 32 \cdot (8 + 10) = 5760$ random bytes in total for the full AES, excluding the randomness used to do the initial masking of the input and the round keys. Naturally, the implementation that computes two blocks in parallel requires double the amount of random bytes. For 8 shares, refreshing takes 32 bytes and a masked AND uses 48 bytes, which makes the total $10 \cdot 32 \cdot (32 + 48) = 25600$ bytes.

3.3   SubBytes

Using the masked AND and refreshing algorithms, we can build our bitsliced SubBytes. Several papers have presented optimized bitsliced representations of the AES S-box. The smallest known to us is by Boyar and Peralta [9]. It uses 83 XORs/XNORs and 32 ANDs, which was later improved to 81 XORs/XNORs and 32 ANDs. The few NOTs can be moved into the key expansion, so we only need to consider XORs and ANDs. We use this implementation as our starting point, as this is also the implementation with the smallest number of binary ANDs, and an AND will be much slower to compute than a XOR.

We have used the compiler provided in [4] to generate a first masked implementation of SubBytes. This tells us when it is necessary to refresh a value, making sure that we do not refresh more often than strictly necessary. For our version of SubBytes, however, the compiler adds a refresh on one of the inputs for every AND. Then we implement an XOR on multiple shares in parallel with a veor instruction. For an AND, we use the algorithms of the previous section. Finally, the code has been manually optimized to limit pipeline stalls.

The S-box implementation has many intermediate variables. With 4 shares and a single block, the d registers are used. There are 32 of them and this turns out to be sufficient to store all the intermediate values. With two blocks or with 8 shares, however, we can use only 16 q registers. This implies that values have to be spilled to the stack. Of course, we want to minimize the overhead caused by this. In [36], an instruction scheduler and register allocator for the ARM Cortex-M4 was used to optimize the number of pushes to the stack. We modified this tool to handle the NEON instructions that we need, and use it to obtain an implementation with 18 push instructions and 18 loads.

According to a cycle-count simulator [38], our SubBytes implementation takes 1035 cycles with one block and 4 shares and 2127 cycles with 8 shares.

3.4   Linear Layer

We now discuss the linear operations of AES. We manually optimized them using a cycle-count simulator to hide as many latencies as possible [38].

AddRoundKey. AddRoundKey loads the round key with the vld1 instruction and adds it to the state using veor. The loads and arithmetic instructions can be interleaved. This helps because they go into separate NEON pipelines. An arithmetic instruction can than be executed in parallel with the load of the next part of the round key. For the loads, we make sure that they are aligned to at least 64 bits. AddRoundKey then only takes 10 cycles.

ShiftRows. With ShiftRows, rotations by fixed distances over 16 bits need to be computed. This can be implemented using `vand`, `vsra`, `vshl`, and `vorr` instructions. The arithmetic pipeline is now clearly the bottleneck. According to the simulator, our ShiftRows takes 150 cycles.

MixColumns. MixColumns requires more rotations by 4 or by 12 over 16 bits. This takes 106 cycles as measured by the simulator.

3.5   Performance

We benchmark our implementations on the BeagleBone Black with the clock frequency fixed at 1 GHz. In other words, we disabled frequency scaling. For the rest, we did not apply any changes to a standard Debian Linux 9 installation. In particular, we did not disable background processes and did not give our process special priority or CPU core affinity. The implementations are run 10000 times and the median cycle counts are given in Table 1.

Table 1. Performance of our masked AES implementations.

	4 shares 1 block	4 shares 2 blocks	8 shares 1 block
Clock cycles (randomness from `/dev/urandom`)	1, 598, 133	4, 738, 024	9, 470, 743
Clock cycles (randomness from normal file)	14, 488	17, 586	26, 601
Clock cycles (pre-loaded randomness)	12, 385	15, 194	23, 616
Random bytes	5, 760	11, 520	25, 600
Stack usage in bytes	12	300	300
Code size in bytes	39, 748	44, 004	70, 188

When using `/dev/urandom`, more than 99% of the time is spent on waiting for randomness, which is delivered at a rate of only 369 cycles per byte in the 8-share case. With a faster RNG, it becomes clear that our implementations are very fast and practical. We reach 474 cycles/byte with 4 shares and 1476 cycles/byte with 8 shares with pre-loaded randomness. Note that all implementations are fully unrolled, so the code size can trivially be decreased to roughly a tenth when this is a concern. However, we do not expect this to be an issue for devices with a Cortex-A8 or similar microprocessors, as they are relatively high-end.

Comparison to Related Work. In the following we discuss how our implementation compares to related work. We note that one should be cautious when it comes to comparing cycle counts, in particular when benchmarks were obtained on different microarchitectures or from simulators.

Goudarzi and Rivain [23] compared the performance of different higher-order masking approaches on ARM architectures. A simplified model is assumed for the number of cycles that specific instructions take, without referring to a specific microarchitecture. Private communication made clear that they are derived from the Keil simulator based on an ARM7TDMI-S. Their fastest bitsliced implementation is claimed to take 120,972 cycles with 4 shares and 334,712 cycles with 8 shares. To achieve this performance, the presence of a fast TRNG is assumed that delivers fresh randomness at 2.5 cycles per byte. Only the cost of a normal ldr instruction it taken into account, which corresponds to our performance with pre-loaded randomness. Despite the differences between ARMv4T and ARMv7-A, it is clear that there is quite a performance gap.

Wang et al. [43] presented a masked AES implementation for NEON that appears to run in 14,855 cycles with 4 shares and 77,820 with 8 shares on a Cortex-A15 simulator. This uses a cheap LFSR-based PRNG to provide randomness of which the authors already say that it should be replaced by a better source of randomness. We require less randomness due to a different masking scheme and apply bitslicing instead of computing SubBytes with tower-field arithmetic. The Cortex-A15 is more modern and powerful than the Cortex-A8. It can decode 3 instructions instead of 2, has out-of-order execution, and its NEON unit has a 128-bit wide datapath instead of 64-bit. However, it has longer pipelines which means that the penalty for, for instance, wrong branch predictions will be higher. We ran their code on our Cortex-A8-based benchmarking device and measured 34,662 cycles for the 4-share implementation and 158,330 cycles for the 8-share implementation, but we cannot fully explain the difference due to the amount of possible causes and the unavailability of more detailed information.

Balasch et al. [2] do use the same microarchitecture, but not the NEON SIMD processor. They do not mention the performance of their implementation. They explicitly say that they focus on the security evaluation and do not aim to achieve a high-throughput implementation.

Finally, Journault and Standaert [26] consider a bitsliced AES implementation with up to 32 shares on an ARM Cortex-M4. They exploit the parallelism of the shares, but not of AES itself as there are only 32-bit registers. An on-board TRNG is used to provide randomness at a reported speed of 20 cycles per byte. They use the refreshing and multiplication algorithms of [5] and almost the same S-box baseline implementation. Eventually, they report that 2,783,510 cycles are required to compute AES with 32 shares, of which 73% are spent on generating randomness. While this is certainly a very interesting idea, we show how the parallelism in SubBytes can additionally be exploited on a higher-end CPU with vector registers when using less shares might be sufficient.

Compared to unmasked implementations, there is of course still a noticeable performance penalty for adding side-channel protections. The unmasked bitsliced AES implementation of Bernstein and Schwabe [8] also exploits NEON to run at 19.12 cycles per byte (i.e., 306 cycles per block) in CTR mode, but that uses counter-mode caching and processes 8 blocks in parallel.

4   Side-Channel Evaluation

4.1   Measurement Setup

Balasch et al. [2] described in detail how they performed DPA attacks on a BeagleBone Black running at 1 GHz. Our experimental setup and measuring environment follow their approach. The board is running Debian Jessie and has several processes running in the background. We power the board using a standard AC adapter and connect it to the measurement PC over Ethernet. A few lines of Python on the BeagleBone open a TCP socket and spawn a new AES process for every input that it receives. The measurement PC connects to the socket and sends inputs over Ethernet.

We use a LeCroy WaveRunner 8404M-MS oscilloscope with a bandwidth of 4 GHz, operating at a sampling rate of 2.5 GSamples/sec. The AES process sets a GPIO port high before the execution of AES and sets it low after AES is finished, so that it can be used as the trigger signal. We place a magnetic field probe from Langer, model RF-B 0.3–3, with a small tip on the back of the BeagleBone board, near capacitor 66. The probe is connected to a Langer amplifier, model PA 303 SMA. The acquired traces were post-processed in order to perform signal alignment. We note that OS-related interrupts in conjunction with time-variant cache behavior result in a fairly unstable acquisition process. Thus, the evaluator has to either discard a large portion of the acquired trace set or resort to more sophisticated alignment techniques such as elastic alignment [41].

4.2   Security Order Evaluation

Since our implementation uses SNI gadgets, it maintains theoretical security against probing attacks of order $d - 1$ or less. The natural starting point of our side-channel evaluation is to identify any discrepancy between the theoretical and the actual security order, i.e., to determine the real-world effectiveness of the masking scheme. To achieve that goal, we need to assess whether the shares leak independently or whether the leakage function recombines them. Such recombinations can be captured by evaluating the security order in the bounded moment model [5] using, e.g., the leakage detection methodology [13,34,44].

Several lines of work have observed divergence between the theoretical order of a masking scheme and its real-world counterpart. Initially, Balasch, Gierlichs, Grosso, Reparaz, and Standaert [1] put forward the issue of distance-based leakages, which can result in the order reduction of a scheme. Specifically, if a $(d - 1)$th-order scheme is implemented on a device that exhibits distance-based leakages, its actual order will reduce to $\lfloor (d - 1)/2 \rfloor$, damaging its effectiveness w.r.t. noise amplification. Such effects have been observed in numerous architectures such as AVR, 8051 [1], ARM Cortex-M4 [16], FPGAs [12] and stem from both architectural choices and physical phenomena. To some extent, they can be mitigated by either increasing the order of the scheme or by "hardening" the implementation against effects that breach the independence of shares [31].

We evaluate the security order using the leakage detection methodology known as TVLA [13], which emphasizes detection over exploitation in order to speed-up the procedure. To make the evaluation feasible w.r.t. data complexity, we focus on the first round of our single-block 4-share implementation and employ the random vs. fixed Welch t-test, which uses random and fixed plaintexts acquired in a non-deterministic and randomly interleaved manner. Consecutively, we perform univariate t-tests of orders 1 through 4 using the incremental, one-pass formulas of Schneider and Moradi [34] at a level of significance $\alpha = 0.00001$. The results are plotted in Fig. 2. Note that the number of samples per trace is fairly high due to the lengthy computation of the 4-share masked AES round and due to the high sampling rate dictated by the clock frequency (1 GHz) and the Nyquist theorem. As a result, the t-test methodology faces the issue of multiple comparisons and we need to control the familywise error rate using the Šidák correction $\alpha_{SID} = 1 - (1 - \alpha)^{1/\#samples}$ [37]. The leakage detection threshold th is then computed using the formula $th = CDF^{-1}_{\mathcal{N}(0,1)}(1 - \alpha_{SID}/2)$, which equals to 6.25 when testing 25k samples per trace [44].

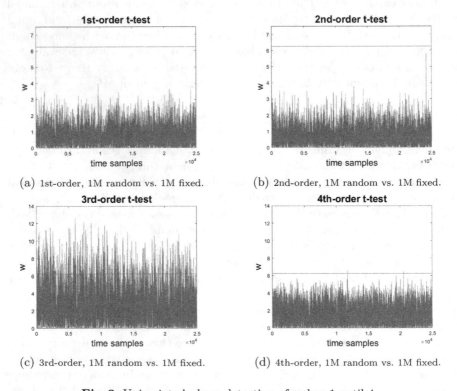

(a) 1st-order, 1M random vs. 1M fixed.   (b) 2nd-order, 1M random vs. 1M fixed.

(c) 3rd-order, 1M random vs. 1M fixed.   (d) 4th-order, 1M random vs. 1M fixed.

Fig. 2. Univariate leakage detection of orders 1 until 4.

In Fig. 2 we observe that for orders 1 and 2, a 1M random vs. 1M fixed t-test does not reject the null hypothesis, thus no leakage is detected in the first two statistical moments. The situation is different for higher orders: both the 3rd and the 4th-order univariate t-tests are able to detect leakage. This demonstrates that the actual security order of the implementation is less than the theoretical one and detecting the presence of 3rd-order leakage is in fact easier than detecting 4th-order leakage. Interestingly, the experimental results are not in direct accordance with the order reduction suggested by [1], i.e., our 3rd-order (4-share) implementation achieves practical order of 2, while the theorized reduction suggests $\lfloor 3/2 \rfloor = $ 1st-order security.

An additional way to approach the order reduction issue is to phrase it as a leakage certification problem [18,19]. The leakage certification procedure allows us to assess the quality of a leakage model w.r.t. estimation and assumption errors. Gauging the effect of estimation errors, i.e., those that arise from insufficient profiling, is straightforward and can be carried out via cross-validation techniques [20]. Assumption errors are more difficult to assess, since they arise from incorrect modeling choices and would ideally require the comparison between the chosen model and an unknown perfect model. To tackle this, the indirect approach of Durvaux, Standaert and Veyrat-Charvillon [19] observes the relation between estimation and assumption errors and if the latter are negligible in comparison, they conclude that the chosen model is adequate.

In our approach, we use the t-test-based certification toolset of Durvaux, Standaert, and Del Pozo [18], which focuses on the assumption and estimation errors for each statistical moment. Initially, we start with an erroneous model for our 4-share implementation: we assume that the leakage is sufficiently captured by a Gaussian template, i.e., a normal distribution that is fully described by the first two statistical moments. The results are visible in the upper part of Fig. 3, using a trace set of size 900,000. In particular, we plot the p-value of a t-test that compares an actual statistical moment (estimated from the trace set) with a simulated statistical moment (estimated by sampling the profiled model). A high p-value (i.e., a mostly white image) indicates that estimation errors overwhelm assumption errors and that the chosen model is adequate. A small p-value indicates that assumption errors are larger than estimation errors, thus the chosen model is erroneous. The process is repeated for all first four statistical moments (mean, variance, skewness, kurtosis) using cross-validation.

In the first two images of Fig. 3 (upper part, mean and variance), the high p-values indicate that these moments are well-captured by the model. Naturally, the fourth image (upper part, kurtosis) is black, indicating that the model disregards the 4th moment of a parallel 4-share implementation which should (in theory) contain useful information. Interestingly, the third image (skewness) is also black, penalizing any model that does not include the 3rd statistical moment, although in a perfect scheme it should not convey any information. We continue this approach with a more adequate model for the 4-share implementation: we assume that the leakage is captured by a Pearson type I distribution [35], i.e., a 4-moment Beta distribution. The results are visible in the lower part of Fig. 3 and show that the assumption errors in the 3rd and 4th moments tend to be smaller than the corresponding estimation errors.

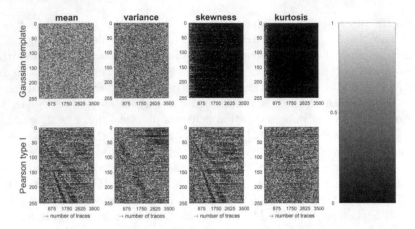

Fig. 3. Leakage certification p-values for Gaussian templates and Pearson type I.

As demonstrated by both the t-test methodology and the leakage certification process, the NEON-based implementations on ARM Cortex-A8 are likely to be subject to order reduction and may require further hardening to prevent dependencies between shares. The potential causes of the order reduction remain unexplored since they may stem from bus/register/memory transitions, pipelined data processing or even electrical coupling effects. Pinpointing the origin of the security reduction remains an open problem in the side-channel field since it essentially requires the countermeasure designer to access/modify the hardware architecture and chip layout, a task that is not possible with proprietary designs.

4.3 Information-Theoretic Evaluation

Having investigated the security order of the single-block 4-share AES implementation, we turn to the evaluation of its 8-share counterpart. The core feature of a masking scheme is the noise amplification stage. Assuming sufficient noise, it has been shown that the number of traces required for a successful attack grows exponentially w.r.t. the order $d - 1$ [11]. As a result, the evaluation of the proposed 8-share implementation can be beyond the measurement capability of most evaluators. To tackle this issue, we will rely on an information-theoretic approach used by Standaert et al. and Journault et al. [26,39,40], assisted by the bound-oriented works of Prouff and Rivain [32], Duc et al. [17], and Grosso and Standaert [24].

Analytically, we start with an unprotected (single-share) AES implementation and estimate the device/setup signal to noise ratio (SNR). We define the random variable S to correspond to the sensitive (key-dependent) intermediate values that we try to recover. Likewise, we define the random variable L to correspond to the time sample that exhibits high leakage (heuristically chosen as the sample with the highest t-test value). Subsequently, we profile Gaussian templates for all sensitive values s that are instances of variable S. In other words, we estimate $\hat{Pr}[L|s]_{model} \sim \mathcal{N}(\hat{\mu}_s, \hat{\sigma}_s^2)$ for all s. Using the estimated moments, we compute the SNR as the ratio $\hat{var}_s(\hat{\mu}_s)/\hat{E}_s(\hat{\sigma}_s^2)$, resulting in SNR ≈ 0.004. We continue to compute the Hypothetical Information (HI) which shows the amount of information leaked if the leakage is adequately represented by the estimated model $\hat{Pr}_{model}$.

$$\text{HI}(S; L) = H[S] + \sum_{s \in \mathcal{S}} Pr[s] \cdot \int_{l \in \mathcal{L}} \hat{Pr}_{model}[l|s] \cdot log_2 \hat{Pr}_{model}[s|l] \; dl,$$

where $\hat{Pr}_{model}[s|l] = \dfrac{\hat{Pr}_{model}[l|s]}{\sum_{s^* \in \mathcal{S}} \hat{Pr}_{model}[l|s^*]}.$

To simplify the evaluation process, we employ the independent shares' leakage assumption so as to extrapolate the information of a single share to the information of a d-tuple of shares. Thus, in order to obtain the HI bounds for security orders 3 and 7, we raise $\text{HI}(S; L)$ to the security order. In addition, the evaluator should take special consideration w.r.t. horizontal exploitation [6,42], which can be particularly hazardous, e.g., in the context of lengthy masked multiplications. To showcase such a scenario, we employ the bound of Prouff and Rivain [32], stating that the multiplication leakage is roughly $1.72d + 2.72$ times the leakage of a d-tuple of shares. The results of the information-theoretic evaluation are visible in Fig. 4.

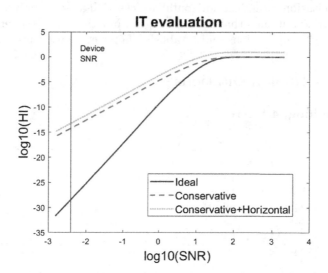

Fig. 4. Information-theoretic evaluation for the 8-share masked implementation.

Figure 4 assesses the performance of the proposed 8-share AES implementation, using information-theoretic bounds. The solid line shows the ideal masking performance, while the dashed line shows a conservative masking performance due to order reduction from order 7 to order 3. Last, the dotted line demonstrates the scenario where the adversary exploits the order-reduced (conservative) version in a horizontal fashion, i.e., (s)he incorporates all intermediate values computed during a masked AES multiplication. For the current SNR of the device, the measurement complexity is bounded by approximately 2^{91} measurements (ideal case), 2^{45} (conservative case) and 2^{42} (conservative horizontal case) [17].

5   Conclusion and Outlook

We have shown how higher-order masking of AES can be sped up using NEON vector registers. With a good randomness source, such implementations are very fast and practical. We also performed a side-channel evaluation to study the security order of the single-block 4-share implementation and an information-theoretic analysis to bound the measurement complexity w.r.t. the 8-share implementation.

Future SCA work can delve deeper into order-reduction issues, in conjunction with multivariate and horizontal exploitation. For instance, with our high-order univariate methodology, it is implicitly assumed that all the shares are manipulated in parallel. While this appears to hold when looking at the NEON assembly specifications, full parallelism may not be enforced on a hardware level. A deeper inspection of the circuitry could potentially clarify the actual parallelism and identify the underlying issues behind order reduction. Moving towards multivariate exploitation, practical horizontal attacks such as soft-analytical attacks need to be carried out such that we can gauge in practice the detrimental effects of lengthy leaky computations and establish a fairer evaluation procedure.

A   NEON Implementations

A.1   Refreshing, 4 Shares

```
//param rand is r register with address of randomness
//param a is d register to refresh
//param tmp is d register that gets overwritten
.macro refresh rand a tmp
  vld1.64 {\tmp}, [\rand]! //get 8 bytes of randomness
  veor \a, \tmp
  vext.16 \tmp, \tmp, #1
  veor \a, \tmp
.endm
```

A.2   Refreshing, 8 Shares

```
//param rand is r register with address of randomness
//param a is q register to refresh
//param tmp is q register that gets overwritten
.macro refresh rand a tmp
```

```
  vld1.64 {\tmp}, [\rand:128]! //get 16 bytes of randomness
  veor \a, \tmp
  vext.16 \tmp, \tmp, #1
  veor \a, \tmp

  vld1.64 {\tmp}, [\rand:128]! //get 16 bytes of randomness
  veor \a, \tmp
  vext.16 \tmp, \tmp, #2
  veor \a, \tmp
.endm
```

A.3   Multiplication, 4 Shares

```
//param rand is r register with address of randomness
//param c is d register where result gets stored
//param a and b are d registers to and, remain unchanged
//param tmp and tmpr are d registers that get overwritten
.macro masked_and rand c a b tmp tmpr
  vand \c, \a, \b //z = x.y
  vld1.64 {\tmpr}, [\rand]! //get 8 bytes of randomness
  vext.16 \tmp, \b, \b, #1
  veor \c, \tmpr  // + r
  vand \tmp, \a
  veor \c, \tmp    // + x.(rot y 1)
  vext.16 \tmp, \a, \a, #1
  vand \tmp, \b
  veor \c, \tmp    // + (rot x 1).y
  vext.16 \tmpr, \tmpr, #1
  veor \c, \tmpr  // + (rot r 1)
  vext.16 \tmp, \b, \b, #2
  vand \tmp, \a
  veor \c, \tmp    // + x.(rot y 2)
  vld1.16 {\tmp[]}, [\rand]! //get 2 bytes of randomness
  veor \c, \tmp    // + (r4,r4,r4,r4)
.endm
```

A.4   Multiplication, 8 Shares

```
//param rand is r register with address of randomness
//param c is q register where result gets stored
//param a and b are q registers to and, remain unchanged
//param tmp and tmpr are q registers that get overwritten
.macro masked_and rand c a b tmp tmpr
  vand \c, \a, \b //K = A.B
  vld1.64 {\tmpr}, [\rand:128]! //get 16 bytes of randomness
  vext.16 \tmp, \b, \b, #1
  veor \c, \tmpr  // + R
  vand \tmp, \a
  veor \c, \tmp    // + A.(rot B 1)
  vext.16 \tmp, \a, \a, #1
```

```
vand \tmp, \b
veor \c, \tmp     // + (rot A 1).B
vext.16 \tmpr, \tmpr, #1
veor \c, \tmpr    // + (rot R 1)
vext.16 \tmp, \b, \b, #2
vand \tmp, \a
veor \c, \tmp     // + A.(rot B 2)
vext.16 \tmp, \a, \a, #2
vand \tmp, \b
veor \c, \tmp     // + (rot A 2).B
vld1.64 {\tmpr}, [\rand:128]! //get 16 bytes of randomness
vext.16 \tmp, \b, \b, #3
veor \c, \tmpr    // + R'
vand \tmp, \a
veor \c, \tmp     // + A.(rot B 3)
vext.16 \tmp, \a, \a, #3
vand \tmp, \b
veor \c, \tmp     // + (rot A 3).B
vext.16 \tmpr, \tmpr, #1
veor \c, \tmpr    // + (rot R' 1)
vext.16 \tmp, \b, \b, #4
vand \tmp, \a
veor \c, \tmp     // + A.(rot B 4)
vld1.64 {\tmpr}, [\rand:128]! //get 16 bytes of randomness
veor \c, \tmpr    // + R''
vext.16 \tmpr, \tmpr, #1
veor \c, \tmpr    // + (rot R'' 1)
.endm
```

References

1. Balasch, J., Gierlichs, B., Grosso, V., Reparaz, O., Standaert, F.-X.: On the cost of lazy engineering for masked software implementations. In: Joye, M., Moradi, A. (eds.) CARDIS 2014. LNCS, vol. 8968, pp. 64–81. Springer, Cham (2015). https://doi.org/10.1007/978-3-319-16763-3_5

2. Balasch, J., Gierlichs, B., Reparaz, O., Verbauwhede, I.: DPA, bitslicing and masking at 1 GHz. In: Güneysu, T., Handschuh, H. (eds.) CHES 2015. LNCS, vol. 9293, pp. 599–619. Springer, Heidelberg (2015). https://doi.org/10.1007/978-3-662-48324-4_30

3. Barthe, G., Belaïd, S., Dupressoir, F., Fouque, P.-A., Grégoire, B., Strub, P.-Y.: Verified proofs of higher-order masking. In: Oswald, E., Fischlin, M. (eds.) EUROCRYPT 2015. LNCS, vol. 9056, pp. 457–485. Springer, Heidelberg (2015). https://doi.org/10.1007/978-3-662-46800-5_18

4. Barthe, G., Belaïd, S., Dupressoir, F., Fouque, P.-A., Grégoire, B., Strub, P.-Y., Zucchini, R.: Strong non-interference and type-directed higher-order masking. In: Proceedings of the 2016 ACM SIGSAC Conference on Computer and Communications Security, CCS 2016, pp. 116–129. ACM (2016). https://doi.org/10.1145/2976749.2978427

5. Barthe, G., Dupressoir, F., Faust, S., Grégoire, B., Standaert, F.-X., Strub, P.-Y.: Parallel implementations of masking schemes and the bounded moment leakage model. In: Coron, J.-S., Nielsen, J.B. (eds.) EUROCRYPT 2017. LNCS, vol. 10210, pp. 535–566. Springer, Cham (2017). https://doi.org/10.1007/978-3-319-56620-7_19
6. Battistello, A., Coron, J.-S., Prouff, E., Zeitoun, R.: Horizontal side-channel attacks and countermeasures on the ISW masking scheme. In: Gierlichs, B., Poschmann, A.Y. (eds.) CHES 2016. LNCS, vol. 9813, pp. 23–39. Springer, Heidelberg (2016). https://doi.org/10.1007/978-3-662-53140-2_2
7. Bernstein, D.J.: Cache-timing attacks on AES. https://cr.yp.to/antiforgery/cachetiming-20050414.pdf (2005)
8. Bernstein, D.J., Schwabe, P.: NEON crypto. In: Prouff, E., Schaumont, P. (eds.) CHES 2012. LNCS, vol. 7428, pp. 320–339. Springer, Heidelberg (2012). https://doi.org/10.1007/978-3-642-33027-8_19
9. Boyar, J., Peralta, R.: A new combinational logic minimization technique with applications to cryptology. In: Festa, P. (ed.) SEA 2010. LNCS, vol. 6049, pp. 178–189. Springer, Heidelberg (2010). https://doi.org/10.1007/978-3-642-13193-6_16
10. Canright, D., Batina, L.: A very compact "perfectly masked" S-Box for AES. In: Bellovin, S.M., Gennaro, R., Keromytis, A., Yung, M. (eds.) ACNS 2008. LNCS, vol. 5037, pp. 446–459. Springer, Heidelberg (2008). https://doi.org/10.1007/978-3-540-68914-0_27
11. Chari, S., Jutla, C.S., Rao, J.R., Rohatgi, P.: Towards sound approaches to counteract power-analysis attacks. In: Wiener, M. (ed.) CRYPTO 1999. LNCS, vol. 1666, pp. 398–412. Springer, Heidelberg (1999). https://doi.org/10.1007/3-540-48405-1_26
12. De Cnudde, T., Bilgin, B., Gierlichs, B., Nikov, V., Nikova, S., Rijmen, V.: Does coupling affect the security of masked implementations? In: Guilley, S. (ed.) COSADE 2017. LNCS, vol. 10348, pp. 1–18. Springer, Cham (2017). https://doi.org/10.1007/978-3-319-64647-3_1
13. Cooper, J., DeMulder, E., Goodwill, G., Jaffe, J., Kenworthy, G., Rohatgi, P.: Test vector leakage assessment (TVLA) methodology in practice (2013). http://icmc-2013.org/wp/wp-content/uploads/2013/09/goodwillkenworthtestvector.pdf
14. Coron, J.-S., Prouff, E., Rivain, M., Roche, T.: Higher-order side channel security and mask refreshing. In: Moriai, S. (ed.) FSE 2013. LNCS, vol. 8424, pp. 410–424. Springer, Heidelberg (2014). https://doi.org/10.1007/978-3-662-43933-3_21
15. Daemen, J., Rijmen, V.: The design of Rijndael. AES – The Advanced Encryption Standard. Springer, Heidelberg (2002). https://doi.org/10.1007/978-3-662-04722-4
16. de Groot, W., Papagiannopoulos, K., de La Piedra, A., Schneider, E., Batina, L.: Bitsliced masking and ARM: friends or foes? In: Bogdanov, A. (ed.) LightSec 2016. LNCS, vol. 10098, pp. 91–109. Springer, Cham (2017). https://doi.org/10.1007/978-3-319-55714-4_7
17. Duc, A., Faust, S., Standaert, F.-X.: Making masking security proofs concrete. In: Oswald, E., Fischlin, M. (eds.) EUROCRYPT 2015. LNCS, vol. 9056, pp. 401–429. Springer, Heidelberg (2015). https://doi.org/10.1007/978-3-662-46800-5_16
18. Durvaux, F., Standaert, F.-X., Del Pozo, S.M.: Towards easy leakage certification. In: Gierlichs, B., Poschmann, A.Y. (eds.) CHES 2016. LNCS, vol. 9813, pp. 40–60. Springer, Heidelberg (2016). https://doi.org/10.1007/978-3-662-53140-2_3
19. Durvaux, F., Standaert, F.-X., Veyrat-Charvillon, N.: How to certify the leakage of a chip? In: Nguyen, P.Q., Oswald, E. (eds.) EUROCRYPT 2014. LNCS, vol. 8441, pp. 459–476. Springer, Heidelberg (2014). https://doi.org/10.1007/978-3-642-55220-5_26

20. Efron, B., Tibshirani, R.J.: An Introduction to the Bootstrap. CRC Press, Boca Raton (1994)
21. Gandolfi, K., Mourtel, C., Olivier, F.: Electromagnetic analysis: concrete results. In: Koç, Ç.K., Naccache, D., Paar, C. (eds.) CHES 2001. LNCS, vol. 2162, pp. 251–261. Springer, Heidelberg (2001). https://doi.org/10.1007/3-540-44709-1_21
22. Goubin, L., Patarin, J.: DES and differential power analysis — the "duplication" method. In: Koç, Ç.K., Paar, C. (eds.) CHES 1999. LNCS, vol. 1717, pp. 158–172. Springer, Heidelberg (1999). https://doi.org/10.1007/3-540-48059-5_15
23. Goudarzi, D., Rivain, M.: How fast can higher-order masking be in software? In: Coron, J.-S., Nielsen, J.B. (eds.) EUROCRYPT 2017. LNCS, vol. 10210, pp. 567–597. Springer, Cham (2017). https://doi.org/10.1007/978-3-319-56620-7_20
24. Grosso, V., Standaert, F.-X.: Masking proofs are tight (and how to exploit it in security evaluations). Cryptology ePrint Archive, Report 2017/116 (2017). http://eprint.iacr.org/2017/116
25. Ishai, Y., Sahai, A., Wagner, D.: Private circuits: securing hardware against probing attacks. In: Boneh, D. (ed.) CRYPTO 2003. LNCS, vol. 2729, pp. 463–481. Springer, Heidelberg (2003). https://doi.org/10.1007/978-3-540-45146-4_27
26. Journault, A., Standaert, F.-X.: Very high order masking: efficient implementation and security evaluation. In: Fischer, W., Homma, N. (eds.) CHES 2017. LNCS, vol. 10529, pp. 623–643. Springer, Cham (2017). https://doi.org/10.1007/978-3-319-66787-4_30
27. Käsper, E., Schwabe, P.: Faster and timing-attack resistant AES-GCM. In: Clavier, C., Gaj, K. (eds.) CHES 2009. LNCS, vol. 5747, pp. 1–17. Springer, Heidelberg (2009). https://doi.org/10.1007/978-3-642-04138-9_1
28. Kim, H.S., Hong, S., Lim, J.: A fast and provably secure higher-order masking of AES S-Box. In: Preneel, B., Takagi, T. (eds.) CHES 2011. LNCS, vol. 6917, pp. 95–107. Springer, Heidelberg (2011). https://doi.org/10.1007/978-3-642-23951-9_7
29. Kocher, P., Jaffe, J., Jun, B.: Differential power analysis. In: Wiener, M. (ed.) CRYPTO 1999. LNCS, vol. 1666, pp. 388–397. Springer, Heidelberg (1999). https://doi.org/10.1007/3-540-48405-1_25
30. Könighofer, R.: A fast and cache-timing resistant implementation of the AES. In: Malkin, T. (ed.) CT-RSA 2008. LNCS, vol. 4964, pp. 187–202. Springer, Heidelberg (2008). https://doi.org/10.1007/978-3-540-79263-5_12
31. Papagiannopoulos, K., Veshchikov, N.: Mind the gap: towards secure 1st-order masking in software. In: Guilley, S. (ed.) COSADE 2017. LNCS, vol. 10348, pp. 282–297. Springer, Cham (2017). https://doi.org/10.1007/978-3-319-64647-3_17
32. Prouff, E., Rivain, M.: Masking against side-channel attacks: a formal security proof. In: Johansson, T., Nguyen, P.Q. (eds.) EUROCRYPT 2013. LNCS, vol. 7881, pp. 142–159. Springer, Heidelberg (2013). https://doi.org/10.1007/978-3-642-38348-9_9
33. Rivain, M., Prouff, E.: Provably secure higher-order masking of AES. In: Mangard, S., Standaert, F.-X. (eds.) CHES 2010. LNCS, vol. 6225, pp. 413–427. Springer, Heidelberg (2010). https://doi.org/10.1007/978-3-642-15031-9_28
34. Schneider, T., Moradi, A.: Leakage assessment methodology. In: Güneysu, T., Handschuh, H. (eds.) CHES 2015. LNCS, vol. 9293, pp. 495–513. Springer, Heidelberg (2015). https://doi.org/10.1007/978-3-662-48324-4_25
35. Schneider, T., Moradi, A., Standaert, F.-X., Güneysu, T.: Bridging the gap: advanced tools for side-channel leakage estimation beyond Gaussian templates and histograms. In: Avanzi, R., Heys, H. (eds.) SAC 2016. LNCS, vol. 10532, pp. 58–78. Springer, Cham (2017). https://doi.org/10.1007/978-3-319-69453-5_4

36. Schwabe, P., Stoffelen, K.: All the AES you need on Cortex-M3 and M4. In: Avanzi, R., Heys, H. (eds.) SAC 2016. LNCS, vol. 10532, pp. 180–194. Springer, Cham (2017). https://doi.org/10.1007/978-3-319-69453-5_10

37. Sidak, Z.: Rectangular confidence regions for the means of multivariate normal distributions. J. Am. Stat. Assoc. **62**(318), 626–633 (1967)

38. Sobole, E.: Cycle counter for Cortex-A8. http://pulsar.webshaker.net/ccc/index.php?lng=us

39. Standaert, F.-X., Malkin, T.G., Yung, M.: A unified framework for the analysis of side-channel key recovery attacks. In: Joux, A. (ed.) EUROCRYPT 2009. LNCS, vol. 5479, pp. 443–461. Springer, Heidelberg (2009). https://doi.org/10.1007/978-3-642-01001-9_26

40. Standaert, F.-X., Veyrat-Charvillon, N., Oswald, E., Gierlichs, B., Medwed, M., Kasper, M., Mangard, S.: The world is not enough: another look on second-order DPA. In: Abe, M. (ed.) ASIACRYPT 2010. LNCS, vol. 6477, pp. 112–129. Springer, Heidelberg (2010). https://doi.org/10.1007/978-3-642-17373-8_7

41. van Woudenberg, J.G.J., Witteman, M.F., Bakker, B.: Improving differential power analysis by elastic alignment. In: Kiayias, A. (ed.) CT-RSA 2011. LNCS, vol. 6558, pp. 104–119. Springer, Heidelberg (2011). https://doi.org/10.1007/978-3-642-19074-2_8

42. Veyrat-Charvillon, N., Gérard, B., Standaert, F.-X.: Soft analytical side-channel attacks. In: Sarkar, P., Iwata, T. (eds.) ASIACRYPT 2014. LNCS, vol. 8873, pp. 282–296. Springer, Heidelberg (2014). https://doi.org/10.1007/978-3-662-45611-8_15

43. Wang, J., Vadnala, P.K., Großschädl, J., Xu, Q.: Higher-order masking in practice: a vector implementation of masked AES for ARM NEON. In: Nyberg, K. (ed.) CT-RSA 2015. LNCS, vol. 9048, pp. 181–198. Springer, Cham (2015). https://doi.org/10.1007/978-3-319-16715-2_10

44. Ding, A.A., Zhang, L., Durvaux, F., Standaert, F.-X., Fei, Y.: Towards sound and optimal leakage detection procedure. In: Eisenbarth, T., Teglia, Y. (eds.) CARDIS 2017. LNCS, vol. 10728, pp. 105–122. Springer, Cham (2018). https://doi.org/10.1007/978-3-319-75208-2_7

On Masked Galois-Field Multiplication for Authenticated Encryption Resistant to Side Channel Analysis

Hirokazu Oshida$^{(\boxtimes)}$, Rei Ueno$^{(\boxtimes)}$, Naofumi Homma, and Takafumi Aoki

Tohoku University, Aramaki Aza Aoba 6–6–05, Aoba-ku, Sendai-shi 980-8579, Japan
oshida@riec.tohoku.ac.jp

Abstract. This paper presents a side-channel attack on masked Galois-field (GF) multiplication used in authenticated encryptions including AES-GCM and a new countermeasure against the proposed attack. While the previous side-channel attack is likely to recover the full key of GHASH in AES-GCM, no countermeasure has been discussed and evaluated until now. In this paper, we first apply a straightforward masking countermeasure to GF multiplication for GHASH and show that the masked GF multiplication is resistant to the previous attack. We then show the straightforward masked GHASH can be defeated by a new attack utilizing the variance of power trace. The feasibility of the new attack is demonstrated by an experiment with power traces measured from a smart card operating the masked GHASH. Finally, we propose a new masking countermeasure against the proposed attack.

Keywords: Galois-field multiplication · AES-GCM · Masking
Side-channel attack · Authenticated encryption

1 Introduction

Authenticated encryptions (AEs) have been widely used in secure information systems demonstrating both confidentiality and integrity. In recent years, AEs are expected to be implemented on even resource-constrained embedded devices for securing Internet of Things (IoT) applications. Currently, AES-GCM is one of the most widely used AEs, with applications including SSL/TLS and SSH [14]. It is composed of AES encryption in the counter mode and authentication tag generation based on a Galois-field (GF) multiply and accumulator (GHASH). Thanks to the block-wise parallelism, AES-GCM achieves higher throughput and implementation efficiency than that of block-chaining modes of operations (e.g., CMAC). Thus, studies on AES-GCM has an influence on other AE designs including candidates for CAESAR competition [7].

AES-GCM is computationally secure against existing cryptanalyses. On the other hand, the possibility of a side-channel attack (SCA) [12] on AES-GCM should also be evaluated like other ciphers. Because of its increasing demand,

© Springer International Publishing AG, part of Springer Nature 2018
J. Fan and B. Gierlichs (Eds.): COSADE 2018, LNCS 10815, pp. 44–57, 2018.
https://doi.org/10.1007/978-3-319-89641-0_3

an AES-GCM module resistant to SCAs is strongly required for secure implementation on smart cards and embedded systems. So far, much work has been devoted to differential power analyses (DPAs) on AES primitives [9,13] and DPA-resistant AES implementations [4,6,16,21,23]. On the other hand, SCAs on GF multiplication in GHASH, which is another major component of AES-GCM, were recently reported in [2,3,17]. These attacks are likely to recover the secret key for authentication tag generation in order to forge tags. However, to the best of the authors' knowledge, no countermeasures against such attacks have been discussed and evaluated with actual devices until now. In the context of AEs, a development of SCA-resistant GF multiplication for GHASH is also important for secure AES-GCM implementations on smart cards and embedded systems.

This paper presents a new attack on GF multiplication in GHASH and a corresponding countermeasure. The contribution of this study is threefold: (i) We first apply a straightforward masking countermeasure to GF multiplication in GHASH in order to evaluate its resistance to the previous attack of [2]. The resistance is evaluated using power traces generated by a simulation. (ii) We then propose a new attack on the straightforward masked GHASH. The basic idea of the proposed attack is to exploit the variance of power consumption like the second-order DPA, given measured masked intermediate values and mask values. For the validity verification, we measure power traces of a straightforwardly masked GHASH implemented on a smart card and apply the proposed attack. Finally, (iii) we present a masking countermeasure which proves resilient even against the proposed attack.

2 Preliminaries and Related Work

2.1 Brief Description and Notation of AES-GCM

Let $(P_1, P_2, \ldots, P_n)$, $(A_1, A_2, \ldots, A_m)$, and $(C_1, C_2, \ldots, C_n)$ be plaintexts, associated data, and ciphertexts, respectively. Here, P_i, A_j, and C_i ($1 \leq i \leq n$ and $1 \leq j \leq m$) denote a 128-bit block. Let K, IV, and T be a 128-bit secret key, a 96-bit initialization vector, and a 128-bit authentication tag, respectively. Figure 1 shows the block diagram of the AES-GCM, where each arrow basically represents a 128-bit data flow. Blocks "AES ENC", "MULT", and "$\oplus$" denote one block AES encryption, GF multiplication, and GF addition (i.e., bit-parallel XOR), respectively. Note here that these GF arithmetic operations are performed over a polynomial basis (PB)-based $GF(2^{128})$ with an irreducible polynomial $x^{128} \oplus x^7 \oplus x^2 \oplus x \oplus 1$.

AES-GCM encryption consists of n AES encryption operations in the counter mode and a tag generation based on GHASH denoted by the blue and red dotted frames in Fig. 1, respectively. The counter values for n AES encryption operations $Y_0, Y_1, Y_2, \ldots, Y_i \ldots, Y_n$ generated from IV, namely, $Y_0 = IV', Y_i = Y_{i-1} + 1 \ (= IV + i)$, where IV' is a 128-bit value obtained by concatenating a 32-bit value $0^{31}1$ to the LSB of a 96-bit IV. Note here that the encryption result of Y_0 is only used as a sub key S for the following tag generation, but not

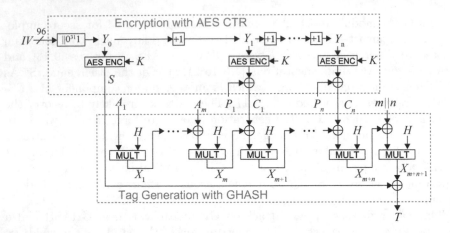

Fig. 1. Block diagram of AES-GCM.

for the counter-mode encryption. On the other hand, in the tag generation part, we first compute a GHASH, that is, a hash value X_{m+n+1}, where H is a secret 128-bit hash key given by the AES encryption result of the 128-bit zero vector with the secret key K. More precisely, we first compute $X_j = (X_{j-1} \oplus A_j)H$ and then $X_{m+i} = (X_{m+i-1} \oplus C_i)H$, where $X_0 = 0$. Finally, we compute the hash value $X_{m+n+1} = (X_{m+n} \oplus m||n)H$, where $m||n$ denotes $m \times 2^{\log(n)} + n$. After the computation of GHASH, we obtain the authentication tag $T = S \oplus X_{m+n+1}$.

The security of AES-GCM should be preserved for not only the confidentiality of the secret key K, but also the confidentiality of the hash key H and sub key S. If either H or S is exposed, attackers can compute (i.e., forge) valid authentication tags for any pairs of associated data and ciphertexts [10]. Forged authentication tags make an AE fatally vulnerable because such an AE cannot provide message integrity. For example, the forging attackers can make victims perform a compromised HTTPS authentication that redirects to malicious websites by deceiving the authentication provided by TLS [5]. Therefore, it is quite important to implement an AES-GCM module which never exposes H and S in addition to K.

2.2　Side-Channel Attack on AES-GCM

AES-GCM consists of AES encryption operations in the counter mode and a GHASH-based tag generation. SCAs on AES primitives (in the counter mode) [9,13] and its countermeasures [4,6,16,21,23] have been studied by many researchers. On the other hand, SCAs on the GHASH-based tag generation to retrieve H were recently reported in [2,3,11], but no countermeasures against them have been discussed and evaluated so far.

In the following, we briefly introduce the state-of-the-art attack presented in 2015 [2]. The attacker observes the power traces of the first GF multiplication of GHASH when the AES-GCM module performs its encryption z times.

Let $A_1^{(s)}$ and $X_1^{(s)}$ be the first block of authentication data for the s-th encryption ($1 \le s \le z$) and the result of the first multiplication (i.e., the product of $A_1^{(s)}$ and H), respectively. The attacker can roughly estimate $HW(X_1^{(s)})$ from the observed power trace, where $HW(x)$ denotes the Hamming weight of x. The main focus of the attack is to compute H from $A_1^{(s)}$ inversely and estimate $HW(X_1^{(s)})$; that is, $X_1^{(s)} = A_1^{(s)}H$. However, $HW(X_1^{(s)})$ cannot always be estimated accurately because of noise included in the power trace. In other words, we should recover H from $A_1^{(s)}$ and the inaccurate $HW(X_1^{(s)})$. Therefore, the attack [2] recovers H with these three steps: (i) select desired $A_1^{(s)}$s according to the observed traces (and discard remaining ones), (ii) build a learning parity with noise (LPN) problem whose solution is H, and (iii) solve the LPN problem to recover H. Here, an LPN problem is represented by a set of equations over $GF(2)$ including incorrect equations (i.e., errors) at a small ratio. In other words, the LPN problem is equal to learning with an error (LWE) problem over $GF(2)$.

Step (i) selects operands $A_1^{(s_1)}, A_1^{(s_2)}, \ldots, A_1^{(s_u)}, \ldots, A_1^{(s_t)}$ ($1 \le u \le t$) in accordance with measured power traces of multiplication $X_1^{(s)} = A_1^{(s)}H$ such that $HW(X_1^{(s_u)})$ would be extremely large or small, where t is the number of selected operands and is determined by z and the signal to-noise ratio (SNR) of the measurement. Here, it is assumed that $HW(X_1^{(s_u)})$ and the corresponding power trace have a positive correlation. In other words, if the power consumption of multiplication $X_1^{(s_u)} = A_1^{(s_u)}H$ is extremely large (or small), $HW(X_1^{(s_u)})$ would be extremely large (or small).

Step (ii) builds an LPN problem in accordance with $A_1^{(s_u)}$. Let $h_v (1 \le v \le 128)$ be the v-th bit of H. Since the multiplication over $GF(2^{128})$ can be represented by a set of 128 linear equations over $GF(2)$, we can build linear equations with variable h_v if we know $X_1^{(s_u)}$. However, in general, we cannot know the secret value $X_1^{(s_u)}$. Then, the attacker builds the linear equations by considering $X_1^{(s_u)}$ as the 128-bit 1's or 0's vector according to the result of Step (i). Note here that these equations include some errors (i.e., wrong equations) with a small discrepancy resulting from the fact that $X_1^{(s_u)}$ is not exactly equal to the 1's or 0's vector. Thus, we can recover h_v (i.e., H) by solving the LPN problem. Since 128 linear equations are obtained from $A_1^{(s_u)}$, the LPN problem is composed of $128 \times t$ equations.

Step (iii) finally solves the LPN problem. The solution of LPN problem (i.e. the hash key h_v) is denoted as a candidate value that satisfies most equations of the LPN problem among all of the candidate values because values except for the solution satisfy about half of the whole equations statistically. This indicates that we can solve the LPN problem by counting the number of satisfied equations for all the candidate values. However, the attacker cannot examine all the candidate values by straightforward brute force since the variables of the LPN problem are given by 128 bits. For reducing the computational complexity, the attack of [2] consists of two steps: (a) to reduce the number of variables (i.e., bit-length) based on a Generalized Birthday Paradox-like (GBP) algorithm [24], and

Table 1. Trade-offs between time and memory for solving LPN problem

Available memory	2^{27}	2^{36}	2^{44}
Computation time	$2^{59.31}$	$2^{51.68}$	2^{50}

(b) to enumerate the number of satisfied equations for each candidate value with a Walsh-Hadamard transform (WHT). In Step (iii)(a), GBP algorithm reduces the number of variables in the LPN problem by adding equations to each other in a similar manner to Gaussian elimination. Here, the number of additions in the GBP algorithm is limited according to the number of erroneous equations in order to avoid diffusing the error too much. In other words, the number of erroneous equations determines the complexity of solving the LPN problem. In Step (iii)(b), WHT enables to perform the enumeration faster than a brute force. However, the space and time complexities of WHT increase exponentially to the bit-length of inputs. Table 1 shows an example of time/memory trade-offs for solving the LPN problem with 2^{20} traces under the condition that the signal-to-noise ratio (SNR) of the measurement is given by 8, where "Computation time" denotes the approximate number of arithmetic operations (i.e. addition,) and "Available memory" denotes the approximate memory size in bytes. The SNR and the number of traces also have an impact on the computational complexities because the number of erroneous equations depends on them. Table 1 indicates that this attack would be feasible for attackers who have sufficient traces and memory even when the SNR of the measurement is not good (SNR = 8). See [2] for details.

3   Masked GHASH

To perform the attack, the attacker should observe the power trace of the multiplication $A_1^{(s)}H$ to estimate $HW(X_1^{(s)})$. A practical idea for a countermeasure is to mask the multiplication of $X_1^{(s)} = A_1^{(s)}H$. Figure 2 shows the block diagram of a straightforwardly masked GHASH, where $M^{(s)}$ denotes the 128-bit mask value, $X_l'^{(s)}(= X_l^{(s)} \oplus M^{(s)}H^l)$ is masked $X_l^{(s)}$, and $U_l^{(s)}(= M^{(s)}H^l)$ is the unmasked value of $X_l'^{(s)}$ for the s-th encryption ($1 \leq l \leq m + n + 1$). Here, we do not consider masking H because there is no known exploitable side-channel leakage from a fixed value of H itself [18]. In addition, according to [8,15,19,22], masking H requires non-negligible overhead compared to the above scheme.

The masked GHASH in Fig. 2 consists of a masked multiplication and an unmasked value calculation in a similar manner to the typical masking schemes for symmetric key ciphers. The multiplications $A_1^{(s)}H$ and $(A_1^{(s)}H \oplus A_2^{(s)})H$ should be masked because they can be represented by linear equations of h_v. Note that $X_2^{(s)}$ can also be exploited by the attack due to the linearity of the squaring operation over $GF(2^{128})$.

To evaluate the resistance of the above masked GHASH, we perform the attack of [2] on an unmasked and a masked 8-bit multiplier by simulation.

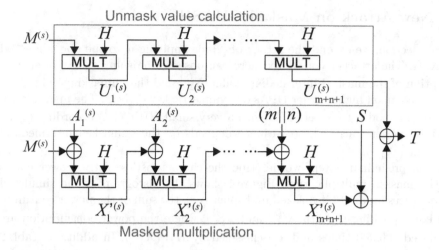

Fig. 2. Masked GHASH.

Figure 3 shows the measures to disclose for (a) the unmasked and (b) masked multipliers, where the horizontal axis denotes the number of traces and the vertical axis denotes the ratio of the number of satisfied equations to that of all equations for all the candidate values to solve this LPN problem. Here, the ratio for the correct key is denoted in black. While we can easily identify the correct key from the unmasked multiplier in Fig. 3(a), we have difficulty in distinguishing the correct and incorrect keys from the masked multiplier in Fig. 3(b). This means that the attacker cannot recover the secret key from the masked multiplier even if the attacker solves the LPN problem. Although we used 8-bit multipliers in this experiment for simplicity, we would obtain the equivalent results for the case of those with other bit-lengths, including 128 bits. Thus, we can confirm the resistance of the above masked GHASH.

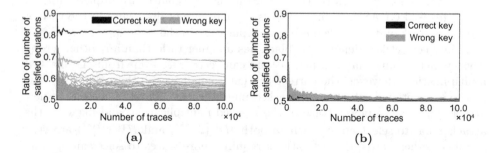

Fig. 3. Measure to disclosure for (a) unmasked and (b) masked multipliers.

4   New Attack on Masked GHASH

In this section, we extend the attack of [2] for applying it to the above masked GHASH. The attacker considered here can observe the sum of the power consumption of the masked intermediate value $X_1^{(s)}$ and the unmasking value $U_1^{(s)}$ like the common higher-order DPAs on symmetric key ciphers. The main idea of the new method is to select $A_1^{(s_u)}$ with a very small $HW(X_1^{(s)})$ according to the observed power trace, whose variance depends on the unmasked intermediate value (i.e., $X_1^{(s)}$).

As a preliminary step, we describe the characteristics of the power traces for the masked multiplication. Figure 4 shows the histogram of the simulated power traces for an 8-bit masked multiplier (i.e., the sum of the power consumption corresponding to both $X'^{(s)}_1$ and $U_1^{(s)}$), where the power consumption are simulated 100,000 times and are classified by $HW(X_1^{(s)})$. In addition, Table 2 shows the mean and variance of power consumption for each $HW(X_1^{(s)})$. From Fig. 4 and Table 2, we can find that the variance decreases linearly by $HW(X_1^{(s)})$ while the means are fixed for every $HW(X_1^{(s)})$. In particular, the variance is the largest when $HW(X_1^{(s)}) = 0$. This result indicates that we can roughly estimate $HW(X_1^{(s)})$ even from the power traces of the masked multiplication.

In this paper, we assume two attack scenarios: known-input and chosen-input. We first describe how to recover H in the known-input scenario (where the attacker cannot control the input). The main difference between the conventional and new attack is in Step (ii). In the case of masked multiplication, $HW(X_1^{(s)})$ would be very small if the corresponding power trace is extremely large or small as shown in Fig. 4. Therefore, Step (ii) of our attack builds an LPN problem by considering $X_1^{(s_u)}$ as the 128-bit 0's vector according to $A_1^{(s_u)}$. Note that our attack considers $X_1^{(s_u)}$ as the 128-bit 0's vector instead of 1's, even if the corresponding power trace is extremely large. Then, the attacker can recover H by solving the LPN problem in Step (iii).

For validation, we perform the new attack using a smart card implementation of the masked GHASH. Figure 5 shows the measure of disclosure in the case of the new attack on the masked 8-bit multiplication in the same manner as Fig. 3. The only correct key denoted by black has a higher ratio than any other wrong keys, which means that the new attack can recover H even from the masked multiplication. However, the correct key has a smaller peak than Fig. 3(a); that is, the conventional attack on unmasked multiplication. This is because the new attack exploits the power trace of the masked multiplication, and likewise, the attacker has to select an $A_1^{(s)}$ where both $HW(X'^{(s)}_1)$ and $HW(U_1^{(s)})$ are very small. In other words, the new attack requires more traces to select an optimal $A_1^{(s)}$ with a small $HW(X_1^{(s)})$ than the conventional attack because $U_1^{(s)}$ is considered to be noise. As a result, the peak of the correct key in Fig. 5 is smaller than that in Fig. 3(a). This indicates that it is more time-consuming to solve the LPN problem in the new attack than that in the conventional attack on the unmasked GHASH.

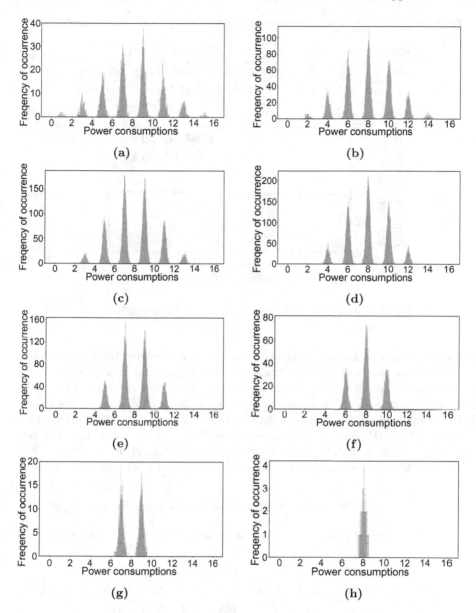

Fig. 4. Histograms of power consumptions of masked multiplication for different $HW(X_1^{(s)})$ from (a) 1 to (h) 8.

The computational complexity of the new attack is evaluated in simulation. The computational complexity for solving the LPN problem heavily depends on the ratio of erroneous equations to all equations. The ratio then depends on the number of traces and the SNR of measurement. In addition, the available

Table 2. Mean and variance of power consumptions for 8-bit masked multiplier

$HW(X_1^{(s)})$	0	1	2	3	4	5	6	7	8
Mean	7.97	7.96	7.99	7.96	7.99	7.99	8.01	8.00	8.00
Variance	7.97	6.87	5.92	4.96	4.00	3.04	2.04	1.04	0.03

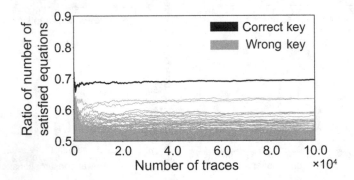

Fig. 5. Measure to disclosure for masked 8-bit multiplication.

memory also has an impact on the time complexity of solving the LPN problem. Table 3 shows the time complexity of the new attack. Time complexity is the approximate number of arithmetic operations. Here "Mem." denotes the available memory and "N/A" denotes Not Attackable. Note that we cannot solve the LPN problem when the SNR and the number of traces are too small due to the limitation of GBP algorithm. However, from Table 3, we can find that the new attack is feasible when the SNR of measurement is enough large (64~). Thus, we can confirm the effectiveness of the new attack on the masked GHASH.

Table 3. Time complexity of proposed attack

SNR	Num. of traces: 2^{18}			Num. of traces: 2^{22}			Num. of traces: 2^{24}		
	Mem. 2^{25}	Mem. 2^{33}	Mem. 2^{46}	Mem. 2^{25}	Mem. 2^{33}	Mem. 2^{46}	Mem. 2^{25}	Mem. 2^{33}	Mem. 2^{46}
8	N/A	N/A	N/A	N/A	N/A	N/A	N/A	N/A	86.0
32	N/A	N/A	N/A	N/A	N/A	81.3	N/A	N/A	74.7
64	48.2	48.0	48.0	47.6	47.6	47.6	44.4	44.4	44.4

In order to validate the new attack, we perform an experimental evaluation using masked AES-GCM implemented on a smart card with an 8-bit microcontroller. Figure 6 shows the overview of the experimental setup consisting of a side-channel attack standard evaluation board (SASEBO-W) [1] equipped with an ATmega163-based smart card, and an Agilent MSO6104A digital oscilloscope for the power trace measurement. For the 8-bit microcontroller, we implemented the masked 128-bit GF multiplication by the shift-and-add method, and then calculated the SNR of the measurement according to [20]. Note that the 128-bit leakage is simulated by summing the intermediate leakage on 8-bit parts of the result. The SNR is 107.9, which means that even the masked AES-GCM implemented on the smart card would be vulnerable to the new attack.

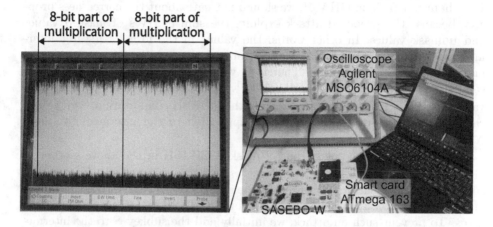

Fig. 6. Experimental setup and example of power trace with masked GHASH.

In addition, we briefly describe the new attack in the chosen-input scenario. The chosen-input attacker can recover H with less computational complexity for solving the LPN problem than the known-input attacker. Since the attacker can observe the variance of the power traces for an $X_1^{(s)}$ by repeating encryption with a fixed input, the attacker can estimate $HW(X_1^{(s)})$ for any $HW(X_1^{(s)})$ from the variance. Thus, the attacker can build an LPN problem with a less erroneous equation in Step (ii) than that in the known-input scenario, and can solve it with a computational complexity close to that of the conventional attack on an unmasked GHASH as described in Sect. 2.2. In addition, it is possible to combine the new attack and chosen-input attack in [2] for achieving a more efficient attack on masked GHASH. Note that we omit the evaluation of computational complexity of the chosen-input attack because this is an easier attack than the known-input variety, and the complexity would be similar to that of the conventional attack [2] on an unmasked GHASH.

5   New Countermeasure

In this section, we present an efficient countermeasure against the above new attack. Figure 7 shows the block diagram of the proposed countermeasure. Unlike the conventional masked GHASH in Sect. 3, the proposed method has the two following features: (i) to compute unmask value $U^{(s)}_{m+n+1}(= M^{(s)}H^{m+n+1})$ from H^{m+n+1} calculated prior to masked multiplication, and (ii) to add an offset S to masked intermediate values in order to prevent the attackers from using masked intermediate value and unmask value. The conventional masking schemes (e.g., trichina gate, ISW, and TI) require the correctness property [19], which indicates that the sum of all shares (i.e., masked and unmask values) should be equal to the original value in order to defeat DPAs. However, in the case of side-channel attack on GHASH, we should not care about the correctness property because the proposed attack exploits the sum of HWs of masked values and unmask values. In other words, the values in the form of [(secret intermediate value) $\oplus$ (mask value)] and [(unmask value)] should not appear in masked GHASH computation. Therefore, we first calculate H^{m+n+1} and then calculate the unmask value $M^{(s)}H^{m+n+1}$. Thus, we have no longer unmask values (i.e., $U^{(s)}_1, U^{(s)}_2, \ldots, U^{(s)}_{m+n}$) during the GHASH computation, which indicates that the proposed attack is not applicable to the intermediate values $X^{(s)}_1, X^{(s)}_2, \ldots, X^{(s)}_{m+n}$.

On the other hand, the output of masked GHASH in the above method is given by $X'^{(s)}_{m+n+1} (= X^{(s)}_{m+n+1} \oplus U^{(s)}_{m+n+1})$ and $U^{(s)}_{m+n+1}$, which can be targeted. In particular, if the attacker can choose the inputs (i.e., A_j and C_i), the proposed attack can be directly applied to the output of GHASH by letting the inputs be zeros. To prevent such an attack, we initially add the subkey S to the intermediate value as an offset, and add $S \oplus SH$ to the output of each multiplication for correcting the offset. As a result, the output of proposed masked GHASH is directly given by $S \oplus X^{(s)}_{m+n+1} \oplus U^{(s)}_{m+n+1}$ and $U^{(s)}_{m+n+1}$ (i.e., masked authentication tag and its unmask value, respectively) without computing the vulnerable values given in the form of [(secret intermediate value) $\oplus$ (mask value)] and [(unmask value)]. Note that $S \oplus X^{(s)}_{m+n+1}$ is the output of AES-GCM, and therefore the output of the proposed masked GHASH is not exploitable by (univariate) side-channel attacks.

The overhead of the proposed countermeasure is evaluated by the additional number of GF multiplication and addition operations. The computation of H^{m+n+1} requires the highest computational cost in the proposed masked GHASH. The computation of H^{m+n+1} with at least $\log(m + n + 1)$ multiplications is pre-computable, On the other hand, the initial addition of mask value and offset, the computation of $S \oplus SH$, the correct of offset (i.e., the addition of $S \oplus SH$ to masked values), the computation of $M^{(s)}H^{m+n+1}$, and the unmask of authentication tag should be performed on-the-fly, which require two addition, one addition and multiplication, $m + n + 1$ addition, one multiplication, and one addition, respectively. Thus, the proposed masked GHASH requires $\log(m + n + 1)$ multiplication operations for pre-computation of H^{m+n+1} and additional $m + n + 5$ addition and two multiplication operations for one-the-fly computation in total. This indicates that the overhead of the masked GHASH is relatively small compared to GHASH computation itself with $m+n+1$ addition and $m + n + 1$ multiplication.

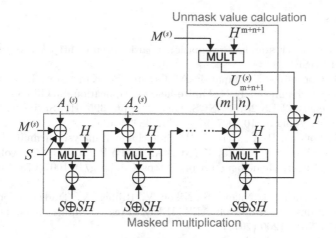

Fig. 7. Proposed countermeasure.

And if the attacker cannot choose the inputs in a practical attack scenario, the overhead can be reduced by unmasking the mask value after the third multiplication (i.e., the computation of masked $X_3^{(s)}$ because there is no longer the intermediate value represented by the linear equation of h_v. The reduced masked GHASH requires three multiplication for computing $U_3^{(s)} (= M^{(s)} H^3)$ and two addition for initial masking and unmasking. Such reduced masked GHASH is useful for devices where the overhead of the countermeasure can be critical if the attacker cannot control the input.

6 Conclusion

This paper presented an SCA on masked GF multiplication in GHASH of AES-GCM and its associated countermeasure. First, we described a masked GHASH resistant to a state-of-the-art SCA. We then proposed an extended attack on the masked GHASH, which exploits the variance of power consumption. We confirmed that the proposed attack was feasible through an experimental evaluation using AES-GCM implemented on a smart card. Finally, we proposed an efficient countermeasure against the proposed attack. In the future, a further evaluation of the proposed countermeasure would be required. A design of an AES-GCM processor with the proposed countermeasure would also be a part of this future work.

Acknowledgment. We would like to show our greatest appreciation to Dr. S. Belaïd, and Dr. B. Gérard for their valuable and insightful comments. This work has been supported by JSPS KAKENHI Grants No. 17H00729.

References

1. Side-channel attack standard evaluation board (sasebo). http://www.rcis.aist.go.jp/special/SASEBO
2. Belaïd, S., Coron, J.-S., Fouque, P.-A., Gérard, B., Kammerer, J.-G., Prouff, E.: Improved side-channel analysis of finite-field multiplication. In: Güneysu, T., Handschuh, H. (eds.) CHES 2015. LNCS, vol. 9293, pp. 395–415. Springer, Heidelberg (2015). https://doi.org/10.1007/978-3-662-48324-4_20
3. Belaïd, S., Fouque, P.-A., Gérard, B.: Side-channel analysis of multiplications in GF(2^{128}). In: Sarkar, P., Iwata, T. (eds.) ASIACRYPT 2014. LNCS, vol. 8874, pp. 306–325. Springer, Heidelberg (2014). https://doi.org/10.1007/978-3-662-45608-8_17
4. Bilgin, B., Gierlichs, B., Nikova, S., Nikov, V., Rijmen, V.: Trade-offs for threshold implementations illustrated on AES. IEEE Trans. Comput. Aided Des. Integr. Syst. **34**(7), 1188–1200 (2015)
5. Böck, H., Zauner, A., Devlin, S., Somorovsky, J., Jovanovic, P.: Nonce-disrespecting adversaries: practical forgeny attacks on GCM in TLS. In: 10th USENIX Workshop on Offensive Technologies (WOOT 16), pp. 1–13. USENIX Association (2016)
6. De Cnudde, T., Reparaz, O., Bilgin, B., Nikova, S., Nikov, V., Rijmen, V.: Masking AES with $d+1$ shares in hardware. In: Gierlichs, B., Poschmann, A.Y. (eds.) CHES 2016. LNCS, vol. 9813, pp. 194–212. Springer, Heidelberg (2016). https://doi.org/10.1007/978-3-662-53140-2_10
7. Cryptographic competitions: Caesar: competition for authenticated encryption: security, applicability, and robustness (2016). https://competitions.cr.yp.to/caesar.html
8. Ishai, Y., Sahai, A., Wagner, D.: Private circuits: securing hardware against probing attacks. In: Boneh, D. (ed.) CRYPTO 2003. LNCS, vol. 2729, pp. 463–481. Springer, Heidelberg (2003). https://doi.org/10.1007/978-3-540-45146-4_27
9. Jaffe, J.: A first-order DPA attack against AES in counter mode with unknown initial counter. In: Paillier, P., Verbauwhede, I. (eds.) CHES 2007. LNCS, vol. 4727, pp. 1–13. Springer, Heidelberg (2007). https://doi.org/10.1007/978-3-540-74735-2_1
10. Joux, A.: A authentication failures in NIST version of GCM (2006). http://csrc.nist.gov/groups/ST/toolkit/BCM/documents/comments/800-38_Series-Drafts/GCM/Joux_comments.pdf
11. Käsper, E., Schwabe, P.: Faster and timing-attack resistant AES-GCM. In: Clavier, C., Gaj, K. (eds.) CHES 2009. LNCS, vol. 5747, pp. 1–17. Springer, Heidelberg (2009). https://doi.org/10.1007/978-3-642-04138-9_1
12. Kocher, P., Jaffe, J., Jun, B.: Differential power analysis. In: Wiener, M. (ed.) CRYPTO 1999. LNCS, vol. 1666, pp. 388–397. Springer, Heidelberg (1999). https://doi.org/10.1007/3-540-48405-1_25
13. Mangard, S., Pramstaller, N., Oswald, E.: Successfully attacking masked AES hardware implementations. In: Rao, J.R., Sunar, B. (eds.) CHES 2005. LNCS, vol. 3659, pp. 157–171. Springer, Heidelberg (2005). https://doi.org/10.1007/11545262_12
14. McGrew, D.A., Viega, J.: The Galois/Counter Mode of operation (GCM) (2005). http://csrc.nist.gov/groups/ST/toolkit/BCM/documents/gcm-revised-spec.pdf
15. Nikova, S., Rijmen, V., Schläffer, M.: Secure hardware implementation of nonlinear functions in the presence of glitches. J. Cryptol. **24**, 292–321 (2011)

16. Oswald, E., Mangard, S., Pramstaller, N., Rijmen, V.: A side-channel analysis resistant description of the AES S-box. In: Gilbert, H., Handschuh, H. (eds.) FSE 2005. LNCS, vol. 3557, pp. 413–423. Springer, Heidelberg (2005). https://doi.org/10.1007/11502760_28
17. Pessl, P., Mangard, S.: Enhancing side-channel analysis of binary-field multiplication with bit reliability. In: Sako, K. (ed.) CT-RSA 2016. LNCS, vol. 9610, pp. 255–270. Springer, Cham (2016). https://doi.org/10.1007/978-3-319-29485-8_15
18. Poschmann, A., Moradi, A., Khoo, K., Lim, C.W., Wang, H., Ling, S.: Side-channel resistant crypto for less than 2,300 GE. J. Cryptol. **24**, 322–334 (2011)
19. Reparaz, O., Bilgin, B., Nikova, S., Gierlichs, B., Verbauwhede, I.: Consolidating masking schemes. In: Gennaro, R., Robshaw, M. (eds.) CRYPTO 2015. LNCS, vol. 9215, pp. 764–783. Springer, Heidelberg (2015). https://doi.org/10.1007/978-3-662-47989-6_37
20. Mangard, S., Oswald, E., Popp, T.: Power Analysis Attacks Revealing the Secrets of Smart Cards. Springer, Heidelberg (2007). https://doi.org/10.1007/978-0-387-38162-6
21. Tiri, K., Verbauwhede, I.: A logic level design methodology for a secure DPA resistant ASIC or FPGA implementation. In: Design, Automation and Test in Europe Conference and Exhibition (DATE), vol. 1, pp. 246–251 (2004)
22. Trichina, E.: Combinational logic design for AES SubBytes transformation on masked data. Cryptology ePrint Archive, Report 2003/236 (2003). http://eprint.iacr.org/2003/236
23. Ueno, R., Homma, N., Aoki, T.: Toward more efficient DPA-resistant AES hardware architecture based on threshold implementation. In: Guilley, S. (ed.) COSADE 2017. LNCS, vol. 10348, pp. 50–64. Springer, Cham (2017). https://doi.org/10.1007/978-3-319-64647-3_4
24. Wagner, D.: A generalized birthday problem. In: Yung, M. (ed.) CRYPTO 2002. LNCS, vol. 2442, pp. 288–304. Springer, Heidelberg (2002). https://doi.org/10.1007/3-540-45708-9_19

Tools for Side-Channel Analysis

On the Use of Independent Component Analysis to Denoise Side-Channel Measurements

Houssem Maghrebi[1(✉)] and Emmanuel Prouff[2,3]

[1] Underwriters Laboratories, La Ciotat, France
houssem.maghrebi@ul.com
[2] ANSSI, Paris, France
emmanuel.prouff@ssi.gouv.fr
[3] CNRS, Inria, Laboratoire d'Informatique de Paris 6 (LIP6), Équipe PolSys,
Sorbonne Universités, UPMC Univ Paris 06, 4 place Jussieu, 75252 Paris, France

Abstract. Independent Component Analysis (ICA) is a powerful technique for blind source separation. It has been successfully applied to signal processing problems, such as feature extraction and noise reduction, in many different areas including medical signal processing and telecommunication. In this work, we propose a framework to apply ICA to denoise side-channel measurements and hence to reduce the complexity of key recovery attacks. Based on several case studies, we afterwards demonstrate the overwhelming advantages of ICA with respect to the commonly used preprocessing techniques such as the singular spectrum analysis. Mainly, we target a software masked implementation of an AES and a hardware unprotected one. Our results show a significant Signal-to-Noise Ratio (SNR) gain which translates into a gain in the number of traces needed for a successful side-channel attack. This states the ICA as an important new tool for the security assessment of cryptographic implementations.

Keywords: Independent Component Analysis · Side-channel analysis
Preprocessing · Noise filtering · Correlation Power Analysis
Boolean masking scheme

1 Introduction

Side-Channel Attacks. Side-Channel Attacks (SCA) are nowadays well known and most designers of secure embedded systems are aware of them. Since the first public reporting of these threats [37] in 1996, a lot of effort has been devoted towards the research about side-channel attacks and the development of corresponding countermeasures. SCA take advantage of the fact that the

---

H. Maghrebi and E. Prouff—This work has been done when the authors was working at Safran Identity and Security.

J. Fan and B. Gierlichs (Eds.): COSADE 2018, LNCS 10815, pp. 61–81, 2018.
https://doi.org/10.1007/978-3-319-89641-0_4

power consumption (or the electromagnetic radiation) of a cryptographic device depends on the internally used secret key. Since this property can be exploited with relatively cheap equipment, these attacks pose a serious practical threat to cryptographic embedded systems. To perform a successful side-channel attack against embedded cryptographic implementations, several steps should be carefully followed [28]. First, the physical leakage (*e.g.* the power consumption or the electromagnetic radiation) of the target device must be measured during the processing of cryptographic algorithms. Second, it is common to preprocess the collected measurements by applying for instance: traces alignment, noise filtering, Points-Of-Interest (POI) selection and dimensionality reduction [41]. Finally, statistical distinguishers are applied on the (preprocessed) traces to discriminate key hypotheses.

Preprocessing Tools in SCA Context. When looking at the broad literature of side-channel attacks, several techniques and tools have been proposed to preprocess the measurements. The goal behind is to reduce the attack complexity in terms of computational time and number of traces needed for a successful attack. From the side-channel evaluation perspective, the preprocessing step is of great importance especially when targeting modern embedded systems (*e.g.* mobile phone) [24] and System-on-Chip (SoC) devices with high clock frequencies [3,39].

We provide hereafter a brief overview of the most commonly used preprocessing techniques in side-channel context:

- **Traces synchronization:** to conceal the traces misalignment typically caused by inaccuracies in triggering the power measurements or by some activated countermeasures (*e.g.* clock jitter), several works have proposed to apply synchronization techniques like the alignment [41] (*i.e.* performing a cross-correlation with sliding widow to search a pattern) or elastic alignment [52] based on the Dynamic Time Warping (DTW) algorithm.
- **Noise filtering:** several techniques have been applied to deal with traces denoising. These techniques range from simple ones like averaging to sophisticated ones like the use of the fourth-order cumulant [38] or the application of some linear filters (*e.g.* Wiener filter or Kalman filter [48]). Recently at CHES 2014, Del Pozo *et al.* have suggested using the Singular Spectrum Analysis (SSA) as a filtering technique to improve the efficiency of side-channel attacks [42]. The results obtained on various scenario (*e.g.* unprotected and masked software implementations of an AES and a Hardware implementation of PRESENT) have shown the overwhelming advantages of using this technique. However, some (hyper) parameters (*i.e.* the choice of the window length for constructing the *trajectory matrix* and the principal components selection for the reconstruction [42]) are ad-hoc and thus, if not properly executed could diminish the associated gains of SSA.
- **POI selection:** the computation complexity of side-channel attacks can be reduced by selecting a small subset of time samples where leakage prevails. To achieve this goal, several works have proposed some preprocessing techniques

amongst which we identify the Sum Of Squared pairwise Differences (SOSD) and the Sum Of Squared pairwise T-differences (SOST) [27] based on the T-Test algorithm [19,47] to choose the most relevant time samples. Other techniques exist and are rather based on SNR computation [41], variance tests [7], correlation and mutual information [20,26].

– **Dimensionality reduction:** the most commonly used methods for dimensionality reduction in side-channel context are the Principal Component Analysis (PCA) and the Linear Discriminant Analysis (LDA) [2,4,14,49] or the Kernel Discriminant Analysis (KDA) [10]. While the first provides a set of vectors (*aka* the principal components) onto which the data are first projected and then only few projections (these that maximize the variance between the mean leakage traces) are kept, the second one projects the data on the directions that maximize the ratio between inter-class and intra-class variances. So, reducing the data complexity aims at decreasing the computation time during the key recovery phase.

Our Contribution. By contrast, the denoising techniques are in general discussed less, despite their importance in reducing the complexity of side-channel attacks especially for Common Criteria evaluation [17]. In this paper, we propose the use of the Independent Component Analysis (ICA) [15,16,36] to denoise side-channel measurements. This technique is widely applied for Blind Source Separation (BSS) (see *e.g.* [32] for an application of the ICA in reducing the noise in natural images) and aims at finding a linear representation of the processed multivariate data so that the resulting components are statistically independent. To the best of our knowledge this is the first complete attempt to apply ICA as a preprocessing technique in side-channel context. Actually, in [23] Gao *et al.* have proposed a new profiled attack based on the ICA and they claimed that it could be used to improve the signal-to-noise (SNR) ratio, but they left this for further research. In another paper [8], Bohy *et al.* have also suggested a similar application but they didn't provide a practical framework on how to efficiently apply it.

Throughout several practical experiments (see Sect. 4), we argue that ICA outperforms the commonly used denoising methods in side-channel context and leads to a significant SNR gain which translates into a significant advantage in terms of number of traces needed to succeed an attack. For instance, we represent in Fig. 1 the results of a first-order Correlation Power Analysis (CPA) attack [9] when targeting an unprotected software implementation of the AES running on an ATMega163 micro-controller. Several denoising techniques have been applied for the sake of comparison.

From Fig. 1, one can conclude that the gain in terms of number of traces needed to succeed the CPA attack, with respect to our specific experiments, is about 120% compared to the SCA state-of-the-art filtering techniques.

Moreover, we compare ICA to the well-known preprocessing techniques used in SCA context to ensure dimensionality reduction and POI selection (*i.e.* PCA [49], LDA [14] and the Projection Pursuit (PP) [22]). Despite the fact that

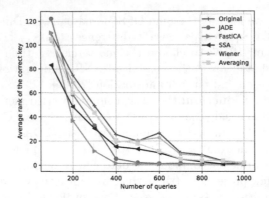

Fig. 1. Evolution of the correct key rank (y-axis) according to an increasing number of traces (x-axis) for several filtering techniques when targeting an unprotected software implementation of the AES.

these methods are applied for different purposes than measurements denoising, we pinpoint several similarities with ICA that we discuss in Sect. 2.4.

2   Independent Component Analysis

2.1   Notations

In the rest of the paper, bold block capitals $\mathbf{X}$ denote matrices and bold lower cases $\mathbf{x}$ denote real row vectors. The identity matrix of dimension n is denoted by $\mathbf{I}_n$. The ith row vector of a matrix $\mathbf{X}$ is denoted by $\mathbf{x}_i$, while its ith coordinate is denoted by $\mathbf{x}[i]$. The transpose and the inverse of a matrix $\mathbf{X}$ are respectively denoted by $\mathbf{X}^T$ and $\mathbf{X}^{-1}$. The capital letters X are used for random variables while the lower-case letter x for their realizations. The mean, the variance and the entropy of a random variable X are respectively denoted by $\mathbb{E}[X]$, $\mathbb{V}[X]$ and $\mathbb{H}[X]$. We any (n, m)-matrix $\mathbf{M}$, we shall denote by $\mathbb{E}[\mathbf{M}]$ the mean of the matrix when drawn uniformly at random in its definition set. The dot/inner product and the matrix product shall be denoted by $\cdot$, while the product over $\mathbb{R}$ and the product between a scalar and a vector shall be denoted by $\times$.

2.2   Overview of ICA

ICA [15,16,36] is one of the most widely used techniques for blind source separation [44]. It assumes that the observed data are drawn from multiple source signals and aims at recovering these individual signals. A typical example is the so-called *cocktail party problem*: in a room, multiple people are speaking simultaneously while there are some recorders in different places of the room capturing the superimposition of their voices. The objective is to recover the speech of each individual speaker from the recorded voices.

We present hereafter a mathematical model of this problem. Let $\mathbf{x}_i$ and $\mathbf{s}_i$ respectively denote an observation and a source p-dimensional vector over $\mathbb{R}$. We define $\mathbf{X} = (\mathbf{x}_i)_{1 \le i \le n}$ and $\mathbf{S} = (\mathbf{s}_i)_{1 \le i \le n}$ as respectively the so-called *observations* (n, p)-*matrix* and the so-called *sources* (n, p)-*matrix* both defined over $\mathbb{R}^{n \times p}$ such that:

$$\mathbf{X} = \mathbf{A} \cdot \mathbf{S}, \tag{1}$$

where $\mathbf{A} = (a_{i,j})_{1 \le i,j \le n}$ is the so-called *mixing matrix* defined over $\mathbb{R}^{n \times n}$. Hence, (1) implies that the observations (*e.g.* the recorded speech) are considered as a linear combination of the sources (*e.g.* the individual voice of each speaker). For instance, the ith p-dimensional row vector of $\mathbf{X}$ rewrites:

$$\mathbf{x}_i = \sum_{j=1}^{n} a_{i,j} \times \mathbf{s}_j. \tag{2}$$

Remark 1. In the rest of this paper, we will often consider the $\mathbf{x}_i$ and $\mathbf{s}_j$ as random variables drawn uniformly from their respective definition set.

The goal of ICA is to solve the following problem:

Problem 1. Approximate the unknown matrix $\mathbf{A}$ in order to recover the latent signals $\mathbf{s}_j$ from the observable data $\mathbf{X}$.

To address Problem 1, the ICA first looks for an estimation $\hat{\mathbf{W}}$ of the so-called *unmixing matrix* $\mathbf{W}$ defined over $\mathbb{R}^{n \times n}$ such that $\mathbf{W} = \mathbf{A}^{-1}$ and secondly recovers an approximation of the sources matrix by computing:

$$\hat{\mathbf{S}} = \hat{\mathbf{W}} \cdot \mathbf{X}.$$

The ICA asymptotically succeeds in solving Problem 1 (*i.e.* $\hat{\mathbf{S}} = \mathbf{S}$) if the two following assumptions are satisfied [34].

Assumption 1 (Statistical independence). *The source signals* $\mathbf{s}_j$ *are mutually independent.*

Assumption 2 (Non-Gaussian distribution). *The source signals* $\mathbf{s}_j$ *have non-Gaussian distributions.*

Remark 2. Remarkably, Assumption 2 can be relaxed by allowing at most one source signal to have a Gaussian distribution [34]. This is an important remark in our case study since, as we will see in the following, one of the source signals corresponds to a noise observation (often assumed to have a Gaussian distribution).

From the ICA model in (1), the following ambiguities may already be discussed:

– **Whitening:** it is impossible to estimate the original variance and sign of the source signals. Indeed, since both $\mathbf{S}$ and $\mathbf{A}$ are unknown, then any scalar multiple of one of the sources s_j can always be cancelled by dividing the corresponding column vector $\mathbf{a}_j$ of $\mathbf{A}$ by the same scalar; namely, for every $\alpha \in \mathbb{R}$ the relation $\mathbf{X} = (\mathbf{A} \cdot \alpha^{-1}) \cdot (\alpha \cdot \mathbf{S})$ holds.

As a consequence, and unlike PCA which focus on the variance maximization problem to find the optimal projections of the data [35], ICA exploits higher-order statistical moments to recover the sources s_j [34]. Indeed, before performing ICA, the observations $\mathbf{X}$ are centered and *whitened*, that is, modified to have identity covariance matrix [34]. This is typically done by applying first the Eigen-Value Decomposition (EVD) of the covariance matrix $\mathbb{E}[\mathbf{X} \cdot \mathbf{X}^T]$ defined by $\mathbb{E}[\mathbf{X} \cdot \mathbf{X}^T] = \mathbf{E} \cdot \mathbf{D} \cdot \mathbf{E}^T$ where $\mathbf{E}$ and $\mathbf{D}$ denote respectively the *orthogonal matrix of eigenvectors* and the *diagonal matrix of eigenvalues*. Then, the *whitened observations* are defined as $\tilde{\mathbf{X}} = \mathbf{E} \cdot \mathbf{D}^{1/2} \cdot \mathbf{E}^T \cdot \mathbf{X}$ and one can easily check that the covariance matrix $\mathbb{E}[\tilde{\mathbf{X}} \cdot \tilde{\mathbf{X}}^T]$ is the identity matrix $\mathbf{I}_n$.

– **Order invariant:** it is impossible to determine the order of the source signals. In fact, since both $\mathbf{S}$ and $\mathbf{A}$ are unknown, then any permutation of the source signals could always be canceled by applying the inverse permutation on the mixing matrix $\mathbf{A}$. Let $\mathbf{P}$ be a permutation matrix defined over $\mathbb{R}^{n \times n}$, then from (1) we have $\mathbf{X} = (\mathbf{A} \cdot \mathbf{P}^{-1}) \cdot (\mathbf{P} \cdot \mathbf{S})$. Consequently, we shall say that $\hat{\mathbf{W}}$ is a good estimation of $\mathbf{W}$ if there exists a matrix $\mathbf{Q}$ permutation of the identity matrix $\mathbf{I}_n$ such that $\hat{\mathbf{W}} = \mathbf{Q} \cdot \mathbf{W}$.

2.3   ICA Estimation

Let us denote by $\mathbf{y}_j$ the jth p-dimensional row vector $\hat{\mathbf{w}}_j \cdot \mathbf{X}$ where $\hat{\mathbf{w}}_j$ is the jth row of $\hat{\mathbf{W}}$. Then, as a direct consequence of (1) and after denoting $\mathbf{z}_j = \hat{\mathbf{w}}_j \cdot \mathbf{A}$, for $j \in [1; n]$ we have:

$$\mathbf{y}_j = \sum_{i=1}^{n} \mathbf{z}_j[i] \times \mathbf{s}_i. \tag{3}$$

Thus, $\mathbf{y}_j$ is a linear combination of the source signals $\mathbf{s}_i$. If a single coefficient $\mathbf{z}_j[i]$ in (3) is non-zero then the sum contains a single signal $\mathbf{s}_i$ and therefore $\mathbf{y}_j$ corresponds to a row of the signal matrix $\mathbf{S}$ we want to recover (equivalently, $\hat{\mathbf{w}}_j$ corresponds to one row of the unmixing matrix $\mathbf{W}$). In other terms if for every $j \in [1; n]$, the sum in (3) contains a single signal $\mathbf{s}_i$ then $\hat{\mathbf{W}}$ is a good estimation of $\mathbf{W}$ modulo a permutation of the rows order.

Since the $\mathbf{s}_i$ are mutually independent (Assumption 1), this linear combination $\mathbf{y}_j$ tends towards a Gaussian distribution when the number of non-zero coefficients $\mathbf{z}_j[i]$ increases (by *Central Limit Theorem*). Conversely, due to Assumption 2 the vector $\mathbf{y}_j$, viewed as a random variable, becomes least Gaussian when the number of non-zero coefficients $\mathbf{z}_j[i]$ tends towards one. Such a non-Gaussianity of a probability density function (pdf) may for instance be measured thanks to the Kurtosis moments. Based on this remark, the core idea of ICA is to find, among all possible estimations $\hat{\mathbf{w}}_j$, the one that maximizes the non-Gaussianity of $\hat{\mathbf{w}}_j \cdot \mathbf{X}$. Such a vector would necessarily correspond to a vector $\mathbf{z}$ which has a single nonzero component and the corresponding vector $\mathbf{y}_j = \hat{\mathbf{w}}_j \cdot \mathbf{X}$ should therefore equal one of the source signals $\mathbf{s}_i$.

More formally, ICA is an optimization algorithm that aims (1) at estimating the unmixing matrix $\mathbf{W}$ by maximizing the non-Gaussianity of $\mathbf{y}_j = \hat{\mathbf{w}}_j \cdot \mathbf{X}$, and (2) at afterwards deducing the sources signals. In fact, the optimization landscape for non-Gaussianity in a n-dimensional space of vectors $\hat{\mathbf{w}}_j \in \mathbb{R}^p$ has $2n$ local maxima (two for each source signal corresponding to $+\mathbf{s}_i$ and $-\mathbf{s}_i$). To find all independent source signals, we need to find all these local maxima.

2.4   Differences Between ICA, Projection Pursuit, PCA and LDA

The Projection Pursuit [22] is a statistical technique that aims at finding the most informative projections of a highly multivariate data. It has been demonstrated in [29] that the most interesting directions are those that show the lowest Gaussianity and this is exactly what the ICA estimation does. Thus, both techniques are remarkably similar and optimize the same criterion despite the fact that they have been developed independently by the Statistics and the Signal Processing communities [34]. Meanwhile, several major differences between these techniques can be pinpointed:

- PP aims at reducing the dimension of the processed data such that only few (*i.e.* mainly one or two) directions are preserved, whereas ICA aims at identifying all source vectors (*i.e.* all directions) with the same dimension as the processed data.
- Unlike ICA, PP makes no assumption about the source signals. Said differently, when ICA assumptions are satisfied, then its estimation returns the independent components of the processed data. Otherwise, what we obtain by applying ICA is the projection pursuit directions.

Regarding PCA [35] and LDA [21], which are widely used in the SCA context for dimensionality reduction and measurement processing [2,4,14,49], several important differences may be noticed. In fact, while PCA aims at finding the most interesting orthogonal projections that maximize the variance of the data, LDA seeks for some directions that maximize the inter-class variance and minimize the intra-class variance of the data. Hence, both techniques exploit the second-order statistic of the processed data unlike ICA that aims rather at estimating higher-order statistics such as the fourth-order cummulant (*i.e.* the Kurtosis) by finding the interesting projections (not necessarily orthogonal) that minimize the Gaussianity of the components [34]. So, PCA and LDA are suitable when the source signals are Gaussian ones and when the signal variance is informative. However, when dealing with strongly non-Gaussian data, the variance may not be the statistic of interest compared to higher-order moments. Indeed, in the ICA model, all timing samples are *a priori* equally important unlike for PCA and LDA where many components will be discarded since judged less informative. Actually, we think that ICA and PCA/LDA are not competitors but complement each other; applying a dimensionality reduction technique (PCA or LDA) after processing ICA to filter the SCA traces may increase the success of the attack.

2.5 ICA Methods

Several algorithms were developed to perform the ICA estimation. We review in this section the most popular ones.

InfoMax. It is based on a neural network approach which tries to maximize the entropy of the network's output [5,43]. Let us view the observations' matrix $\mathbf{X} \in \mathbb{R}^{n \times p}$ as an input layer, then the p-dimensional rows $\mathbf{y}_j$, $j \in [1; n]$, of the matrix $\mathbf{Y}$ defined in Sect. 2.3 satisfies $\mathbf{y}_j = f_j(\hat{\mathbf{w}}_j \cdot \mathbf{X})$, where f_j is some non-linear function and the vectors $\hat{\mathbf{w}}_j$ can be viewed as the weight vectors of the neurons. So, finding the weight matrix $\hat{\mathbf{W}} = (\hat{\mathbf{w}}_j)_{1 \leq j \leq n}$ that maximizes the *negentropy* of $\mathbf{Y}$ for a well chosen set of f_j functions leads to an ICA estimation. The InfoMax approach is equivalent to the maximum likelihood estimation, not detailed in this work for lack of room, which could be also used to estimate the ICA model [12].

FastICA. It is the most commonly used approach, based on the maximization of the negentropy, to estimate the ICA [31,33]. Indeed, it is faster than the conventional ICA algorithms and can be used to perform projection pursuit as well [30].

Joint Approximate Diagonalization of Eigenmatrices (JADE). It is based on the diagonalization of the cumulant matrices [13]. In fact, the diagonal elements of a cumulant matrix characterize the distribution of a signal, while the off-diagonal elements indicate the statistical dependencies between signals. So, JADE algorithm uses the second and the fourth cumulant matrix. First, the data are transformed into a reduced set of PCA loadings (*i.e.* a diagonalization of the second-order cumulant matrix with a selection of the interesting directions) that are then whitened to have equal variances. Second, the fourth-order cumulant matrix is diagonalized via a rotation matrix (using the Jacobi algorithm) yielding the mixing matrix.

3 Filtering Leakage Using ICA

3.1 SCA Model vs. ICA Model

In a side-channel context, the matrix of observations $\mathbf{X} \in \mathbb{R}^{n \times p}$ in (1) is assumed to be related to the manipulation of a sensitive variable Z ranging over some finite set. We recall that the values taken by Z correspond to the output of a processing $\varphi(m,k)$ involving a plaintext m and a secret parameter k. The dimension n of $\mathbf{X}$ corresponds to the number of observations of the manipulation, while p denotes the length of each observation. It is often assumed that an observation $\mathbf{x}$, viewed as a random variable defined over $\mathbb{R}^p$, is well modelled by a linear combination of two mutually independent parts:

- a part $Z \mapsto \mathcal{D}(Z) \in \mathbb{R}^p$ which is a deterministic function representing the un-noisy leakage on Z during its manipulation by the system and,
- a random part $\mathbf{r}$ representing the noise in the observations and being associated with a Gaussian distribution $\mathcal{N}(\mathbf{0}, \boldsymbol{\Sigma})$ (in our case we make the classical assumption that $\boldsymbol{\Sigma}$ is diagonal which essentially implies that the instantaneous noises in the observation vectors are mutually independent).

Hence, the noisy observation of the manipulation of Z can be associated with a random variable $\mathbf{x}$ defined over $\mathbb{R}^p$ as:

$$\mathbf{x} = a_1 \times \mathcal{D}(Z) + a_2 \times \mathbf{r}, \tag{4}$$

where (a_1, a_2) are some weighting coefficients defined over $\mathbb{R}^2$ (and a_2 is often assumed to be equal to one). After assuming that the n rows of $\mathbf{X}$ are n independent realizations of the random variable $\mathbf{x}$ defined in (4), it may be checked that $\mathbf{X}$ fits well the ICA model defined in (1) and (2) by setting $\mathcal{D}(Z) = \mathbf{s}_1^{(m)}$ and $\mathbf{r} = \mathbf{s}_2$.[1] So, the ICA noise reduction technique described in previous sections should allow for an easy detection of the interesting components.

Remark 3. The deterministic part $\mathcal{D}(Z)$ is often assumed to be well estimated by a linear combination in $\mathbb{R}$ of the bits of Z. Under this modelling, the different sources $\mathbf{s}_i$ are no longer 2 but $\log_2(Z)$ (*i.e.* composed of the bits of Z and the noise). In this context, the ICA could be used to isolate the noise signal from the other ones.

Remark 4. We stress the fact that one can extend the leakage model defined in (4) to the following one:

$$\mathbf{x} = a_1 \times \mathcal{D}(Z_1) + a_2 \times \mathcal{D}'(Z_2) + a_3 \times \mathbf{r},$$

where (a_1, a_2, a_3) is a triplet of weighting coefficients defined over $\mathbb{R}$, where $\mathcal{D}(Z_1)$ is the deterministic part of the targeted variable Z_1 and where $\mathcal{D}'(Z_2)$ is the deterministic part of a non-targeted variable Z_2 (aka algorithmic noise). This model can be used, for instance, when an adversary tries his attack on several SBoxes processed in parallel in a hardware setting context.

At this point, it must be observed that, unlike SSA (which transforms individual traces [42]), the ICA cannot be applied on a single observation in our context (*i.e.* on matrices $\mathbf{X}$ with a single row) since at least $n > t$ measurements are generally required to recover t source signals [25]. So according to

---

[1] Note that we used the notation $\mathbf{s}_1^{(m)}$ to alert on the fact that the signal s_1 corresponds to the plaintext m.

our modelling where $t = 2$, at least two measurements are required, for each possible value z of Z (or equivalently for each possible m), to recover the power consumption of $\mathcal{D}(Z = z) = \mathcal{D}(\varphi(m, k))$. Let us assume that we collected two such power observations by executing the processing two times for a randomly chosen plaintext m. We then get a matrix of observations $\mathbf{X}$ composed of two rows $\mathbf{x_1}$ and $\mathbf{x_2}$) which are realizations of the same random variable defined in (4) and hence satisfy:

$$\mathbf{x_1} = a_{1,1} \times \underbrace{\mathcal{D}(Z = z \text{ where } z = \varphi(m, k))}_{\text{realization of } \mathbf{s}_1^{(m)}} + a_{1,2} \times \underbrace{\mathbf{r_1}}_{\text{realization of } \mathbf{s}_2} \qquad (5)$$

and

$$\mathbf{x_2} = a_{2,1} \times \underbrace{\mathcal{D}(Z = z \text{ where } z = \varphi(m, k))}_{\text{realization of } \mathbf{s}_1^{(m)}} + a_{2,2} \times \underbrace{\mathbf{r_2}}_{\text{realization of } \mathbf{s}_2} \qquad (6)$$

with $\mathbf{r_1}$ and $\mathbf{r_2}$ being two realizations of the same noise random variable $\mathbf{r} \sim \mathcal{N}(\mathbf{0}, \mathbf{\Sigma})$. As recalled in Sect. 2, the ICA technique recovers the source signals $\mathcal{D}(Z = z)$ and $\mathbf{r}$ by estimating the unmixing matrix $\mathbf{W} = \mathbf{A}^{-1}$ s.t.

$$\mathbf{A} = \begin{pmatrix} a_{1,1} & a_{1,2} \\ a_{2,1} & a_{2,2} \end{pmatrix}.$$

3.2   First Approach to Apply ICA in SCA Context

To apply ICA for denoising side-channel measurements, a first approach may consist in using two identical probes to capture the leakage during the execution of a cryptographic implementation. So, for each execution (e.g. a plaintext encryption) two measurements (one per probe) are collected satisfying (5) and (6). Then, an ICA algorithm is applied to recover the noise-free signal.

To efficiently apply this approach, both probes must be positioned above the same location of the chip surface to collect the same activity. We believe that this constraint is sometime hard to fulfill in practice and is also highly dependent on the size of the targeted chip under evaluation.

3.3   Second Approach to Apply ICA in SCA Context

We present in Algorithm 1 a second framework for using the ICA technique in order to filter the side-channel measurements.

Our algorithm takes as input the matrix of observations $\mathbf{X}$ (with row elements denoted by $\mathbf{x}_i$) and the corresponding set of plaintexts (or ciphertexts) $\mathcal{M} = \{m_i\}$ used during the execution of the targeted cryptographic operation. The goal is to output a set of noise-free measurements. To do so, for each possible value m of the plaintext we collect all[2] the observations $\mathbf{x}_i$ that have been

---

[2] Another option could consist in only using a few number of measurements (e.g. 100) for each value m in order to speed up the execution of our algorithm.

Algorithm 1. Denoising side-channel traces using ICA technique

---

Require: $\mathbf{X}$: the noisy measurements dataset and $\mathbf{M}$: the set of plaintexts (or cipher-texts) m such that $Z = \varphi(m, k)$ for some public function φ and some target secret k

Ensure: filtered measurement dataset
1: **for** each value m **do**
2:     From $\mathbf{X}$ take the observations $\mathbf{x}_i$ that have been captured during the processing of m and store them in a new observation matrix $\mathbf{X}^{(m)}$
3: **end for**
4: **for** each value m **do**
5:     Apply ICA on $\mathbf{X}^{(m)}$ to remove the noise signal ($\mathbf{s}_2$) and keep the genuine signal ($\mathbf{s}_1^{(m)}$)
6:     In $\mathbf{X}^{(m)}$, replace each row by $\mathbf{s}_1^{(m)}$
7: **end for**
8: **return** $(\mathbf{X}^{(m)})_m$

---

captured during the processing of this value (*i.e.* for which $m_i = m$) and we store them in a new observations matrix $\mathbf{X}^{(m)}$. Then, for each of the $\mathbf{X}^{(m)}$, one of the ICA methods described in Sect. 2.5 (*e.g.* FastICA or JADE) is applied to recover the source signals: the noise $\mathbf{s}_2$ and the genuine signal $\mathbf{s}_1^{(m)}$. At this step, the genuine signal can be identified by mere visual inspection and/or by fixing a threshold to distinguish it from the noise signal[3].

Actually, this phase is quite essential since as discussed in Sect. 2.2 one of the ambiguities of the ICA technique is that the recovered source signals are outputted in a random order. Then, the noise component $\mathbf{s}_2$ is removed and only the genuine signal $\mathbf{s}_1^{(m)}$ is kept. Finally, we replace all the measurements in $\mathbf{X}^{(m)}$ that have been captured during the processing of m by the noise-free signal $\mathbf{s}_1^{(m)}$. Once, we have performed this procedure for all m values, we obtain a set of filtered measurements.

In the sequel, we will rather use the second approach for applying the ICA technique. Our choice was motivated by the fact that it is faster than the first approach and requires fewer measurements.

4   Practical Experiments

4.1   Experimental Setup

Targeted Implementations. To evaluate the efficiency of the ICA framework described in Sect. 3.3, we have targeted two different implementations: (1) a

---

[3] This threshold is defined for one m value (*e.g.* $m = 0$) and then applied for the other ones. We stress the fact that other approaches could be applied to distinguish the genuine signal from the noise. For instance, one can (1) compute the correlation between the noisy signal and the obtained source signals or (2) apply a dimensionality reduction algorithm (*e.g.* PCA or LDA).

software AES implementation first unprotected and secondly protected by first-order Boolean masking and (2) a hardware unprotected one.

While for the software unprotected AES implementation (running on an ATMega163 micro-controller) the power traces were acquired using our in-house equipment[4], we used the power measurements publicly provided in the website of DPA-contest V2 [51] for the hardware one. The rationale behind using the DPA contest V2 campaign is twofold: (1) to evaluate the efficiency of ICA on a very noisy setup [51] and (2) to ease the reproduction of our results by the side-channel community. Finally, our first-order Boolean masking scheme was implemented on the ChipWhisperer-Lite Board (CW1173) [45] and the power traces were collected using our in-house equipment. The goal is to assess the efficiency of ICA technique in the presence of side-channel countermeasures.

Denoising Setup and Evaluation Metric. Regarding the ICA methods, we have considered mainly the FastICA and the JADE algorithms. The source code of these algorithms are publicly available [1,11]. We have just adapted them to our context (*i.e.* by setting the number of the output components and the dimensions of the processed traces). Once, the traces have been filtered using our framework described in Algorithm 1, we conducted a CPA attack over several independent sets of traces. Then, we have computed the averaged rank of the correct key among all key hypotheses (*aka* the *guessing entropy metric* [50]).

ICA vs. State-of-the-art Denoising Techniques. For the sake of comparison, we have applied the *averaging method*[5], the *Wiener filter* [48] and the SSA technique to filter the power traces of both AES implementations[6]. Moreover, we have performed the CPA attack on noisy traces without preprocessing. The goal was to evaluate the efficiency of ICA w.r.t. the commonly used filtering techniques in side-channel context.

4.2   Unprotected AES Implementation on ATMega163

To fulfill the requirement pointed out in the second part of Sect. 3.1 to apply the ICA technique, we chose to repeat each acquisition two times with the same AES input. We got 10.000 power traces, aka 5.000 pairs of acquisitions. Then, for a sample size n ranging from 50 to 1000, we ran Algorithm 1 for a subset of our acquisitions such that $|\mathbf{X}| = |\mathbf{M}| = n$ and we filtered the traces by applying one of the denoising techniques described in Sect. 2.5. To quantify the mean behavior of the algorithm, we repeated each experiment 100 times (for each sample size n

---

[4] A LeCroy WavePro 725Zi oscilloscope with maximum 40 GS/s sampling rate and an active differential probe Lecroy ZD1500 have been used to measure the voltage drop over a 1Ω resistor in the VDD path.

[5] It merely consists in replacing the fifth step in Algorithm 1 by an averaging of the traces in $\mathbf{X}^{(m)}$.

[6] We recall that other filtering techniques exist, *e.g.* the wavelet [18], but are not considered in our work since are heuristic methods.

and each denoising technique). For an illustration, an exemplary power trace of the implementation and the source signals (*i.e.* the noise and the filtered trace) recovered by the FastICA method are shown in Appendix A.

Regarding the SSA, we followed the approach described in [42]: (1) the window length WL was fixed by applying the rule-of-thumb $WL = [\log(n)^c]$ with $c = 1.5$, and (2) during the reconstruction phase only the second component is used. In fact, it was argued in [42] that the first component usually corresponds to low-frequency noise and thus should not be considered during the reconstruction phase. This observation was confirmed during our experiments.

The efficiency of a CPA attack targeting the first AES SBox[7] after each filtering technique is depicted in Fig. 1 with respect to the number of traces before denoising (as described below, the CPA efficiency has been averaged over 100 experiments).

From Fig. 1, the following observations may be emphasized:

- the CPA attack performs well when the traces are filtered using ICA techniques (*i.e.* either FastICA or JADE). In fact, one can see that less traces are needed to disclose the good value of the key when ICA is applied to filter the traces.
- when the SSA is used to denoise the measurements, the gain in terms of SNR is low (compared to the ICA techniques) which translates into a small (or even no) gain in terms of number of traces needed to discover the key with respect to those needed when no preprocessing is done. This can be explained by the fact that SSA is a heuristic tool and that the results are highly dependent on the choice made to set the window length and/or to select the components standing for the useful information. Indeed, in [42], authors have argued that the selection of the most informative components may be simply done by a mere visual inspection of the obtained singular spectrum. However, this ad-hoc approach is subject to errors due to biased selection of the appropriate components. The same conclusion holds for the choice of the window length for constructing the trajectory matrix. Despite the fact that some rules and guidelines exist, the optimal choice is highly dependent on the processed data [53].
- regarding the use of the averaging method and the Wiener filter to denoise the traces, the related attack results are less efficient compared to those obtained when ICA is applied.

4.3   Unprotected AES Implementation on FPGA

For this second scenario, we performed a similar evaluation with the minor difference that we have first estimated the SNR of the traces before and after applying the FastICA technique for denoising. This choice was motivated by the fact that the DPA contest V2 traces are more noisy compared to these

---

[7] We stress the fact that same results were obtained when targeting the other SBoxes and are not shown here for lack of room.

acquired on the ATMega163 micro-controller. Let us recall that the leakage satisfies $\mathbf{x} = a_1 \times \mathcal{D}(Z) + a_2 \times \mathbf{r}$, then it is well known that the *instantaneous* SNR (*i.e.* the SNR for each of p coordinates of the observation vector) is a p-dimensional vector such that its ith coordinate is defined as:

$$\text{SNR}[i] = \frac{\mathbb{V}_Z[\mathbb{E}[\mathbf{x}[i] \mid Z]]}{\mathbb{E}_Z[\mathbb{V}[\mathbf{x}[i] \mid Z]]}. \tag{7}$$

Remark 5. By definition of $\mathbf{x}$, it may be checked that, for every z, $\mathbb{E}[\mathbf{x} \mid Z = z]$ equals $a_1 \times \mathbb{E}[\mathcal{D}(z)] + a_2 \times \mathbb{E}[\mathbf{r}]$, and hence that $\mathbb{V}_Z[\mathbb{E}[\mathbf{x}[i] \mid Z]]$ equals $a_1^2 \mathbb{V}[\mathcal{D}(Z)[i]]$ if the noise $\mathbf{r}$ is independent of Z (which are classical and reasonable assumptions). On the other hand, it can be checked that, for every z, $\mathbb{V}[\mathbf{x}[i] \mid Z = z]$ equals $a_2^2 \mathbb{V}[\mathbf{r}[i]]$. Consequently, (7) is equivalent to $\text{SNR}[i] = \frac{a_1^2}{a_2^2} \frac{\mathbb{V}[\mathcal{D}(Z)[i]]}{\mathbb{V}[\mathbf{r}[i]]}$, under the independent and additive noise assumption. This can be rephrased as the ratio between the variance of the information and the variance of the noise.

Remark 6. In [6], the authors propose to use the *Normalized Inter-Class Variance* (NICV) instead of the SNR. This essentially replaces the denominator in (7) by $\mathbb{V}[\mathbf{x}[i]]$, that is $a_2^2 \mathbb{V}[\mathbf{r}[i]] + a_1^2 \mathbb{V}[\mathcal{D}(Z)[i]]$ since the noise is considered independent of Z. Eventually, this gives $\text{NICV}[i] = \frac{1}{\text{SNR}[i]+1}$.

So, to obtain a first intuition about the efficiency of the ICA as a denoising technique we have compared the obtained SNR with and without applying the FastICA. For the sake of comparison, we also added the SNR when the averaging technique is applied. The results are shown on Fig. 2.

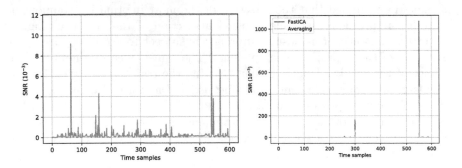

Fig. 2. Signal-to-Noise Ratio estimation without filtering (left) and when applying the FastICA and averaging techniques (right).

From Fig. 2, one can conclude that the SNR gain is close to a factor of 100. In general, higher SNR should translate into a successful attack requiring much less traces. To confirm this claim, we have performed a CPA attack by targeting the output of the first AES SBox. For the sake of comparison, we considered the same filtering techniques as those used in the first case study (Sect. 4.2). Regarding the SSA, the window length has been set using the previously described rule-of-thumb and only the second component was selected for the re-construction phase. The attack results for each filtering technique are depicted in Fig. 3 (left-hand side).

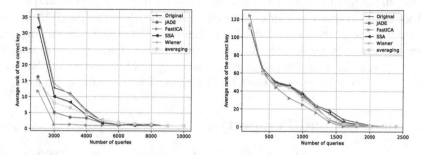

Fig. 3. Evolution of the correct key rank (y-axis) according to an increasing number of traces (x-axis) for each filtering technique when targeting the first AES SBox (unprotected implementation at left-hand side and protected one at right-hand side).

As expected the connection between the SNR gain and the number of traces needed for a successful attack is confirmed. In fact, when applying the FastICA technique less traces are needed to recover the good value of the key (*i.e.* 1.000 traces instead of 3.000 for the non-preprocessed traces). Actually, in several works [40, 41] the relation between the number of traces required to achieve 90% of success rate for the CPA attack ($N_{90\%}$) and the SNR has been exhibited and, for every coordinate $i \in [1; p]$, it rewrites:

$$N_{90\%} \approx \frac{2\beta_{90\%}^2}{\text{SNR}[i]}, \tag{8}$$

where $\beta_{90\%}$ is a quantile of a normal distribution for the 2-sided confidence interval [41]. So, (8) confirms our experimental findings, the higher the SNR is, the less traces are required to succeed a CPA attack. Regarding the SSA, the averaging method and the Wiener filter, the gains are not that large.

4.4   Masked AES Implementation on the ChipWhisperer-Lite Board (ATMega128)

We focus in this section on the practical evaluation of the ICA against a first-order Boolean masking scheme[8] implemented on the ChipWhisperer-Lite board

---

[8] Particular attention has been paid on the implementation to ensure that no first-order leakage occurred.

(CW1173) [45]. To do so, we have acquired a set of power measurements standing for the loading of the masks and the processing of the first AES round. For our attack phase, we assumed that the leaking points related to the loading of the masks are known. Then, we have performed a second-order CPA attack with centered product as a combination function [46]. The attack results when applying different filtering techniques are depicted in Fig. 3 (right-hand side).

From Fig. 3 (right-hand side), one can conclude that the FastICA is more efficient than the other tested denoising techniques. Noticeably, the gain in terms of number of traces needed to succeed a second-order CPA attack is not very high (as it was the case for the second scenario)[9]. This could be explained by the fact that the noise level of the ChipWhisperer-Lite board is quite low.

5   Conclusion and Perspectives

In this work, we proposed an in-depth study of the application of ICA in side-channel context. In particular, we discussed the relationship between the ICA and the commonly used preprocessing techniques (*e.g.* PCA, LDA and projection pursuit). Then, we proposed a framework to use the ICA as a preprocessing technique to reduce the noise level of side-channel measurements. Finally, we validated its interest in three different scenarios. Namely, we considered an unprotected software AES implementation, the noisy traces of the DPA contest v2 and a first-order Boolean masking implementation. The obtained results have shown that the ICA introduces a significant SNR gain which implies a gain in terms of the number of measurements required to succeed a side-channel attack.

---

[9] On other protected implementations, we observed that the gain with ICA techniques is more important. However, we cannot communicate information related to these implementations and the tested chips since these are confidential IPs.

A   Example of Trace Denoising Based on the FastICA Method

For illustration, an exemplary power trace and the resulting filtered trace after applying ICA are shown in Fig. 4.

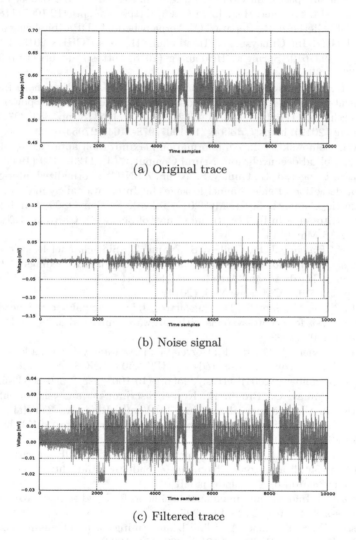

(a) Original trace

(b) Noise signal

(c) Filtered trace

Fig. 4. Unprotected AES implementation: original power trace, noise signal and filtered trace.

References

1. Python implementation of FastICA algorithm. http://scikit-learn.org/stable/modules/generated/sklearn.decomposition.FastICA.html
2. Archambeau, C., Peeters, E., Standaert, F.-X., Quisquater, J.-J.: Template attacks in principal subspaces. In: Goubin, L., Matsui, M. (eds.) CHES 2006. LNCS, vol. 4249, pp. 1–14. Springer, Heidelberg (2006). https://doi.org/10.1007/11894063_1
3. Balasch, J., Gierlichs, B., Reparaz, O., Verbauwhede, I.: DPA, bitslicing and masking at 1 GHz. In: Güneysu, T., Handschuh, H. (eds.) CHES 2015. LNCS, vol. 9293, pp. 599–619. Springer, Heidelberg (2015). https://doi.org/10.1007/978-3-662-48324-4_30
4. Batina, L., Hogenboom, J., van Woudenberg, J.G.J.: Getting more from PCA: first results of using principal component analysis for extensive power analysis. In: Dunkelman, O. (ed.) CT-RSA 2012. LNCS, vol. 7178, pp. 383–397. Springer, Heidelberg (2012). https://doi.org/10.1007/978-3-642-27954-6_24
5. Bell, A.J., Sejnowski, T.J.: An information-maximization approach to blind separation and blind deconvolution. Neural Comput. **7**(6), 1129–1159 (1995)
6. Bhasin, S., Danger, J.-L., Guilley, S., Najm, Z.: NICV: normalized inter-class variance for detection of side-channel leakage. In: International Symposium on Electromagnetic Compatibility (EMC 2014/Tokyo). Session OS09: EM Information Leakage. Hitotsubashi Hall (National Center of Sciences), Chiyoda, Tokyo, Japan. IEEE, 12–16 May 2014
7. Bhasin, S., Danger, J.-L., Guilley, S., Najm, Z.: Side-channel leakage and trace compression using normalized inter-class variance. In: Proceedings of the Third Workshop on Hardware and Architectural Support for Security and Privacy, HASP 2014, pp. 7:1–7:9. ACM, New York (2014)
8. Bohy, L., Neve, M., Samyde, D., Quisquater, J.J.: Principal and independent component analysis for crypto-systems with hardware unmasked units. In: Proceedings of e-Smart 2003 (2003)
9. Brier, E., Clavier, C., Olivier, F.: Correlation power analysis with a leakage model. In: Joye, M., Quisquater, J.-J. (eds.) CHES 2004. LNCS, vol. 3156, pp. 16–29. Springer, Heidelberg (2004). https://doi.org/10.1007/978-3-540-28632-5_2
10. Cagli, E., Dumas, C., Prouff, E.: Kernel discriminant analysis for information extraction in the presence of masking. In: Lemke-Rust, K., Tunstall, M. (eds.) CARDIS 2016. LNCS, vol. 10146, pp. 1–22. Springer, Cham (2017). https://doi.org/10.1007/978-3-319-54669-8_1
11. Cardoso, J.F.: Python and Matlab implementations of JADE algorithm. https://github.com/camilleanne/pulse/blob/master/jade.py and http://perso.telecom-paristech.fr/~cardoso/Algo/Jade/jadeR.m
12. Cardoso, J.F.: Infomax and maximum likelihood for blind source separation. IEEE Sig. Process. Lett. **4**(4), 112–114 (1997)
13. Cardoso, J.F., Souloumiac, A.: Blind beamforming for non-Gaussian signals. IEE Proc. F - Radar Sig. Process. **140**(6), 362–370 (1993)
14. Choudary, O., Kuhn, M.G.: Efficient template attacks. In: Francillon, A., Rohatgi, P. (eds.) CARDIS 2013. LNCS, vol. 8419, pp. 253–270. Springer, Cham (2014). https://doi.org/10.1007/978-3-319-08302-5_17
15. Comon, P.: Independent component analysis, a new concept? Sig. Process. **36**(3), 287–314 (1994)
16. Comon, P., Jutten, C.: Handbook of Blind Source Separation: Independent Component Analysis and Applications. Academic Press, Cambridge (2010)

17. China Consulting Consortium: Common Criteria (*aka* CC) for Information Technology Security Evaluation (ISO/IEC 15408) (2013). http://www.commoncriteriaportal.org/

18. Debande, N., Souissi, Y., Elaabid, M.A., Guilley, S., Danger, J.-L.: Wavelet transform based pre-processing for side channel analysis. In: HASP, Vancouver, British Columbia, Canada, pp. 32–38. IEEE, 2 December 2012. https://doi.org/10.1109/MICROW.2012.15

19. Ding, A.A., Chen, C., Eisenbarth, T.: Simpler, faster, and more robust t-test based leakage detection. In: Standaert, F.-X., Oswald, E. (eds.) COSADE 2016. LNCS, vol. 9689, pp. 163–183. Springer, Cham (2016). https://doi.org/10.1007/978-3-319-43283-0_10

20. Durvaux, F., Standaert, F.-X.: From improved leakage detection to the detection of points of interests in leakage traces. In: Fischlin, M., Coron, J.-S. (eds.) EURO-CRYPT 2016. LNCS, vol. 9665, pp. 240–262. Springer, Heidelberg (2016). https://doi.org/10.1007/978-3-662-49890-3_10

21. Fisher, R.A.: The use of multiple measurements in taxonomic problems. Ann. Eugenics **7**(7), 179–188 (1936)

22. Friedman, J.H., Tukey, J.W.: A projection pursuit algorithm for exploratory data analysis. IEEE Trans. Comput. **23**(9), 881–890 (1974)

23. Gao, S., Chen, H., Wu, W., Fan, L., Cao, W., Ma, X.: My traces learn what you did in the dark: recovering secret signals without key guesses. In: Handschuh, H. (ed.) CT-RSA 2017. LNCS, vol. 10159, pp. 363–378. Springer, Cham (2017). https://doi.org/10.1007/978-3-319-52153-4_21

24. Genkin, D., Pachmanov, L., Pipman, I., Tromer, E., Yarom, Y.: ECDSA key extraction from mobile devices via nonintrusive physical side channels. In: Proceedings of the 2016 ACM SIGSAC Conference on Computer and Communications Security, CCS 2016, pp. 1626–1638. ACM, New York (2016)

25. Georgiev, P., Theis, F.J.: Blind source separation of linear mixtures with singular matrices. In: Puntonet, C.G., Prieto, A. (eds.) ICA 2004. LNCS, vol. 3195, pp. 121–128. Springer, Heidelberg (2004). https://doi.org/10.1007/978-3-540-30110-3_16

26. Gierlichs, B., Batina, L., Tuyls, P., Preneel, B.: Mutual information analysis. In: Oswald, E., Rohatgi, P. (eds.) CHES 2008. LNCS, vol. 5154, pp. 426–442. Springer, Heidelberg (2008). https://doi.org/10.1007/978-3-540-85053-3_27

27. Gierlichs, B., Lemke-Rust, K., Paar, C.: Templates vs. stochastic methods. In: Goubin, L., Matsui, M. (eds.) CHES 2006. LNCS, vol. 4249, pp. 15–29. Springer, Heidelberg (2006). https://doi.org/10.1007/11894063_2

28. Goodwill, G., Jun, B., Jaffe, J., Rohatgi, P.: A testing methodology for side-channel resistance validation. In: NIST Non-Invasive Attack Testing Workshop, September 2011. http://csrc.nist.gov/news_events/non-invasive-attack-testing-workshop/papers/08_Goodwill.pdf

29. Huber, P.J.: Projection pursuit. Ann. Stat. **13**(2), 435–475 (1985)

30. Hyvärinen, A.: New approximations of differential entropy for independent component analysis and projection pursuit. In: Jordan, M.I., Kearns, M.J., Solla, S.A. (eds.) Advances in Neural Information Processing Systems 10, pp. 273–279. MIT Press (1998)

31. Hyvarinen, A.: Fast and robust fixed-point algorithms for independent component analysis. Trans. Neur. Netw. **10**(3), 626–634 (1999)

32. Hyvärinen, A.: Sparse code shrinkage: denoising of nongaussian data by maximum likelihood estimation. Neural Comput. **11**(7), 1739–1768 (1999)

33. Hyvärinen, A., Oja, E.: A fast fixed-point algorithm for independent component analysis. Neural Comput. **9**(7), 1483–1492 (1997)
34. Hyvärinen, A., Oja, E.: Independent component analysis: algorithms and applications. Neural Netw. **13**, 411–430 (2000)
35. Jolliffe, I.T.: Principal Component Analysis. Springer Series in Statistics. Springer, Heidelberg (2002). ISBN 0387954422
36. Jutten, C., Herault, J.: Blind separation of sources, part i: an adaptive algorithm based on neuromimetic architecture. Sig. Process. **24**(1), 1–10 (1991)
37. Kocher, P., Jaffe, J., Jun, B.: Differential power analysis. In: Wiener, M. (ed.) CRYPTO 1999. LNCS, vol. 1666, pp. 388–397. Springer, Heidelberg (1999). https://doi.org/10.1007/3-540-48405-1_25
38. Le, T.-H., Cledière, J., Servière, C., Lacoume, J.-L.: Noise reduction in side channel attack using fourth-order cumulant. IEEE Trans. Inf. Forensics Secur. **2**(4), 710–720 (2007). https://doi.org/10.1109/TIFS.2007.910252
39. Longo, J., De Mulder, E., Page, D., Tunstall, M.: SoC it to EM: electromagnetic side-channel attacks on a complex system-on-chip. In: Güneysu, T., Handschuh, H. (eds.) CHES 2015. LNCS, vol. 9293, pp. 620–640. Springer, Heidelberg (2015). https://doi.org/10.1007/978-3-662-48324-4_31
40. Maghrebi, H., Servant, V., Bringer, J.: There is wisdom in harnessing the strengths of your enemy: customized encoding to thwart side-channel attacks. In: Peyrin, T. (ed.) FSE 2016. LNCS, vol. 9783, pp. 223–243. Springer, Heidelberg (2016). https://doi.org/10.1007/978-3-662-52993-5_12
41. Mangard, S., Oswald, E., Popp, T.: Power Analysis Attacks: Revealing the Secrets of Smart Cards. Springer, Heidelberg (2006). https://doi.org/10.1007/978-0-387-38162-6. http://www.dpabook.org/. ISBN 0-387-30857-1
42. Merino Del Pozo, S., Standaert, F.-X.: Blind source separation from single measurements using singular spectrum analysis. In: Güneysu, T., Handschuh, H. (eds.) CHES 2015. LNCS, vol. 9293, pp. 42–59. Springer, Heidelberg (2015). https://doi.org/10.1007/978-3-662-48324-4_3
43. Nadal, J.-P., Parga, N.: Nonlinear neurons in the low-noise limit: a factorial code maximizes information transfer. Netw.: Comput. Neural Syst. **5**(4), 565–581 (1994)
44. Naik, G.R., Wang, W.: Blind Source Separation: Advances in Theory, Algorithms and Applications. Springer Publishing Company, Heidelberg (2014). Incorporated
45. O'Flynn, C., Chen, Z.D.: ChipWhisperer: an open-source platform for hardware embedded security research. In: Prouff, E. (ed.) COSADE 2014. LNCS, vol. 8622, pp. 243–260. Springer, Cham (2014). https://doi.org/10.1007/978-3-319-10175-0_17
46. Prouff, E., Rivain, M., Bévan, R.: Statistical analysis of second order differential power analysis. IEEE Trans. Comput. **58**(6), 799–811 (2009)
47. Schneider, T., Moradi, A.: Leakage assessment methodology. In: Güneysu, T., Handschuh, H. (eds.) CHES 2015. LNCS, vol. 9293, pp. 495–513. Springer, Heidelberg (2015). https://doi.org/10.1007/978-3-662-48324-4_25
48. Souissi, Y., Guilley, S., Danger, J.-L., Duc, G., Mekki, S.: Improvement of power analysis attacks using Kalman filter. In: ICASSP, IEEE Signal Processing Society, Dallas, TX, USA, 14–19 March 2010, pp. 1778–1781. IEEE (2010). https://doi.org/10.1109/ICASSP.2010.5495428
49. Standaert, F.-X., Archambeau, C.: Using subspace-based template attacks to compare and combine power and electromagnetic information leakages. In: Oswald, E., Rohatgi, P. (eds.) CHES 2008. LNCS, vol. 5154, pp. 411–425. Springer, Heidelberg (2008). https://doi.org/10.1007/978-3-540-85053-3_26

50. Standaert, F.-X., Malkin, T.G., Yung, M.: A unified framework for the analysis of side-channel key recovery attacks. In: Joux, A. (ed.) EUROCRYPT 2009. LNCS, vol. 5479, pp. 443–461. Springer, Heidelberg (2009). https://doi.org/10.1007/978-3-642-01001-9_26
51. TELECOM ParisTech SEN research group. DPA Contest (2nd edition) 2009–2010. http://www.DPAcontest.org/v2/
52. van Woudenberg, J.G.J., Witteman, M.F., Bakker, B.: Improving differential power analysis by elastic alignment. In: Kiayias, A. (ed.) CT-RSA 2011. LNCS, vol. 6558, pp. 104–119. Springer, Heidelberg (2011). https://doi.org/10.1007/978-3-642-19074-2_8
53. Wang, R., Ma, H.-G., Liu, G.-Q., Zuo, D.-G.: Selection of window length for singular spectrum analysis. J. Franklin Inst. **352**(4), 1541–1560 (2015)

Micro-architectural Power Simulator for Leakage Assessment of Cryptographic Software on ARM Cortex-M3 Processors

Yann Le Corre[✉], Johann Großschädl, and Daniel Dinu

CSC and SnT, University of Luxembourg,
6, Avenue de la Fonte, 4364 Esch-sur-Alzette, Luxembourg
{yann.lecorre,johann.groszschaedl,dumitru-daniel.dinu}@uni.lu

Abstract. Masking is a common technique to protect software implementations of symmetric cryptographic algorithms against Differential Power Analysis (DPA) attacks. The development of a properly masked version of a block cipher is an incremental and time-consuming process since each iteration of the development cycle involves a costly leakage assessment. To achieve a high level of DPA resistance, the architecture-specific leakage properties of the target processor need to be taken into account. However, for most embedded processors, a detailed description of these leakage properties is lacking and often not even the HDL model of the micro-architecture is openly available. Recent research has shown that power simulators for leakage assessment can significantly speed up the development process. Unfortunately, few such simulators exist and even fewer take target-specific leakages into account. To fill this gap, we present *MAPS*, a micro-architectural power simulator for the M3 series of ARM Cortex processors, one of today's most widely-used embedded platforms. *MAPS* is fast, easy to use, and able to model the Cortex-M3 pipeline leakages, in particular the leakage introduced by the pipeline registers. The M3 leakage properties are inferred from its HDL source code, and therefore *MAPS* does not need a complicated and expensive profiling phase. Taking first-order masked Assembler implementations of the lightweight cipher SIMON as example, we study how the pipeline leakages manifest and discuss some guidelines on how to avoid them.

Keywords: Leakage assessment · Architecture-specific leakage
Pipeline leakage · Power simulator · Cortex-M3

1 Introduction

Side-channel attacks [14] pose a serious threat to the security of cryptographic primitives, in particular when they are executed on mobile or embedded devices that are physically accessible to an attacker. A typical example of such devices are wireless sensor nodes, which are often deployed in unattended areas and do not come with any measures or techniques to minimize the leakage of sensitive

© Springer International Publishing AG, part of Springer Nature 2018
J. Fan and B. Gierlichs (Eds.): COSADE 2018, LNCS 10815, pp. 82–98, 2018.
https://doi.org/10.1007/978-3-319-89641-0_5

information through power or electromagnetic (EM) side channels. One of the most sophisticated forms of side-channel attack is Differential Power Analysis (DPA), first described in the open cryptographic literature almost 20 years ago by Kocher et al. [13]. A standard DPA attack involves two steps, namely (i) an acquisition step, in which the attacker measures the power consumption of the target device while it executes a cryptographic algorithm, and (ii) an analysis step, in which she uses advanced statistical techniques to recover the sensitive (i.e. key-dependent) data processed during the execution of the algorithm from the acquired power consumption traces. There exists a large body of literature demonstrating successful DPA attacks against (unprotected) implementations of both secret-key and public-key cryptographic primitives, see e.g. [15] and the references therein. In the case of block ciphers, it was shown that a few dozens of power traces can be sufficient to reveal the full secret key [7].

Due to the efficacy of DPA attacks, it is necessary to protect an implementation of a block cipher through the integration of countermeasures. One of the most well-known and widely used DPA countermeasures is *masking*, which can be realized in both hardware and software [8,11,22]. Masking aims to conceal every key-dependent variable with a random value, called mask, to de-correlate the sensitive data of the algorithm from the data that is actually processed on the device. The basic principle is related to the idea of secret sharing because every sensitive variable is split up into $n \geq 2$ "shares" so that any combination of up to $d = n - 1$ shares is statistically independent of any secret value. These n shares have to be processed separately during the execution of the algorithm (to ensure their leakages are independent of each other) and then recombined in the end to yield the correct result. What makes masking attractive is that its security can be proven in the framework of Isai, Sahai, and Wagner [12]. However, despite the theoretical security guarantees, it turned out that masking is challenging to implement in practice without introducing unintended (and often unobvious) leakage. For example, it was shown in [16] that a masked hardware implementation of the AES can be broken by exploiting glitches at the outputs of logic gates. On the other hand, software implementations of masked ciphers can also be vulnerable to DPA attacks because of unintended violations of the independent leakage requirement mentioned above, typically caused by certain micro-architectural effects and features [4,18,21]. Therefore, it is important to check whether a masked implementation meets its theoretical security promises also in practice (i.e. does not show any DPA-exploitable leakage), which can be done by performing a leakage assessment test [6] or a full DPA attack.

Developing a masked software implementation of a block cipher is a tedious and highly iterative endeavor. The developer tries to eliminate existing leakage and then performs a leakage assessment, and thereafter the same cycle starts again until no leakage can be detected anymore [4,7]. In order to decrease the development time, a power simulator like ELMO [17] can be used to generate the power traces. However, to get realistic traces, the simulator should be able to take certain micro-architectural effects into account, in particular the inter-instruction dependencies in the power consumption (and, hence, leakage) of the target processor. For example, due to pipelining effects, the power consumption caused by the execution of a certain instruction does not solely depend on the operands/results and from/to which register(s) they are read/written, but also on preceding and succeeding instructions that are in the pipeline at the same time. ELMO takes these effects into account by using measured power characteristics and by grouping instructions together. In the case of ARM Cortex M0 and M4 microcontrollers, which are currently supported by ELMO, up to three instructions need to be considered since the pipeline has three stages.

Even though ELMO is a undoubtedly a useful tool, it suffers from a couple of shortcomings. In particular, getting realistic instruction-level power models is a non-trivial task and requires a lot of measurements. Furthermore, in order to model differential data-dependent effects of "neighboring" instructions, ELMO uses power models for groups of instructions, whereby the size of the groups is determined by the number of instructions that can be in the processor pipeline at the same time (i.e. the number of pipeline stages). This approach achieves promising results, as demonstrated through several experiments by the authors of [17], but seems only viable for processors with few (e.g. up to three) pipeline stages. However, there exists a large number of embedded processors with five (e.g. ARM9), eight (e.g. ARM11), or even eleven (e.g. Cortex-R7/R8) pipeline stages, which makes it very costly to develop accurate power models for groups of instructions. Our simulator *MAPS* (Micro-Architectural Power Simulator) is based on a different approach and takes the inter-instruction dependency of the power consumption into account by utilizing a more refined micro-architectural model of the target processor. Specifically, *MAPS* models all pipeline registers and validates these models through simulations with an HDL description of the target micro-architecture. Thus, *MAPS* has two advantages over ELMO: (i) the power model does not require any measurements, especially no measurements of inter-instruction dependencies, and (ii) *MAPS* is also suitable for processors with deep(er) pipelines consisting of more than three stages.

Our Contributions. We present the basic concepts of *MAPS*, which is to the best of our knowledge the first open-source power simulator for leakage assessment targeting the Cortex-M3 architecture, one of the most popular platforms in the embedded domain. Besides being fast and easy to use, *MAPS* is capable to model (certain) architecture-specific leakages based on a structural analysis of an HDL description of the Cortex-M3 pipeline. As a second contribution, we analyze the impact of pipeline registers on the leakage of masked ciphers.

2   State of the Art

Over the years, numerous power simulators have been developed; the interested reader can find a survey in [24, Sect. 5.3]. We focus here on recent simulators that perform high-level simulations rather than analog or transistor/gate-level simulations. While low-level simulators are, in general, more accurate, they are relatively slow and rely on VLSI-technology-specific data (e.g. netlists, parasitic components, back-annotated delays), which is usually not publicly available.

Gagnerot introduced in his thesis [10] a power simulator that was developed for leakage assessment of cryptographic implementations. It is able to generate power traces by monitoring all read/write operations on the registers and buses of a complete system (e.g. a smart card). No concrete details of the system are described because the power simulator was developed in collaboration with an industry partner. However, what was stated is that it contained a 16-bit RISC processor, UART interfaces, as well as two coprocessors. The simulator accepts a compiled binary object file as input. Neither the simulator nor its source code are publicly available; hence, it is not known how detailed the modeling of the processor is, e.g. whether it includes the pipeline registers or not.

SILK stands for "Simple Leakage Simulator" and was presented by Veshchikov in 2014 [23]. It is not tied to a specific processor architecture but generates power traces using a high level of abstraction. The power model is very flexible and can be easily adapted to support different leakage scenarios. SILK accepts a C file as input. The source code is publicly available on Github[1].

Also Reparaz described in [19] a simulator capable to generate power traces from a high-level C description of a cryptographic algorithm. The values of the intermediate variables are traced after the implementation has been compiled with a modified version of the LLVM compiler. Thus, the simulator is not tied to a specific architecture. Yet, it is fast and also provides debugging capabilities that help a developer to pinpoint the sources of leakage.

ELMO ("Emulator for Power Leakage for Cortex M0") was introduced in 2016 by McCann et al. [17]. It is dedicated to the Cortex-M0 and M4 families of processors and takes a compiled binary object file as input. ELMO is based on an existing ARM v6-M emulator, which was "back-annotated" with leakage information. This leakage information was extracted using elaborate statistical processing that was applied to power measurements performed on a hardware setup. Therefore, ELMO belongs to the category of profiled simulators. Due to limitations of the underlying emulator, it supports only the Thumb instruction set but not Thumb-2. The reported leakages are potentially very accurate since the hardware measurements include various leakage effects such as glitches and coupling. However, adding a new target to ELMO is very challenging because it requires an elaborate measurement setup and the statistical processing has to be done again since it depends on the characteristics of the target instruction set and micro-architecture, e.g. pipeline depth. ELMO is publicly available[2].

3   Cortex-M3 Architecture-Specific Leakages

3.1   Cortex-M3 Overview

The Cortex-M3 is a 32-bit RISC processor developed by ARM that implements version v7-M [1] of the ARM instruction set. It is one of the most widely-used

---

[1] https://github.com/nikita-veshchikov/silk.

[2] https://github.com/bristol-sca/ELMO.

embedded platforms because it combines an efficient and compact instruction set with a high-quality tool chain. The Cortex-M3 has a Harvard architecture with both 16-bit and 32-bit instructions as well as a 32-bit data path. It does not include a data cache and comes with a pre-fetch buffer instead of a more complex instruction cache. Like other 32-bit ARM processors, the Cortex-M3 is equipped with 16 registers; besides 13 general-purpose registers (r0–r12) there is a stack pointer (r13), a link register (r14), and a program counter (r15).

The arithmetic and logical instructions operate solely on registers. A barrel shifter located between the register file and the Arithmetic-Logic Unit (ALU) allows one to combine an ALU operation with a shift or rotation of the second operand. Most ALU instructions execute in one cycle; the only exceptions are mul (multiply), div (divide), and operations targeting the program counter.

The pipeline is made of three stages. In the first stage, the instruction gets fetched from instruction memory. Thereafter, the instruction is decoded in the second stage, and finally executed in the third stage. Conditional branches are speculated (i.e. one of the alternative instructions is speculatively executed and eventually discarded if it turns out that the speculation was wrong). Store to memory instructions (e.g. str) are buffered and executed in one cycle, whereas load from memory instructions (e.g. ldr) introduce a wait-state. The typical Clock-Per-Instruction (CPI) figure for embedded software is close to 1.

3.2 Cortex-M3 HDL Analysis

ARM makes the entire HDL source code of the Cortex-M3 processor available to universities via the *DesignStart Pro Academic* program. The source package contains the M3 core, which is described in a set of Verilog files, and a minimal system that connects the core with the memories through AMBA ("Advanced Microcontroller Bus Architecture") buses. The system also includes peripherals like communication and debugging interfaces to enable developers to trace the execution of a program. By default, the Verilog simulation of the system loads and executes a C program cross-compiled for the ARM v7-M architecture.

Since we have access to the HDL source code, all registers related with the data path can be isolated and then traced. At the logic level, any information leakage could be related to the values held by the registers. The dependencies between the succeeding instructions and the sensitive data will be captured too since these registers also define the pipeline stages. All registers in the core can be easily found by looking for signals defined with the Verilog keyword *reg* and assigned in an "*always @(posedge <clock>)*" block. Of these registers, only the ones involved in the manipulation of data are relevant from a leakage-detection point of view. We can further discriminate by selecting the registers that have a width of 32 bits. In addition, since the ALU operates exclusively on operands read from registers, only the 32-bit registers connected to the two output ports of the register file have to be analyzed. Based on these criteria, the 16 registers of the register file (i.e. r0 to r15), along with two registers ra and rb located between the register file and the ALU and three registers inside the ALU, are retained. However, the latter three registers are solely used during multi-cycle

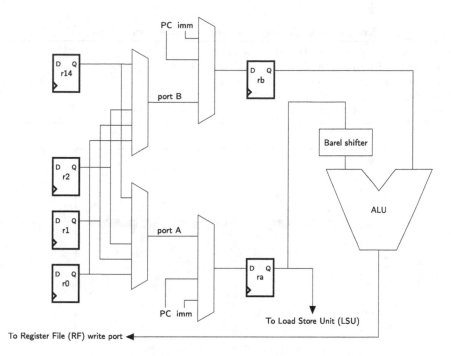

Fig. 1. Simplified structure of the Cortex-M3 pipeline

ALU instructions like umull, umlal, or udiv. Since such instructions are quite uncommon in the context of symmetric cryptosystems, we decided to not trace these three registers. The program counter r15 is also not traced by default in order to limit the length of the power traces. A major requirement for secure cryptographic software is that the control flow is independent of any sensitive data; if this is the case then the program counter can not leak anyway.

The registers ra and rb are pipeline registers isolating the decode from the execute stage. Their existence and location could have also been inferred from the fact that an ALU instruction can be executed while the succeeding instruction can access the registers. However, our analysis of the HDL code confirmed their exact location and allowed us to find out what values are written to them in each instruction. A simplified version of the pipeline is shown in Fig. 1.

3.3   Cortex-M3 Pipeline Leakages

The registers ra and rb are specific to the pipeline architecture of the M3 processor. They are a possible source of leakage since they combine operand values of consecutive instructions. Indeed, the power consumption associated with the writing to these registers is directly related to the Hamming distance between the current operand value and the previous one. Both the first and the second operand of ALU instructions can be affected. Since the register ra connects the register file with the barrel shifter, even an ALU instruction with a shifted or rotated second operand may leak through this register.

Listing 1. Code fragment with second-operand leakage

```
; r2 and r3 contain the two shares
; r4 and r5 contain random and unrelated values
; r6 and r7 are initialized to 0
and r6, r4, r2, lsl 4
orr r7, r5, r3, ror 5
```

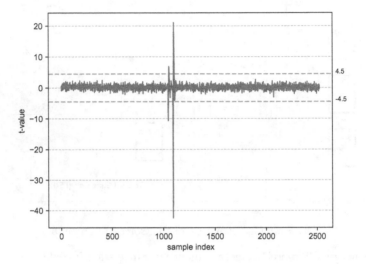

Fig. 2. T-test confirming second-operand leakage (hardware measurements)

Register Transfer Notation 1. Equivalent to Listing 1

1: $rb \leftarrow r4$
2: $ra \leftarrow r2$
3: $r6 \leftarrow rb \wedge (ra \ll 4)$
4: $rb \leftarrow r5$
5: $ra \leftarrow r3$ $\triangleright Power(ra) = HW(r2 \oplus r3)$
6: $r7 \leftarrow rb \vee (ra \gg 5)$

Listing 1 illustrates such a leakage. In this code fragment, the two registers r2 and r3 hold the shares of a secret value, which is $(r2 \oplus r3)$. Register r4 and r5 contain arbitrary values unrelated with the content of other registers. From an architectural view, there should be no leakage. However, our measurements on an actual Cortex-M3 processor show that there is a leakage, as illustrated in Fig. 2. The measurements were taken on an Atmel Cortex-M3 SAM3X8E chip using a Langer EM probe connected to a LeCroy WR 8254M oscilloscope sampling at 500 MSamples/s. This leakage is not difficult to explain when we take all register transfers involving ra and rb into account. Listing 1 is equivalent to the Register Transfer Notation 1. As expected, $(r2 \oplus r3)$ leaks through ra.

Listing 2. Code fragment with `str` instruction leakage

```
; r2 and r3 contain the two shares
str  r2, [r0, 0]
str  r3, [r0, 4]
```

Register Transfer Notation 2. Equivalent to Listing 2

1: $rb \leftarrow r0$
2: $ra \leftarrow r2$
3: $rb \leftarrow r0$
4: $ra \leftarrow r3$ ▷ $Power(\mathbf{ra}) = HW(\mathbf{r2} \oplus \mathbf{r3})$

In general, every instruction using a value read from a general-purpose register is affected, not only the ALU instructions. For example, all memory store instructions will leak when executed one right after another, as in Listing 2 and its equivalent Register Transfer Notation 2. The leakage of the `str` instructions extends further to the `push` and the store-multiple (`stm`) instructions since the latter are actually a shorthand for a sequence of `str` instructions.

3.4   Guidelines to Reduce Cortex-M3 Pipeline Leakage

The Cortex-M3 pipeline leakages can be reduced or even entirely circumvented in a few different ways, listed below in ascending order of their implementation cost in terms of execution time and code size.

1. Simply swap the operands of commutative instructions.
2. Schedule instructions so that the two shares are not processed by successive instructions. This may be difficult to achieve because of the relatively small number of general-purpose registers.
3. Overwrite the pipeline registers with unrelated values, which can sometimes be done by just using more complex instructions for certain operations. To give a concrete example, the statement "`mov r0, 0`" to clear register `r0` can be replaced by "`eor r0, rx, rx`" where `rx` is an arbitrary register. In the former version using `mov`, the registers `ra` and `rb` are not written since the immediate value 0 gets directly transferred from the instruction decoder to the register `r0`. In the second version, `ra` and `rb` are written with the value of `rx` before `r0` is cleared. This version can, depending on which register is actually used as `rx`, increase code size by two bytes at most.
4. Explicitly set the registers `ra` and `rb` to a value unrelated to any sensitive data. This can be done by a statement of the form "`orr r0, r0, r0`" where `r0` contains some random data; for example, `r0` could be the address of an input buffer. The cost is a clock cycle and two or four bytes of code size.

Note that inserting a `nop` instruction will not prevent the leakage since the `nop` instruction does not pass the instruction decoder and, consequently, it can not modify the two pipeline registers `ra` and `rb`.

4   Our Simulator: *MAPS*

In this section, we provide an overview of the main properties (i.e. features and limitations) of *MAPS* and briefly describe its operation.

4.1   Features

MAPS has been created to aid and simplify the development of masked implementations of cryptographic primitives. Its main features are as follows.

Easy to Use. The implementation and testing of a masked primitive requires advanced skills in cryptographic engineering. In addition, it is a highly iterative task that takes a lot of time, effort, and scrutiny. Our simulator is easy to use (even for non-experts) and provides a convenient way to do automated leakage assessment of cryptographic implementations. In this way, *MAPS* simplifies the whole development and testing process.

Advanced Debug Support. In this paper, the word debug has actually two meanings; the first relates to the debugging of the functionality of the primitive to achieve (algorithmic) correctness. Our simulator is able to interact with the GNU debugger GDB through a GDB server. The other meaning refers to identifying which instructions cause information leakage. *MAPS* generates an index file linking the program counter and the power trace sample index, which allows for easy identification of the instruction that leaks.

Fast(er) Development Cycles. Securely-masked versions of a cryptographic algorithm are typically implemented in Assembly language to have full control over the instructions that will be executed. The allocation of registers and the selection of operands may require several tries, but long simulation times make it costly to try various "what-if" scenarios. *MAPS* is very fast so that an entire "compile-simulate-test" cycle can be completed in just a few minutes.

Only One Set of Source Files. In absence of a leakage simulator for Cortex-M3, implementers commonly resort to emulated leakages, which, as mentioned in Sect. 2, are typically generated using a high-level C implementation instead of the Assembler implementation that will actually be deployed. Having to deal with two separate code bases can easily lead to mistakes due to inconsistencies and may require adaptations of one or both source codes. Using *MAPS* avoids such problems since the leakage assessment can be carried out with exactly the same implementation that will finally end up on the target device.

Target-Specific Leakages. Our simulator reports algorithmic leakages and as many as possible target-specific leakages. The power waveforms are computed from the trace of all registers related to the data being processed, including the pipeline registers.

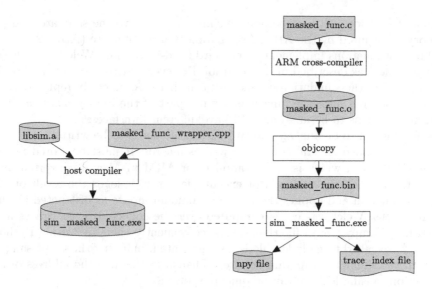

Fig. 3. *MAPS* flow

Open-Source. *MAPS* is open-source software[3] and may be used and modified without restrictions. In addition, anyone can contribute to the further development of *MAPS* by adding not-yet-supported instructions or new features.

4.2 Simulation Flow

A high-level view of the operation of *MAPS* is depicted in Fig. 3. At first, one has to produce a simulator executable, which is labeled *sim_masked_func.exe* in Fig. 3. The executable is tasked with loading and simulating the function to be analyzed. It "glues" together the Cortex-M3 simulation engine, the interface functions, and the test functions, all written in C++ 11.

The Cortex-M3 simulation engine is a C++ object with the usual methods such as `load()`, `step()`, `run()`, and so on. It is also responsible for tracing the register writes: each time a register is written, the Hamming distance between the previous register value and the new value is added as a new sample to the power trace. A power trace is a `std::vector` that can be manipulated after the end of the simulation. The Cortex-M3 simulation engine as well as some useful functions, such as a default `main()` function handling common command-line options, are grouped together in a library named *libsim.a*.

The file *masked_func_wrapper.cpp* contains both the test functions and the interface functions. The latter functions wrap the call to the simulator engine so that the function to be analyzed regarding leakage appears like a host-domain function. It "abstracts" the process of passing parameters from the host to the

---

[3] The full source code of *MAPS* is available on Github under the GNU General Public License version 3 (GPLv3): https://github.com/cryptolu/maps.

simulated function. All parameters are simply copied into the simulated target memory as required by the ARM Application Binary Interface (ABI) [2].

The test functions implement a standard fixed-vs-random Welch t-test leakage assessment as described in detail in [6]. However, the assessment method is independent of the simulation engine and can therefore be easily replaced. The test functions and interface functions are not part of the library *libsim.a* since different functions to be analyzed will have different interfaces.

The function to be analyzed regarding leakage needs to be written in C and can contain inlined Assembly code as well as macros. It must be stored in the file *masked_func.c*, which is cross-compiled for ARM v7-M and converted into binary format. When the simulator executable is run, it loads the result of the cross-compilation and applies the fixed and random inputs as instructed by the test functions. Welch's t-test is computed over the collected power traces and stored in a Numpy (*.npy*) file that can be conveniently visualized using Python scripts. A so-called trace index file is also generated, mapping the t-test sample index to the simulated program counter. Thanks to this file, the address of an instruction causing leakage can be quickly spotted.

4.3   Validation

In order to ensure that the Cortex-M3 processor is correctly modeled, both its functionality and leakage generation features were carefully tested in a specific test environment. All supported instructions were collected in a C file that was cross-compiled for the Cortex-M3. Then, they were simulated using *MAPS* as well as ARM's Verilog-based minimal system testbench. For each simulation, a trace of the registers was created and the two traces were compared. The trace generated by our simulator exactly matched the one produced by the system testbench, which guarantees that *MAPS* behaves like the actual processor.

4.4   Limitations

The current version of *MAPS* has the following limitations:

- Only the Cortex-M3 target is supported.
- Not all instructions of the Cortex-M3 described in [1] are supported. The currently-not supported instructions include conditional instructions, table branch instructions, saturation instructions, multiply instructions, packing instructions, as well as hint instructions. However, all these instructions are unlikely to be found in an implementation of a symmetric primitive.
- The simulator traces only the registers. Glitches or the power consumption of the ALU are not taken into account. For example, a "cmp r2, r3" leaks (r2 − r3) on the actual hardware, but does not leak on the simulator.
- No peripheral components or interfaces are modeled, and data can only be transferred between host and targets using the ABI and target memory.
- The simulator traces only registers of the Cortex-M3 core. Other registers located outside of the core, e.g. in a memory interface, are not considered.
- The simulator is not cycle-accurate.

4.5   Performance

The simulation speed of *MAPS* is summarized in Table 1. All test cases correspond to a fixed-vs-random Welch t-test as in [6] for one million measurements (i.e. two million executions of the simulated function). The tests were executed on an Intel i7-6700 processor running at 3.4 GHz. For comparison, it should be noted that the acquisition speed of the setup employed by the organizers of the DPA contest v4 to measure AES power traces was about 0.9 traces/s [24].

Table 1. *MAPS* simulation performance for three first-order masked block ciphers (generation of one million traces)

Algorithm	No. of instructions	Simulation time [s]	Traces/s
SIMON-64/128	1194	113	17700
RECTANGLE-64/128	2279	220	9091
SPECK-64/128	6055	488	4098

We used for our performance evaluation first-order masked implementations of three well-known lightweight block ciphers, namely SIMON and SPECK [5], as well as RECTANGLE [25]. SIMON-64/128 is a hardware-oriented cipher with an And-Rotation-Xor structure. The version we tested is a 2-share masked implementation protected with the Trichina AND gate [22]. SPECK-64/128 is a more software-optimized cipher based on an Addition-Rotation-Xor structure. The tested implementation is protected by a 2-share Boolean masking, whereby the modular addition is performed directly on the Boolean shares according to the Kogge-Stone Adder (KSA) technique introduced in [9]. RECTANGLE-64/128 is a bit-sliced lightweight cipher designed on basis of a substitution-permutation network. The tested implementation is protected by a 2-share Boolean masking using the Trichina AND gate [22] and the OR gate from Baek et al. [3] with an additional random variable to mirror the AND gate.

5   Case Study

In this section, we show how *MAPS* can be used to implement a secure version of SIMON-64/128 on a Cortex-M3 processor. All results we will present in the following are based on a leakage assessment using Welch's t-test on power traces generated by *MAPS* in a fixed-vs-random setting. For each experiment, 10,000 traces with fixed inputs and 10,000 traces with random inputs were collected.

First, Fig. 4(a) shows the result of a naive implementation of SIMON-64/128 protected using Trichina AND gates. This naive implementation minimizes the number of execution cycles and places intermediate results of the computation in the next free register. Any Hamming distance effect due to the reuse of some registers was not taken into account and *MAPS* was configured to not trace the pipeline registers `ra` and `rb`. Unsurprisingly, this implementation leaks.

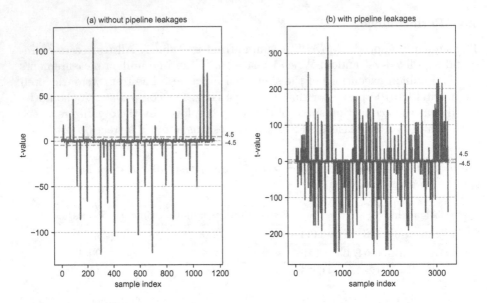

Fig. 4. Leakage assessment of the naive implementation of SIMON-64/128, simulated (a) without and (b) with pipeline leakages

Figure 4(b) visualizes the result of the leakage assessment test for the same naive implementation, but this time the tracing of the pipeline registers ra and rb is enabled in the simulator. Many more leakage points can be observed.

Next, the naive implementation was improved by fixing the leakages due to the reuse of registers. The obtained result of the leakage assessment is depicted in Fig. 5(a), whereby the simulator was configured to not trace register ra and rb. Now the leakages seem to be fixed. However, Fig. 5(b) illustrates that this improved version still leaks through the pipeline registers when their tracing is enabled. In fact, most of the leakage comes from the two pipeline registers.

Table 2. Comparison of three masked implementations of SIMON-64/128

Version	No. of instructions	Penalty factor
(1) naive	1106	1.00
(2) fixed register-reuse leakages	1194	1.08
(3) fixed pipeline leakages	1285	1.16

Table 2 lists the number of instructions executed by the three SIMON implementations. Version (1) is the naive implementation and version (2) the naive implementation with fixed register-reuse leakage effects. Version (3) represents an improvement of version (2) to fix all pipeline leakages using the techniques

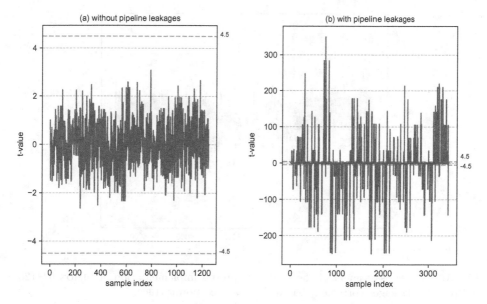

Fig. 5. Leakage assessment of the improved implementation of SIMON-64/128 (register-reuse leakages corrected), simulated (a) without and (b) with pipeline leakages

given in Subect. 3.4. It should be noted that the number of instructions differs from the number of clock cycles. For example, replacing one `stm` instruction by several `str` instructions does not increase the number of cycles.

Figure 6 shows the result of the t-test for the further-improved implementation of SIMON-64/128 where we tried to fix all pipeline leakages. The t-test was performed using measured traces (acquired with the hardware setup that was also used for the t-test shown in Fig. 2) in a fixed-vs-random setting. As can be seen in Fig. 6, this implementation is still not entirely leakage-free, but the t value exceeds the threshold of 4.5 only insignificantly compared to the naive implementation in Fig. 2. Performing the t-test with this implementation on simulated traces did not show any leakage anymore, i.e. the t value was always well below the threshold of 4.5. Therefore, an implementer can conveniently use *MAPS* in the early stages of the leakage elimination process until the t-test on simulated traces is free of leakage. The final step is then the "fine-tuning" of the implementation until the t-test on measured traces does not show any leakage anymore. However, thanks to *MAPS*, an implementer needs to measure traces only at the very end of the implementation process, but not in the early stages of the implementation, which significantly reduces the development time.

With our setup, the measurement of power traces took roughly eight hours for 8,000 encryptions with a fixed input and 8,000 encryptions with a random inputs. Each encryption was repeated eight times and then averaged to reduce the noise. On the other hand, obtaining simulated traces with *MAPS* for 8,000 fixed-input/random-input encryptions took just 1.2 seconds altogether, which is 24,000 times faster than the eight hours we needed to measure the traces.

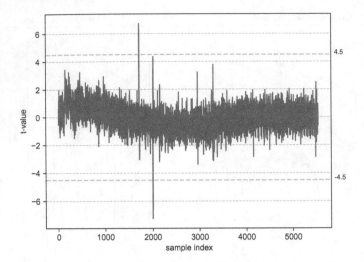

Fig. 6. Leakage assessment of the further-improved implementation of SIMON-64/128 (all pipeline leakages corrected) based on measured power traces

6   Conclusions and Future Work

In this paper, we presented the design of *MAPS*, a simulator for fast leakage assessment of cryptographic software on ARM Cortex-M3 processors, which are widely used in the embedded domain. We demonstrated that our simulator can greatly speed up the implementation of masked block ciphers by identifying the architecture-specific leakages early in the development phase. Furthermore, we analyzed Cortex-M3-specific leakages introduced by the pipeline registers and showed that they are significant. In this way, we contribute to a better understanding of which micro-architectural properties and features of a Cortex-M3 processor actually cause the leakage that can be exploited in a DPA attack. We also provided a number of guidelines on how to take the pipeline leakages into consideration when developing a masked implementation of a cipher.

Our approach to analyze architecture-specific leakages can be easily applied to other targets without the need of complex profiling procedures, provided the HDL code of the processor is available. A possible candidate is Cortex-M0 since it is also part of the *DesignStart Pro Academic* program. The simulation speed may be further improved by optimizing the t-test implementation following the recent proposal of Reparaz et al. [20].

References

1. ARM Limited. ARM v7-M Architecture Reference Manual (2010). http://static. docs.arm.com/ddi0403/eb/DDI0403E_B_armv7m_arm.pdf
2. ARM Limited. Procedure Call Standard for the ARM Architecture (2015). http:// infocenter.arm.com/help/topic/com.arm.doc.ihi0042f/IHI0042F_aapcs.pdf

3. Baek, Y.-J., Noh, M.-J.: Differential power attack and masking method. Trends Math. **8**(1), 1–15 (2005)
4. Balasch, J., Gierlichs, B., Grosso, V., Reparaz, O., Standaert, F.-X.: On the cost of lazy engineering for masked software implementations. In: Joye, M., Moradi, A. (eds.) CARDIS 2014. LNCS, vol. 8968, pp. 64–81. Springer, Cham (2015). https://doi.org/10.1007/978-3-319-16763-3_5
5. Beaulieu, R., Shors, D., Smith, J., Treatman-Clark, S., Weeks, B., Wingers, L.: The SIMON and SPECK lightweight block ciphers. In: Proceedings of the 52nd Annual Design Automation Conference, San Francisco, CA, USA, 7–11 June 2015, pp. 175:1–175:6. ACM (2015)
6. Becker, G., Cooper, J., DeMulder, E., Goodwill, G., Jaffe, J., Kenworthy, G., Kouzminov, T., Leiserson, A., Marson, M., Rohatgi, P., Saab, S.: Test vector leakage assessment (TVLA) methodology in practice. In: International Cryptographic Module Conference (2013)
7. Biryukov, A., Dinu, D., Großschädl, J.: Correlation power analysis of lightweight block ciphers: from theory to practice. In: Manulis, M., Sadeghi, A.-R., Schneider, S. (eds.) ACNS 2016. LNCS, vol. 9696, pp. 537–557. Springer, Cham (2016). https://doi.org/10.1007/978-3-319-39555-5_29
8. Chari, S., Jutla, C.S., Rao, J.R., Rohatgi, P.: Towards sound approaches to counteract power-analysis attacks. In: Wiener, M. (ed.) CRYPTO 1999. LNCS, vol. 1666, pp. 398–412. Springer, Heidelberg (1999). https://doi.org/10.1007/3-540-48405-1_26
9. Coron, J.-S., Großschädl, J., Tibouchi, M., Vadnala, P.K.: Conversion from arithmetic to Boolean masking with logarithmic complexity. In: Leander, G. (ed.) FSE 2015. LNCS, vol. 9054, pp. 130–149. Springer, Heidelberg (2015). https://doi.org/10.1007/978-3-662-48116-5_7
10. Gagnerot, G.: Étude des attaques et des contre-mesures assoccées sur composants embarqués. Ph.D. thesis, Université de Limoges (2013)
11. Goubin, L., Patarin, J.: DES and differential power analysis the "Duplication" method. In: Koç, Ç.K., Paar, C. (eds.) CHES 1999. LNCS, vol. 1717, pp. 158–172. Springer, Heidelberg (1999). https://doi.org/10.1007/3-540-48059-5_15
12. Ishai, Y., Sahai, A., Wagner, D.: Private circuits: securing hardware against probing attacks. In: Boneh, D. (ed.) CRYPTO 2003. LNCS, vol. 2729, pp. 463–481. Springer, Heidelberg (2003). https://doi.org/10.1007/978-3-540-45146-4_27
13. Kocher, P., Jaffe, J., Jun, B.: Differential power analysis. In: Wiener, M. (ed.) CRYPTO 1999. LNCS, vol. 1666, pp. 388–397. Springer, Heidelberg (1999). https://doi.org/10.1007/3-540-48405-1_25
14. Le, T., Canovas, C., Clédière, J.: An overview of side channel analysis attacks. In: Abe, M., Gligor, V.D. (eds.) Proceedings of the 2008 ACM Symposium on Information, Computer and Communications Security, ASIACCS 2008, Tokyo, Japan, 18–20 March 2008, pp. 33–43. ACM (2008)
15. Mangard, S., Oswald, E., Popp, T.: Power Analysis Attacks - Revealing the Secrets of Smart Cards. Springer, Heidelberg (2007). https://doi.org/10.1007/978-0-387-38162-6
16. Mangard, S., Pramstaller, N., Oswald, E.: Successfully attacking masked AES hardware implementations. In: Rao, J.R., Sunar, B. (eds.) CHES 2005. LNCS, vol. 3659, pp. 157–171. Springer, Heidelberg (2005). https://doi.org/10.1007/11545262_12

17. McCann, D., Oswald, E., Whitnall, C.: Towards practical tools for side channel aware software engineering: 'Grey Box' modelling for instruction leakages. In: Kirda, E., Ristenpart, T. (eds.) 26th USENIX Security Symposium, USENIX Security 2017, Vancouver, BC, Canada, 16–18 August 2017, pp. 199–216. USENIX Association (2017)

18. Papagiannopoulos, K., Veshchikov, N.: Mind the gap: towards secure 1st-order masking in software. In: Guilley, S. (ed.) COSADE 2017. LNCS, vol. 10348, pp. 282–297. Springer, Cham (2017). https://doi.org/10.1007/978-3-319-64647-3_17

19. Reparaz, O.: Detecting flawed masking schemes with leakage detection tests. In: Peyrin, T. (ed.) FSE 2016. LNCS, vol. 9783, pp. 204–222. Springer, Heidelberg (2016). https://doi.org/10.1007/978-3-662-52993-5_11

20. Reparaz, O., Gierlichs, B., Verbauwhede, I.: Fast leakage assessment. In: Fischer, W., Homma, N. (eds.) CHES 2017. LNCS, vol. 10529, pp. 387–399. Springer, Cham (2017). https://doi.org/10.1007/978-3-319-66787-4_19

21. Seuschek, H., De Santis, F., Guillen, O.M.: Side-channel leakage aware instruction scheduling. In: Brorsson, M., Lu, Z., Agosta, G., Barenghi, A., Pelosi, G. (eds.) Proceedings of the 4th Workshop on Cryptography and Security in Computing Systems (CS2@HiPEAC 2017), pp. 7–12. ACM Press (2017)

22. Trichina, E., Korkishko, T., Lee, K.H.: Small size, low power, side channel-immune AES coprocessor: design and synthesis results. In: Dobbertin, H., Rijmen, V., Sowa, A. (eds.) AES 2004. LNCS, vol. 3373, pp. 113–127. Springer, Heidelberg (2005). https://doi.org/10.1007/11506447_10

23. Veshchikov, N.: SILK: high level of abstraction leakage simulator for side channel analysis. In: Preda, M.D., McDonald, J.T. (eds.) Proceedings of the 4th Program Protection and Reverse Engineering Workshop, PPREW@ACSAC 2014, New Orleans, LA, USA, 9 December 2014, pp. 3:1–3:11. ACM (2014)

24. Veshchikov, N.: Use of simulators for side-channel analysis: leakage detection and analysis of cryptographic systems in early stages of development. Ph.D. thesis, Université Libre de Bruxelles (2017)

25. Zhang, W., Bao, Z., Lin, D., Rijmen, V., Yang, B., Verbauwhede, I.: RECTANGLE: a bit-slice lightweight block cipher suitable for multiple platforms. Sci. China Inf. Sci. **58**(12), 1–15 (2015)

Fault Attacks and Hardware Trojans

Lattice-Based Fault Attacks Against ECMQV

Weiqiong Cao, Hua Chen[✉], Jingyi Feng, Limin Fan, and Wenling Wu

Trusted Computing and Information Assurance Laboratory, Institute of Software, Chinese Academy of Sciences, South Fourth Street 4#, ZhongGuanCun, Beijing 100190, People's Republic of China
{caowq,chenhua,fengjingyi,fanlimin,wwl}@tca.iscas.ac.cn

Abstract. ECMQV is a standardized key agreement protocol based on ECC with an additional implicit signature authentication. In this paper we investigate the vulnerability of ECMQV against fault attacks and propose two efficient lattice-based fault attacks. In our attacks, by inducing a storage fault to the ECC parameter a before the execution of ECMQV, we can construct two kinds of weak curves and successfully pass the public-key validation step in the protocol. Then, by solving ECDLP and using a guess-and-determine method, some information of the victim's temporary private key and the implicit-signature result can be deduced. Based on the retrieved information, we build two new lattice-attack models and recover the upper half of the static private key. Compared with the previous lattice-attack models, our models relax the attack conditions and do not require the exact partial knowledge of the nonces. The validity of the attacks is proven by experimental simulations, which show our attacks pose real threats to the unprotected ECMQV implementations since only one permanent fault is sufficient to retrieve half bits of the secret key.

Keywords: ECC · Fault attack · Lattice attack · ECMQV

1 Introduction

Smart cards and mobile devices are playing indispensable roles today, since a lot of important data such as mobile payment data and bank account information is stored on them. Hence, it is necessary to protect their security with cryptographic algorithms. Among various algorithms, elliptic curve cryptosystem (ECC) [1] is a popular one because it ensures the same level of security with less key bits and faster run time than RSA.

It is necessary to analyze not only the theoretical security but also the implementation security resisting physical attacks. When ECC is implemented on embedded devices, physical attacks may gain some information by physical tools to recover the secrets. Among various physical attacks, fault attack (FA) is a powerful one which exploits the faulty results caused by fault injection using laser injection, strong electromagnetic radiation and glitches. So far,

© Springer International Publishing AG, part of Springer Nature 2018
J. Fan and B. Gierlichs (Eds.): COSADE 2018, LNCS 10815, pp. 101–116, 2018.
https://doi.org/10.1007/978-3-319-89641-0_6

many different types of fault attacks (FAs) against ECC have been proposed and weak curve attack (WCA) based on low-order feature is a common one. In CRYPTO'2000 [2], the WCA based on the faulty basic point was first proposed by Biehl et al. After that, the WCAs based on the faulty curve parameters a and p were also proposed in [3,4]. Differential fault attack (DFA) [2,5,6] is another powerful FA. It recovers the scalar by inducing faults to alter the sign bit or instruction flow during the implementation of a scalar multiplication (SM) kG, and analyzing the difference between the correct and faulty results of the SM. Furthermore, the combination of FA and other attacks has also been used to analyze various algorithms of ECC. In CHES'2011 [7], the combination of FA and simple power analysis (SPA) has been proposed to attack a SM. Besides, FA combining with lattice attack (LA) [6] is also applied to signature algorithms. Nevertheless, to our knowledge, there seems to be no FA on the authenticated key agreement protocol ECMQV.

ECMQV is an extension of MQV proposed by Law, Menezes et al. [8], which has been standardized in IEEE 1363 [9], ANSI X9.63 [10], Chinese standard GM/T 0009-2012 (SM2) [11], etc. It is based on the Diffie-Hellman key agreement protocol on ECC (ECDH) with an additional implicit signature authentication. There mainly exist two kinds of attacks on ECMQV at present. Man-in-the-middle attack based on the application of ECMQV is the first one, such as forgery attack [12] and unknown key-share attack [13]. The other one is the traditional algorithm analysis based on the structure of ECMQV. WCA is naturally the common one and was proposed against one-pass ECMQV in PKC'2003 [14], in which the attacker pretending one party in the agreement sends two low-order points as public keys to the other-party victim. After several runs of the protocol, the victim's private key can be recovered by guessing the implicit-signature results and using Chinese Remainder Theorem (CRT). However, the attack cannot be applied to ECMQV with authentication and public key validation. Meanwhile, Leadbitter and Smart presented a LA against ECMQV in ISC'2003 [15]. If the attacker has partial knowledge of the victim's nonces: the temporary private key and the implicit-signature result, then the LA can be mounted to recover the upper half of the victim's static private key. The remainder bits can be obtained by Baby-Step/Giant-Step algorithm with a run time of $O(n^{1/4})$, where n is the order of basic point in the ECMQV protocol. After that, the combinations of WCA and LA are mentioned in INDOCRYPT'2006 [16] and JMC'2007 [17], respectively. However, such attacks have the following limits: (1) The victim's temporary private key is required to be known to the attacker; (2) There exists no or only part public-key validations to make the victim accept the low-order public keys; (3) The order of the low-order points must have the factor 2^l to ensure l bits of the nonce known for LA, where l is a positive integer. Apparently, the limits above are impractical for an integrated ECMQV. In view of the importance of public-key validation in ECMQV, we think it is interesting if some faults are induced so that the public-key validations are passed. Moreover, because of the existence of the implicit signature, the lattice-based fault attacks against ECDSA probably can be applied to ECMQV.

Our contributions. In this paper, we present two new lattice-based fault attacks against ECMQV. Our attack procedures can be divided into two stages. In the first stage, a storage fault is induced to the ECC parameter a before the running of ECMQV and two kinds of weak curves are constructed. The low-order points on the first weak curve can thereby pass the public-key validation steps in ECMQV. By solving ECDLP and using a guess-and-determine method, some reduced information of the victim's temporary private key r_B and the implicit-signature result s_B can be deduced. In the second stage, we build two new LA models with the retrieved information and successfully recover the upper half of the static private key d_B in ECMQV.

In our attacks, the LA models are more relaxed because it is unnecessary for the attacker to know the partial bits of the nonces s_B and r_B exactly, while it is required in the previous models [15–17]. The first model only utilizes the reduced values $s = s_B \mod d$ and $r = r_B \mod d$, where d is the greatest common divisor derived from the weak curves constructed in the first stage. In our case, only when d is equal to 2^l (l is a positive integer), the model is equivalent to the previous model which means the l bits of the nonces have to be known. Except that, the attacker does not need to know any bit of the nonces. The second model is totally different from the previous ones, in which $s = s_B \mod d$ and $r = r_B \mod n_2$ are required. Here d is a small factor of the order of the first weak curve and n_2 is the order of basic point G on the second weak curve. When the sum of bit lengths of n_2 and d is greater than a lower bound, the LA model will work. We also prove the correctness and effectiveness of the two attacks by software simulations. The simulations show that our attacks only require one permanent effective fault to retrieve half bits of the secret key. Thus, the corresponding countermeasure should be considered in practical implementations.

The remainder of the paper is organized as follows: Sect. 2 introduces the ECMQV protocol and some basic theory about lattices. In Sect. 3, the first lattice-based fault attack against ECMQV is presented, and the second one is presented in Sect. 4. The corresponding feasibility is verified by simulations in Sect. 5. Finally, conclusion is given in Sect. 6.

2 Preliminaries

2.1 ECMQV Authenticated Key Agreement Protocol

In this section, we will discuss the elliptic curves in prime field $F_p(p > 3)$ and ECMQV protocol. Elliptic curve $E(a, b)$ is defined by Weierstrass equation

$$E(a, b) : y^2 = x^3 + ax + b \mod p, \tag{1}$$

where $a, b \in F_p$, and $4a^3 + 27b^2 \neq 0 \mod p$.

The additive group $E(F_p)$ consists of the set of points and infinity point $\mathcal{O}$ on $E(a, b)$.

$$E(F_p) = \left\{ (x, y) | x, y \in F_p, y^2 = x^3 + ax + b \mod p \right\} \cup \{\mathcal{O}\}. \tag{2}$$

Given a basic point $G \in E(F_p)$ with order n, $<G>$ is the group taking G as its generator. For any point $Q \in <G>$, there exists a scalar $k \in [0, n-1]$, so that $Q = kG$. The scalar multiplication (SM) kG is an elementary operation on $E(a, b)$ and is composed of point doublings and additions. There are many algorithms for calculating SM, such as binary algorithm, wNAF window algorithm and Montgomery algorithm [18]. The security of ECC is based on the elliptic curve discrete logarithm problem (ECDLP): knowing the basic point $G \in E(F_p)$ and point $Q \in E(F_p)$, it is hard to find the scalar $k \in [0, n-1]$ satisfying $Q = kG$. As the best general attack on ECDLP, the combination of Pohlig Hellman algorithm and Pollard's rho algorithm reduces the ECDLP in the group $<G>$ into in a subgroup with prime order q, where q is the biggest prime factor of order n and the time complexity is $O(q^{1/2})$. Therefore, the security of ECC depends on the bit-size of q, so the curve parameters and basic point G of ECC are usually selected to make q as big as possible.

Next, we will introduce the three pass **ECMQV** protocol [18]. ECMQV is usually used for negotiating the shared session key between party A and B. In ECMQV, $\#E(F_p)$ is the order of $E(F_p)$, cofactor h is equal to $\#E(F_p)/n$, and $(a, b, p, G, n, \#E(F_p), h)$ are the optional parameters. A and B all have two private-public key pairs, the temporary and the static key pairs, respectively. The temporary key pair is variable with every key agreement. It is assumed that (P_A, d_A), (R_A, r_A) are the static and temporary key pairs of A and (P_B, d_B), (R_B, r_B) are the corresponding key pairs of B, respectively, where $P_A = d_A G$, $R_A = r_A G$, $P_B = d_B G$ and $R_B = r_B G$. In order to resist WCA, it is necessary for both A and B to perform public key validation on each other's static and temporary public keys. As stated in [18], Algorithm 1 is usually used for validating public key.

Algorithm 1. Public Key Validation [18]

Require: parameters a, b, p, n, h and public key Q
Ensure: the validation of Q is pass or not.

1. Verify $Q \neq \mathcal{O}$;
2. Verify that the x/y-values x_Q and y_Q of Q are the elements of field F_p, namely, $x_Q, y_Q \in [0, p-1]$;
3. Verify that Q lies on the elliptic curve $E(a, b)$ defined by a, b and p;
4. If any one of the verifications above fails, then return false; else return true.

Besides, we also define

$$f = \lfloor \log_2 n \rfloor + 1.$$

For any point $Q \in E(F_p)$, let

$$\overline{Q} = x_Q \bmod 2^{\lceil f/2 \rceil} + 2^{\lceil f/2 \rceil}, \tag{3}$$

where x_Q is the x-value of Q, and f is the bit length of n.

There exists an implicit signature with their own static private key to ensure the session key shared by A and B. After that, a key derivation function (KDF) based on hash function is executed to generate the shared key. $KDF(S)$ is the concatenation of the values of hash functions $H(S, i)$, where i is a counter that is accumulated until the sum of the bit lengths of hash values equals the bit length of required key. Meanwhile, as the optional steps, the results are processed by a message authentication code (MAC) algorithm and the result of MAC is sent to the other party for further verification. The whole protocol is specified in Algorithm 2, where ID_A and ID_B are the IDs of A and B, respectively.

Algorithm 2. ECMQV Key Agreement [18]

Require:

$$A \rightarrow B : R_A, ID_A;$$
$$B \rightarrow A : R_B, ID_B, t_B;$$
$$A \rightarrow B : t_A.$$

Ensure: share key K

1. A selects randomly $r_A \subset [1, n - 1]$, calculates $R_A = r_A G$, and sends R_A, ID_A to B;
2. B calculates the following:
   2.1 validates the public key R_A with Algorithm 1;
   2.2 selects randomly $r_B \in [1, n - 1]$ and calculates $R_B = r_B G$;
   2.3 calculates $s_B = r_B + \overline{R_B} d_B \mod n$ and $V = h s_B (R_A + \overline{R_A} P_A)$, and verifies $V \neq \mathcal{O}$;
   2.4 calculates $K = KDF(V, ID_A, ID_B)$;
   2.5 (options)calculates $t_B = MAC(2, V, ID_A, ID_B, R_B, R_A)$;
   2.6 sends $R_B, ID_B(, \text{options } t_B)$ to A;
3. A calculates the following:
   3.1 validates the public key R_B with Algorithm 1;
   3.2 calculates $s_A = r_A + \overline{R_A} d_A \mod n$ and $V = h s_A (R_B + \overline{R_B} P_B)$, and verifies $V \neq \mathcal{O}$;
   3.3 calculates $K = KDF(V, ID_A, ID_B)$;
   3.4 (options)calculates $t = MAC(2, V, ID_A, ID_B, R_B, R_A)$, and verifies $t = t_B$;
   3.5 (options) calculates $t_A = MAC(3, V, ID_A, ID_B, R_A, R_B)$, and sends t_A to B;
4. (options) B calculates $t = MAC(3, V, ID_A, ID_B, R_A, R_B)$, verifies $t = t_A$.

2.2   Lattices

In this section, we will introduce some basic definitions of lattice. Lattice is an old mathematical concept. Let vectors $b_1, b_2, ..., b_d \in \mathbb{R}^m$ are linearly independent, then the set $\mathcal{L}$

$$\mathcal{L} = \mathcal{L}(b_1, b_2, ..., b_d) = \{z = \sum_{i=1}^{d} x_i \cdot b_i | x_i \in \mathbb{Z}\} \tag{4}$$

is called a lattice and regards the vectors $\boldsymbol{b}_i(i = 1, 2, ..., d)s$ as its basis, where $\mathbb{R}^m$ is the m dimensional space in real number field $\mathbb{R}$. Matrix $B = (\boldsymbol{b}_1, \boldsymbol{b}_2, ..., \boldsymbol{b}_d)^T$ is denoted as the basis matrix of $\mathcal{L}$. For any $z \in \mathcal{L}$, there exists $\boldsymbol{x} \in \mathbb{Z}^d$ so that $\boldsymbol{z} = \boldsymbol{x}B$. d is the dimension of $\mathcal{L}$. If $m = d$, then $\mathcal{L}$ is full rank. $\mathcal{L}$ is an integer lattice when any vector $\boldsymbol{b}_i(i = 1, ..., d)$ belongs to $\mathbb{Z}^m$.

There are two famous problems in lattice $\mathcal{L}$, the shortest vector problem(SVP) and the closest vector problem(CVP). For SVP, given the basis $\boldsymbol{b}_is$ of $\mathcal{L}$, find a nonzero vector $\boldsymbol{v} \in \mathcal{L}$ so that $\|\boldsymbol{v}\| = \lambda_1(\mathcal{L})$, where $\lambda_1(\mathcal{L})$ is the length of shortest vector in lattice $\mathcal{L}$ and $\|.\|$ is denoted as Euclidean norm. It has been proven that LLL algorithm [19] and LLL-based BKZ algorithms [20] can solve approximate SVP in polynomial time. Similarly, CVP is defined as follow: given the basis $\boldsymbol{b}_is$ of $\mathcal{L}$ and a target vector $\boldsymbol{u} \in \mathbb{R}^m$, find a nonzero vector $\boldsymbol{v} \in \mathcal{L}$ satisfying $\|\boldsymbol{v} - \boldsymbol{u}\| = \lambda(\mathcal{L}, \boldsymbol{u})$, where $\lambda(\mathcal{L}, \boldsymbol{u})$ is the closest distance from vector $\boldsymbol{u}$ to lattice $\mathcal{L}$. CVP is harder than SVP and the approximate CVP can be solved by using LLL-based Babai's nearest plane algorithm [21] in polynomial time. Hence, CVP is usually reduced into SVP by the embedding technique in practice [22]. Given the basis $\boldsymbol{b}_is$ of $\mathcal{L}$ and the target vector $\boldsymbol{u}$, a new lattice $\mathcal{L}'$ can be built with new basis $\boldsymbol{b}_1', \boldsymbol{b}_2', ..., \boldsymbol{b}_{d+1}'$, where $\boldsymbol{b}_i' = (\boldsymbol{b}_i, 0)(i = 1, ..., d)$ and $\boldsymbol{b}_{d+1}' = (\boldsymbol{u}, \beta)$. β is a parameter to be determined. If $\boldsymbol{v}$ is the closest vector in $\mathcal{L}$ from $\boldsymbol{u}$, then $(\boldsymbol{u} - \boldsymbol{v}, \beta)$ is the shortest vector in $\mathcal{L}'$.

It has been proved [23] that a full-rank random lattice $\mathcal{L} \in \mathbb{R}^m$ satisfies with overwhelming probability

$$\lambda_1(L) \approx \sqrt{\frac{d}{2\pi e}} vol(\mathcal{L})^{\frac{1}{d}}, \tag{5}$$

where $vol(\mathcal{L})$ is the determinant of $\mathcal{L}$ satisfying $vol(\mathcal{L}) = \prod_{i=1}^{d} \|\boldsymbol{b}_i^*\|$. $\boldsymbol{b}_i^*s$ are the corresponding Gram-Schmidt basis derived from matrix B.

Furthermore, the theorem above can be extended to CVP. Babai has proved [21] that given a target vector $\boldsymbol{u}$, the lattice vector $\boldsymbol{v}$ can be determined in polynomial time when satisfying the in equation

$$\|\boldsymbol{v} - \boldsymbol{u}\| \leq c_1 \|b_N^*\|^2 \leq \sqrt{\frac{d}{2\pi e}} vol(\mathcal{L})^{\frac{1}{d}}. \tag{6}$$

3   First Lattice-Based Fault Attack Against ECMQV

As mentioned above, there exist public key validations described in Algorithm 1 for resisting WCA, and the point V generating shared key cannot be gained directly except the MAC results in Algorithm 2. Therefore, the DFA making use of the difference between correct and faulty points, and the WCA utilizing the feature of low-order point, all cannot be applied to the ECMQV protocol. However, if we disturb the curve parameter a into a' by fault injection before the execution of ECMQV protocol, then the following public-key validations in

ECMQV will be executed on a new weak curve $E_1(a', b)$. Obviously, the low-order points on $E_1(a', b)$ can pass the public key validation. In addition, the basic point $G(x_G, y_G)$ does not lie on the original curve $E(a, b)$ but on another new weak curve $E_2(a', b')$, where $b' = y_G^2 - x_G^3 - a'x_G$. Thereby, as long as ECMQV protocol can run repeatedly on the two weak curves, we can recover the upper half of the static private key.

In this section, we present the first lattice-based fault attack against ECMQV. To recover the full key, the attack usually composes of three stages. First, FA is carried out to retrieve some reduced information of the nonces. Next, a LA model different from the one in ISC'2003 [15] is built to reveal the upper half of d_B with the retrieved information. Finally, the remaining bits of d_B can be solved by a Baby-Step/Giant-Step algorithm, which is same with the stage presented in ISC'2003 [15] and is not the focus of our study. Hence, our attack just takes the first two stages into account. The following sections describe the FA and its corresponding LA.

3.1 Fault Attack Scenario

Our attack assumes that the attacker as party A intends to acquire the static private d_B of party B and the SM calculation involves the parameter a^1. Moreover, there exist no additional countermeasures for resisting WCA except the common Algorithm 1. Party A disturbs the parameter a stored in the cryptographic device of party B to generate a faulty a' which is unknown to party A. Meanwhile, the static public key P_A invoked by party B can be changed by party A, which exists in practical applications, such as $P_A = R_A$ in the ECMQV of SSH protocol. Finally, it is assumed that the curve parameter b is quadratic residue, that is, there exists $g \in F_p$ so that $b = g^2 \mod p$. This is true for most of the curves recommended in standards. The point $C(0, \pm g)$ is so-called common point lying on the curve $E(\tilde{a}, b)$ for any $\tilde{a} \in F_p$ as mentioned in [24].

3.2 Fault Attack Against ECMQV

The FA includes the following steps, in which fault injection and sending low-order public keys to B are online, and the remaining steps are off-line for analysis.

Step 1: disturb a into a' by fault injection (online). At the beginning of ECMQV in the cryptographic device, the parameter a is written into RAM through the bus. If the attacker mounts FI on the bus/RAM during/after the write operation to disturb a into a', a' will replace a for the following operations of ECMQV and remains unchanged until the device resets or powers down.

Based on the faulty parameter a', we have the first weak curve

$$E_1(a', b) : y^2 = x^3 + a'x + b. \tag{7}$$

n_1 is the order of $E_1(F_p)$.

---

[1] a is usually not involved in the SM calculation directly when $a = p - 3$.

Meanwhile, because of the faulty a', the SM $R_B = r_B G$ is computed on the second new curve $E_2(a', b')$ instead of the original curve $E(a, b)$.

$$E_2(a', b') : y^2 = x^3 + a'x + b'. \tag{8}$$

n_2 is the order of G on $E_2(a', b')$.

In order to determine the values of a' and b', the attacker first sends the common point $C(0, \pm\sqrt{b})$ lying on $E_1(a', b)$ to B. Obviously, B would accept the point C after validation and send its temporary public key R_B to the attacker. Thereby, the points $G(x_G, y_G)$ and $R_B(x_{R_B}, y_{R_B})$ on the weak curve $E_2(a', b')$ are all known to the attacker. Apparently, a' and b' can be determined by the equations

$$\begin{aligned} y_G{}^2 &= x_G{}^3 + a'x_G + b' \mod p \\ y_{R_B}{}^2 &= x_{R_B}{}^3 + a'x_{R_B} + b' \mod p. \end{aligned} \tag{9}$$

Let $d \in \mathbb{Z}$ be the greatest common divisor of n_1 and n_2, that is, $d = \gcd(n_1, n_2)$, then there exists m_2 so that $n_2 = m_2 d$. To ensure the success of the next LA, we should find an effective faulty a' to make d as big as possible under the feasible time complexity $O(d)$. Otherwise, reset the device and restart FI.

Step 2: send low-order public keys on weak curve $E_1(a', b)$ to B (online). After determining an effective a', the attacker intentionally selects a point R_A lying on $E_1(a', b)$ with order d as its temporary public key and a point P_A satisfying $P_A = uR_A$ as its static public key, where $u \in [1, d-1]$ and $\gcd(d, h + hu\overline{R_A}) = 1$, and then sends them to B. According to Algorithm 2, B calculates the shared key K and outputs R_B, ID_B, and t_B(options) to the attacker.

Step 3: deduce the reduced information r of the temporary private-key r_B (off-line). Given that $R_B = r_B G$, it follows that $m_2 R_B = r_B(m_2 G)$. Because of the low-order point $m_2 G$, it is easy to solve the ECDLP and gain the result $r = r_B \mod d$, i.e., $r_B = r + \lambda d$, where $\lambda < n/d$.

Step 4: guess and determine the reduced information s of the implicit-signature result s_B (off-line). Since $P_A = uR_A$ and $\gcd(d, h + hu\overline{R_A}) = 1$, $h(R_A + \overline{R_A}P_A)$ lies on $E_1(a', b)$ and its order $\frac{d}{\gcd(d, h+hu\overline{R_A})}$ equals d. Guess the reduced value $s = s_B \mod d$ and calculate the following formulas

$$\begin{aligned} V &= hs(R_A + \overline{R_A}P_A), \\ K &= KDF(V, ID_A, ID_B), \\ t &= MAC(2, V, ID_A, ID_B, R_B, R_A). \end{aligned} \tag{10}$$

As long as $t = t_B$, the corresponding guessed s is the correct value and $s_B = s + \mu d$, where $\mu < n/d$.

As an option in Algorithm 2, B may terminate the ECMQV agreement without calculating t_B. In that case, the attacker needs to implement the encryption/decryption using the shared key K with B. If the results of encryption/decryption are correct, the guessed s is also correct. Besides, in case the static public key P_A is sent to B before FI and cannot be changed by the attacker, the attacker could construct a low-order point $R_A + \overline{R_A}P_A$ with order n_3 on a new weak curve by uprating R_A. d will become the greatest common divisor of n_2 and n_3 for analysis by then.

To sum up, by the fault attack above, the attacker can get some reduced information of r_B and s_B, i.e., r and s, which can be applied to build the model of lattice attack.

3.3   Lattice Attack Against ECMQV

As stated above, although the attacker does not know the exact partial bits of r_B and s_B as presented in ISC'2003 [15], the LA still can be mounted with the reduced information retrieved by FA.

Assuming that the ECMQV protocol based on the faulty parameter a' is executed N times, the attacker gets N reduced results (r_i, s_i) by FA. For $i = 1, \ldots, N$, the i-th temporary private key $r_{B,i}$ and the i-th implicit-signature result $s_{B,i}$ satisfy the following equations, respectively.

$$r_{B,i} = r_i + \lambda_i d,$$
$$s_{B,i} = s_i + \mu_i d. \tag{11}$$

where $\lambda_i, \mu_i < n/d$.

As shown in Algorithm 2, it is known

$$s_{B,i} = r_{B,i} + \overline{R_{B,i}}d_B \quad \bmod n, \tag{12}$$

where $R_{B,i}$ is the i-th temporary public key, and $\overline{R_{B,i}} \in [2^{\lceil f/2 \rceil}, 2^{\lceil f/2 \rceil+1} - 1]$ is derived from the Eq. (3).

Substituting the Eqs. (11) into (12), we have

$$(\mu_i - \lambda_i)d = r_i - s_i + \overline{R_{B,i}}d_B \quad \bmod n. \tag{13}$$

Hence, there exists $h_i \in \mathbb{Z}$ satisfying the equation

$$(\mu_i - \lambda_i) = (d^{-1}\overline{R_{B,i}} \quad \bmod n)d_B + h_i n - d^{-1}(s_i - r_i) \quad \bmod n. \tag{14}$$

Since $\lambda_i, \mu_i < n/d$, we have

$$|h_i n + (d^{-1}\overline{R_{B,i}} \quad \bmod n)d_B - d^{-1}(s_i - r_i) \quad \bmod n| < n/d. \tag{15}$$

A model of LA can be built by the inequation (15). Let $A_i = d^{-1}(s_i - r_i) \bmod n$, $B_i = d^{-1}\overline{R_{B,i}} \bmod n$. For $i = 1, \ldots, N$, a lattice $\mathcal{L}$ can be spanned by the row vectors $\boldsymbol{b}_1, \ldots, \boldsymbol{b}_{N+1}$ of matrix

$$M = \begin{pmatrix} n & 0 & \cdots & 0 \\ 0 & \ddots & & \vdots \\ \vdots & & n & 0 \\ B_1 & \cdots & B_N & 1/d \end{pmatrix}.$$

Let $\boldsymbol{x} = (h_1, \ldots, h_N, d_B) \in \mathbb{Z}^{N+1}$, then $\boldsymbol{x}M$ is a nonzero vector in $\mathcal{L}$ and $\boldsymbol{v} = \boldsymbol{x}M = (B_1 d_B + h_1 n, \ldots, B_N d_B + h_N n, d_B/d)$. In addition, let the non-lattice vector $\boldsymbol{u} = (A_1, \ldots, A_N, 0) \in \mathbb{Z}^{N+1}$. Naturally, the in Eq. (15) can be rewritten into

$$\|\boldsymbol{v} - \boldsymbol{u}\| < \sqrt{N+1}n/d \tag{16}$$

As mentioned in Sect. 2, if $\sqrt{N+1}n/d < \sqrt{\frac{N+1}{2\pi e}} vol(\mathcal{L})^{\frac{1}{N+1}}$, i.e., $N > \frac{f + \log 2\pi e}{l_d - \log 2\pi e}$, then $\boldsymbol{v}$ can be determined by solving CVP, where $vol(\mathcal{L}) = det(M) = n^N/d$ and $l_d = \lceil \log d \rceil$ is the bit length of d. Nevertheless, due to $\overline{R_{B,i}} \in [2^{\lceil f/2 \rceil}, 2^{\lceil f/2 \rceil + 1} - 1]$, there is only the upper half of d_A recovered in the lattice attack as proved in ISC'2003 [15].

4   Second Lattice-Based Fault Attack Against ECMQV

In this section, we will introduce the second lattice-based FA against ECMQV. The target of fault injection is still the parameter a and the FA scenario is same with the first attack. However, the two constructed weak curves and the model of LA have some different features.

4.1   Fault Attack Against ECMQV

Similarly, the steps of fault attack are mainly divided into two parts, online and off-line.

The online steps
    As stated above, after disturbing a into a' by fault injection repeatedly, we obtain the two weak curves $E_1(a', b)$ and $E_2(a', b')$. But unlike the first attack, it assumes that the order n_1 of $E_1(a', b)$ have a small factor d and the ECDLP on $E_2(a', b')$ is solvable, that is, the time complexity $O(d)$ and $O(\sqrt{q})$ are feasible for calculation, where q is the greatest prime factor of order n_2 of the basic point G on $E_2(a', b')$.
    Next, using the same method as the first attack, the attacker selects the low-order point R_A and P_A on $E_1(a', b)$ as its public keys and sends them to B, where the selected R_A and P_A are same as those in the first attack. Finally, the attacker receives the corresponding R_B, ID_B, and t_B(options) from B.

The off-line analysis steps
    First, the reduced information of temporary private key r_B is deduce by solving ECDLP. Given that $R_B = r_B G$ and the time complexity $O(\sqrt{q})$ is feasible, we can deduce the value $r \in [1, n_2 - 1]$ by using Pohlig-Hellman algorithm and Pollard's rho algorithm, so $r_B = r + \lambda n_2$, where $\lambda \in \mathbb{Z}$ and $\lambda < n/n_2$.
    Next, the correct value $s \in d$ is determined by using the same guess-and-determine method as the first attack, and then $s_B = s + \mu d$, where $\mu < n/d$.
    Although it is uncertainty whether there exists an available common divisor between n_2 and d, a model of lattice attack still can be built.

4.2 Lattice Attack Against ECMQV

In the same way, after the faulty ECMQV runs N times, we have the following equations for $i = 1, \ldots, N$.

$$r_{B,i} = r_i + \lambda_i n_2,$$
$$s_{B,i} = s_i + \mu_i d. \tag{17}$$

Where $\lambda_i, \mu_i \in \mathbb{Z}$, $\lambda_i < n/n_2$ and $\mu_i < n/d$.

Substitute the Eq. (17) into the equation $s_{B,i} = r_{B,i} + \overline{R_{B,i}} d_B \bmod n$, then

$$s_i + \mu_i d = r_i + \lambda_i n_2 + \overline{R_{B,i}} d_B \bmod n (i > 1)$$
$$s_1 + \mu_1 d = r_1 + \lambda_1 n_2 + \overline{R_{B,1}} d_B \bmod n (i = 1). \tag{18}$$

We have the following $N - 1$ equations by eliminating d_B.

$$\mu_i = d^{-1}(r_i - s_i) - d^{-1}\overline{R_{B,1}}^{-1}\overline{R_{B,i}}(r_1 - s_1) - d^{-1}\overline{R_{B,1}}^{-1}\overline{R_{B,i}} n_2 \lambda_1 \\ + d^{-1} n_2 \lambda_i + \overline{R_{B,1}}^{-1}\overline{R_{B,i}} \mu_1 \bmod n (1 < i \le N) \tag{19}$$

Let $A_i = d^{-1}\overline{R_{B,1}}^{-1}\overline{R_{B,i}}(r_1 - s_1) - d^{-1}(r_i - s_i) \bmod n$, $B_i = -d^{-1}\overline{R_{B,1}}^{-1}\overline{R_{B,i}} n_2 \bmod n$, $C = d^{-1} n_2 \bmod n$ and $D_i = \overline{R_{B,1}}^{-1}\overline{R_{B,i}} \bmod n$, then there exists $h_i \in \mathbb{Z}$ so that

$$\mu_i = B_i \lambda_1 + C\lambda_i + D_i \mu_1 + h_i n - A_i. \tag{20}$$

Since $\mu_i < n/d$, we have

$$|B_i \lambda_1 + C\lambda_i + D_i \mu_1 + h_i n - A_i| < n/(2d). \tag{21}$$

Similarly, for $i = 2, \ldots, N$, we can construct a lattice $\mathcal{L}$ spanned by the row vectors $\boldsymbol{b}_1, \ldots, \boldsymbol{b}_{2N}$ of matrix

$$M = \begin{pmatrix} \delta n & & \cdots & & 0 \\ 0 & \ddots & & & \\ & & \delta n & & \\ \delta D_2 \cdots \delta D_N \; \delta & & & & \vdots \\ \delta B_2 \cdots \delta B_N \; 0 \; \gamma & & & \\ \delta C & & & \ddots & \\ & \ddots & & & \gamma \\ 0 & & \delta C \; 0 & \cdots & \gamma \end{pmatrix},$$

where $\gamma, \delta \in \mathbb{R}$. Let $\boldsymbol{x} = (h_2, \ldots, h_N, \mu_1, \lambda_1, \ldots, \lambda_N) \in \mathbb{Z}^{2N}$, then $\boldsymbol{v} = \boldsymbol{x} M = (\delta(h_2 n + D_2 \mu_1 + B_2 \lambda_1 + C\lambda_2), \ldots, \delta(h_N n + D_N \mu_1 + B_N \lambda_1 + C\lambda_N), \delta \mu_1, \gamma \lambda_1, \ldots, \gamma \lambda_N)$. In addition, let non-lattice vector $\boldsymbol{u} = (\delta A_2, \ldots, \delta A_N, 0, \cdots, 0) \in \mathbb{Z}^{2N}$, then $\boldsymbol{v} - \boldsymbol{u} = (\delta \mu_2, \ldots, \delta \mu_N, \delta \mu_1, \gamma \lambda_1, \ldots, \gamma \lambda_N)$. Supposing that $\beta \in \mathbb{R}, \delta = d\beta$ and $\gamma = n_2 \beta$, we have

$$\|\boldsymbol{v} - \boldsymbol{u}\| < \sqrt{2N} n\beta \tag{22}$$

It is assumed that $l_2 = \lceil \log n_2 \rceil$ and $l_d = \lceil \log d \rceil$. If $l_2 + l_d > f + \log 2\pi e$ and $N > f/(l_2 + l_d - f - \log 2\pi e)$, then $\|\boldsymbol{v} - \boldsymbol{u}\| < \sqrt{2N}n\beta < \sqrt{\frac{2N}{2\pi e}}vol(L)^{\frac{1}{2N}}$, where $vol(L) = \det(M) = \beta^{2N}n^{N-1}d^N n_2^N$. Hence, $\boldsymbol{v}$ can be determined by solving CVP, and then $d_B = \overline{R_{B,1}}^{-1}(s_1 - r_1 + \delta\mu_1/\beta - \gamma\lambda_1/\beta) \mod n$. Similarly, since $\overline{R_{B,i}}$ belongs to $[2^{\lceil f/2 \rceil}, 2^{\lceil f/2 \rceil+1} - 1]$, only the upper half of d_A can be recovered by the LA.

5   Feasibility Analysis and Simulation of Attacks

In this section, we will verify the feasibility of our proposed attacks by software simulations. First, we carry out some simulations in two standard curves to analyze the rate of effective faulty parameter $a's$ for the attacks. Next, based on the effective faulty $a's$, we verify the two attacks by experiments.

We choose the curves in prime field with 256-bit keys recommended in FIPS 186-2 and SM2 as the FI objects, and then simulate the flipped single fault and 32-bit random fault of parameter a, respectively. For the flipped single fault, every bit of a is flipped in turn, so there are 256 kinds of different faulty $a's$. As for the random fault, a continuous 32-bit part of a is randomized, which is also simulated 256 times. After that, we compute the orders n_1, n_2 of the two constructed curves by using the MIRACL implementation of SEA algorithm [25], respectively.

As stated above in the first attack, the number N of ECMQV protocol needed for LA is greater than $\frac{f+\log 2\pi e}{l_d - \log 2\pi e}$. Hence, the case $l_d \geq 5 (i.e., \lceil \log d \rceil > \lfloor \log 2\pi e \rfloor)$ is required for the two weak curves. Moreover, the greater d, the smaller N. Figure 1 displays the cumulative outcome probability that the greatest common divisor d is bigger than a certain bit length for the two faulty types of the two standard curves. To better understand these results, we list the faulty number N_d, d_{max}(namely the biggest d) and the bit length $\lceil \log d_{max} \rceil$ of d_{max} when $l_d \geq 5$ as shown in Table 1. From the results the probability of faulty $a's$ available for the first attack exceeds 4%, and the optimal $d_{max}s$ for the four faulty types are sufficient to mount lattice attack successfully.

As for the second attack, our analysis concerns the probability that the ECDLP with time complexity $O(2^{l_q/2})$ is solved by modern computers, where $l_q = \lceil \log q \rceil$ and q is the biggest prime factor of order n_2 on $E_2(a', b')$. We assume that the computation limit for solving ECDLP is bound to 112 bits complexity [26], thus we consider the faulty $a's$ whose q is smaller than 112 bits are effective for the attack. Meanwhile, in order to ensure the success rate of LA, $l_2 + l_d > f + \log 2\pi e$ is also required under the premise of feasible computation complexity $O(2^{l_d})$. Similarly, Fig. 2 displays the cumulative outcome probability that the biggest factor q is smaller than a certain bit-length. It can be observed that the probability to obtain sufficiently small sizes of q exceeds 19%. Table 2 lists the number N_{l_q} of all the faulty $a's$ under the conditions $l_q \leq 112$, $l_d < 40$ and $l_2 + l_d > f + \log 2\pi e$, in which q_{min} is the smallest q satisfying the conditions above. L equals the biggest $l_2 + l_d - f - \lfloor \log 2\pi e \rfloor$ when $q = q_{min}$.

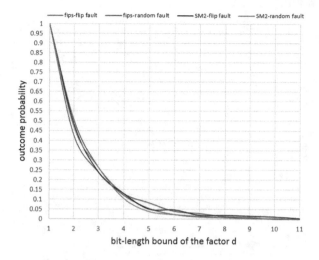

Fig. 1. Cumulative probability of the bit length of each common factor d in the first attack

Table 1. Effective faulty $a's$ for the first attack

Curve	Data			
	N_d	$N_d/256$	d_{max}	$\lceil \log d_{max} \rceil$
FIPS-flipped fault	14	5.5%	0×374	10
FIPS-random fault	21	8.2%	$0 \times 1E9$	9
SM2-flipped fault	13	5.1%	0×409	11
SM2-random fault	10	4.0%	$0 \times 2B0$	10

Compared to the first attack, the probability $N_{l_q}/256$ of effective faulty $a's$ in the second attack is greater than $N_d/256$, but at the same time the computation complexity is higher as well.

To sum up, there are at least 24% faulty $a's$ available for both of the above attacks in all. Which attack to choose depends on the case generated by the faulty a'.

Finally, we carry out the two attacks based on the flipped single fault of the FIPS 186-2 curve, in which the lattice attacks invoke the Babai algorithm based on BKZ reduced basis in NTL library [27]. In the first LA, the upper half of d_A can be recovered correctly by LA as long as $l_d \geq 5$, and at least $N = 62$ is needed when $l_d = 5(l_d - \lfloor \log 2\pi e \rfloor = 1)$. The N needed is far smaller than the theoretical one(i.e., $N > \frac{f + \lfloor \log 2\pi e \rfloor}{l_d - \lfloor \log 2\pi e \rfloor} = 260$). Meanwhile, we choose the faulty case $\lceil \log q \rceil = 58$, $l_2 = 253$, $l_d = 8$ and $L = 1$ for the second attack. The experiments show that at least $N = 90$ is needed for a successful LA when $l_d + l_2 - f - \lfloor \log 2\pi e \rfloor = 1$. This is also far smaller than $\frac{f}{l_d + l_2 - f - \lfloor \log 2\pi e \rfloor} = 256$. Thus, the results from lattice attack in practice are actually better than those in theory.

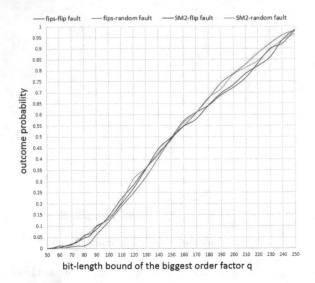

Fig. 2. Cumulative probability of the bit length of each biggest factor q in the second attack

Table 2. Effective faulty a's for the second attack

Fault type	Data					
	N_{l_q}	$N_{l_q}/256$	$q = q_{min}$			
			$\lceil \log q_{min} \rceil$	l_2	l_d	L
FIPS-flipped fault	56	21.9%	58	253	8	1
FIPS-random fault	43	16.8%	55	256	39	35
SM2-flipped fault	49	19.1%	60	255	39	26
SM2-random fault	60	23.4%	57	256	39	35

6   Conclusion

In this paper, we present two new lattice-based fault attacks on ECMQV, which are based on the possibility of storage error of parameter a. Both of the attacks construct two weak curves with the faulty parameter a'. Because of the greatest common divisor d of the two curves, the first attack reduces the temporary private key and implicit-signature result (r_B, s_B) into $(r_B \mod d, s_B \mod d)$, respectively. The second attack reduces (r_B, s_B) into $(r_B \mod n_2, s_B \mod d)$ by solving ECDLP on the second weak curve $E_2(a', b')$ and using the guess-determine method. Next, the two new lattice attacks with the reduced information of (r_B, s_B) are launched to recover half bits of the static private key d_B. Finally, the experiments confirm the feasibility of our attacks. For a 256-bit standard key length, 62 faulty agreements with a 5 bit-length common divisor d are sufficient to recover 128 bits of the private key d_B in the first attack, and 90 faulty agreements are sufficient to determine half of d_B using the second attack when the sum of the bit lengths of the small factor d and order n_2 equals 261.

The ideas of such attacks also can be applied to the other ECC algorithms, such as ECDSA and SM2 signature. Note that although the point R_A sent to victim from attacker can pass through the public key validation, the general countermeasure such as the point validation toward the points G, Q_B during the calculation of SM $Q_B = r_B G$ is effective at resisting our attacks. For this reason, our further research will focus on how to mount attacks when there are some countermeasures in SM. For example, we can consider fault attacks based on the storage error of parameter p.

Acknowledgments. We thank the anonymous reviewers for their careful reading and insightful comments. This work is supported by China's National Cryptography Development Fund (No. MMJJ20170214 and No. MMJJ20170211), National Natural Science Foundation (No. 61672509) and National Science and Technology Major Project (No. 2014ZX01032401-001).

References

1. Miller, V.S.: Use of elliptic curves in cryptography. In: Williams, H.C. (ed.) CRYPTO 1985. LNCS, vol. 218, pp. 417–426. Springer, Heidelberg (1986). https://doi.org/10.1007/3-540-39799-X_31
2. Biehl, I., Meyer, B., Müller, V.: Differential fault attacks on elliptic curve cryptosystems. In: Bellare, M. (ed.) CRYPTO 2000. LNCS, vol. 1880, pp. 131–146. Springer, Heidelberg (2000). https://doi.org/10.1007/3-540-44598-6_8
3. Ciet, M., Joye, M.: Elliptic curve cryptosystems in the presence of permanent and transient faults. Des. Codes Crypt. **36**(1), 33–43 (2005)
4. Kim, T., Tibouchi, M.: Bit-flip faults on elliptic curve base fields, revisited. In: Boureanu, I., Owesarski, P., Vaudenay, S. (eds.) ACNS 2014. LNCS, vol. 8479, pp. 163–180. Springer, Cham (2014). https://doi.org/10.1007/978-3-319-07536-5_11
5. Blömer, J., Otto, M., Seifert, J.-P.: Sign change fault attacks on elliptic curve cryptosystems. In: Breveglieri, L., Koren, I., Naccache, D., Seifert, J.-P. (eds.) FDTC 2006. LNCS, vol. 4236, pp. 36–52. Springer, Heidelberg (2006). https://doi.org/10.1007/11889700_4
6. Schmidt, J., Medwed, M.: A fault attack on ECDSA. In: 2009 Workshop on Fault Diagnosis and Tolerance in Cryptography (FDTC), pp. 93–99. IEEE (2009)
7. Fan, J., Gierlichs, B., Vercauteren, F.: To infinity and beyond: combined attack on ECC using points of low order. In: Preneel, B., Takagi, T. (eds.) CHES 2011. LNCS, vol. 6917, pp. 143–159. Springer, Heidelberg (2011). https://doi.org/10.1007/978-3-642-23951-9_10
8. Elkamchouchi, H.M., Abu Elkair, E.F.: An efficient protocol for authenticated key agreement. Des. Codes Crypt. **28**(2), 119–134 (2003)
9. IEEE Std: 1363-2000 - IEEE standard specifications for public-key cryptography, pp. 1–228. IEEE Computer Society, August 2000
10. Alberta Teachers' Association: Public key cryptography for the financial services industry, key agreement and key transport using elliptic curve cryptography. Speculum **81**(2), 566–569 (2006)

11. Office of State Commercial Cryptgraphy Administration: Public Key Cryptographic Algorithm SM2 Based on Elliptic Curves (2010, in Chinese). http://www.oscca.gov.cn/UpFile/2010122214822692.pdf
12. Yeh, H.T., Sun, H.M., Hwang, T.: Improved authenticated multiple-key agreement protocol. Comput. Math. Appl. **46**(2), 207–211 (2003)
13. Kaliski, B.S.: An unknown key-share attack on the MQV key agreement protocol. ACM Trans. Inf. Syst. Secur. **4**(3), 275–288 (2001)
14. Antipa, A., Brown, D., Menezes, A., Struik, R., Vanstone, S.: Validation of elliptic curve public keys. In: Desmedt, Y.G. (ed.) PKC 2003. LNCS, vol. 2567, pp. 211–223. Springer, Heidelberg (2003). https://doi.org/10.1007/3-540-36288-6_16
15. Leadbitter, P.J., Smart, N.P.: Analysis of the insecurity of ECMQV with partially known nonces. In: Boyd, C., Mao, W. (eds.) ISC 2003. LNCS, vol. 2851, pp. 240–251. Springer, Heidelberg (2003). https://doi.org/10.1007/10958513_19
16. Menezes, A., Ustaoglu, B.: On the importance of public-key validation in the MQV and HMQV key agreement protocols. In: Barua, R., Lange, T. (eds.) INDOCRYPT 2006. LNCS, vol. 4329, pp. 133–147. Springer, Heidelberg (2006). https://doi.org/10.1007/11941378_11
17. Menezes, A.: Another look at HMQV. JMC **1**(1), 47–64 (2007)
18. Hankerson, D., Menezes, A.J., Vanstone, S.: Guide to Elliptic Curve Cryptography. Springer, Heidelberg (2004). https://doi.org/10.1007/b97644
19. Lenstra, H.W., Lenstra, A.K., Lovfiasz, L.: Factoring polynomials with rational coefficients. Mathematische Ann. **261**, 515–534 (1982)
20. Schnorr, C.P.: A hierarchy of polynomial time lattice basis reduction algorithms. Theor. Comput. Sci. **53**(2–3), 201–224 (1987)
21. Babai, L.: On Lovász' lattice reduction and the nearest lattice point problem (shortened version). Combinatorica **6**(1), 1–13 (1986)
22. Nguyen, P.Q., Stern, J.: Lattice reduction in cryptology: an update. In: Bosma, W. (ed.) ANTS 2000. LNCS, vol. 1838, pp. 85–112. Springer, Heidelberg (2000). https://doi.org/10.1007/10722028_4
23. Ajtai, M.: Generating random lattices according to the invariant distribution. Draft of March (2006)
24. Battistello, A.: Common points on elliptic curves: the Achilles' heel of fault attack countermeasures. In: Prouff, E. (ed.) COSADE 2014. LNCS, vol. 8622, pp. 69–81. Springer, Cham (2014). https://doi.org/10.1007/978-3-319-10175-0_6
25. Schoof, R.: Counting points on elliptic curves over finite fields. J. de Theorie des Nombres de Bordeaux **7**(1), 219–254 (1995)
26. Bos, J.W., Kaihara, M.E., Kleinjung, T., Lenstra, A.K., Montgomery, P.L.: Solving a 112-bit prime elliptic curve discrete logarithm problem on game consoles using sloppy reduction. Int. J. Appl. Crypt. **2**(3), 212–228 (2012)
27. Shoup, V.: Number Theory C++ Library (NTL) version 9.6.4. (2016). http://www.shoup.net/ntl/

Thermal Scans for Detecting Hardware Trojans

Maxime Cozzi$^{(\boxtimes)}$, Jean-Marc Galliere, and Philippe Maurine

LIRMM, 161 Rue Ada, Montpellier, France
`maxime.cozzi@lirmm.fr`

Abstract. It is well known that companies have been outsourcing their IC production to countries where it is simply not possible to guarantee the integrity of final products. This relocation trend creates a need for methodologies and embedded design solutions to identify counterfeits but also to detect potential Hardware Trojans (HT). Hardware Trojans are tiny pieces of hardware that can be maliciously inserted in designs for several purposes ranging from denial of service, programmed obsolescence etc. They are usually stealthy and characterized by small area and power overheads. Their detection is thus a challenging task.

Various solutions have been investigated to detect Hardware Trojans. We focus in this paper on the use of thermal near field scans to that aim. Therefore we first introduce and characterize a low cost, large bandwidth (20 kHz) thermal scanning system with the high detectivity required to detect small Hardware Trojans. Then, we experimentally demonstrate its efficiency on different test cases.

Keywords: Trojan detection · Lock-in thermography
Thermal mapping · Thermal modeling

1 Introduction

Hardware security recently emerged as an important research problem. Attacks such as Side Channel proved that it was possible to break trusted ciphering algorithms such as Rijndael and therefore raised the problem of securing electronic devices [1]. This concern is even greater in the economic context where the quest for better performances pushes CMOS technology close to its limits and to an exponential growth of Integrated Circuits (IC) complexity and cost. Consequently, more and more companies are fabless and are outsourcing their production to foreign countries. As a result, ensuring the integrity of integrated products has become a critical issue because most of electronic systems, even critical ones, rely on ICs. We obtained these last years more and more evidence that counterfeits, cloning and Trojan insertion have become a credible vector of attack against electronic systems [2–4].

The increasing complexity of ICs and the scaling of technology have made Trojan detection a particularly challenging task as both their size and power

© Springer International Publishing AG, part of Springer Nature 2018
J. Fan and B. Gierlichs (Eds.): COSADE 2018, LNCS 10815, pp. 117–132, 2018.
https://doi.org/10.1007/978-3-319-89641-0_7

overhead have become infinitesimal in their respective applicative context, thus creating the need for high performance methodologies (inspired from Side Channel Attacks for most of them) [2–4] and embedded design solutions [5,6].

Infra-Red (IR) thermography has proven to be efficient in detecting small defects in ICs [7]. It has also demonstrated to be efficient, *by simulation only,* for Trojan identification in [8]. One drawback is their reliance on IR camera set-ups which have a very limited frame rate, a limited number of pixels and are costly. Within this context we propose in this paper a low cost and high detectivity thermal platform characterized by a bandwidth of 20 kHz as well as Side Channel Attacks (SCA) inspired techniques to exploit IR data collected.

The organization of this paper is as follows. Section 2 provides a theoretical background on thermal emissions. It also gives a state of the Art relative to our application domain and illustrates that DC silicon thermal response can be modeled by a first order system to deduce a usage policy of tunable IR platforms to manage their spatial resolution and detectivity. Section 3 details the proposed low cost and high detectivity experimental IR set-up. Then, Sect. 4 gives experimental results demonstrating the efficiency of the proposed IR set-up. Finally, in Sect. 5, performance of the proposed platform regarding Trojan detection is given, as well as the SCA inspired techniques defined for this purpose.

2   State of the Art

This section aims at introducing ICs thermal mapping. Many other thermal investigation methods have been proposed, such as thermoreflectance presented in [9]. Here, we only present techniques that are relevant to our measurement system.

2.1   Light Emission from Above 0 °K Bodies

It is well known that every body above absolute 0 °K emits light [10]. This principle is described by Planck's law which shows that the wavelength of the light emitted by a black body is linked to its temperature by the following formula:

$$I_{\lambda,b} = 2.h.c_0^2.\lambda^{-5}.e^{\frac{-h.c_0}{k.\lambda.T}} \tag{1}$$

where c_0 is the electromagnetic radiation propagation speed in a vacuum, h and k respectively are the Plank and Boltzmann constants, and λ is the wavelength of the emitted light. Considering a classical environment for the Device Under Test (DUT), e.g. a room temperature of 25 °C, we get from (1) that light emission should be observed in the (IR) spectrum. Silicon is transparent to wavelengths above 1100 nm. It is therefore possible to detect hot spots using IR sensors, through the backside of DUTs [7].

One of the challenges in IR thermography is compensating for natural emissivity of materials. Indeed, if every body does emit light depending on its temperature, it does not radiate the same intensity depending on its constitution. For that matter, we define emissivity as the ratio between the intensity of the radiation emitted by the studied material and the intensity of the radiation emitted by a black body at the same temperature. A precise thermal map of a DUT composed of different materials with high contrast in emissivity can be difficult to obtain as weak thermal sources can be concealed by surrounding hot spots emissions. This is particularly true for modern ICs because of the high emissivity contrast between metals and silicon. To overcome this phenomenon, we use lock-in thermography techniques as proposed in [11] and detailed in Sect. 2.3.

2.2   DC Measurements

The simplest method in order to detect circuit activity is to directly acquire all thermal emissions from the chip using an IR camera. Work in [12] presents a methodology for post silicon power characterization. Based on temperature measurements obtained using a $-196\,°C$ cooled SC5600 FLIR IR camera with a resolution of 640×512 pixels, the authors managed to retrieve a power density cartography of a die for different workloads. For that, they show that the heat diffusion equation can be approximated by the following linear matrix formulation

$$Rp + e = t \tag{2}$$

where R is the matrix of the thermal resistivities between different locations, p is the desired power map, e is the error in temperature measurement and t is the temperature matrix. Previous methodology used least squares estimation to find the p value that gives temperatures as close as possible to measured temperatures t. According to the authors, this technique poses several problems because of the inherent thermal spatial low-pass filter effect of silicon dies that leads to critical loss of information, especially in high frequencies. Hence, many power patterns can lead to the same thermal image, thus rendering the problem of temperature to power conversion ill-posed. To replace this method Reda et al. proposed instead minimizing the total squared error between temperature computed using (2) and measured ones combined with techniques from regularization theory [14].

In [13,15] authors managed to obtain a high resolution thermal map of a dual-core AMD Athlon II 240 running at 2.1 GHz, using the same IR acquisition platform. The circuit has a power consumption of 65 W and measured temperature gradients were up to $16\,°C$. In these papers, the authors demonstrated how different workloads can lead to variations in hot spot location. Several configurations, assigning the workload only to one core or both of them, were used by Reda et al., highlighting the possibility of active area tracking by IR thermography because hot spots were found on top of active areas while sectors of lower activity such as memory remained cooler. They then applied their method of temperature to power inversion in order to recover the power density map of the chip.

We find that this method of IR image acquisition is flawed, as a DC offset is generated by the static power consumption of the chip (including constant power consumption of the IC such as the clock tree), and the diffusion of the heat generated by this phenomenon can lead to weak spot concealing. Moreover, this method requires steady environmental conditions as both the detector and the thermal emissions are sensible to room temperature variations. This is especially true because our area of investigation mainly includes ICs such as FPGAs or microcontrollers which have a significantly lower power consumption than ICs considered in [13,15]. These devices consume few hundreds of milliampere, whereas microprocessor can draw up to several dozens of ampere. So it is obvious that this methodology (DC measurements) is highly unsuitable for weak thermal spot detection because of the high contrast of material emissivity, static thermal emissions, and heat diffusion.

However, if DC measurements are not suitable for hot spot mapping, they are of a great utility to learn about the thermal behavior of the DUT and thus for guiding dynamic measurements, i.e. to apply the lock-in thermography approach described in the next section. Indeed, a few DC measurements of the DUT step response enables us to quickly set up a first order model of its thermal behavior; such a model is of great help in deciding which (f_{lockin}, gain) couple should be used to obtain lock-in maps of high quality.

By way of illustration Fig. 1 gives, for several current steps, the responses of the DUT considered in the rest of the paper as well as the responses deduced from the identified first order model. In the present case, the IC thermal behavior of the DUT is characterized by a cutting frequency of 5 mHz. This is extremely low and implies the use of an amplification chain of at least 60 dB to obtain lock in thermography maps at 10 Hz. Implementation and protocol used to produce Fig. 1 is described in Sect. 4.

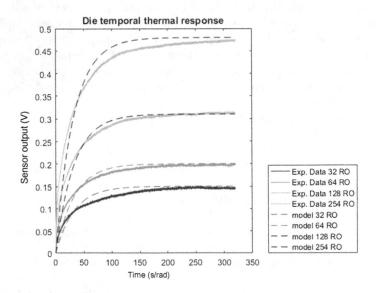

Fig. 1. Experimental and calculated thermal responses of the DUT to several step inputs.

2.3   Lock-in Thermography

Lock-in thermography is a correlation technique that allows retrieving periodic signals deeply drowned in noise. The principle, which is illustrated in Fig. 2, is very close to lock-in detection. It mainly consists of imposing a periodic thermal modulation to the DUT. With only the knowledge of the modulation frequency, it is then possible to retrieve the amplitude A and phase ϕ of the thermal signal and thus to fully rebuild the thermal behavior of the DUT [11].

Considering two processing channels, lock-in correlation consists of integrating the multiplication of sensor output by the correlation signal on the first channel and by the 90° phase shifted correlation signal on the second channel. Results are respectively named S_0 and S_{90} and are given by Eqs. (3)–(5) where K_j is the correlation signal, $F_{i,j}$ is the incoming signal, n is the number of samples and N is the number of lock-in periods the measurement is averaged over.

$$S = \frac{1}{n \cdot N} \sum_{i=1}^{n} \sum_{j=1}^{N} K_j F_{i,j} \tag{3}$$

$$S_0 = A \cdot cos(\phi) \tag{4}$$

$$S_{90} = A \cdot sin(\phi) \tag{5}$$

From (4) and (5) we easily infer Eqs. (6) and (7) that provide amplitude and phase of the thermal wave.

$$A = \sqrt{S_0^2 + S_{90}^2} \tag{6}$$

$$\phi = Arctan(\frac{S_0}{S_{90}}) \tag{7}$$

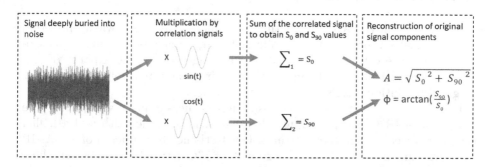

Fig. 2. Discrete lock-in process

This methodology was first implemented by Busse et al. in [16] and used to implement the first lock-in camera system in 1992. This was then deepened by

Breintenstein et al. in [11, 17] to investigate small resistive defects in solar panels. In this work, authors show that lock-in thermography can be used to highlight small hot spots created by resistive paths in silicon dies, dynamic operations of a particular circuit element turned on and off at 54 Hz, and gate oxide integrity defects in Cu-grown silicon MOS structures.

Following on [12, 13, 15], the authors demonstrated in [18] that increasing the lock-in frequency reduces considerably the heat diffusion distance comparing results from DC to 8 Hz. According to Breitenstein in [11] the lock-in frequency must be chosen respectively to a trade off between the Signal to Noise Ratio (SNR) and the spatial resolution. Indeed, if raising the lock-in frequency certainly reduces the heat diffusion distance, it also impacts the thermal load's duration on the die, thus the amount of signal that can be measured. In [19], it was demonstrated both theoretically and experimentally, that for their specific IR acquisition platform, SNR rises at first with the lock-in frequency but starts decreasing after a corner frequency around 3 Hz. The corner frequency obviously relies on detectivity, bandwidth and the amplifiers of the measurement chain.

So, using lock-in correlation to create a thermal map of the DUT brings forward several advantages. First, as mentioned earlier, it allows detection of signals deeply buried in noise which is critical in low power IC characterization. Secondly, the use of lock-in thermography discards any thermal emission that is not modulated at f_{lockin}. This means that, not only the final thermal map is free from any DC offset, but the user is able to target a specific area of the chip by adapting the modulation (induced through power supply modulation, software modulation, data or address modulation, etc.) used to create the thermal wave. In addition, heat diffusion is controllable by modifying the lock-in frequency. Finally, retrieving the signal phase is a tremendous advantage that allows us to completely discard the emissivity contrast, which is a critical problem while facing complex ICs as aforementioned in Sect. 2.1.

3   Experimental Set-Up

From the state of the Art, we get that IR cameras have been widely preferred to single pixel sensors as they provide faster image acquisition and easier calibration. On the other hand, the latter advantages are at the expanse of cost (around 70k USD), bulk and bandwidth as their frame-rate rarely exceed 100 Hz using full resolution [11, 18].

In this paper, we propose a low cost compact measurement set-up, based on a mono pixel IR sensor providing a large acquisition bandwidth and a higher detectivity at equivalent temperatures. Our testbench is composed of a InAs IR sensor working in the 1–3.8 µm spectrum at −60 °C, a trans-impedance amplifier providing a 2.10^8 V. A gain and a remote controlled oscilloscope, for a total cost of 3.5k USD, not counting the oscilloscope which is basic measurement equipment. This set-up is able to detect signals from DC up to 20 kHz.

In order to draw a thermal map, we use the lock-in correlation algorithm to compute amplitude and phase values at every position on the die. One drawback of our system is the acquisition time of a full map, which is around 12 h for a 160×160 pixels thermal map (acquiring 10 measurements at $f_{lockin} = 10\,\text{Hz}$ at each position). However, the mapping time is customizable by modifying the number of acquired traces, the cartography spatial step, the trace length, and f_{lockin}.

4 IC Thermal Characterization

As explained in Sect. 2.3, the f_{lockin} value has an influence on several parameters. The higher the frequency the shorter is the heat diffusion distance [18]. Therefore, to increase the spatial resolution of thermal maps, it is necessary to increase f_{lockin}. On the other hand, increasing the heat modulation frequency leads to shorter periods of heating and thus to weaker IR amplitude and SNR. In this section we demonstrate that this trade off can be managed rationally through a first order modeling of the thermal behavior of ICs.

4.1 Experimental Protocol

For many designs or research objectives, FPGAs are suitable integration targets as they are nearly 100% customizable. This is the case for our work. We have thus implemented our several designs on a Xilinx Virtex 5 FPGA after having removed the metallic package to get a direct access to the backside. This FPGA has a die area equal to $16 \times 16\,\text{mm}^2$ and is designed with a 65 nm CMOS technology.

The aim of our first experiment was to estimate the detectivity of our platform and to observe the thermal behavior of the FPGA. We integrated 255 Ring Oscillators (RO) to use them as micro-heaters [18]. Each RO was composed of two inverters and one Nand2 gate allowing us to enable/disable it. All ROs were placed as homogeneously as possible in a constrained area. The main idea was to integrate a local and controllable source of heat by driving the number of active ROs. Indeed, ROs are constant micro-heater thanks to their constant power consumption. By modifying the number of active ROs we were able to linearly control the local power density.

The lock-in toggling frequency of ROs was fixed at 10 Hz. This toggling imposed with an external signal generator creates a current variation and thus a heat wave. The amplitude of this current variation was measured after removal of the on-board voltage regulator. The toggling of a single RO generated a current variation equal to approximately 3.23 mA, while the core was biased by a 316 mA current under a voltage of 1 V.

4.2 Electrical Activity Detection by Heat Detection

Thermal maps with $n = 1, 8, 16, 32$ and 255 active ROs were collected and drawn. In order to diminish experimental measurement time, only the top right quarter of the die was mapped. The results for $n = 1, 8, 16$ and 32 ROs are presented Fig. 3.

On the amplitude map, heat generation is clearly and visually distinguishable when at least 16 ROs are activated. Even if a few heat sources can be spotted on the 8 ROs map, they can not be directly separated from heat diffusion of the surrounding hot spots or measurement noise without application of statistical or signal processing techniques.

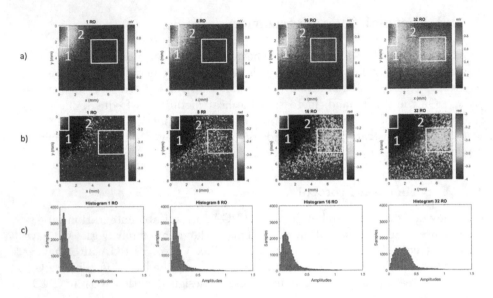

Fig. 3. (a) Amplitude map, (b) Phase map, (c) Amplitude histograms; 1: Heat source generated by the control logic. 2: Localization of implemented ROs used as thermal heaters. (Color figure online)

On the other hand, looking at phase maps in Fig. 3(b), one can observe that the presence of the 8 ROs is more visible than on the amplitude maps reported in (a). In (b), dark blue areas correspond to heat diffusion zones whereas dark red zones represent areas free of heat diffusion and hot spots. This confirms that the study of phase signal is a key element in separating diffusion heat from heat sources. The higher information of the reported phase maps is a direct illustration of former comments related to emission contrast. It proves that the phase image can provide much more accurate information in several situations.

However, the main point here is that the distributions in Fig. 3(c) of the lock-in amplitudes over the IC surface are also highly interpretable. Indeed, the effect of 8, 16 and 32 ROs on the distribution shapes is clearly visible. From these observations, we believe it is possible to extrapolate whether a circuit is infected or not by a stealthy hardware Trojans (HT) using statistical means. This point will be further discussed in Sect. 5.

Using the same IR measurement platform, we were able to acquire thermal maps for $n = 255$ ROs with a f_{lockin} up to 210 Hz. In comparison, works reported in [18,19] used a maximal f_{lockin} of 8 Hz. This considerably increases our detection capability (as shown Fig. 4) as we are able to detect weaker hot spots diffusing on a very limited area at higher f_{lockin} frequencies. This is presented in the top left map of Fig. 4 that shows a regular pattern in the target FPGA heat diffusion, which is less visible in the 10 Hz bottom left thermal map. Without any access to the layout of this FPGA we are not able to explain the origin of this pattern at this time.

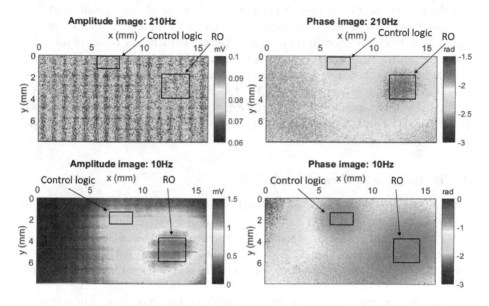

Fig. 4. Thermal maps at 10 Hz and 210 Hz

5 Trojan Detection

This section describes the methodology we proposed to detect rough and stealthy hardware Trojans. It also gives and discusses experimental results obtained on the considered DUT.

5.1 Hardware Trojan Characteristics

A Trojan is a tiny integrated circuit maliciously added to an existing design without knowledge of the company owing its intellectual propriety. This circuit's purpose can be variable, including denial of service, programmed obsolescence etc. They usually aim to avoid being detected, both from a power overhead and surface point of view. As a consequence, detecting them is a challenging task and requires a comprehensive knowledge on the subject.

A Trojan is made up of two components: the trigger and the payload [20]. The trigger is the part of the circuit waiting for the occurrence of an event to activate the malicious function of the Trojan, i.e. its payload. This trigger could be 'always-on' or active when a part or a functional block of the IC is under use. This is, a priori, the only part of the HT we can detect since the payload remains quiet before its triggering. The trigger could be sequential or combinatorial. In the rest of the paper we consider a sequential trigger, i.e. a trigger waiting for a sequence of states.

The payload is the hostile part of the HT which is activated by the trigger when the firing condition is met. A HT can be spread inside the circuit as well as restrained to a particular area. It could be hidden in the functional block where it is waiting the triggering condition (e.g. a particular sequence of values of different registers in the block). In that case we say it is 'stealthy'. It can also be placed far from the functional block(s) from which it is waiting for the triggering condition. In that case we say it is 'externalized'. Most former papers on HT detection using SCA focused on externalized HTs. In the following paragraphs, we consider both externalized HTs and stealthy HTs, placed in a restraint area of the device, and with a sequential trigger.

5.2   Testchips and Emulation of HTs

To demonstrate the efficiency of thermal maps in detecting HTs we chose to emulate the infection by an HT of a simple design mapped into a Xilinx virtex 5 FPGA. This simple design is made of a hardware 128-bit AES block and its associated control logic. This AES is clock gated. This means that its electrical activity, and thus its heating effect, can be fully stopped by disabling its clock signal.

Two different implementations of this simple design were done. The resulting floorplans are shown in Fig. 5. For both implementations, the HT is a 16-bit Linear Feedback Serial Register (LFSR) clocked with the same clock signal as the AES as explained in [6]. It is therefore only active when the AES is operating. It occupies 4 slices of the FPGA among the 17280 available slices. This represents less than 0.023% of the total resources (surface). For a convincing demonstration that the proposed lock-in thermography platform is able to detect stealthy HTs, we implemented the HT with an enable signal to be sure that the golden design and the infected designs are exactly the same from a hardware routing point of view and thermally differs only when the HT is enabled.

The two implementations of the design differ by the placement of the HT with respect to the AES block. In the first implementation, the HT is placed far from the AES block (Fig. 5 left). This case corresponds to an HT externalized in a block which is inactive when the AES is operating (or externalized in an empty place of the circuit, an improbable situation in real ICs). In the second implementation (Fig. 5 right), the place and route constraints were set so that the HT is merged in the middle of the AES. This situation corresponds to an adversary trying to hide the HT activity within the activity of another functional block, i.e. trying to render its HT to be as stealthy as possible. This case corresponds to a more challenging situation regarding HT detection.

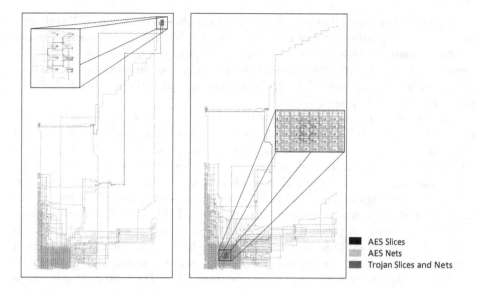

Fig. 5. Left: testchip with a externalized HT. Right: testchip with a stealthy HT.

5.3 Detection Methodology

The principle of the detection methodology consists of comparing golden thermal maps drawn from measurements done on a IC from a trusted production lot (i.e. a golden chip) with the corresponding thermal maps obtained above the DUT, i.e. above an IC coming from a potentially infected lot.

These thermal maps correspond to several computational activities of the design. The latter should be chosen so that it activates all the functional blocks of the design or has high coverage of its surface.

According to the size of the infection which is expected or researched, i.e. according the stealthiness of the HT, the comparison between the golden IC and the DUT can be done with different levels of accuracy. It can be done visually to detect externalized un-stealthy HTs or by simple difference of means between corresponding positions of the maps for quite stealthy HTs. Alternatively, it can be done using statistical tests such as the Welch's t-test for stealthy HTs. The next sections detail the application of this methodology to our two testcases and give the obtained experimental results.

5.4 Experimental Results

Case 1: Externalized HT. This first case considers a HT externalized in an inactive area when the HT is active. This is thus the case of a rough HT. To detect it, a basic use of our IR measurement platform could be sufficient. Such a use, which can also be applied to detect rough counterfeit products (but not clones), consists of (a) visually comparing a golden thermal map with the ones obtained for a potentially infected IC or (b) computing a basic difference of means between the two thermal maps.

Thermal maps were therefore acquired on the same FPGA with HT activated or not. The acquisition of one map consists of collecting $n = 10$ lock-in traces (vectors length of $N = 1000$). The lock-in frequency was fixed at $10\,Hz$. This means that the AES (or the AES and the HT in case of an infection) is disabled during $0.05\,s$ (cold phase of the lock-in process) and active during $0.05\,s$ (hot phase of the lock-in process).

Figure 6 gives the thermal maps of the whole die. They are made of 160×160 pixels. The first left column of this figure gives the amplitude of the thermal wave at each coordinate with a color scale corresponding to the dynamic of all measurements. The second column gives the same results but with a color scale allowing us to detect the HT which is in the rectangle labeled (3) in the maps. The rectangles labeled (2) point out areas where large buffers are used to drive IO pads allowing to get out output values of the AES. The third column gives the phase of the thermal wave with respect to the lock-in signal. One can observe the significant impact of the HT on the phase map, impact which is much more visible than on the amplitude map. These results demonstrate that our IR platform is efficient in detecting rough or externalized HTs (and probably rough counterfeits) by simple visual inspection of thermal maps and this especially by considering the phase map.

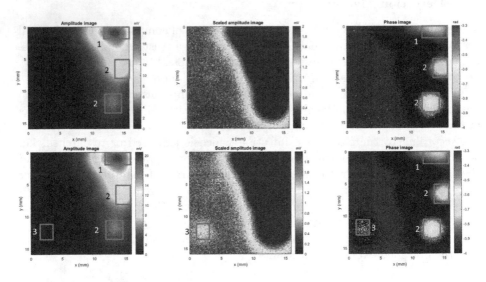

Fig. 6. First row: thermal maps (amplitude and phase) obtained with the golden circuit. Second row: thermal maps obtained with the infected circuit. Label (1) shows the position of the AES, label (2) shows the position of large output buffers and label (3) shows the position of the externalized HT. (Color figure online)

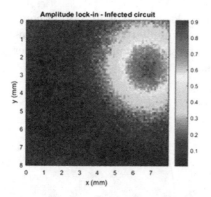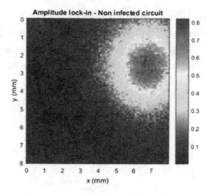

Fig. 7. Left: amplitudes of the thermal waves collected above the golden IC. Right: amplitudes of the thermal waves collected above the infected IC.

Case 2: Stealthy HT. Figure 7 gives the thermal maps (amplitude only) of the quarter of the IC surface containing the AES and the stealthy HT which is hidden in the AES. For this experiment, the output signals of the AES were gated using a Nand gate to suppress the electrical activity of the IO pad's buffers. As shown, there are no visual difference between these two maps. The heat generated by the HT is masked within the AES's heat. Thus an enhanced comparison technique must be used to detect the thermal impact of the HT.

The main idea to compare these thermal maps is to apply a Welch's t-test between corresponding positions of the maps in order to detect small heat differences due to the HT. However this cannot be done in a straight forward manner. Indeed, thermal maps were not done the same day and in a controlled environment. Thus temperature changes significantly during their acquisitions and one must take these changes into account prior to applying the Welch's t-test application.

Because we observed that this global shift of the room temperature during the cartography process acts as a multiplicative coefficient on the lock-in amplitudes, the applied procedure to conceal the effects of temperature changes is quite simple. It consists of considering the amplitudes of thermal maps as statistical distributions and standardizing them in order to get the best match between the two distributions; one distribution being associated with the golden IC and the other with the DUT. Concealing the room's temperature shift allows us to minimize, as best as possible, the differences between the thermal maps (distributions) prior to applying the Welch's t-test.

The standardization of all the lock-in values, $A_l(x,y)$, obtained at coordinate (x,y) is done using the following formula:

$$A_l^S(x,y) = \frac{A_l(x,y) - <\bar{A}_l>}{\sigma(<\bar{A}_l>)} \qquad (8)$$

where $<\bar{A}_l>$ is the empirical mean of mean amplitudes obtained over the whole map; $\sigma(<\bar{A}_l>)$ is the standard deviation of the mean amplitudes obtained over the whole map and $A_l^S(x, y)$ is the standardized lock-in value of $A_l(x, y)$ at coordinate (x, y). By way of illustration Fig. 8 gives the cumulative density functions (cdf) associated with two set of measures above the same circuit before and after concealing effects of the temperature variation.

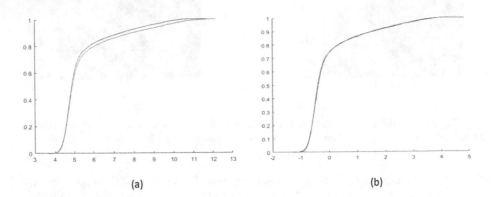

(a)   (b)

Fig. 8. (a) cdfs of two thermal maps of the same IC before temperature effect concealing (b) after concealing of temperature effect

After correction, by standardization of the effect of room temperature change, the Welch's t-test can be applied to detect the remaining changes due to the presence of an HT. Applying this test means herein computing, for each (x, y) coordinate of the maps, the statistic of the the Welch's t-test, $T_{(x,y)}$ between two samples of A_l^G and A_l^P.

Then the obtained $T_{(x,y)}$ value is compared to a critical value T_{crit} defined according to the chosen confidence level fixed by α that sets the critical p-value for the test. Typically, α is set to 0.05 or 0.01. This means that we accept 5% (or 1%) of chance that the detected difference is a false positive. If $|T_{(x,y)}| > |T_{crit}|$, the samples do not have the same mean and one can conclude that at this coordinate there is an extra source of heat, i.e. in our application case an HT.

Figure 9(a) gives the $T_{(x,y)}$ map obtained by comparing two thermal maps performed with the same golden IC. From this map, it clearly appears that the means of all corresponding samples of the two maps are the same. This result indicates that the IC are the same.

Figure 9(b) gives the $T_{(x,y)}$ map obtained by comparing with the Welch's t-test the thermal maps associated to the stealthy HT of Fig. 5 with the one associated to the golden IC. From this map it is clear that there is an HT close to $(x, y) = (70, 30)$ which is close to the effective HT position. This demonstrates the correctness of the proposed HT detection technique and the interest of lock-in thermography for detecting HT and for locating small electrical activities in IC in general.

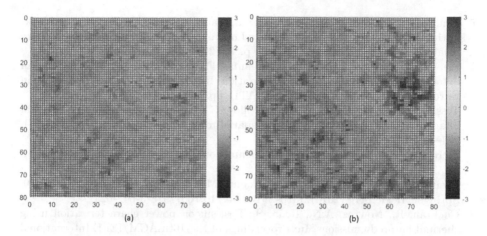

Fig. 9. (a) Welch t-test between two golden chips, (b) Welch t-test between a golden IC and a IC infected by a stealthy HT.

6   Conclusion

In this paper we have introduced a cost effective IR measurement platform characterized by a large bandwidth and a high detectivity. It has been designed to be able to locate small electrical activities within ICs using lock-in correlation. An application has been shown to the detect a stealthy hardware Trojan hidden in a functional block. Results obtained are very encouraging and demonstrate the usefulness of lock-in thermography in the field of secure device characterization.

References

1. Loai, A., Houssain, H., Al-Somani, T.F.: Review of Side Channel Attacks and Countermeasures on ECC, RSA, and AES Cryptosystems
2. Nowroz, A.N., Hu, K., Koushanfar, F., Reda, S.: Novel techniques for high-sensitivity hardware Trojan detection using thermal and power maps. IEEE Trans. Comput.-Aided Des. Integr. Circuits Syst. **33**(12), 1792–1805 (2014)
3. Ngo, X.T., Najm, Z., Bhasin, S., Guilley, S., Danger, J.L.: Method taking into account process dispersion to detect hardware Trojan Horse by side-channel analysis. J. Cryptogr. Eng. **6**, 239–247 (2016)
4. Balasch, J., Gierlichs, B., Verbauwhede, I.: Electromagnetic circuit fingerprints for hardware Trojan detection. In: IEEE International Symposium on Electromagnetic Compatibility (EMC), Dresden, pp. 246–251 (2015)
5. Zhang, X., Tehranipoor, M.: RON: an on-chip ring oscillator network for hardware Trojan detection. In: Design, Automation and Test in Europe, Grenoble, pp. 1–6 (2011)
6. Lecomte, M., Fournier, J., Maurine, P.: An on-chip technique to detect hardware Trojans and assist counterfeit identification. IEEE Trans. Very Large Scale Integr. VLSI Syst. **25**(12), 3317–3330 (2017)

7. Tan, M.C., Tay, M.Y., Qiu, W., Phoa, S.L.: Fault localization using infra-red lock-in thermography for SOI-based advanced microprocessors. In: Physical and Failure Analysis of Integrated Circuits, IPFA, p. 15 (2011)
8. Hu, K., Nowroz, A.N., Reda, S., Koushanfar, F.: High-sensitivity hardware Trojan detection using multimodal characterization. In: Design, Automation and Test in Europe Conference and Exhibition, DATE, pp. 1271–1276 (2013)
9. Tessier, G., Bardoux, M., Bou, C., Filloy, C., Fournier, D.: Back side thermal imaging of integrated circuits at high spatial resolution. Appl. Phys. Lett. **90**(17), 171–172 (2007)
10. Incropera, F.P., Dewitt, D.P.: Fundamentals of Heat and Mass Transfer, 5th edn, pp. 700–746. Wiley, Hoboken (2001)
11. Breitenstein, O., Warta, W., Langenkamp, M.: Lock-in Thermography, vol. 10. Springer, Heidelberg (2010). https://doi.org/10.1007/978-3-642-02417-7
12. Cochran, R., Nowroz, A.N., Reda, S.: Post-silicon power characterization using thermal infrared emissions. In: Proceedings of the 16th ACM/IEEE International Symposium on Low Power Electronics and Design, pp. 331–336 (2010)
13. Reda, S., Cochran, R., Nowroz, A.N.: Improved thermal tracking for processors using hard and soft sensor allocation techniques. IEEE Trans. Comput. **60**(6), 841–851 (2011)
14. Bertero, M., Boccacci, P.: Introduction to Inverse Problems in Imaging. Institute of Physics Publishing, Bristol (1998)
15. Reda, S.: Thermal and power characterization of real computing devices. IEEE J. Emerg. Sel. Top. Circuits Syst. **1**(2), 76–87 (2011)
16. Busse, G., Wu, D., Karpen, W.: J. Appl. Phys. **71**, 3962 (1992)
17. Huth, S., Breitenstein, O., Huber, A., Dantz, D., Lambert, U., Altmann, F.: Lock-in IR-thermography-a novel tool for material and device characterization. In: Diffusion and Defect Data Part B Solid State Phenomena, pp. 741–746 (2002)
18. Nowroz, A., Woods, G., Reda, S.: Improved post-silicon power modeling using AC lock-in techniques. In: 48th ACM/EDAC/IEEE Design Automation Conference, DAC, pp. 101–107 (2011)
19. Nowroz, A.N., Woods, G., Reda, S.: Power mapping of integrated circuits using AC-based thermography. IEEE Trans. Very Large Scale Integr. (VLSI) Syst. **21**(8), 1398–1409 (2013)
20. Chakraborty, R.S., Narasimhan, S., Bhunia, S.: Hardware Trojan: threats and emerging solutions. In: IEEE International High Level Design Validation and Test Workshop, HLDVT 2009, pp. 166–171 (2009)

Side-Channel Analysis Attacks

SCATTER: A New Dimension in Side-Channel

Hugues Thiebeauld[1], Georges Gagnerot[1], Antoine Wurcker[1]([✉]),
and Christophe Clavier[2]

[1] eshard, Martillac, France
{hugues.thiebeauld,georges.gagnerot,antoine.wurcker}@eshard.com
[2] Université de Limoges, XLIM-CNRS, Limoges, France
christophe.clavier@unilim.fr

Abstract. Side-channel techniques have been progressing over the last
few years, leading to the creation of a variety of statistical tools, aiming
at extracting secrets handled in cryptographic algorithms. Noticeably,
the vast majority of side-channel techniques requires to get the traces
aligned together prior to applying statistics. This prerequisite turns out
to be challenging in the practical realization of attacks as implementations tend to include hardware or software countermeasures to increase
this difficulty. This is typically achieved by adding random jitters or random executions with fake operations. In this paper, we introduce the
new side-channel technique *scatter*, whose potential is to tackle alignment issues. By construction, *scatter* brings an additional dimension
and opens the door to a large set of potential new attack techniques. The
effectiveness of *scatter* has been proven on both simulated traces and real
world secure products. In summary *scatter* is a new side-channel technique offering a valuable alternative when the trace alignment represents
an issue. Furthermore, *scatter* represents a suitable option for low-cost
attacks, as the requirements in terms of equipment and expertise are
significantly reduced.

Keywords: Side-channel · *Scatter* · Mutual information
Pearson chi-squared

1 Introduction

Over the past few years, *Side-Channel Attacks* have been proven effective on
a wide range of hardware devices [17–19]. Recent works have highlighted that
software based products can also be subject to these attacks [5]. When successful,
the impact of side-channel attacks is severe as it leads to the disclosure of the
secret cryptographic key. In case of partial recovery, several techniques [33] can
be used to achieve the whole key recovery. As a result, a flaw can be exploited
and leads to losses. In order to avoid any exposure on the field, it is recommended
to implement the right protections and validate them by practical testing.

© Springer International Publishing AG, part of Springer Nature 2018
J. Fan and B. Gierlichs (Eds.): COSADE 2018, LNCS 10815, pp. 135–152, 2018.
https://doi.org/10.1007/978-3-319-89641-0_8

The number of side-channel attack techniques to take into consideration reaches a significant number. Beginning with the original *Simple Power Analysis* (SPA) [23] and *Differential Power Analysis* (DPA) [24], several other techniques have been developed over the past few years. The most famous distinguishers are CPA [6], standing for *Correlation Power Analysis* and exploiting Pearson coefficient, the MIA [20], standing for *Mutual Information Analysis* and taking benefit of the Shannon entropy and the LRA for *Linear Regression Analysis* [14,36]. These attacks can be run on devices without any prerequisite knowledge about their implementation. Some other attacks (such as the *Templates Attacks* and more generally *Profiled Attacks*) [7] make use of a profiling stage used to learn about the target and exploit this knowledge on a secret during a matching or exploitation phase. Finally, another testing methodology with the *T-Tests* has been introduced [4,15,21,22] to provide an efficient way to characterize potential leakages.

In parallel, research works have been run to design countermeasures defeating these attack techniques. Most common ones consist of adding misalignment using hardware and software techniques [10,12,37] and/or to de-correlate the information from the traces using random values by masking the data manipulated [1,9,11,16,23,35]. In the masking case, more complex but realistic, attacks named *Higher-Order Side-Channel Analysis* introduced by Messerges [29], studied [34] and later improved [3,27,30,32,38] are still applicable. Generally speaking, traces alignment remains a critical phase when conducting first or higher order practical side-channel attacks.

We present in this paper a new side-channel analysis technique named *scatter* which has the potential to tackle most of the alignment issues, such as random jitters or random order execution. We believe that *scatter* opens doors to improvements of side-channel analyses as they are implemented including for higher order side-channel attacks. It could lead developers to revisit the way they implement countermeasures. This article shows the new technique efficiency on simulated traces, and some practical testing as well.

This paper is organized as follows. Section 2 gives necessary background on side-channel analysis. We present in Sect. 3 the principles of our *scatter* method. Section 4 presents a first validation of *scatter* efficiency based on simulations when practical results on physical measurements from a real hardware device are given in Sect. 6. Section 5 shows a comparison with some other window-based techniques, such as Fast Fourier Transform (FFT) or average. We discuss the impact of this new technique on secure products and state-of-the art countermeasures in Sect. 7, and conclude in Sect. 8.

2   Side-Channel Analysis Practical Issues

Most of the time, except for simple side-channel attacks using one single trace, attack techniques mostly rely on the assumption that the data traces have been aligned before applying a statistical analysis tool. In other words, it requires the estimated variable to be located at the same (X-axis) index along a certain number of traces - being the minimum number of aligned traces required to exploit the leakage with the statistical test. The success rate drops when a proper alignment is not possible. And this condition increasingly becomes an issue when the cryptography is executed on recent secure devices and on complex devices such as a SoC (System on Chip) in a mobile platform, due to complex mechanisms involved such as multi-stage pipeline or speculative execution.

When conducted practically, the alignment step may be time consuming and difficult. This requires a specific expertise and may increase dramatically the number of traces required to expose the key when not properly done. Moreover, the alignment represents a significant part of the effort for performing an attack. Conscious of this, some interesting, but limited, work has been developed to investigate automated ways to run the alignment. The most remarkable is the elastic alignment [39] exploiting fast *Dynamic Time Warping*. Some other techniques explored the use of *wavelets* [13, 26, 31]. All these techniques represent good tools, but remain hard to apply in a generic way, are computationally demanding and sometimes turn out to be inefficient.

On the other hand, some other studies investigated the opportunity to work in the frequency domain via Fourier transformations. Interesting results were obtained on second order attacks in [3]. Indeed, Discrete Fourier transformations represent a valuable tool when fine alignment is hard to achieve. By construction, it integrates a piece of trace in time domain into its equivalent in frequency domain. All values gathered within the window, even non-aligned, are spread over their corresponding set of frequencies. Practically, this technique shows interesting results, but the results are hard to predict as its success depends on non controllable parameters such as the phase, the impact of the interfering noise, or the under sampling when the number of point is too small. Whereas a practical study would be worth of interest, no deep comparison is done in this article. Indeed, both techniques are only comparable by the fact they are window-based. For the rest, they remain different by construction. To avoid misleading technical results on specific targets, this article focuses on exposing *scatter* technique and shows it works practically. Limited comparisons are developed in simulation though.

Since the alignment is a critical condition for most side-channel attacks, a large set of protections exploits this by making this task as difficult as possible. Excluding the inherent protocol based countermeasures (padding, session-keys) we can categorize the side-channel countermeasures in the two following categories:

- **Signals desynchronization:** it aims at avoiding as much as possible an efficient alignment between the same point of interest of the execution among the different traces (executions). This can be achieved with hardware security features: noise generators, dummy cycles, clock jittering or power filtering. It can also be done using software security measures: dummy operations, inserting fake or variable instructions amongst the real one, execute the operations in random order but constant time [10, 12, 37]. Doing so, it makes the alignment task difficult or even impossible when the same operation is hidden in the middle of fake but similar operations.

– **Signals de-correlation:** the principle is to make the leakage independent from the sensitive data to prevent attackers from predicting intermediate values manipulated during the known algorithm execution. Masking and randomization techniques are in this category. It consists of the application to the sensitive data of a randomly chosen value, named the mask.

As a result, there remains a significant technical challenge of extracting a secret key when the information is present in the traces but the alignment is not obvious. *Scatter* addresses this technical problem, by reducing or at most removing the need of alignment.

Notations. In this paper the following notations are being used:

– $\mathcal{P}$ denote the set of the n plaintext values $\{\mathcal{P}_0, \ldots, \mathcal{P}_{n-1}\}$,
– $\mathcal{S}$ denote the set of n side-channel traces $\{\mathcal{S}_0, \ldots, \mathcal{S}_{n-1}\}$,
– $\mathcal{U}$ denote the set containing all the possible ordinates values of points of $\mathcal{S}$,
– $\mathcal{S}_{i,j}$ the jth point of ith trace $\mathcal{S}_i$ of the set $\mathcal{S}$,
– $\mathcal{L}_i$ denote the set of $\#\mathcal{L}_i$ points of interest in the trace $\mathcal{S}_i$, so the points related to the side-channel leakage,
– $\mathcal{O}_i$ denote the set of $\#\mathcal{O}_i$ points of no-interest in the trace $\mathcal{S}_i$, so the points not related to the side-channel leakage,
– The set of value of $\mathcal{S}_i$ is equal to $\mathcal{L}_i \cup \mathcal{O}_i$,
– $G = \{g_0, \ldots, g_{b-1}\}$ is the set of $b = 2^\ell$ possible guesses for k, a targeted secret key ℓ-bit part of whole key K,
   $\Rightarrow$ e.g. $G = \{0, \ldots, 255\}$ for a guess on 8-bit key part.
– $f(\mathcal{P}_i, g)$ is the intermediate calculation targeted for the statistical analysis, for instance the output of the SubBytes in the first round of the AES,
– $w(.)$ is the function used to model the way the information leaks, for instance $w(x)$ is the Hamming weight of point value x in case of a Hamming weight based leakage,
– H is the set of possible values $h = w(x)$ for $x = f(\mathcal{P}_i, g)$, for instance $H = \{0, \ldots, 8\}$ for $h = w(x)$ in the case where x are byte values.

3   *Scatter* Principle

Scatter lies on the exploitation of side-channel leakages using an new representation of the measurements points and the way to process them. More precisely, it integrates the measurements of a set of points and convert it into the corresponding distribution depicting the number of times each value occurred. The set of point can be chosen without limitations as long as it includes the leakage into it. Unlike other window-based techniques, the technique remains relevant when points are selected without being adjacent. This method is defeating first order leakages, the case of higher order leakages is evoked in Sect. 7.

It is processed for each trace by choosing a relevant set of points of interest, encompassing leakages. Figure 1 shows a window selection in traces and
the corresponding conversion into their respective distributions. We will denote
hereafter *distribution of a trace* the outcome of the distribution process for a
trace.

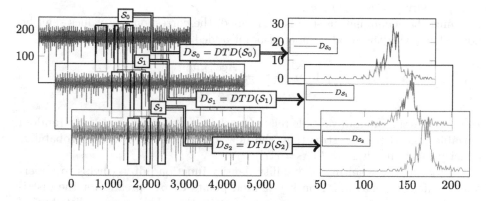

Fig. 1. Illustration of transformation from temporal traces portions to untemporal
distributions.

Doing so, a new dimension is created. Indeed the useful information counts
the same wherever it stands in the selected set of points. In the following, we use
the defined notation $\mathcal{L}_i$ and $\mathcal{O}_i$ respectively for the leakage related measurement
part and not related part in a trace $\mathcal{S}_i$. The corresponding number of points are
respectively $\#\mathcal{L}_i$ and $\#\mathcal{O}_i$.

The corresponding distribution for the ith realization can be expressed as:

$$DTD(\mathcal{S}_i) = DTD(\mathcal{L}_i) + DTD(\mathcal{O}_i)$$

For the next step of the attack, the distribution of each trace needs to be
sorted against the estimated value over all key guesses. The estimated value is
denoted h. In this paper, h will be chosen as the Hamming weight of the targeted
variable. This choice is not restrictive; other models could be applied, such as
the value itself or any subset. Moreover, it is important to mention that *scatter*
is built in such a way that it does not assume anything about the linearity of the
model. In other words, *scatter* works indifferently on either linear or non linear
leakages.

Sorting the traces requires the creation of so called *accumulators*. An accumulator Acc is a two dimensional vector defined for each guess $g \in G$ and for each
value $h \in H$. It holds the frequency of each possible ordinate value $u \in U$. The
integer value $\mathrm{Acc}_{(g,h)}[u]$ is then counting the number of times the value u was
found in the trace selections whose intermediate value was h when the guess g is
considered: $h = w \; o \; f(\mathcal{P}_i, g)$. As an example, attacking an AES implementation
by 8-bit key chuncks ($\#G = 256$) with traces acquired on a 10-bit oscilloscope

$(\#U = 2^{10} = 1024)$ and with a leakage in Hamming weight of the SubBytes output $(\#H = 9)$ would require a accumulator composed of $256 \times 9 \times 1024$ integers. In the following, $\mathrm{Acc}_{(g,h)}$ denotes the vector of $\#U$ counters corresponding to the guess g and the intermediate value h.

In the course of the attack, each trace is distributed only once. The $\#U$ sized vector generated is then accumulated $\#G$ times: once for each guess value g into $\mathrm{Acc}_{(g,h)}$ with $h = w \ o \ f(\mathcal{P}_i, g)$.

Once the accumulation step is performed, the corresponding values shall be normalized with the total number of point added in the accumulator:

$$\mathrm{pdf}_{(g,h)}[u] = \frac{\mathrm{Acc}_{g,h}[u]}{\sum\limits_{u' \in U} \mathrm{Acc}_{g,h}[u']}$$

Denoting X the random variable related to the measurement, and Y the random variable related to the estimation, the new expression leads to the probability density function $\mathrm{pdf}(x) = P(X = x|Y)$.

Exploring the resulting probability density function $\mathrm{pdf}_{(g,h)}$ helps to understand different behaviors. Non key-related points $\mathcal{O}$ are spread over the distribution and converge towards an average distribution. This average distribution is shaped according to the nature of the signal and remains the same regardless the key guess. All the key-related points $\mathcal{L}$ follow however a specific behavior depending on the correctness of the key guess, thus allowing to distinguish the good candidate from wrong ones.

In order to illustrate the distinguishability by a visual manner we built simulations by creating a set of 10 point traces without noise. One point over 10 was the Hamming weight of an intermediate byte value of an algorithm[1] representing the $\mathcal{L}$ set of points and 9 over 10 was the Hamming weight of random byte values representing the $\mathcal{O}$ set of points.

The Fig. 2 shows resulting accumulators after accumulation of several traces. On the left-hand side and in the middle are the representations of two accumulators $\mathrm{Acc}_{g,h}$ that are histograms of 9 values. We chose $h = 4$ and g as the right candidate k on the left and a wrong candidate in the middle. We can see that the $\mathcal{O}$ distribution is almost the same for both candidates when $\mathcal{L}$ points distribution is significantly different. Indeed, for the latter all values are correctly guessed and pile up in a unique peak when the wrong guess may be spread over a set of shorter peaks. Finally, the pdf transformations of the two resulting accumulators is represented on the right-hand side of Fig. 2 and shows the difference. It shows that there is an opportunity to distinguish the good from the wrong candidates.

Given this behavior, the next step is to discriminate the $\mathrm{pdf}_{(k,h)}$ related to the correct key from all other $\mathrm{pdf}_{(g,h)}$. To achieve this, different distinguisher functions may be used combining the partial results obtained for several h values. For instance, authors in [25] suggested several methods to compare different

---

[1] Here, one byte of the output of AES SubBytes operation was chosen as an example without loss of generality.

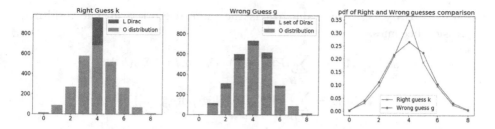

Fig. 2. Pdf functions for the right and a wrong key guess

distributions. In the context of this article, two functions will be explored using classical statistical tools in the information technology. Both are giving the best candidate returning the highest value. The first one makes use of Pearson's chi-squared (χ^2) statistical test expressing how much a distribution differs from a general distribution. The general formula is given as follows:

$$\chi^2 = \sum_{u \in U} \frac{(B[u] - E[u])^2}{E[u]}$$

$B[u]$ being the observed frequency of u and $E[u]$ the expected frequency of u. The application to *scatter* takes each $\mathrm{pdf}_{(g,h)}$ as the observation and analyze how much it differs from the expected frequency, expressed as the average distribution of all $\mathrm{pdf}_{(g,h \in H)}$:

$$\chi^2_{(g,h)} = \sum_{u \in U} \frac{(\mathrm{pdf}_{(g,h)}[u] - \frac{1}{\#H} \cdot \sum_{h' \in H} \mathrm{pdf}_{(g,h')}[u])^2}{\frac{1}{\#H} \cdot \sum_{h' \in H} \mathrm{pdf}_{(g,h')}[u]}$$

Doing so, it is expected that the factor reaches the highest value for the correct key guess.

As the distinguishability may occur for most values of h values, it can be valuable to combine the information as follows:

$$scatter_{\chi^2}(g) = \prod_{h \in H} \chi^2_{(g,h)}$$

The second example of distinguisher exploits the Mutual Information (MI) as introduced in [20]. The difference of entropy remains an appropriate factor, in spite of the presence of $\mathcal{O}$. The difference of entropy is given by the formula:

$$\mathrm{MI} = \sum_Y P(Y) \cdot \sum_X P(X|Y) \cdot \log(P(X|Y)) - \sum_X P(X) \cdot \log(P(X))$$

Mutual Information can be simply applied to *scatter* as any individual value $\mathrm{pdf}_{(g,h)}[u]$ represents the probability $P(X = u|Y = h)$. The rest can be translated as follows: $P(Y) = P(Y = h)$ and $P(X = u) = \frac{1}{\#H} \cdot \sum_{h' \in H} \mathrm{pdf}_{(g,h')}[u]$

for any arbitrary g as this value yields the same regardless g. The resulting expression becomes:

$$scatter_{MI}(g) = \sum_{h \in H} P(Y = h) \cdot (\nabla_1(g, h) - \nabla_2(h))$$

$$\nabla_1(g, h) = \sum_{u \in U} \text{pdf}_{(g,h)}[u] \cdot \log(\text{pdf}_{(g,h)}[u])$$

$$\nabla_2(h) \quad = \sum_{u \in U} P(X = u) \cdot \log(P(X = u))$$

In the following sections, results with both distinguishers (χ^2 and MI) are given, showing similar performance.

4 Attack Simulation

Practical validations of *scatter* were first run on simulated traces. The aim was twofold: first, to confirm that the technique is valid, even when the leakage is in minority within the chosen set of point. Doing so, it gives an idea of an exploitation in case of misalignment or shuffling protections. Second, it allowed to validate its resilience in the presence of noise.

To do this study, we chose to apply the technique on a variable window of adjacent points. The window size represents the strength of the misalignment. Indeed, the unique point of leakage is equally spread over the window. As a result, the probability of having the leakage at a given time is $1/f$ for a window size f. As a result, the maximum number of traces with the leakage point properly aligned converges to $1/f$.

In order to give an order of magnitude, a correlation attack was computed on the same set of point. Obviously its performance drops with a growing window. The chosen leakage model is the Hamming weight. Therefore, there was no need to explore other distinguishers than the Pearson coefficient.

Scatter concerns all algorithms subject to side-channel analyses. AES algorithm was chosen for this study. The simulations for window size is f were generated following the process:

1. Generate a secret key, the value is kept for checking the validity of the results but is not exploited for the attack.
2. Generate a 16-byte long random plaintext.
3. Compute and save the output of one SBOX from SubBytes operation during the first round of AES-128 computation.
4. Generate and save $f - 1$ random bytes.
5. Convert all values into their Hamming weight.
6. Apply a random Gaussian noise level to simulate non-perfect measurements.
7. Apply countermeasures such as shuffling.
8. Go back to step 2 until enough simulation traces are generated.

The Gaussian noise was added using the following formula:

$$\mathcal{L}_j = \alpha \times HW(\text{data}) + \beta + \mathcal{N}(0, \sigma^2) \tag{1}$$

$$\mathcal{O}_j = \alpha \times HW(\text{random data}) + \beta + \mathcal{N}(0, \sigma^2) \tag{2}$$

All points share the same α and β parameters and σ is the standard deviation of the Gaussian noise applied with a mean set to 0.

The simulations results are averaged over different campaigns in order to smooth down potential statistical inconsistencies. On following figures, the X-axis represents in logarithmic scale, the size f of the window of interest for *scatter* methods (bottom scale of the trace) and $1/f$ being the number of traces aligned at each instant. This is relevant for CPA results (top scale of the trace). The Y-axis represents the number of traces necessary to extract the key value. The Y-axis is in normal scale. The score is defined when the correct key value remains above all guesses for the given key byte. One can notice that the lowest this number, the most successful the attack.

4.1   In Time Integration: Keep Information

Figures 3a and b illustrate the effectiveness of the techniques with different levels of Gaussian noise (respectively $\sigma = 0$ and $\sigma = 3$). All computations were made using both *scatter*$_{\chi^2}$ and *scatter*$_{\text{MI}}$ distinguishers.

Remarkably, *scatter*'s outcomes remain solid with a growing window size, even though it implies the integration of an increasing number of non informative points ($\mathcal{O}$). In this configuration, *scatter*$_{\text{MI}}$ configuration stays slightly better

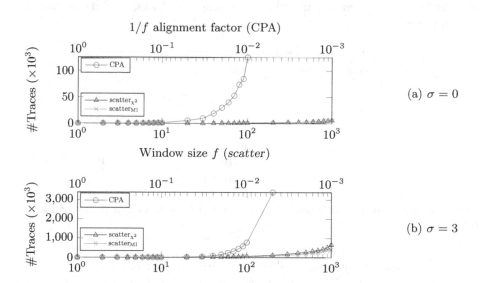

Fig. 3. Simulation of the impact of window size parameter f onto CPA and *scatter* methods under $\sigma = 0$ and $\sigma = 3$ noises

than $scatter_{\chi^2}$, but remains comparable. Unsurprisingly, CPA results decrease significantly (the number of traces needed grows faster) when the shift in time grows. Indeed, a poor alignment quickly undermines the effectiveness of the attack.

Depending on the level of noise σ, the number of traces necessary to retrieve the key changes. However, the general outcome remains similar with $scatter$ techniques showing valuable results even with large windows. It shows as well that the technique is sensitive to noise in the same order of magnitude as the Pearson coefficient.

In case of a fairly good alignment, it is expected the classical technique, such as CPA or MIA, will give better results. However, these results confirm that $scatter$ represents a clear benefit when the alignment condition cannot be satisfactorily fulfilled, due to a poor quality of traces or shuffling countermeasures.

4.2 In Time Integration: Accumulate Information

The previous simulations took into account one single leakage point. With the integration in time, $scatter$ has the ability to combine different leakage points in time and consequently take benefit of the information available. And this can be achieved, even though the respective measurement levels are not identical.

To illustrate this, corresponding simulation traces were generated using the same methodology. For this purpose, the traces were forged using two set of points of equal cardinality: $f/2$, the sets having point parameters equal to (α_1, β_1) and (α_2, β_2) respectively. Compared to the previous analysis, the window of interest contains two leakage points. Figure 4 captures the corresponding results computed with a noise $\sigma = 0$. In dashed, the outcome of the attacks using one single leakage point is depicted and, in plain, two leakage points are present within the window of interest.

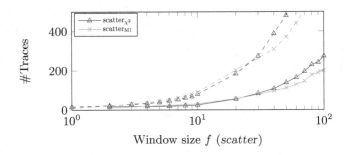

Fig. 4. Comparison results when integrating one (dashed) vs two points of leakage (plains)

The outcome of this analysis shows a positive impact of having two leakage points instead of one. Using either $scatter_{\chi^2}$ or $scatter_{\mathrm{MI}}$ distinguishers, the gain is significant. This result could be obviously enhanced in the event of more leakages.

4.3   In Time Integration: Face the Shuffling Countermeasure

Shuffling countermeasure has been shown as an efficient way to protect algorithms. This is typically implemented by randomizing the execution order of independent operations. As an example this works well when executing SBOX operations during the SubBytes of an AES. In the same vein, any sensitive operation can be concealed, by hiding it randomly in the middle of fake but similar operations. Doing this makes the identification of the correct operation difficult, or even impossible, and prevents the alignment between different execution traces.

By either integrating the whole area in the trace, or by picking up the small pieces for each individual operation, *scatter* has the potential to defeat such protection. Indeed, fake values are likely independent from the targeted value, and consequently do not interfere negatively during the discrimination of the right key guess. Equivalent to random noise, it can be considered that the results depicted in Fig. 3 remain valid to highlight *scatter* performances in case of shuffling.

5   A Comparison with Window-Based Techniques

A comparison between *scatter* and other window-based preprocessing technique, such as average or FFT was found to be uneasy. Indeed, the latter require some consistency when choosing the set of points. Typically, a FFT does not make any sense when picking up points here and there. It deserves to choose a sequence of points in the trace that are sensible to be translated into the frequency domain.

In order to keep a scientific interest, simulation traces were generated allowing averaging and FFT techniques to be relevant. No practical comparisons were made, as the results can vary significantly from one device to the other. Indeed, average or FFT are subject to limitation dependent on the nature of the signal and the outcome depends on a lot of parameters, such as the magnitude of the leakages, the phase of the interfering noise, the number of leaking points, etc. A proper practical study will then be subject to further works.

The main purpose of the following test was to provide a first level of comparison by defining a realistic simulation model and highlight how much the different techniques perform in that case. To serve this purpose a model with two sets of parameters was defined. One stating the jitter and the related window size. And a second describing the leakage model, including the value representation and the noise.

Different levels of jitter were chosen, more particularly 3, 10, 30 or 50 points. The maximum jitter value is denoted J and a dedicated set of test was performed for the given value J. With J defined, sets of traces were generated with $(2*J)-1$ points per traces. The right value is located at the same index $J-1$ for all traces. A random jitter was simulated by taking J points from an index randomly chosen between $[0, J]$. Doing so, the model integrates a jitter J and the information is always present once within the window of size J.

Regarding the trace profile, the intention was to remain generic and therefore to cover most of practical cases. The Hamming weight of values was applied with couples (α, β), with (α, β) defined random in time but remaining the same from a trace to the other:

$$T_{i,j} = \alpha_j \times \mathrm{HW}(x_{i,j}) + \beta_j + \mathcal{N}(0, \sigma^2)$$

with:

- $T_{i,j}$, the point j within the trace i
- $\mathrm{HW}(x)$ function returning the Hamming weight of the value x
- $\mathcal{N}(0, \sigma^2)$ representing a normal random noise factor.

The Gaussian noise has been chosen at $\sigma = 1$ representing a fair amount of noise without being excessive.

Taking into account that a trace is not only made of leakage points, even unrelated to the targeted variable, α was chosen equal to 0 for 70% of the points, and α randomly chosen between $[2, 6]$ for the 30% remaining points.

β was chosen randomly between $[50, 200]$ for all points. α and β range of values were defined with the aim to represent an information fitting an 8-bit oscilloscope with values staying within the range $[0, 255]$. The realization of the noise $\mathcal{N}(0, \sigma^2)$ being a real value, data in the traces were truncated to stay within the range $[0, 255]$.

$x_{i,j}$ are 8-bit values chosen randomly within $[0, 255]$. The point of interest is located at the index $j = J$.

For this study, our choice was to compare *scatter* with respectively a CPA average and the Fast Fourier Transformation (FFT) CPA. For a proper comparison, it was important to keep the same window of points for all techniques. The window remains fix in this set of results. Applying a moving average would not help the comparison, as the same could be applied to all techniques.

For the CPA average [8], all points within the window were summed together and the CPA subsequently applied. On the other hand, a FFT was performed and the CPA applied to the resulting real value. The first point of the FFT was excluded as the frequency 0 is equivalent to the averaged window and therefore would give the same result as the CPA average.

The results shown in Figs. 5, 6, 7 and 8 are the outcome of 200 runs with the same parameters. These runs aim at smoothing down the statistical discrepancy. The selected jitter levels J have been applied. When the maximum jitter level was increased, it resulted to get a larger window and therefore required more traces to get a strong success rate for all techniques. Doing so, the corresponding impact of the window size could be observed.

For all jitter levels, it can be observed that *scatter* success rate is higher than the other techniques after processing of a reasonable amount of traces.

As a result, this case shows that *scatter* technique represents a value when jitter and desynchronization could not be fully removed.

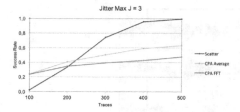

Fig. 5. Comparison with jitter = 3

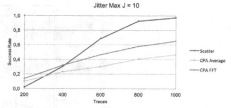

Fig. 6. Comparison with jitter = 10

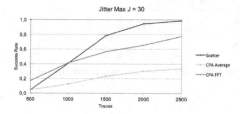

Fig. 7. Comparison with jitter = 30

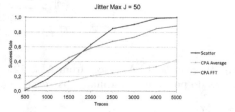

Fig. 8. Comparison with jitter = 50

6   Practical Results

Further testing were performed on a hardware device. This was an unprotected AES-128 implementation running on an 8-bit AVR micro-controller. Physical measurements were performed using intentionally a low-end near-field electromagnetic probe and a low cost acquisition hardware. The global cost of the equipment used for this campaign turns around $1 000. The setup was chosen to represent a real case scenario with poor quality of traces.

The choice was made to acquire traces with an external trigger and no jitter. AES-128 encryptions were performed with a fixed key and random plaintexts. In a post processing, the aim was to downgrade the initial alignment with a random shift in time as previously done on the simulation traces. As it can be observed on Fig. 9, the traces quality is very poor. Without any signal processing, there is no easy way to align these traces since no pattern was found exploitable. With a random shift in time, the model looked realistic to represent an attack scenario with jittering and no good way to perform the alignment.

Figure 9 shows the processing of one round of AES-128 encryption. The operations are not visible but it gives an idea of the number of points involved. In a similar way as the previous testing, *scatter*'s performance is analyzed with the integration of a growing number of adjacent points. A random shift in time is applied to spread the leakage uniformly within the window of interest.

For having a clear view of the integration in time, Fig. 10 illustrates *scatter* techniques evolution together with the time representation of the AES encryption. Looking at this figure, it becomes clear that *scatter* techniques remains very efficient when integrating the whole SubBytes operation, including the 16

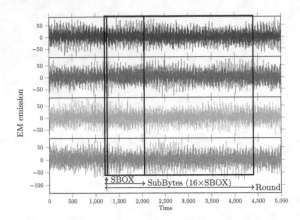

Fig. 9. Near field EM traces from AES-128 execution showing that even synchronized traces do not share identifiable patterns

SBOXes. This means that any random order execution countermeasure would have no effect, and the attack results be the same. Furthermore, the technique is still valid albeit less efficient when integrating the whole round operation. This gives a lot of latitude for exploring the leakage area with raw window sizes.

As a result, this practical session led to several valuable observations. First of all, *scatter* is confirmed to be beneficial when handling raw traces with non obvious alignment. This can be exploited to characterize the leakages in an exploration mode or even to break the implementation when a good alignment could not be performed. Besides, it demonstrates that *scatter* has the potential to defeat several countermeasures, such as random executions or shuffling.

7   Impact on Current State-of-the-Art

This new technique appears to be particularly suitable when leakages are present but remained hard to exploit due to the quality of the traces or the difficulty to align them together in a proficient way. In that cases, the attack turns out to be an alternative to capture the leakage and extract the secrets. Furthermore the technique may be particularly attractive to defeat many shuffling protections, typically by selecting the same sequence of points from each occurrence.

The success of the attack varies from one device to another and practical work is still necessary to assess how much *scatter* represents a clear benefit compared to other windows techniques, such as the ones using either the Fast Fourier Transformation as the integration in time.

It is strongly recommended to take into account this new attack when building a secure implementation. Moreover, the relevance of protections relying mostly on hiding countermeasures should be questioned.

A mitigation can be found by avoiding any kind of single order leakage. Doing so, the leakage would remain non exploitable applying the technique in its simple

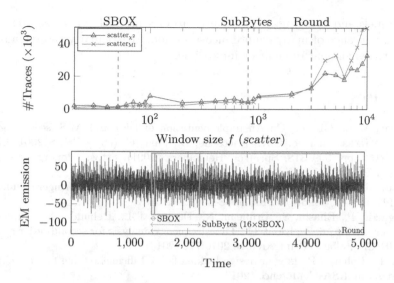

Fig. 10. Practical result of a growing window integration reaching sequentially the size of a suboperation (SBOX), algorithm step (SubBytes), a round and more

form. However, it is important to notice that higher order attacks are possible. Our recent work showed that the technique can be successfully extended and threaten implementations with second order leakages. This is still subject to work in progress.

8   Conclusion

This article introduces *scatter*, a new side-channel technique taking benefit of the integration in time of several data or measurements. On both simulated and practical cases, the testing results have shown a high effectiveness, particularly when the set of traces has not been or could not be aligned prior to the attack. Unlike a large number of existing attacks, the *scatter* technique is still able to extract the secret key, even when the traces are non-aligned. As a result, the technical difficulties related to practical side-channel realizations are significantly lowered. This provides new opportunities of attack when alignment is not possible properly due to the nature of the traces. On the other hand, it makes the attacks cheaper in terms of equipment cost and expertise level. As a result, it is very likely that *scatter* will make practical realizations of side-channels more affordable.

The technique is generic and consequently concerns all algorithms, both symmetrical and asymmetrical. Furthermore, it opens up new exploitation opportunities, particularly when combining different pieces of information available during a sensitive algorithm execution. Extensions to higher order attacks are powerful and were briefly introduced in this article. Representing a new step in side-channels and bringing a complement to existing techniques, *scatter* questions the relevance of many countermeasures, more particularly those aiming at making the alignment difficult or impossible.

References

1. Akkar, M.-L., Giraud, C.: An implementation of DES and AES, secure against some attacks. In: Koç, Ç.K., Naccache, D., Paar, C. (eds.) CHES 2001. LNCS, vol. 2162, pp. 309–318. Springer, Heidelberg (2001). https://doi.org/10.1007/3-540-44709-1_26
2. Batina, L., Robshaw, M. (eds.): CHES 2014. LNCS, vol. 8731. Springer, Heidelberg (2014). https://doi.org/10.1007/978-3-662-44709-3
3. Belgarric, P., Bhasin, S., Bruneau, N., Danger, J.-L., Debande, N., Guilley, S., Heuser, A., Najm, Z., Rioul, O.: Time-frequency analysis for second-order attacks. IACR Cryptology ePrint Archive 2016:772 (2016)
4. Jun, B., Rohatgi, P.: Is your design leaking keys? Efficient testing for side-channel leakage. In: RSA Conference (2013)
5. Bos, J.W., Hubain, C., Michiels, W., Teuwen, P.: Differential computation analysis: hiding your white-box designs is not enough. In: Gierlichs, B., Poschmann, A.Y. (eds.) CHES 2016. LNCS, vol. 9813, pp. 215–236. Springer, Heidelberg (2016). https://doi.org/10.1007/978-3-662-53140-2_11
6. Brier, E., Clavier, C., Olivier, F.: Correlation power analysis with a leakage model. In: Joye, M., Quisquater, J.-J. (eds.) CHES 2004. LNCS, vol. 3156, pp. 16–29. Springer, Heidelberg (2004). https://doi.org/10.1007/978-3-540-28632-5_2
7. Chari, S., Rao, J.R., Rohatgi, P.: Template attacks. In: Kaliski, B.S., Koç, K., Paar, C. (eds.) CHES 2002. LNCS, vol. 2523, pp. 13–28. Springer, Heidelberg (2003). https://doi.org/10.1007/3-540-36400-5_3
8. Clavier, C., Coron, J.-S., Dabbous, N.: Differential power analysis in the presence of hardware countermeasures. In: Koç, Ç.K., Paar, C. (eds.) CHES 2000. LNCS, vol. 1965, pp. 252–263. Springer, Heidelberg (2000). https://doi.org/10.1007/3-540-44499-8_20
9. Coron, J.-S.: Resistance against differential power analysis for elliptic curve cryptosystems. In: Koç, Ç.K., Paar, C. (eds.) CHES 1999. LNCS, vol. 1717, pp. 292–302. Springer, Heidelberg (1999). https://doi.org/10.1007/3-540-48059-5_25
10. Coron, J.-S.: A new DPA countermeasure based on permutation tables. In: Ostrovsky, R., De Prisco, R., Visconti, I. (eds.) SCN 2008. LNCS, vol. 5229, pp. 278–292. Springer, Heidelberg (2008). https://doi.org/10.1007/978-3-540-85855-3_19
11. Coron, J.-S., Goubin, L.: On Boolean and arithmetic masking against differential power analysis. In: Koç, Ç.K., Paar, C. (eds.) CHES 2000. LNCS, vol. 1965, pp. 231–237. Springer, Heidelberg (2000). https://doi.org/10.1007/3-540-44499-8_18
12. Coron, J.-S., Kizhvatov, I.: An efficient method for random delay generation in embedded software. In: Clavier, C., Gaj, K. (eds.) CHES 2009. LNCS, vol. 5747, pp. 156–170. Springer, Heidelberg (2009). https://doi.org/10.1007/978-3-642-04138-9_12
13. Debande, N., Souissi, Y., Abdelaziz Elaabid, M., Guilley, S., Danger, J.-L.: Wavelet transform based pre-processing for side channel analysis. In: 45th Annual IEEE/ACM International Symposium on Microarchitecture, MICRO 2012, Workshops Proceedings, Vancouver, BC, Canada, 1–5 December 2012, pp. 32–38. IEEE Computer Society (2012)

14. Doget, J., Prouff, E., Rivain, M., Standaert, F.-X.: Univariate side channel attacks and leakage modeling. J. Cryptogr. Eng. **1**(2), 123–144 (2011)
15. Standaert, F.-X.: How (not) to use Welch's T-test in side-channel security evaluations (2017)
16. Fumaroli, G., Martinelli, A., Prouff, E., Rivain, M.: Affine masking against higher-order side channel analysis. In: Biryukov, A., Gong, G., Stinson, D.R. (eds.) SAC 2010. LNCS, vol. 6544, pp. 262–280. Springer, Heidelberg (2011). https://doi.org/10.1007/978-3-642-19574-7_18
17. Genkin, D., Pachmanov, L., Pipman, I., Tromer, E.: Stealing keys from PCs using a radio: cheap electromagnetic attacks on windowed exponentiation. In: Güneysu, T., Handschuh, H. (eds.) CHES 2015. LNCS, vol. 9293, pp. 207–228. Springer, Heidelberg (2015). https://doi.org/10.1007/978-3-662-48324-4_11
18. Genkin, D., Pipman, I., Tromer, E.: Get your hands off my laptop: physical side-channel key-extraction attacks on PCs. In: Batina and Robshaw [2], pp. 242–260
19. Genkin, D., Shamir, A., Tromer, E.: RSA key extraction via low-bandwidth acoustic cryptanalysis. In: Garay, J.A., Gennaro, R. (eds.) CRYPTO 2014, Part I. LNCS, vol. 8616, pp. 444–461. Springer, Heidelberg (2014). https://doi.org/10.1007/978-3-662-44371-2_25
20. Gierlichs, B., Batina, L., Tuyls, P., Preneel, B.: Mutual information analysis. In: Oswald, E., Rohatgi, P. (eds.) CHES 2008. LNCS, vol. 5154, pp. 426–442. Springer, Heidelberg (2008). https://doi.org/10.1007/978-3-540-85053-3_27
21. Gierlichs, B., Lemke-Rust, K., Paar, C.: Templates vs. stochastic methods. In: Goubin, L., Matsui, M. (eds.) CHES 2006. LNCS, vol. 4249, pp. 15–29. Springer, Heidelberg (2006). https://doi.org/10.1007/11894063_2
22. Goodwill, G., Jun, B., Jaffe, J., Rohatgi, P.: A Testing methodology for side channel resistance validation. In: NIST Non Invasive Attack Testing Workshop (2011)
23. Kocher, P.C.: Timing attacks on implementations of Diffie-Hellman, RSA, DSS, and other systems. In: Koblitz, N. (ed.) CRYPTO 1996. LNCS, vol. 1109, pp. 104–113. Springer, Heidelberg (1996). https://doi.org/10.1007/3-540-68697-5_9
24. Kocher, P., Jaffe, J., Jun, B.: Differential power analysis. In: Wiener, M. (ed.) CRYPTO 1999. LNCS, vol. 1666, pp. 388–397. Springer, Heidelberg (1999). https://doi.org/10.1007/3-540-48405-1_25
25. Linge, Y., Dumas, C., Lambert-Lacroix, S.: Using the joint distributions of a cryptographic function in side channel analysis. In: Prouff, E. (ed.) COSADE 2014. LNCS, vol. 8622, pp. 199–213. Springer, Cham (2014). https://doi.org/10.1007/978-3-319-10175-0_14
26. Liu, W., Wu, L., Zhang, X., Wang, A.: Wavelet-based noise reduction in power analysis attack. In: Tenth International Conference on Computational Intelligence and Security, Kunming, Yunnan, China, 15–16 November 2014, CIS 2014, pp. 405–409. IEEE Computer Society (2014)
27. Lomné, V., Prouff, E., Rivain, M., Roche, T., Thillard, A.: How to estimate the success rate of higher-order side-channel attacks. In: Batina and Robshaw [2], pp. 35–54
28. Mangard, S., Standaert, F.-X. (eds.): CHES 2010. LNCS, vol. 6225. Springer, Heidelberg (2010). https://doi.org/10.1007/978-3-642-15031-9
29. Messerges, T.S.: Using second-order power analysis to attack DPA resistant software. In: Koç, Ç.K., Paar, C. (eds.) CHES 2000. LNCS, vol. 1965, pp. 238–251. Springer, Heidelberg (2000). https://doi.org/10.1007/3-540-44499-8_19
30. Moradi, A., Mischke, O., Eisenbarth, T.: Correlation-enhanced power analysis collision attack. In: Mangard and Standaert [28], pp. 125–139

31. Muijrers, R.A., van Woudenberg, J.G.J., Batina, L.: RAM: rapid alignment method. In: Prouff, E. (ed.) CARDIS 2011. LNCS, vol. 7079, pp. 266–282. Springer, Heidelberg (2011). https://doi.org/10.1007/978-3-642-27257-8_17

32. Oswald, E., Mangard, S., Herbst, C., Tillich, S.: Practical second-order DPA attacks for masked smart card implementations of block ciphers. In: Pointcheval, D. (ed.) CT-RSA 2006. LNCS, vol. 3860, pp. 192–207. Springer, Heidelberg (2006). https://doi.org/10.1007/11605805_13

33. Poussier, R., Standaert, F.-X., Grosso, V.: Simple key enumeration (and rank estimation) using histograms: an integrated approach. In: Gierlichs, B., Poschmann, A.Y. (eds.) CHES 2016. LNCS, vol. 9813, pp. 61–81. Springer, Heidelberg (2016). https://doi.org/10.1007/978-3-662-53140-2_4

34. Prouff, E., Rivain, M., Bevan, R.: Statistical analysis of second order differential power analysis. IEEE Trans. Comput. **58**(6), 799–811 (2009)

35. Rivain, M., Prouff, E.: Provably secure higher-order masking of AES. In: Mangard and Standaert [28], pp. 413–427

36. Schindler, W., Lemke, K., Paar, C.: A stochastic model for differential side channel cryptanalysis. In: Rao, J.R., Sunar, B. (eds.) CHES 2005. LNCS, vol. 3659, pp. 30–46. Springer, Heidelberg (2005). https://doi.org/10.1007/11545262_3

37. Tunstall, M., Benoit, O.: Efficient use of random delays in embedded software. In: Sauveron, D., Markantonakis, K., Bilas, A., Quisquater, J.-J. (eds.) WISTP 2007. LNCS, vol. 4462, pp. 27–38. Springer, Heidelberg (2007). https://doi.org/10.1007/978-3-540-72354-7_3

38. Tunstall, M., Whitnall, C., Oswald, E.: Masking tables—an underestimated security risk. In: Moriai, S. (ed.) FSE 2013. LNCS, vol. 8424, pp. 425–444. Springer, Heidelberg (2014). https://doi.org/10.1007/978-3-662-43933-3_22

39. van Woudenberg, J.G.J., Witteman, M.F., Bakker, B.: Improving differential power analysis by elastic alignment. In: Kiayias, A. (ed.) CT-RSA 2011. LNCS, vol. 6558, pp. 104–119. Springer, Heidelberg (2011). https://doi.org/10.1007/978-3-642-19074-2_8

Quadrivariate Improved Blind Side-Channel Analysis on Boolean Masked AES

Christophe Clavier[1]([✉]) [iD], Léo Reynaud[1], and Antoine Wurcker[2]

[1] Université de Limoges, XLIM-CNRS, Limoges, France
christophe.clavier@unilim.fr, leo.reynaud@xlim.fr
[2] eshard, Martillac, France
antoine.wurcker@eshard.com

Abstract. Previous blind side-channel analysis have been proposed to recover a block cipher secret key while neither the plaintext nor the ciphertext is available to the attacker. A recent improvement has been proposed that deals with several first-order Boolean masking schemes. Unfortunately the proposed attacks only work if at least two intermediate states that involve a same key byte are protected by a same mask. In this paper we describe a quadrivariate analysis which involves a pair of key bytes and allows to threaten improved Boolean masked implementations where all masks on inputs of AddRoundKey, SubBytes and MixColumns (respectively r_m, r_x and r_y) related to a same key byte are independant.

Our attack comes in two flavors: in a first variant the attacker learns Hamming distances between pairs of expanded key bytes of his choice while in the other variant he learns whether two pairs of extended key bytes share the same unknown Hamming distance. We provide an analysis and simulation results which demonstrate that the ciphering key can be recovered in both settings.

Keywords: Unknown plaintext · Joint distributions
Maximum likelihood · Boolean masking

1 Introduction

Traditional side-channel analysis on block ciphers [1,4,5] use a divide-and-conquer strategy where a guess on a subkey (e.g. a key byte) is (in)validated by correlating in some way a series of leakage measurements (e.g. power consumptions) with a series of corresponding key-dependent intermediate values that are derived from the guess and from either the plaintext or the ciphertext.

When neither the plaintext nor the ciphertext are available to the attacker such attacks can not apply anymore. In such so-called *blind* contexts, one can only exploit side-channel traces and try to find key dependencies between the leakages of two or more *unknown nor predictable* intermediate values. In the case

© Springer International Publishing AG, part of Springer Nature 2018
J. Fan and B. Gierlichs (Eds.): COSADE 2018, LNCS 10815, pp. 153–167, 2018.
https://doi.org/10.1007/978-3-319-89641-0_9

of the AES block cipher, such key dependency occurs between an input byte of the AddRoundKey and the corresponding output byte of the subsequent SubBytes operation. This is exactly this dependency that has been firstly exploited by Linge et al. [7]. They noticed that the joint distribution of the Hamming weights of these two intermediate bytes depends on the involved key byte and proposed an attack where an observed experimental distribution built from the side-channel traces is compared to each 256 theoretical distributions (also called *models*). The attacker then selects the key byte value that corresponds to the model that best fits the empirical distribution. Later Le Bouder [6] proposed to use the maximum likelihood criterion instead of the distance-based comparison of distributions. Recently Clavier and Reynaud [3] further improved this attack by exploiting other kinds of joint distributions and by attacking some Boolean masked implementations.

Our Contribution. While [3] was the first attempt to defeat a first-order Boolean masked implementation in the blind context, it is interesting to notice that information about the key can be retrieved only if the masks that apply to each component of the considered joint distribution are not independent. Keeping their notations where m, x and y respectively denote an input byte of the AddRoundKey and the corresponding input and output bytes of the subsequent SubBytes, their so-called m-x or m-y attacks[1] on protected implementations do work only if m and x, or m and y, are masked by the same value. This is an important limitation as a state-of-the-art first-order protected implementation should usually mask these intermediate bytes by independent random values which we denote by r_m, r_x and r_y respectively. As noticed by the authors, this case corresponds to the scheme d of their Fig. 5 which is not impacted by their attacks.

In this paper we build on [3] and describe an alternative way of exploiting joint distributions that fills this gap and leads to attacks that apply even when r_m, r_x and r_y are independent masks. We propose to attack key bytes by pairs (k, k') where k and k' designate any two bytes of the expanded key. This means that the (m, x, y) and (m', x', y') areas involving k and k' may be located anywhere in the computation process: at any round, and at any byte index of the state. For our attack to succeed, we need to assume that k and k' areas are masked in the same way, i.e. $(r_m, r_x, r_y) = (r'_m, r'_x, r'_y)$. As a consequence, only a perfect full wide masking with 160 independent masks triplets can thwart our proposed attacks. This usually corresponds to quite costly and complex implementations.

This paper is organized as follows. Section 2 provides a background on blind side-channel analysis and reminds how the maximum likelihood criterion is used in Clavier et al. attacks. In Sect. 3 we introduce our combined attacks that target

---

[1] An m-x attack – respectively an m-y or m-x-y attack – is one that is based on the joint distribution of $(\mathrm{HW}(m), \mathrm{HW}(x))$ – respectively on the joint distribution of $(\mathrm{HW}(m), \mathrm{HW}(y))$ or of $(\mathrm{HW}(m), \mathrm{HW}(x), \mathrm{HW}(y))$. With this notation, Linge's first blind side-channel analysis was an m-y attack.

pairs of key bytes by exploiting quadrivariate joint distributions. We focus on the combined m-x attack – which reveals to be more efficient that the m-y one – and show that it only gives information about the Hamming distance between the key bytes. We also propose an alternative variant that compares together joint distributions related to two pairs (k_1, k_1') and (k_2, k_2') but only reveals whether both Hamming distances are equal or not. As both variants of our m-x attack only give partial information about the key bytes, Sects. 4 and 5 provide analyses showing that such partial information is sufficient to recover the ciphering key in both settings. Finally, Sect. 6 concludes this work and proposes countermeasures to our attacks.

Remark: The practicality of blind joint distributions analysis has been demonstrated on real traces in [3,7]. The point of our contribution is not to argue whether attacks of this kind are easy or difficult to put in practice, but rather to provide new ideas of joint distributions based attacks that allow to extend their applicability. As a consequence – and this does not mean that it is an easy task in practice –, in the sequel we assume that the attacker is able to precisely locate the relevant points of interest and, if needed, to infer the parameters of the leakage functions in order to derive Hamming weights. Also, to measure the effectiveness of our ideas, we only provide simulation-based experimental results.

2   Background on Blind Side-Channel Analysis

The original attack of Linge et al. [7] consists in building the joint distributions of $\mathrm{HW}(m)$ and $\mathrm{HW}(y)$ for each value of k. This is done by counting the number of times every couple $(\mathrm{HW}(m), \mathrm{HW}(y))$ occurs when m takes all values uniformly. Given an experimental distribution one can compare it to each model and select the one which minimizes a distance-based criterion. They have studied a large number of distances and proposed the better ones. They also described the so-called *slice method* that infers Hamming weights – which follow a binomial law – from the set of ordered leakages. The great advantage is that this attack can be applied at any round and that no plaintext nor ciphertext has to be known.

Clavier and Reynaud [3] go further in this way using the maximum likelihood (ML) criterion instead of distances between distributions. They also introduce the so-called *variance method*, which is better suited to the ML criterion, to infer Hamming weights from leakages. They show that it gives better results than any distance previously studied and apply their attack on a real device. Then they investigate the case of masked implementations and show that the joint distributions of $\mathrm{HW}(m \oplus r)$ and $\mathrm{HW}(y \oplus r)$ still depends on the key. Simulations prove that attacking is still feasible but requires a lot more traces than in the unmasked case.

They also propose a variant on m and x that only gives the Hamming weight of k but is much more effective in term of required traces. This is explained by the typical forms of the distributions[2] and the fact that the attacker must

---

[2] In that case, the distributions show linear structures like "walls".

distinguish between only nine of them. They also point that this m-x variant is not affected by the masking as the distributions of $(\mathrm{HW}(m), \mathrm{HW}(m \oplus k))$ and of $(\mathrm{HW}(m \oplus r), \mathrm{HW}(m \oplus k \oplus r))$ are the same.

As the maximum likelihood method shows to be more efficient than distance-based comparison of distributions, let's remind its principle in the case of a m-y attack (it is similar for other variants). Given a noisy measurement (h_m, h_y) of the Hamming weights, one can evaluate the probability of each key hypothesis according to this observation by using Bayes' formula:

$$\Pr(k|(h_m, h_y)) \propto \Pr((h_m, h_y)|k) \cdot \Pr(k)$$

When a series of observations is considered, the posterior probability of the key is computed as the product of the terms $\Pr((h_m, h_y)|k)$, each of them being evaluated, thanks to the law of total probabilities, by considering all possibilities for the actual couple (h_m^*, h_y^*) of Hamming weights:

$$\Pr((h_m, h_y)|k) = \sum_{h_m^*, h_y^*} \Pr((h_m, h_y)|(h_m^*, h_y^*)) \cdot \Pr((h_m^*, h_y^*)|k)$$

In this equation the first term of each product is derived from the distributions of the noises, which are usually taken as Gaussian, while the second term comes from precomputed models. At the end the attacker selects the key that has the largest posterior probability.

3   Combined S-Boxes Attacks

As stated in the introduction, basic joint distributions analysis with masking is not possible when masks r_m, r_x and r_y are independent. However, even in this case, it may be a common practice – to avoid a too time or memory costly implementation – to reuse the same mask triplet either from one round to another and/or from one byte index to another. We thus propose to combine the points of interest of two areas that involve two key bytes and are protected by a same triplet. It happens that corresponding quadrivariate – or possibly sextivariate in the m-x-y case – joint distributions are still dependent on the key bytes, thus giving information about them.

3.1   Combined m-y Maximum Likelihood Attack

Description. The maximum likelihood *combined* m-y attack is an adaptation of the *basic* one described in [3]. The difference is that instead of building joint distributions of $(\mathrm{HW}(m \oplus r_m), \mathrm{HW}(y \oplus r_y))$, which are the same for all k because of the independence of the masks, we build quadrivariate joint distributions of $(\mathrm{HW}(m \oplus r_m), \mathrm{HW}(m' \oplus r_m), \mathrm{HW}(y \oplus r_y), \mathrm{HW}(y' \oplus r_y))$, where $y = S(m \oplus k)$ and $y' = S(m' \oplus k')$. Building these distributions is done by counting the number of times each quadruplet of Hamming weights occurs when m, m', r_m and r_y all vary. An interesting property is that these 2^{16} distributions come in classes of

2^8 equivalent distributions that share the same differential $k \oplus k'$. An argument proving this fact is that in the counting process the quadruplets of Hamming weights for any input (m, m', r_m, r_y) when the pair of keys is (k, k') is exactly the same than for the input $(m \oplus \delta, m' \oplus \delta, r_m \oplus \delta, r_y)$ when the key pair is $(k \oplus \delta, k' \oplus \delta)$. This means that the models for (k, k') and $(k \oplus \delta, k' \oplus \delta)$ are identical whatever δ. As a consequence only the differential between the two key bytes can be recovered by this attack.

Experimental Results. We have simulated the maximum likelihood combined m-y attack with three different levels of noise, $\sigma \in \{0.2, 0.5, 1.0\}$. For each noise level we averaged the results over 100 runs with randomly generated key pairs. Figure 1 shows the evolution of the rank of the correct key differential, as well as the success rate, as a function of the number of traces.

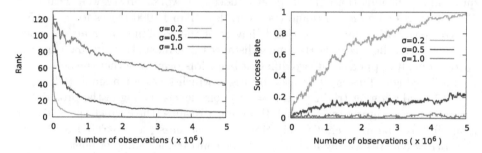

Fig. 1. Rank (left) and success rate (right) of the ML combined m-y attack. Average over 100 runs for three noise levels $\sigma = 0.2$, 0.5 and 1.0.

We notice that except for the smallest noise level $\sigma = 0.2$ where good success rates are obtained after about four millions traces, the combined m-y attack can hardly retrieve the correct differential.

3.2   Combined m-x Maximum Likelihood Attack

Description. Here, we propose the maximum likelihood combined m-x variant as a natural extension of the basic m-x attack described in [3]. Instead of building models that are based on the joint distributions of $(\mathrm{HW}(m \oplus r_m), \mathrm{HW}(x \oplus r_x))$, which are all the same, we combine two key bytes areas and use the joint distributions of $(\mathrm{HW}(m \oplus r_m), \mathrm{HW}(m' \oplus r_m), \mathrm{HW}(x \oplus r_x), \mathrm{HW}(x' \oplus r_x))$ generated by a counting process where m, m', r_m and r_x all vary.

We recall that the basic m-x attack can distinguish between only 9 different models that correspond to the Hamming weight of the key byte. Likewise, the combined m-x attack can distinguish between only 9 different models that correspond to the Hamming distance between k and k'. To prove this we make two observations: (i) the same argument as for the combined m-y attack also applies here, from which we infer that the models are invariant by any transformation $(k, k') \mapsto (k \oplus \delta, k' \oplus \delta)$, (ii) as the only operation between m and x is a XOR and we are considering observations which are Hamming weights, it is also the case that the models are invariant by any transformation $(k, k') \mapsto (\pi(k), \pi(k'))$ where π is any bit permutation of a byte. Combining these two observations, we conclude that two key pairs having the same Hamming distance will also share the same model.

One may wonder whether retrieving only Hamming distances between pairs of key bytes suffices to recover the ciphering key. Section 4 analyses the point and answers positively to this question.

Experimental Results. We have simulated the maximum likelihood combined m-x attack with three noise levels $\sigma \in \{0.5, 1.0, 2.0\}$. Success rates averaged over 1000 runs are given on Fig. 2. One can notice that the combined m-x attack is quite more efficient than the m-y one. Indeed, it works pretty well with only 100 000 traces when $\sigma = 1.0$ and even with less than 10 000 traces for $\sigma = 0.5$.

We have noticed an interesting behavior of the combined m-x attack when one focuses on the incorrect Hamming distances that most strongly challenge the correct one. It happens that two different behaviors occur whether the noise level is small or high. This is illustrated by Fig. 3 which gives for a small (left part, $\sigma = 0.5$) and a higher (right part, $\sigma = 1.0$) noise levels the log of the probability (relative to the highest one) of each Hamming distance (the correct one is 3). For a small noise the most challenging Hamming distances are separated by 2 from the correct one, respecting its parity. On the contrary, for a higher noise level the most challenging Hamming distances are the closest ones, separated by 1 from the correct one. We observe same results when the correct Hamming distance is different from 3. We thus have a parity-driven behavior for small noises, and a proximity-driven behavior for higher ones.

3.3   Collision-Based Combined m-x Attack

Section 3.2 proposes a combined m-x attack based on the maximum likelihood criterion. As explained in [3], in order to apply the ML method the attacker must convert leakages into real-valued Hamming weights beforehand. This is usually done by inverting the leakage function which necessitates to estimate the parameters α and β of the linear leakage model. In some cases, this may be a difficult task resulting in roughly estimated parameters that may cause the attack to give bad results or even totally fail. Apart from a difficult estimation of α and β, another problem arises when the leakage is not a linear function of the Hamming weight of the data.

To deal with such difficult cases, we propose a collision-based variant of the combined m-x attack. In the sequel we do not need the attacker to invert the leakage function. We even do not assume that it is linear. However we make the assumption that both leakage functions $\mathcal{L}_m$ and $\mathcal{L}_x$ related to the manipulations of m and x respectively are the same from one key byte area to another.

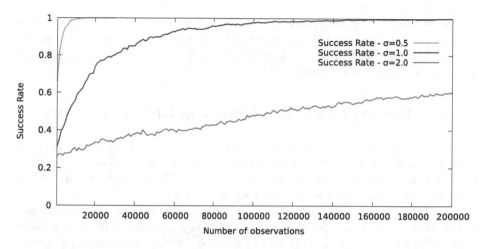

Fig. 2. Success rate for the ML combined m-x attack. Average over 1000 runs for three noise levels $\sigma = 0.5$, 1.0 and 2.0.

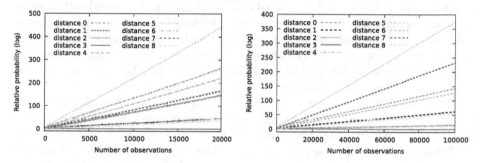

Fig. 3. Probability of the different Hamming distances in cases of a small (left, $\sigma = 0.5$) and a higher (right, $\sigma = 1.0$) noise levels.

If this property holds then the joint distributions can be compared directly in the leakages domain rather than in the Hamming weights domain.

Precisely, given a pair of key bytes (k_1, k_1'), one can build the empirical quadrivariate joint distribution of $(\mathcal{L}_m(m_1), \mathcal{L}_m(m_1'), \mathcal{L}_x(x_1), \mathcal{L}_x(x_1'))$. This joint distribution of *leakages* is as well characterized by $\mathrm{HD}(k_1, k_1')$ than may be the corresponding joint distribution of Hamming weights. Then, one can also build the empirical joint distribution of leakages $(\mathcal{L}_m(m_2), \mathcal{L}_m(m_2'), \mathcal{L}_x(x_2), \mathcal{L}_x(x_2'))$ related to another pair of key bytes (k_2, k_2'). Comparing both distributions together should reveal whether $\mathrm{HD}(k_1, k_1') = \mathrm{HD}(k_2, k_2')$, without knowing the Hamming distance value itself.

We did not simulate this collision-based combined m-x attack, but we think that, provided that the attacker is able to determine a threshold value on the distance between both distributions that allows him to decide between collision and non-collision cases, then this kind of attack should reveal identities of Hamming distances between key byte pairs. While this seems to be a even less informative knowledge than Hamming distances revealed by the ML combined m-x attack of Sect. 3.2, we study in Sect. 5 how to exploit it and conclude that it is also sufficient to recover the ciphering key.

4   Key Recovery Based on Hamming Distances Values

Section 3.2 gives ability to an attacker to retrieve Hamming distances between some key bytes. In this section, we describe how to use such, potentially partially obtained, information to recover the AES main key. We consider in simulations that the information used is recovered without error[3].

The blind attacker scenario might be applied different ways, leading to different constraints on number of remaining valid key candidates. In the usual scenario, the protocol might be designed to not be delivering plaintext or ciphertext or both to attacker so that he can not brute force even a small list of key candidates. This is why we will try in the sequel to reduce the number of remaining candidates to 1. Beside, other relaxed configurations can be considered as some implementation might, for a cost reduction consideration, over-protect only outer rounds and not the inner rounds of an algorithm. In that case, the attacker may have access to plaintext/ciphertext pairs, allowing him to brute force a remaining key list, while he can still be considered as blind for the inner unprotected rounds since he can not predict their inputs/outputs.

We make the use of guess-compute-and-backtrack strategies to recover the main key from a partial information on the expanded key bytes. For example such methods were used in [2,8] to recover AES main key from partial knowledge of Hamming weight of expanded key bytes. This consists in considering *guesses* of expanded key byte value, *computing* other key bytes that are related by the known equations of the AES key schedule process *and backtrack* in case an obtained information about those key bytes is not respected. It gives the attacker a list of keys compatible with observations, potentially reduced to only one key.

Our simulation process consist in: (i) take a random key, (ii) record the Hamming distances related to the model of attacker considered, (iii) explore the solution tree with guided guess-compute-and-backtrack method and finally, (iv) count how many keys are given as output. We always checked that the correct key actually belongs to the remaining candidates list. Simulation results are given for a single 3, 5 GHz core and use less than 1 MiB of RAM memory.

We consider two constraint masking schemes. A first one, with 3×11 bytes of mask entropy, is studied in Sect. 4.1 and corresponds to a mask triplet (r_m, r_x, r_y) that is the same for all key bytes of a same round, but different from one round to another. Then, in Sect. 4.2 we study the 3×16-byte entropy dual scheme where all mask triplets of a same round are different from each others, but they are reused for all rounds. Note that the 3×1-byte entropy simple masking scheme

---

[3] Later, we show how to detect small errors. Once detected erroneous Hamming distances can simply be ignored.

Round 0					Round 1					Round 2						Round 10			
$\oplus r_0$	$\oplus r_0$	$\oplus r_0$	$\oplus r_0$		$\oplus r_1$	$\oplus r_1$	$\oplus r_1$	$\oplus r_1$		$\oplus r_2$	$\oplus r_2$	$\oplus r_2$	$\oplus r_2$			$\oplus r_{10}$	$\oplus r_{10}$	$\oplus r_{10}$	$\oplus r_{10}$
$\oplus r_0$	$\oplus r_0$	$\oplus r_0$	$\oplus r_0$		$\oplus r_1$	$\oplus r_1$	$\oplus r_1$	$\oplus r_1$		$\oplus r_2$	$\oplus r_2$	$\oplus r_2$	$\oplus r_2$	$\cdots$		$\oplus r_{10}$	$\oplus r_{10}$	$\oplus r_{10}$	$\oplus r_{10}$
$\oplus r_0$	$\oplus r_0$	$\oplus r_0$	$\oplus r_0$		$\oplus r_1$	$\oplus r_1$	$\oplus r_1$	$\oplus r_1$		$\oplus r_2$	$\oplus r_2$	$\oplus r_2$	$\oplus r_2$			$\oplus r_{10}$	$\oplus r_{10}$	$\oplus r_{10}$	$\oplus r_{10}$
$\oplus r_0$	$\oplus r_0$	$\oplus r_0$	$\oplus r_0$		$\oplus r_1$	$\oplus r_1$	$\oplus r_1$	$\oplus r_1$		$\oplus r_2$	$\oplus r_2$	$\oplus r_2$	$\oplus r_2$			$\oplus r_{10}$	$\oplus r_{10}$	$\oplus r_{10}$	$\oplus r_{10}$

Fig. 4. Positions of the 11 independent mask triplets on the expanded key.

where all mask triplets are the same can be easily broken: there always remains only one valid solution, and it is retrieved in a fraction of second.

4.1 3 × 11-Byte Entropy Masking Scheme

The 11 independent mask triplets scenario corresponds to attacking an implementation refreshing mask triplets between each round computation. Figure 4 highlights, in grey levels, the key byte areas that share the same mask triplets. Note that on this figure, r_i is actually a shortcut referring to the mask triplet $(r_m, r_x, r_y)_i$ used around K_i.[4]

In this section we show results of simulations of key recovery attempt that can be achieved by an attacker. Several configurations of attacker are considered, all relying on the ability to retrieve Hamming distances between key bytes belonging to the same round. Distances between key bytes from different round keys cannot be recovered here.

Full Information. First we consider an attacker that achieves to recover the maximum of information, i.e. the 120 Hamming distances between the 16 bytes of a round key and for each round key, leading to $11 \times 120 = 1320$ distances. The exploration strategy follows: each key byte guessed allows to apply a constraint on other bytes of the same round key as the Hamming distances between them are known. This reduces the number of candidate for those bytes. When several bytes of a round key are guessed, it allows to compute (no guess needed this time) some of the key bytes from other rounds. As Hamming distance between each pair of key byte from the same round are known, it can be used as a control to stop the exploration as soon as an inconsistency is detected. The guessing order strategies to create a raise of the number of constraints as soon as possible plays a important role to limit the growth of the candidate tree, this question is discussed in [2,8]. Using all information available, the guess phase takes less than 1 s on the 1 000 random cases considered and always gives the correct key as unique solution.

---

[4] Or only the mask couple $(r_m, r_x)_{10}$ for K_{10}.

One Key Information. As gathering Hamming distance might be a demanding task, we consider here an attacker that retrieves the Hamming distances into only one round key. One can remark that it can be any round key as candidates for the main key can be easily derived from candidates for any round key. Table 1 gives the results of 1 000 simulations, the number of key candidates remaining after the exploration and the average execution time.

Table 1. Results of exploration using one round key Hamming distances information

Number of remaining keys	Average time of execution (s)	Encountered case /1 000
5 160 960	36.0	1
10 321 920	80.4	997
20 643 840	108.5	2

In almost all cases (99.7%) the number of keys compatibles with the Hamming distance observation is 10 321 920 and this list needs 80.4 s to be established.

Several Keys Information. In order to further reduce the number of valid candidates we now consider an attacker that is able to use another arbitrary round key. Due to the key schedule relations, the list of candidates for one round key can easily generate a list of candidates for any other. Then, this list can be checked against the new Hamming distance constraints. This additive operation takes a negligible time. Table 2 shows that in most cases (78.4%), the correct key remains as unique candidate.

Table 2. Results of exploration using Hamming distances information inferred from two round keys.

Number of remaining keys	1	2	3	4	6	8	12
Encountered case/1 000	784	189	1	17	7	1	1

Time Exploration Optimization. Attacker may explore faster than generating list of millions of candidates from only one key in case information of a second key is available. As keys are related, guessing bytes from the first key in an appropriate order allows to start to compute part of the second key in use and then apply constraints sooner. The list of remaining candidates is not modified but the exploration tree has branches cut off earlier leading to smaller execution time for research. Indeed, the average exploration time falls from ~80 s to less than one second in case where two consecutive keys are used.

Detection of Erroneous Hamming Distances. In our simulations of the combined m-x attack with $\sigma = 1.0$ we have noticed that when the Hamming distance was not correctly determined, the error was only of ± 1 bit (proximity-driven behavior). As a result, if the number of incorrectly determined distances is not too large, one can detect them based on the parity consistency that must hold within any key byte triangle. Indeed for any three bytes it must be the case that the three Hamming distances that relate them together do not all have the same parity. For instance, it may be the case that $HD(k_1, k_2) = 5$, $HD(k_2, k_3) = 7$ and $HD(k_3, k_1) = 4$ but it can not be the case that they are equal to 5, 7 and 3. Before launching the tree exploration for compatible keys, one can perform a sanity check by verifying the parity property for any triangle of key bytes. Once an inconsistent triangle is detected, one can easily identify and eliminate its incorrect edge. Indeed an incorrect edge would still violate the parity property when associated with other opposite vertices.

Classes of Solutions. One can remark in Table 1 that the 3 different number of remaining keys are precisely related by a factor of 2:

$$20\,643\,840 = 2 \times 10\,321\,920 = 4 \times 5\,160\,960$$

The most common figure ($10\,321\,920$) can be explained. For each valid key candidate, any key that has a same XOR difference on all its bytes is also a solution. Moreover, any bit permutation π applied onto all bytes of a valid candidate gives another valid candidate. We thus have equivalence classes of $256 \times 8! = 10\,321\,920$ solutions. The case of $5\,160\,960$ remaining candidates occurs when two bits are equals on all the 16 bytes of the key candidate, in that case the number of possible permutations is reduced by a factor 2. The case of $20\,643\,840$ remaining candidates occurs when two keys are solutions of the Hamming distance constraints but without being related by any XOR difference nor permutation of bits. One then has two independent classes of solutions.

4.2 3 × 16-Byte Entropy Masking Scheme

Figure 5 highlights, in grey levels, the key bytes that share the same mask triplet in the case of 3×16-byte entropy masking scheme.

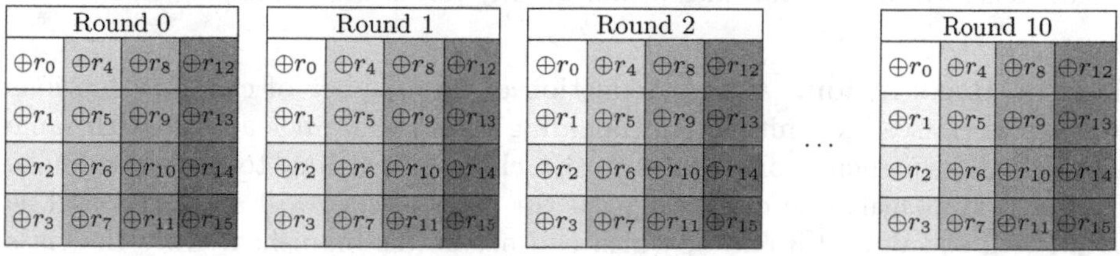

Fig. 5. Positions of the 16 independent mask triplets on the expanded key.

The main difference between those two masking scheme is that we have 16 sets of Hamming distances between 11 bytes ($16 \times 55 = 880$ relations) instead of 11 sets of Hamming distances between 16 bytes (1320 relations) for previous scheme. Using all the information was well enough to retrieve the correct key as sole candidate on our $1,000$ random simulations. But, the fact that the distances relate less bytes at a time alters the tree growth limitation and leads to an average execution time of 31 s compared to less than one second for the other scheme.

Considering one set of 11 related bytes, guessing one value applies a constraint on other bytes of the set by the Hamming distances that relates them. The difference with previous scheme is that those bytes are not in the same round key and do not lead to candidates for one round key. Nevertheless, the known key schedule equations that relate bytes of the expanded key allow an attacker to infer other key bytes from the one guessed. From one set of 11 bytes, one infers candidates for 66 out of the 176 expanded key bytes. A second set that combines well with the first one gives candidates for the whole expanded key.

5 Key Recovery Based on Hamming Distances Collisions

In this section we show how to handle the configuration where an attacker can only recover Boolean information of equality of Hamming distances between key bytes. We focus on the 3×11-byte entropy masking scheme, detailed in Sect. 4.1, as results for the other masking scheme are similar.

5.1 Hamming Distance Classes

Given Boolean information of Hamming distance equalities, one can separate the set of all pairs of key bytes pairs for which the information is known, into classes of identical (but unknown) distances. In the ideal case, all 1320 unknown Hamming distances can be separated in nine classes, one for each possible Hamming distance, without knowing which class corresponds to which distance.

Brute Force. Brute force can be considered with $9! = 362\,880$ possible valuations of the classes. Each valuation leads to a configuration where Hamming distances are known, allowing to apply the key recovery methods depicted in Sect. 4. This high number of combinations might be still feasible, depending on the attacker available information, but greatly raises the processing time.

Classes Recognition. A huge reduction of the number of classes valuations consists in classes recognition. As Hamming distances do not appear with same theoretical frequencies, one can sort the classes according to their cardinals. This should identify the classes, except for pairs of classes 0 and 8, as well as 1 and 7, 2 and 6, and 3 and 5, which can not be distinguished. Only the class of Hamming distance 4 is directly recognizable as the one the most represented.

Once classes are recognized, it remains merely 16 classes – coming from 4 pairwise permutations – that can not be differentiated.

Such recognition is reliable when enough information is used. Table 3 gives simulated percentage of correct classes recognition as defined above with increasing number of round key information used simultaneously.

Table 3. Percentage of correct class recognition as a function of the number of round key information used.

Number of round keys information used	1	2	3	4	...	11
Percentage of correct class recognition	47.4	74.8	86.0	91.5	...	99.9

Class Recognition Simulation Results. When the class recognition is successful, one has to perform 16 key recovery attacks with known Hamming distances like in Sect. 4.

Let's consider an attacker taking the collision information from two consecutive round keys. The class recognition is then correct in 74.8% of cases, and the processing time to generate all valid keys is about 6 s on average. It may happen that some of the 15 wrong valuations that have to be considered lead to some incorrect but valid keys. Table 4 shows the equivalent results of Table 2 where Hamming distances were known. While the results are slightly degraded due to these extra potential false positives, a unique key is still identified in the majority of cases.

Table 4. Results of exploration using two round key information considering the 16 classes valuations.

Number of remaining keys	1	2	3	4	6	8	12
Encountered case/1 000	648	293	1	47	8	2	1

As the execution time is reasonable, cases where classes are not correctly recognized (here 25.2%) can also be considered. Such situation might be detected as giving no valid solution. As the error in the class recognition might be small, one can try to permute sets with close cardinals in order to find the right valuation.

6   Conclusion

We have presented new ways to perform blind side-channel analysis in the presence of Boolean masking. These combined variants, which simultaneously target two areas around two key bytes (not necessarily at the same round), allow to recover key information even when the three masks that apply to m, x and y are independent. This is a major and significant improvement upon single key byte attacks developed in [3].

The maximum likelihood based combined m-y attack recovers the XOR differential between the key bytes but we have observed that it is not that much efficient. On the contrary, its m-x counterpart is much more efficient but can only recover the Hamming distance between the key bytes. We also envisaged an other m-x variant, based on comparison of leakage distributions, which recovers even less information – only whether the Hamming distances between two key bytes pairs are equal – but presents the advantage that the attacker does not need to infer Hamming weights from leakages[5].

Since both variants of our combined m-x attack give a very partial information about the key material, we have studied whether an attacker could nevertheless recover the ciphering key by repeatedly applying those attacks on several key bytes pairs. We demonstrated by simulations that the answer to this question is positive in both masking schemes we considered, and that the attacker does not need to recover the relevant information from all key bytes pairs, but typically from those related to any two successive rounds.

We have also discussed about possible detection of errors on the estimated Hamming distances. We argued that it is easy to detect (a not too large number of) errors of ±1 bit, and observed that these errors are the first to occur with the proximity-driven behavior of higher noise.

As it is important for the developer of secured applications to protect against our attacks, we suggest two non exclusive kinds of countermeasures: (i) a complete full masking of any intermediate value by independent masks, and (ii) any measure that spoils the time alignment (random delays, shuffling,...) and makes harder for the attacker to identify the points of interests on each trace.

References

1. Brier, E., Clavier, C., Olivier, F.: Correlation power analysis with a leakage model. In: Joye, M., Quisquater, J.-J. (eds.) CHES 2004. LNCS, vol. 3156, pp. 16–29. Springer, Heidelberg (2004). https://doi.org/10.1007/978-3-540-28632-5_2
2. Clavier, C., Marion, D., Wurcker, A.: Simple power analysis on AES key expansion revisited. In: Batina, L., Robshaw, M. (eds.) CHES 2014. LNCS, vol. 8731, pp. 279–297. Springer, Heidelberg (2014). https://doi.org/10.1007/978-3-662-44709-3_16
3. Clavier, C., Reynaud, L.: Improved blind side-channel analysis by exploitation of joint distributions of leakages. In: Fischer, W., Homma, N. (eds.) CHES 2017. LNCS, vol. 10529, pp. 24–44. Springer, Cham (2017). https://doi.org/10.1007/978-3-319-66787-4_2
4. Gierlichs, B., Batina, L., Tuyls, P., Preneel, B.: Mutual information analysis. In: Oswald, E., Rohatgi, P. (eds.) CHES 2008. LNCS, vol. 5154, pp. 426–442. Springer, Heidelberg (2008). https://doi.org/10.1007/978-3-540-85053-3_27

---

[5] The leakage function does not even need to be a linear function of the Hamming weights. Though it must be the same in the target areas of all key bytes.

5. Kocher, P., Jaffe, J., Jun, B.: Differential power analysis. In: Wiener, M. (ed.) CRYPTO 1999. LNCS, vol. 1666, pp. 388–397. Springer, Heidelberg (1999). https://doi.org/10.1007/3-540-48405-1_25
6. Le Bouder, H.: Un formalisme unifiant les attaques physiques sur circuits cryptographiques et son exploitation afin de comparer et rechercher de nouvelles attaques. Ph.D. thesis, École Nationale Supérieure des Mines de Saint-Étienne (2014)
7. Linge, Y., Dumas, C., Lambert-Lacroix, S.: Using the joint distributions of a cryptographic function in side channel analysis. In: Prouff, E. (ed.) COSADE 2014. LNCS, vol. 8622, pp. 199–213. Springer, Cham (2014). https://doi.org/10.1007/978-3-319-10175-0_14
8. VanLaven, J., Brehob, M., Compton, K.J.: A computationally feasible SPA attack on AES VIA optimized search. In: Sasaki, R., Qing, S., Okamoto, E., Yoshiura, H. (eds.) SEC 2005. IAICT, vol. 181, pp. 577–588. Springer, Boston, MA (2005). https://doi.org/10.1007/0-387-25660-1_38

Differential Power Analysis of XMSS and SPHINCS

Matthias J. Kannwischer[1,2], Aymeric Genêt[3,4], Denis Butin[1(✉)],
Juliane Krämer[1], and Johannes Buchmann[1]

[1] TU Darmstadt, Darmstadt, Germany
{dbutin,jkraemer,buchmann}@cdc.informatik.tu-darmstadt.de
[2] University of Surrey, Guildford, UK
m.j.kannwischer@surrey.ac.uk
[3] EPFL, Lausanne, Switzerland
aymeric.genet@epfl.ch, aymeric.genet@nagra.com
[4] Kudelski Group, Cheseaux-sur-Lausanne, Switzerland

Abstract. Quantum computing threatens conventional public-key cryptography. In response, standards bodies such as NIST increasingly focus on post-quantum cryptography. In particular, hash-based signature schemes are notable candidates for deployment. No rigorous side-channel analysis of hash-based signature schemes has been conducted so far. This work bridges this gap. We analyse the stateful hash-based signature schemes XMSS and $XMSS^{MT}$, which are currently undergoing standardisation at IETF, as well as SPHINCS—the only practical stateless hash-based scheme. While timing and simple power analysis attacks are unpromising, we show that the differential power analysis resistance of XMSS can be reduced to the differential power analysis resistance of the underlying pseudorandom number generator. This first systematic analysis helps to further increase confidence in XMSS, supporting current standardisation efforts. Furthermore, we show that at least a 32-bit chunk of the SPHINCS secret key can be recovered using a differential power analysis attack due to its stateless construction. We present novel differential power analyses on a SHA-2-based pseudorandom number generator for XMSS and a BLAKE-256-based pseudorandom function for SPHINCS-256 in the Hamming weight model. The first attack is not threatening current versions of XMSS, unless a customised pseudorandom number generator is used. The second one compromises the security of a hardware implementation of SPHINCS-256. Our analysis is supported by a power simulator implementation of SHA-2 for XMSS and a hardware implementation of BLAKE for SPHINCS. We also provide recommendations for XMSS implementers.

Keywords: Post-quantum cryptography · Hash-based signatures
DPA

© Springer International Publishing AG, part of Springer Nature 2018
J. Fan and B. Gierlichs (Eds.): COSADE 2018, LNCS 10815, pp. 168–188, 2018.
https://doi.org/10.1007/978-3-319-89641-0_10

1   Introduction

Due to the wide applicability of Shor's algorithm [29], conventional public-key cryptography (e.g., RSA, DSA, and ECDSA) is vulnerable to attacks using quantum computers. Some cryptographic schemes, known as *post-quantum* [7], are believed to remain safe in the presence of quantum computers. Post-quantum cryptography was already introduced in the 70s, but not deployed at that time. Engineering progress in quantum computing [21] is creating a new sense of urgency. Current standardisation efforts—for instance at NIST [27] and IETF [14]—signal a shift towards real-world use [8]. It is therefore important to further analyse the security of candidate schemes.

In particular, the side-channel resistance of hash-based signature (HBS) schemes has not been evaluated systematically so far. HBS schemes rely on the security of an underlying hash function, and use a binary hash tree structure. While these schemes are conjectured to be "naturally" side-channel resistant [14], a deeper look is desirable to uncover potential weaknesses and increase confidence in them. We provide a side-channel analysis (SCA) of two prominent HBS schemes: XMSS (including its variant XMSS^{MT}) and SPHINCS. We chose them because XMSS is being standardised, SPHINCS is the only practical *stateless* HBS scheme (see Sect. 2 for an explanation of statefulness), and both are recommended by the PQCRYPTO EU project [28].

1.1   Related Work

The side-channel resistance of HBS schemes is rarely addressed. Eisenbarth et al. [11] investigate the side-channel leakage of a customised Merkle-based HBS scheme. Leakage experiments using an AES-based hash function are performed. XMSS is not directly analysed, and only a brief SCA is provided.

For other categories of post-quantum cryptography, SCAs are mainly available for implementations of lattice-based and code-based schemes. In particular, the NTRUEncrypt [20,30] and McEliece [22] schemes have been thoroughly examined. Several differential power analysis (DPA) attacks have been proposed on hash-based message authentication codes (HMACs) based upon SHA-2 [2,23] and SHA-3 [32,33]. However, none of them directly applies to HBS.

We only address purely passive attacks. The fault attack vulnerability of SPHINCS was recently analysed by Castelnovi et al. [9].

1.2   Outline

The remainder of the paper is organised as follows. We start by recalling basics about the schemes under consideration and the more elementary schemes they rely upon: W-OTS$^+$, XMSS, XMSS^{MT}, and SPHINCS (Sect. 2). We next analyse the side-channel resistance of XMSS and XMSS^{MT} (Sect. 3) and describe a DPA on a SHA-2-based pseudorandom number generator (PRNG) which applies to both schemes. SPHINCS-256 is then analysed in the same respect (Sect. 4); we introduce a novel DPA on a BLAKE-256-based pseudorandom function (PRF).

Impact analyses and discussions of implications for implementers appear in both main sections. We then conclude (Sect. 5).

2 XMSS, XMSS^{MT} and SPHINCS

In HBS schemes, many one-time signature key pairs are combined into a single structure, using a binary hash tree. Numerous improvements upon seminal constructions by Lamport [19] and Merkle [25] have culminated in modern schemes such as XMSS [4], its hierarchical variant XMSS^{MT} [15] and SPHINCS [3].

These are the schemes analysed in this paper; in particular, for XMSS and XMSS^{MT}, we examine the recently proposed IETF standard [14]. XMSS has minimal security requirements, since it only requires a second-preimage resistant hash function for its security. XMSS and XMSS^{MT} are *stateful*: after signing, the secret key is updated. If this update is not carried out properly, the security of the cryptographic scheme degrades or vanishes. As a result, extra care is required [24]. Stateful hash-based signature schemes are particularly suited to the use case of software update authentication, where signing frequency is low. SPHINCS is conveniently stateless, but its signatures are significantly larger and speed also suffers.

We start by recalling a one-time signature scheme which is typically not used on its own, but constitutes a cornerstone of these three schemes: W-OTS$^+$ [13]. Due to space limitations, we only describe parts of the schemes relevant for SCA. Self-contained algorithm descriptions and security proofs can be found in the original papers.

2.1 W-OTS$^+$

W-OTS$^+$ improves upon the W-OTS [10]. It is parametrised by the Winternitz parameter $w = 2^\omega$, which enables a time/space trade-off. Large values of w yield small keys and signatures, but slow down the scheme. Given a keyed hash function $f_k : \{0,1\}^n \times \{0,1\}^n \to \{0,1\}^n$, W-OTS$^+$ defines the chaining function c_k^i:

$$c_k^0(x, \mathbf{r}) = x, \qquad c_k^i(x, \mathbf{r}) = f_k(c_k^{i-1}(x, \mathbf{r}) \oplus r_i), \quad \mathbf{r} = (r_1, \ldots, r_j), j > i.$$

We recall the W-OTS$^+$ key generation and signature generation algorithms, which involve secret information and are, thus, relevant for SCA.

W-OTS$^+$ Key Generation. Given the security parameter n and length ℓ, the secret key $\mathbf{X} = (x_0, \ldots, x_{\ell-1}) \in_R \{0,1\}^{n \times \ell}$, the randomisation bitmasks $\mathbf{r} = (r_1, \ldots, r_{w-1}) \in_R \{0,1\}^{n \times w-1}$ and the key $k \in_R \{0,1\}^n$ arc chosen uniformly at random. The public key $\mathbf{Y}$ is computed from $\mathbf{X}$ by applying c_k $(w - 1)$ times:

$$\mathbf{Y} = (y_0, \ldots, y_{\ell-1}) \in \{0,1\}^{n \times \ell}, \quad y_i = c_k^{w-1}(x_i, \mathbf{r}), \quad 0 \le i < \ell.$$

The secret key is $\mathbf{X}$ and the public key is $(\mathbf{Y}, \mathbf{r}, k)$. To compress the public key, $\mathbf{r}$ and k can also be replaced by an n-bit seed to generate $\mathbf{r}$ and k pseudorandomly.

W-OTS$^+$ Signature Generation. Given the secret key $\mathbf{X}$ and the digest $D \in \{0,1\}^n$ of a message M, the digest D is divided into ℓ_1 blocks of w bits each: $D = b_{\ell-1} \parallel \cdots \parallel b_{\ell-\ell_1}$. Using D, a checksum $C = b_{\ell_2-1} \parallel \cdots \parallel b_0$ is calculated. The blocks $b_{\ell-1}, \ldots, b_0$ are then used to calculate the signature:

$$\sigma_{W\text{-}OTS+} = \left(c_k^{b_{\ell-1}}(x_{\ell-1}, \mathbf{r}), \ldots, c_k^{b_1}(x_1, \mathbf{r}), c_k^{b_0}(x_0, \mathbf{r}) \right).$$

2.2 XMSS

XMSS is a stateful digital signature scheme built upon the one-time signature scheme W-OTS (or its optimised version W-OTS$^+$) as a building block. XMSS was introduced by Buchmann et al. in 2011 [4]; it is EU-CMA secure, forward-secure and efficient.

Given the security parameter n, XMSS requires a cryptographic hash function $h : \{0,1\}^{2n} \to \{0,1\}^n$. Denoting H the XMSS tree height, up to 2^H messages can be signed, using as many W-OTS$^+$ key pairs.

XMSS Key Generation. Given H, the key generation algorithm first generates 2^H W-OTS$^+$ key pairs (sk$_{\text{W-OTS+},i}$, pk$_{\text{W-OTS+},i}$), where $0 \le i < 2^H$. The W-OTS$^+$ public keys are then used to construct an XMSS tree. The inner nodes of the XMSS tree are computed as

$$v_h[j] = h\left((v_{h-1}[2j] \oplus b_{l,h}) \parallel (v_{h-1}[2j+1] \oplus b_{r,h})\right),$$

where $b_{l,h}$ and $b_{r,h}$ are *public* randomisation elements derived from a public seed using a PRNG. Each leaf of the XMSS $v_0[i]$ $(0 \le i < 2^H)$ tree is derived from the corresponding W-OTS$^+$ public keys using another XMSS tree, which is called *L-tree*. An L-tree compresses an $n \times \ell$ bit public key to a single n bit value using the same construction for the inner nodes. Since ℓ is not a power of 2 in general, the rightmost leaves of the L-tree are lifted up to form a binary tree.

The XMSS public key is the root of the XMSS tree $v_h[0]$ and the public seed required to generate the randomisation elements in W-OTS$^+$, the XMSS tree, and the L-trees. The XMSS secret key is comprised of all W-OTS$^+$ secret keys sk$_{\text{W-OTS+}}$ and the index s of the next unused leaf (initially $s = 0$). Since storing all W-OTS$^+$ secret keys results in an enormous key ($2^H \cdot \ell \cdot n$ bits), it is recommended to use a PRNG to generate them and just store the n-bit seed.

XMSS Signature Generation. Given the secret key (sk$_{\text{W-OTS+}}$, s) and the digest $D \in \{0,1\}^n$ of a message M, XMSS first computes the W-OTS$^+$ signature $\sigma_{\text{W-OTS+}}$ for M using sk$_{\text{W-OTS+},s}$. It is imperative to increment s in the XMSS secret key to ensure that this one-time key pair is not used again in subsequent signature generations. In addition to pk$_{\text{W-OTS+},s}$, the verifier requires several nodes of the XMSS tree to reconstruct the root of the hash tree. This is achieved by appending the authentication path $A_s = (a_0, \ldots, a_{h-1})$ to the signature, which contains one node in each layer of the hash tree. The a_h are either left or right neighbours of the nodes in the path from $v_0[s]$ to $v_h[0]$:

$$a_h = \begin{cases} v_h[s/2^h - 1], & \text{if } \lfloor s/2^h \rfloor \equiv 1 \pmod 2 \\ v_h[s/2^h + 1], & \text{if } \lfloor s/2^h \rfloor \equiv 0 \pmod 2. \end{cases}$$

The XMSS signature is, thus, $\sigma = (s, \sigma_{\text{W-OTS}^+}, \text{pk}_{\text{W-OTS}^+,s}, A_s)$.

2.3   XMSS^{MT}

While optimised implementations of XMSS provide sufficient performance during signature generation and signature verification, key generation is slow for high trees, e.g., $H > 20$. Since this is problematic in some use cases, an extension of XMSS was proposed using multiple layers of XMSS trees. This tree chaining idea was initially used in the CMSS scheme [6]. Combined with improved distributed signature generation, it resulted in the XMSS^{MT} scheme [15]. It is also specified in the Internet-Draft by Hülsing et al. [14].

A hyper-tree is used. Its upper layers are used to sign the roots of the layers below, and only the lowest layer is used to actually sign messages. Thus, an XMSS^{MT} hyper-tree consists of $T \geq 2$ layers of XMSS trees with heights $H_0, \ldots, H_{T-1}$, where H_0 is the height of the trees at the lowest level. The Internet-Draft further restricts the heights to be equal, i.e., $H_0 = H_1 = \cdots = H_{T-1}$. The W-OTS$^+$ key pairs corresponding to the leaves of layer i are used to sign the roots of the trees on layer $i-1$. The root of layer $T-1$ is the XMSS^{MT} public key. Using XMSS^{MT} is especially sensible if a large number of messages is to be signed. In that case, the use of a PRNG is recommended. Otherwise, the required storage and slow random number generation outweigh the performance gain of XMSS^{MT}.

2.4   SPHINCS

In 2014, Bernstein et al. introduced SPHINCS [3], a practical *stateless* HBS scheme. SPHINCS uses components as XMSS^{MT}, but includes a layer of few-times signatures named HORST beneath the extended Merkle multi-trees, whose instances are pseudorandomly selected to sign messages.

SPHINCS-256. The SPHINCS authors have suggested a standard instantiation for their scheme in [3] that achieves 128 bits of post-quantum security. This instance is called SPHINCS-256 and requires two secret keys $(\text{sk}_1, \text{sk}_2)$ of 32 bytes each. Since SPHINCS-256 is stateless, the hash-based instances within the scheme are referred to with an addressing scheme. The ith W-OTS$^+$ instance at the leaf of the jth sub-tree at layer l is addressed with the binary concatenation of all these indices, i.e., $A(i, j, l) = (l \parallel j \parallel i)$ where the first 4 most significant bits refer to layer l, the next 55 bits to sub-tree j, and the last 5 bits its leaf i.

To sign a given message M, a pseudorandom value R is generated according to M and sk_2. This value represents the selected branch of our hyper-tree, i.e., it allows the computation of the HORST instance address A_{HORST} and the

W-OTS$^+$ addresses A_i^l at each layer $0 \leq l < T$ and for each leaf $0 \leq i < 2^{H_i}$. The secret seeds of these instances are computed using this address. In SPHINCS-256, $\text{SEED}_A = \text{BLAKE-256}(\text{sk}_1 \,\|\, A)$ where BLAKE-256 is the cryptographic hash function [1] used as a PRF. When fed to a PRNG, this seed generates the secret key of the addressed instance.

3   Side-Channel Analysis of XMSS

3.1   Assumptions

To provide a sound analysis of side-channel resistance that is relatively independent of the actual implementation, we first assume that the used hash functions and PRNG suffer no side-channel leakage at all. Obviously, this assumption does not hold for any real world implementations, but it allows us to separate the analysis of the schemes (Sects. 3.2–3.4) from the analysis of the hash function and PRNG (Sect. 3.5). We perform a bottom-up SCA, i.e., we start by analysing W-OTS$^+$ and then extend the analysis to XMSS and XMSS^{MT}. An extended version of this analysis is contained in [16].

3.2   W-OTS$^+$

As illustrated in Fig. 1, the only secret data processed inside W-OTS$^+$ are the secret key parts x_i. The used randomisation elements $\mathbf{r}$ and keys k are public values and, thus, are of no interest for an attacker. The x_i are only used as input to the chaining function c_k.

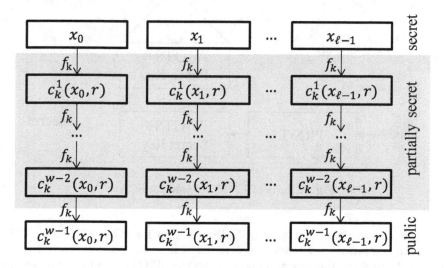

Fig. 1. Parts of W-OTS$^+$ relevant for SCA

To mount a DPA attack, a function depending upon a part of the secret key and a known variable input data must be found. At first sight, $c_k^i(x, \mathbf{r})$ seems to be a perfect target for a power analysis attack. For $i = 1$, the signer calculates $x \oplus r_i$, where x is some secret key block and r_i is a randomisation bitmask known to the adversary. However, this function is only called twice: once during key generation and once during signature generation. This limited number of executions alone prevents the majority of side-channel attacks due to measurement noise. Additionally, r_i is the same for both evaluations. This prevents DPA attacks, which rely upon different inputs to the target function. Also, simple power analysis (SPA) attacks are unable to recover any relevant portion of the secret key.

3.3   XMSS

We just saw that W-OTS$^+$ barely leaks information via power side-channels. Since XMSS is built using many W-OTS$^+$ keys, intuitively XMSS provides this resistance as well. However, one major difference that makes XMSS more vulnerable than W-OTS$^+$ is that W-OTS$^+$ key generation is called much more often during authentication path computation.

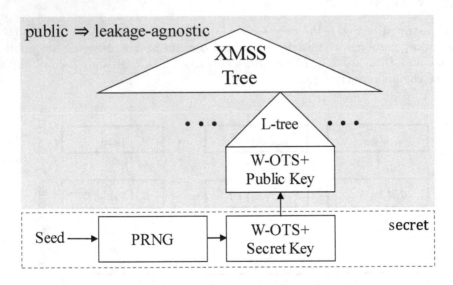

Fig. 2. Parts of XMSS relevant for SCA

Figure 2 summarises the parts of XMSS relevant for SCA. The entire XMSS tree is public and, thus, leakage-agnostic. Even if leaked entirely, the adversary does not learn anything secret. This includes the W-OTS$^+$ public keys and the intermediate values in the L-trees, which are used to compute the XMSS tree leaves. The relevant parts are shown in the lower part of the figure and include the seed used for the pseudorandom W-OTS$^+$ secret key generation and the W-OTS$^+$ secret keys itself.

It was found above that the power leakage resistance of W-OTS$^+$ can mainly be guaranteed because both the key generation and the signature generation are only executed once. For an XMSS signature using the W-OTS$^+$ secret key at index s, the signer first computes the W-OTS$^+$ signature, using sk$_{OTS,s}$, and then the authentication path for $v_0[s]$. The authentication path calculation requires that all other $v_0[i]$ are computed too. While some nodes of the authentication path can be reused, some must be recomputed. Assuming the signer does not reuse nodes at all, we know that, at the time of the signature generation for index s, the sk$_{OTS,s}$ already leaked a few times before.

Assuming the most powerful side-channel adversary [31] who can choose the leakage function arbitrarily and adaptively change it for each signature generation, this leads to a leakage of $2^{H+1} \cdot \lambda$ bits, where λ is a bound for the bits leaked per W-OTS$^+$ key generation and signature generation. Even a small bound λ trivially breaks the security of XMSS for any reasonable choice of H and n. However, in practice such an adversary does not exist. When considering a real-world leakage model, the attack becomes infeasible: During each signature generation the W-OTS$^+$ chaining function is called with the exact same inputs to produce the same W-OTS$^+$ public keys. While this is useful for filtering out noise, which is inevitable in every power analysis attack, the leaked information is still meagre.

When combining this finding with the assumption that the PRNG and hash function have no leakage and the findings above, we find that XMSS has the same leakage as W-OTS$^+$, but the adversary can use the multiple computations to reduce the noise.

3.4   Applicability to XMSS^{MT}

The conclusions we drew so far can be generalised to XMSS^{MT}, since an XMSS^{MT} signature generated using a hyper-tree with T layers can be viewed as T independent XMSS signatures from a side-channel perspective. One major difference is that the W-OTS$^+$ signature generations on the upper layers are executed more than once (if no caching is implemented). Intuitively, this seems to provide more leakage than the single tree variant of XMSS. However, since no relevant leakage could be identified during W-OTS$^+$ signature generation, XMSS^{MT} provides similar side-channel resistance.

3.5   Hash Function and PRNG Side-Channel Resistance

So far, we concluded that W-OTS$^+$, XMSS, and XMSS^{MT} provide strong side-channel resistance, under the assumption that the used hash function and the PRNG are side-channel resistant. Although the actual fulfilment of this requirement is implementation-specific, we now discuss the general side-channel resistance of the used building blocks.

Hash Function. The used hash function is the only function within W-OTS$^+$ which processes secret data. However, a hash function per se cannot be vulnerable or resistant to side-channel attacks, since it can be used in numerous ways which do not necessarily involve a secret key. In the XMSS Internet-Draft [14], the keyed hash function f_k of W-OTS$^+$ is implemented using either a hash function of the SHA-2 or SHA-3 function family using the construction $f_k(x) = f(0^n \parallel k \parallel x)$, where f is SHA-256, SHA-512, SHAKE-128, or SHAKE-256. However, the key k is generated from a public seed, while the actual secret data is x.

Several side-channel attacks, all of which being DPA attacks, have been proposed on both SHA-2 and SHA-3 hash function in the context of HMACs [2,23,32,33]. However, they are not applicable to the W-OTS$^+$ chaining function, since each secret key part is only used with constant randomisation bitmasks (k and r). Additionally, SPA attacks are unable to recover any significant amount of secret key bits due to the absence of conditional branches depending upon the secret key for both SHA-2 and SHA-3. Note that the hash function may be replaced in future XMSS standards. It is thus imperative to analyse whether the replacement still provides similar side-channel resistance.

PRNG. The PRNG which may be used for generating the W-OTS$^+$ secret keys is not specified by the XMSS Internet-Draft [14]. Thus, an implementer may freely choose a secure PRNG which matches the security parameter n.

For $n = 256$ and the SHA-2 hash function family, the XMSS Internet-Draft recommends the use of the following construction to generate a pseudorandom value for the index i from a seed: SHA-256 ($0x000..03 \parallel seed \parallel i$). For other parameters, similar recommended constructions are given.

This construction can be analysed with respect to side-channel attacks building upon the conclusions for the W-OTS$^+$ chaining function. The non-existence of conditional branches depending upon the input of the hash function implies that no SPA can be mounted upon any of the recommended PRNG. However, all constructions are good candidates for DPA attacks, since the hash functions are evaluated for the same seed with different indices.

3.6   DPA Attack on SHA-2 PRNG

To the best of our knowledge, only hash function side-channel resistance in the context of HMAC has been addressed in the literature. We adapt the attack on a SHA-2 HMAC [2] for the recommended XMSS PRNG. We briefly recall the attack by Belaïd et al.:

An HMAC for the message m can be computed by applying a hash function H twice [18]: HMAC(m, k) $= H((k \oplus opad) \parallel H((k \oplus ipad) \parallel m))$. The bitmasks *opad* and *ipad* denote constants $0x5c5c\ldots5c$ and $0x3636\ldots36$. When using a Merkle-Damgård-based hash function, the key is padded to the block length of the hash function (e.g., 512 bits for SHA-256), such that each evaluation of H results in at least 2 evaluations of the compression function cf.

Algorithm 1. SHA-256 compression function cf [26]. Relevant operations for recovering $D^{(0)}$ are highlighted in blue.

1: Input: IV (256 bit), m_i (512 bit)
2: $W_t \leftarrow m_i^{(t)} \quad 0 \leq t \leq 15$
3: $W_t \leftarrow \sigma_1(W_{t-2}) + W_{t-7} + \sigma_0(W_{t-16}) + W_{t-15} \quad 16 \leq t \leq 63$
4: $A \leftarrow IV^{(0)}; B \leftarrow IV^{(1)}; C \leftarrow IV^{(2)}; D \leftarrow IV^{(3)};$
5: $E \leftarrow IV^{(4)}; F \leftarrow IV^{(5)}; G \leftarrow IV^{(6)}; H \leftarrow IV^{(7)};$
6: **for** $t = 0; t < 64; t + +$ **do**
7: $\quad T1 \leftarrow H + \Sigma_1(E) + Ch(E,F,G) + K_t + W_t$
8: $\quad T2 \leftarrow \Sigma_0(A) + Maj(A,B,C)$
9: $\quad H \leftarrow G; \quad G \leftarrow F; \quad F \leftarrow E; \quad E \leftarrow D + T1;$
10: $\quad D \leftarrow C; \quad C \leftarrow B; \quad B \leftarrow A; \quad A \leftarrow T1 + T2$
11: **end for**
12: **return** $[IV^{(0)}+A, \quad IV^{(1)}+B, \quad IV^{(2)}+C, \quad IV^{(3)}+D,$
$\qquad\qquad IV^{(4)}+E, \quad IV^{(5)}+F, \quad IV^{(6)}+G, \quad IV^{(7)}+H]$

The inner hash-evaluation of the HMAC is illustrated in Fig. 3. First, the compression function cf is called with the masked key ($k \oplus ipad$) and the fixed initialisation vector (IV). Then, for each block in the message m, an additional call to cf iteratively combines the resulting IV from the previous iteration with 512 bits of the message m. Since the first evaluation only processes the key, but no variable data, it is not possible to mount a DPA attack on the computations inside. Instead, Belaïd et al. target the second evaluation of cf, which processes the first block of m and the result of the first evaluation of cf, denoted by IV_1. The computations inside cf can be used to entirely recover IV_1 which is enough to forge the inner part of the HMAC.

The actual attack is based upon intermediate values inside the SHA-2 compression function cf shown in Algorithm 1. For definitions of $Ch, Maj, \Sigma_0, \Sigma_1, \sigma_0,$ and σ_1, see [26]. Let $D^{(i)}$ denote the value of D before iteration $t = i$, thus $D^{(0)} = IV_1^{(3)}$. Similarly, $T1^{(i)}$ is the value of $T1$ that was computed during iteration $t = i - 1$. Additionally, let values that are different for each HMAC generation be denoted by bold letters (e.g., $\mathbf{W_t}$), while values that are the same

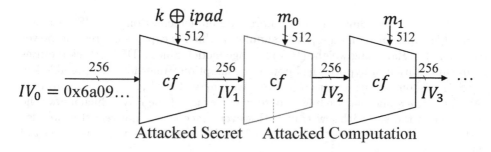

Fig. 3. DPA on SHA-256 HMAC (simplified from [2])

for all generations are in standard letters (e.g., $T1$). To attack the HMAC, the adversary now mounts several DPA attacks building upon each other to recover $A^{(0)}, \ldots, H^{(0)}$. These values are enough to forge the hash output of the inner hash function output for arbitrary message. The outer hash is attacked similarly.

As an illustration, we briefly describe how $D^{(0)}$ can be recovered and refer to [2] for the full attack. We define $\delta^{(1)} := H^{(0)} + \Sigma_1(E^{(0)}) + Ch(E^{(0)}, F^{(0)}, G^{(0)}) + K_0$, i.e., line 7 computes $\mathbf{T1}^{(1)} \leftarrow \delta^{(1)} + \mathbf{W_0}$. A DPA can easily recover $\delta^{(1)}$, since $\delta^{(1)}$ is fixed and $\mathbf{W_t}$ is known and variable. Once the adversary knows $\delta^{(1)}$, they can compute $\mathbf{T1}^{(1)}$ for each known word $\mathbf{W_0}$. The second DPA attack then recovers $D^{(0)}$ from $\mathbf{E}^{(1)} \leftarrow D^{(0)} + \mathbf{T1}^{(1)}$ using known values for $\mathbf{T1}^{(1)}$. Building upon the recovered values of $\mathbf{T1}^{(1)}$, another 7 DPAs in the first and second iteration can be used to recover the values of $A^{(0)}, B^{(0)}, C^{(0)}, E^{(0)}, F^{(0)}, G^{(0)}$ and $H^{(0)}$ (see [2]).

Application to Hash-Based PRNG: To the best of our knowledge, no power analysis attack on hash-based PRNG has been presented so far. However, the HMAC construction above resembles the PRNG suggested by the XMSS Internet-Draft [14] for the generation of W-OTS$^+$ secret keys. Trying to apply the attack of Belaïd et al. [2], we notice that the message words W_0 and W_1, which were used to mount the DPA attack, are always zero for any reasonable parameter choice ($h \leq 448$). If these known values are fixed, a DPA attack does not work.

The attack can be adapted to use $\mathbf{W_{14}}$ and $\mathbf{W_{15}}$ instead, assuming $i < 2^{64}$. The adversary is able to recover $A^{(14)}, \ldots, H^{(14)}$ from the computations in iteration 14 and 15. Although this does not allow to recover IV_1, it is still sufficient to recompute all pseudorandom secret keys, since $W_k = 0$ for $0 \leq k \leq 13$ which consequently means that $A^{(14)}, \ldots, H^{(14)}$ are the same for all values of i.

For our proof-of-concept, we assume that the PRNG is called for uniformly random values between 0 and $2^{64} - 1$. In XMSS it is called for subsequent values which are no bigger than 2^{20}. However, using these parameters, our attack is unable to recover all bits of $A^{(14)}, \ldots, H^{(14)}$. We leave the analysis on how much bits can be recovered for a certain parameter set to future work.

Implementation. To validate that our attack indeed can be used to recover all W-OTS$^+$ secret keys, we created a proof-of-concept implementation of the attack. The source code of our implementation is available [17].

Power Simulation. Since an actual hardware implementation of XMSS was not available, we implemented a power simulator which is capable of creating power traces in the Hamming weight (HW) leakage model. Since a DPA attack requires the computation of hypothetical power consumption values for each possible key hypothesis, our implementation recovers each byte of $A^{(14)}, \ldots, H^{(14)}$ separately. At first, we assume that we have a byte-wise leakage of the HW, which allows the recovery of the key with few traces. However, since this is not realistic, we also extend this to work with the leakage of the HW per 32-bit word using partial DPA.

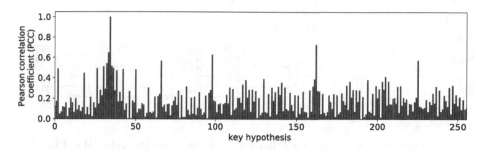

Fig. 4. Maximum PCC of all possible key hypotheses in the 8-bit HW leakage model. The correct sub-key (34) can be easily detected

Some of the DPA used to attack the PRNG target a 32-bit modular addition and some target bitwise AND. They require slightly different hypothesis calculation due to carry handling. For details we refer to our source code [17].

Results. We started evaluating our proposed attack in the 8-bit HW leakage model. Figure 4 illustrates the maximum correlation values of each possible key hypothesis for computing the least significant byte of $\delta^{(15)}$, i.e., this is a DPA on a part of a 32-bit modular addition. We use the Pearson correlation coefficient (PCC) throughout the experiments for this paper. The correct hypothesis results in a correlation of 1.0, which is significantly higher than any other correlation, which allows the recovery of the least significant byte of $\delta^{(15)}$. Correlation values when using physically measured traces will be smaller than 1.0 due to noise. The detection of the correct sub-key will therefore be harder, and, in consequence, may require more traces. Figure 4 also shows that correlation values are small (<0.4) for most key candidates and only higher for 16 key candidates in this experiment. Thus, even if the noise is too high to successfully require the correct sub-key, it still allows a drastic reduction in the search space which can then be enumerated to find the correct key.

Next, we wanted to evaluate the success probability of the entire attack, which includes 9 DPA on 32-bit operation, i.e., 36 DPA when using the 8-bit HW leakage model. The success rates of the single DPA are not independent of each other due to two reasons: Firstly, when attacking addition, the higher significant bytes can only be recovered reliably if the lower significant byte key guesses are correct, since only then we can correctly calculate the carry bits. Secondly, the attacked operations depend on each other, e.g., the DPA attack on $D^{(14)}$ requires that the DPA on $\delta^{(15)}$ was successful. Thus, the success rate of the entire attack is certainly smaller than for each individual DPA.

Figure 5 shows the success rate of the full key recovery attack using different numbers of traces, where one trace corresponds to an execution of the PRNG with an uniformly random index between 0 and $2^{64} - 1$. When using only $T = 8$ traces per experiment, the recovery failed for 100% of our trials, whereas using $T = 10$ already resulted in a success probability of almost 60%. This further increased to 93.3% for $T = 512$. However, we noticed that the DPA on AND

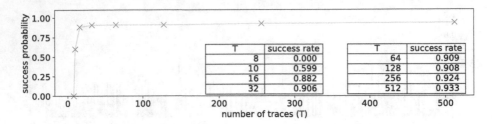

Fig. 5. Success rate of the full DPA key recovery attack on the vulnerable PRNG in the 8-bit HW leakage model

operations always failed to recover the key if the sub-key is equal to zero. This is because for a zero key value the calculated value always has a HW of zero. Since this is a constant value, no correlation can be found with DPA. However, this can be detected by the adversary, and they can conjecture that the key must be zero. We did not implement this optimisation in our proof-of-concept implementation, thus, since the attacked values are uniformly distributed and we have a total of 16 DPA on AND, the probability of having all key bytes $\neq 0$ is $\left(\frac{255}{256}\right)^{16} \approx 0.939$. Therefore, we conjecture that the best achievable success rate in this set-up is about 93.9%, no matter how many traces are used. The actual numbers from these experiments can only provide a lower bound, since our traces contain no noise. In real-world measurements, the required number of traces is larger depending on noise.

Partial DPA. So far, we assumed that the implementation leaks the HW of each byte separately, such that we can mount independent DPA upon them. However, since SHA-2 only involves 32-bit arithmetic, a byte-wise implementation is unrealistic. Most implementations will use 32-bit words and, thus, only leak the HW of the entire words.

Luckily, the strategy can be adapted and still be used to recover each byte separately using partial DPA [2], although requiring a much higher number of traces. We integrated this in our proof-of-concept implementation and were able to reproduce the results of [2].

3.7   Impact

Our proof-of-concept implementation shows that if the SHA-2-based PRNG ($\texttt{SHA-256}\,(0x000..03 \parallel seed \parallel i)$) is called for indices i which vary in 64 bits, an adversary is able to recover an intermediate value which allows one to calculate the output of the PRNG for arbitrary indices. Applied to XMSS and XMSS^{MT}, this allows an adversary to recover all W-OTS$^+$ secret keys which trivially compromises the security of the scheme.

However, in both schemes, the PRNG is never called for indices larger than 2^{20}, which prevents the presented attack. If a different PRNG is used, it may be vulnerable to our attack with current XMSS parameters. For example, if the

PRNG is modified to SHA-256 ($0x000..03 \parallel seed \parallel$ SHA-256(i)), the inner hash evaluation results in uniformly random inputs to the outer hash evaluation which makes our attack practical. This emphasises that if a different PRNG is used, not only the black-box security needs to be considered, but also its side-channel resistance.

3.8 Recommendations

Since XMSS is currently being standardised, practical implementations which need to be protected against power analysis attacks are likely to be created soon. Our results suggest that the most critical part to protect is the PRNG. While the proposed XMSS standard leaves open the actual choice of the PRNG, we showed that the PRNG selection is critical for side-channel resistance. It is crucial to use a PRNG which is well-studied with respect to side-channel attacks, like the one recommended by the XMSS Internet-Draft.

We also found that optimised authentication path computation (e.g., using the BDS algorithm [5]) greatly decreases the side-channel leakage of XMSS because it minimises the accesses to the secret keys and, consequently, executions of the PRNG. Although this optimisation is deemed optional by the XMSS Internet-Draft, every implementation should use it.

Timing attacks were not discussed in this paper, but protecting implementations against them is also necessary. Since constant time implementations exist for all used hash functions, PRNGs, and PRFs, protecting XMSS and SPHINCS against such attacks is straightforward.

4 SPHINCS-256: A DPA on BLAKE

In the previous section, we analysed the side-channel resistance of XMSS and $XMSS^{MT}$ and presented a DPA attack on a SHA-256-based PRNG which is used within both XMSS and $XMSS^{MT}$. To extend the analysis, we evaluate SPHINCS-256 in the same regard.

SPHINCS relies on $XMSS^{MT}$, HORST, and a stateless way of addressing hash-based instances within the scheme. Since the HORST hash tree construction does not leak anything about its secret key, we can assume this component to be side-channel resistant. Moreover, $XMSS^{MT}$ can also be assumed secure by the previous analysis. This leaves us only with the stateless way of computing the PRNG seeds, which we now analyse. This analysis was initially studied in [12].

SPHINCS-256 PRF. In SPHINCS-256, the W-OTS$^+$ and HORST secret seeds are generated with BLAKE-256($sk_1 \parallel A$) where $sk_1 \in \{0,1\}^{256}$ is the SPHINCS secret key, $A \in \{0,1\}^{64}$ the address of the instance, and BLAKE-256 the hash function [1]. Recovering sk_1 would therefore result in a total security break. We now present a 6-DPA attack on the BLAKE hash function in the context of SPHINCS-256 that recovers one 32-bit chunk of the secret key sk_1.

4.1 DPA

The BLAKE-256 compression procedure takes 12 similar rounds during which the input is mixed. Similarly as in Sect. 3, the goal is to subsequently recover intermediate values at certain points in the procedure, to eventually recover one secret chunk. As these values are mixed with variable values early in the procedure, the DPAs focus on the first two rounds. Within SPHINCS-256, the first round is summarised in Algorithm 2. Here, the values v_i for $0 \leq i < 15$ are initialised with known constant values. A general mixing subroutine Mix involved in these steps is shown in Algorithm 3. Here, $M_i \in \{0,1\}^{32}$ for $0 \leq i < 15$ is a chunk of the input padded with a constant and known padding. The function $\sigma_z(i)$ is a permutation that depends on the round $0 \leq z < 12$. Again, the values of C_i for $0 \leq i < 15$ are given constants.

Algorithm 2. Round $z = 0$ of BLAKE-256 compression algorithm [1].

Input: $(s_0, \ldots, s_7)$—secret key sk_1 split into 8 chunks of 32 bits each
Input: (a_0, a_1)—address A split into two chunks of 32 bits each

1: $\mathtt{Mix}(v_0, v_4, v_8, v_{12}; s_0, s_1)$ 5: $\mathtt{Mix}(v_0, v_5, v_{10}, v_{15}; a_0, a_1)$
2: $\mathtt{Mix}(v_1, v_5, v_9, v_{13}; s_2, s_3)$ 6: $\mathtt{Mix}(v_1, v_6, v_{11}, v_{12}; \texttt{0x80000000}, \texttt{0x00000000})$
3: $\mathtt{Mix}(v_2, v_6, v_{10}, v_{14}; s_4, s_5)$ 7: $\mathtt{Mix}(v_2, v_7, v_8, v_{13}; \texttt{0x00000000}, \texttt{0x00000001})$
4: $\mathtt{Mix}(v_3, v_7, v_{11}, v_{15}; s_6, s_7)$ 8: $\mathtt{Mix}(v_3, v_4, v_9, v_{14}; \texttt{0x00000000}, \texttt{0x00000140})$

Algorithm 3. Mix procedure involved in Algorithm 2.

Input: (v_a, v_b, v_c, v_d)—intermediate values of 32 bits each
Input: $(M_{\sigma_z(e)}, M_{\sigma_z(e+1)})$—hash function input chunks of 32 bits each

1: $v_a \leftarrow (v_a + v_b) + (M_{\sigma_z(e)} \oplus C_{\sigma_z(e+1)})$ 5: $v_a \leftarrow (v_a + v_b) + (M_{\sigma_z(e+1)} \oplus C_{\sigma_z(e)})$
2: $v_d \leftarrow (v_d \oplus v_a) \lll 16$ 6: $v_d \leftarrow (v_d \oplus v_a) \lll 8$
3: $v_c \leftarrow v_c + v_d$ 7: $v_c \leftarrow v_c + v_d$
4: $v_b \leftarrow (v_b \oplus v_c) \lll 12$ 8: $v_b \leftarrow (v_b \oplus v_c) \lll 7$

In Algorithm 2, line 5 involves v_0, v_5, v_{10}, and v_{15}, which all respectively depend on two constant chunks of sk_1, and the address. When the Mix procedure is unrolled, the operation $v_0 \leftarrow (v_0 + v_5) + (a_0 \oplus C_9)$ at line 1 involves $(v_0 + v_5)$, and $(a_0 \oplus C_9)$: the first half of the address A masked with a constant. By targeting this addition, we can recover $(v_0 + v_5)$ with a first DPA. Once recovered, the following values for v_5, v_{10}, and v_{15} can be consecutively recovered with additional DPAs. Since the rest of the Mix procedure does not involve any other unknown value, and since these values are not mixed again during round 0, they are, therefore, all known at the beginning of round 1.

On round 1 of the BLAKE-256 compression algorithm, $\mathtt{Mix}(v_1, v_5, v_9, v_{13}; s_4, s_5)$ is called. Line 1 in Algorithm 3 for this call involves v_5 which has been recovered from before, and v_1 which can be recovered with a fifth DPA. Finally, a sixth DPA on $(v_1 + v_5) + (s_4 \oplus C_5)$ can recover s_4, which consists of one chunk of 32 bits of the secret key sk_1.

Setup and Implementation. The SCA was performed on an Arduino Due micro-controller, based on the Atmel SAM3X8E Cortex-M3 CPU. Power consumption was collected by placing a local near-field probe on the chip at the position shown in Fig. 6. The attack considers the BLAKE-256 reference implementation [1] with an additional assumption: the addition of $(v_a + v_b)$ at lines 1 and 4 in Algorithm 3 is performed before the rest. This makes the recovery of v_a or v_b alone harder, but should not affect our results. We provide the code that was used for evaluating the attack at [17].

Fig. 6. Position of an EM probe on a SAM3X8E Cortex-M3 microcontroller at which strong EM radiations could be collected

4.2 Real-Device Analysis and Results

To confirm the practicality of the attack, we performed the first two DPAs of our attack on real traces. We collected $t = 10000$ different traces of the two targeted operations, where the secret key sk_1 was fixed and the addresses A were drawn uniformly at random. This number can be obtained by signing around 2000 different messages, as BLAKE-256 is called on 7 different layers with a different a_0 for a single signature. We use the HW leakage model.

We evaluated the relation between the power traces and the guesses on, first, $(v_0 + v_5)$, and, then, on v_{15}, using Pearson's correlation with a partial DPA on

16 bits, as explained in Sect. 3. The leakages of both the addition and the XOR operation are shown in Fig. 7. The upper plots show the main correlation peaks of 1000 guesses on the most significant bits of the targeted value, while the lower plots show the power consumption average.

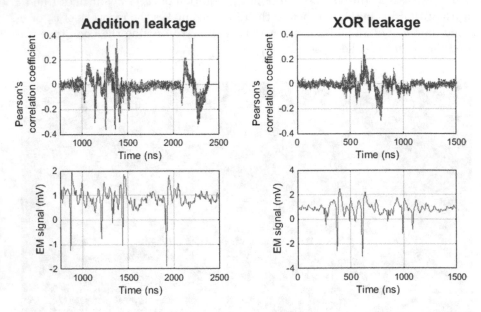

Fig. 7. Power traces average and main PCC peaks on the first half of the targeted values for the addition and XOR operations ($t = 10000$)

By computing the maximum PCC of the 2^{16} possible values for the most significant bits of $v_0 + v_5$ (in the case of the addition) and v_{15} (in the case of the XOR operation) we obtain Fig. 8. In both cases, the candidate with the bigger correlation factor in *absolute value* always happens to be the right value. Similar results were found with the least significant bits, which confirms that the overall attack can be successfully mounted, as the other DPAs target the same kind of operations.

4.3   Impact

The described attack recovers s_4, the fifth 32-bit chunk of sk_1. This makes the stateless construction of SPHINCS-256 vulnerable to DPA. Recovering this chunk potentially leads to the recovery of other chunks, but additional investigation is required.

4.4   Countermeasures

In order to mitigate the effect of this attack, we suggest *hiding* the order of the Mix procedures. During a BLAKE-256 round, the first four calls—as well as the

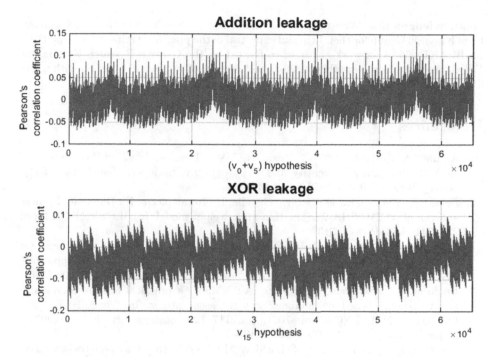

Fig. 8. Maximum PCC of all possible hypotheses on the first half of the targeted values. On the upper plot (addition), the most positively correlated value corresponds to the correct half of $(v_0 + v_5)$, while the lower plot (XOR), the most negatively correlated value corresponds to the correct half of v_{15}

next four—do not depend on each other. Their order can thus be rearranged randomly. This forces an attacker to synchronise the collected traces, making the DPAs more complex.

5   Conclusion

In this paper, we analysed the side-channel resistance of two modern HBS schemes, XMSS and SPHINCS, with a focus on DPA resistance. We presented a novel DPA vulnerability of a SHA-2-based PRNG for XMSS, as well as an attack on the BLAKE-256-based PRF used within SPHINCS-256. While the first attack is not threatening current versions of XMSS, the second one is practical for the actual parameters of SPHINCS-256.

Besides these two found vulnerabilities, we performed a thorough analysis of the building blocks of both XMSS and SPHINCS. Our results confirm the conjecture that XMSS provides strong protection against differential power analysis attacks. This further increases the confidence in the security of stateful HBS schemes, which contributes to a rigorous standardisation process.

Acknowledgments. We would like to thank Hervé Pelletier and Roman Korkikian from Kudelski Group for their help and expertise in the practical verification of the DPA on BLAKE-256. This work has been co-funded by the German Research Foundation (DFG) as part of project BU 630/28-1, and as part of projects P1 and S6 within the CRC 1119 CROSSING.

References

1. Aumasson, J.-P., Meier, W., Phan, R.C.-W., Henzen, L.: The Hash Function BLAKE. Information Security and Cryptography. Springer, Heidelberg (2014). https://doi.org/10.1007/978-3-662-44757-4
2. Belaïd, S., Bettale, L., Dottax, E., Genelle, L., Rondepierre, F.: Differential power analysis of HMAC SHA-2 in the Hamming weight model. In: SECRYPT 2013, pp. 230–241. SciTePress (2013)
3. Bernstein, D.J., et al.: SPHINCS: practical stateless hash-based signatures. In: Oswald, E., Fischlin, M. (eds.) EUROCRYPT 2015. LNCS, vol. 9056, pp. 368–397. Springer, Heidelberg (2015). https://doi.org/10.1007/978-3-662-46800-5_15
4. Buchmann, J., Dahmen, E., Hülsing, A.: XMSS - a practical forward secure signature scheme based on minimal security assumptions. In: Yang, B.-Y. (ed.) PQCrypto 2011. LNCS, vol. 7071, pp. 117–129. Springer, Heidelberg (2011). https://doi.org/10.1007/978-3-642-25405-5_8
5. Buchmann, J., Dahmen, E., Schneider, M.: Merkle tree traversal revisited. In: Buchmann, J., Ding, J. (eds.) PQCrypto 2008. LNCS, vol. 5299, pp. 63–78. Springer, Heidelberg (2008). https://doi.org/10.1007/978-3-540-88403-3_5
6. Buchmann, J., García, L.C.C., Dahmen, E., Döring, M., Klintsevich, E.: CMSS – an improved Merkle signature scheme. In: Barua, R., Lange, T. (eds.) INDOCRYPT 2006. LNCS, vol. 4329, pp. 349–363. Springer, Heidelberg (2006). https://doi.org/10.1007/11941378_25
7. Buchmann, J.A., Lauter, K.E., Mosca, M.: Postquantum cryptography – state of the art. IEEE Secur. Priv. **15**(4), 12–13 (2017)
8. Butin, D.: Hash-based signatures: state of play. IEEE Secur. Priv. **15**(4), 37–43 (2017)
9. Castelnovi, L., Martinelli, A., Prest, T.: Grafting trees: a fault attack against the SPHINCS framework. Cryptology ePrint Archive, Report 2018/102 (2018). https://eprint.iacr.org/2018/102
10. Dods, C., Smart, N.P., Stam, M.: Hash based digital signature schemes. In: Smart, N.P. (ed.) Cryptography and Coding 2005. LNCS, vol. 3796, pp. 96–115. Springer, Heidelberg (2005). https://doi.org/10.1007/11586821_8
11. Eisenbarth, T., von Maurich, I., Ye, X.: Faster hash-based signatures with bounded leakage. In: Lange, T., Lauter, K., Lisoněk, P. (eds.) SAC 2013. LNCS, vol. 8282, pp. 223–243. Springer, Heidelberg (2014). https://doi.org/10.1007/978-3-662-43414-7_12
12. Genêt, A.: Hardware attacks against hash-based cryptographic algorithms. Technical report, École polytechnique fédérale de Lausanne (2017). Master thesis
13. Hülsing, A.: W-OTS+ – shorter signatures for hash-based signature schemes. In: Youssef, A., Nitaj, A., Hassanien, A.E. (eds.) AFRICACRYPT 2013. LNCS, vol. 7918, pp. 173–188. Springer, Heidelberg (2013). https://doi.org/10.1007/978-3-642-38553-7_10

14. Hülsing, A., Butin, D., Gazdag, S., Rijneveld, J., Mohaisen, A.: Internet-draft: XMSS: extended hash-based signatures (2018). https://datatracker.ietf.org/doc/draft-irtf-cfrg-xmss-hash-based-signatures/
15. Hülsing, A., Rausch, L., Buchmann, J.: Optimal parameters for $XMSS^{MT}$. In: Cuzzocrea, A., Kittl, C., Simos, D.E., Weippl, E., Xu, L. (eds.) CD-ARES 2013. LNCS, vol. 8128, pp. 194–208. Springer, Heidelberg (2013). https://doi.org/10.1007/978-3-642-40588-4_14
16. Kannwischer, M.J.: Physical attack vulnerability of hash-based signature schemes. Technical report, Technische Universität Darmstadt (2017), Master thesis. https://www.cdc.informatik.tu-darmstadt.de/fileadmin/user_upload/Group_CDC/Documents/theses/Matthias_Kannwischer.master.pdf
17. Kannwischer, M.J., Genêt, A., Butin, D., Krämer, J., Buchmann, J.: GitHub repositories for DPA code of SHA-256 PRNG and BLAKE-256 PRF. https://github.com/hbs-sca
18. Krawczyk, H., Bellare, M., Canetti, R.: HMAC: Keyed-hashing for message authentication. RFC 2104 (1997). http://www.ietf.org/rfc/rfc2104.txt
19. Lamport, L.: Constructing digital signatures from a one way function. Technical report, SRI International CSL (1979). https://www.microsoft.com/en-us/research/publication/constructing-digital-signatures-one-way-function/
20. Lee, M., Song, J.E., Choi, D., Han, D.: Countermeasures against power analysis attacks for the NTRU public key cryptosystem. IEICE Trans. **93-A**(1), 153–163 (2010)
21. Maurand, R., Jehl, X., Kotekar-Patil, D., Corna, A., Bohuslavskyi, H., Laviéville, R., Hutin, L., Barraud, S., Vinet, M., Sanquer, M., De Franceschi, S.: A CMOS silicon spin qubit. Nat. Commun. **7**, 13575 (2016)
22. von Maurich, I., Güneysu, T.: Towards side-channel resistant implementations of QC-MDPC McEliece encryption on constrained devices. In: Mosca, M. (ed.) PQCrypto 2014. LNCS, vol. 8772, pp. 266–282. Springer, Cham (2014). https://doi.org/10.1007/978-3-319-11659-4_16
23. McEvoy, R., Tunstall, M., Murphy, C.C., Marnane, W.P.: Differential power analysis of HMAC based on SHA-2, and countermeasures. In: Kim, S., Yung, M., Lee, H.-W. (eds.) WISA 2007. LNCS, vol. 4867, pp. 317–332. Springer, Heidelberg (2007). https://doi.org/10.1007/978-3-540-77535-5_23
24. McGrew, D., Kampanakis, P., Fluhrer, S., Gazdag, S.-L., Butin, D., Buchmann, J.: State management for hash-based signatures. In: Chen, L., McGrew, D., Mitchell, C. (eds.) SSR 2016. LNCS, vol. 10074, pp. 244–260. Springer, Cham (2016). https://doi.org/10.1007/978-3-319-49100-4_11
25. Merkle, R.C.: A certified digital signature. In: Brassard, G. (ed.) CRYPTO 1989. LNCS, vol. 435, pp. 218–238. Springer, New York (1990). https://doi.org/10.1007/0-387-34805-0_21
26. National Institute of Standards and Technology: FIPS PUB 180-4: Secure hash standard (2015). http://nvlpubs.nist.gov/nistpubs/FIPS/NIST.FIPS.180-4.pdf
27. NIST computer security division: Post-quantum cryptography standardization – call for proposals announcement (2017). https://csrc.nist.gov/Projects/Post-Quantum-Cryptography/Post-Quantum-Cryptography-Standardization
28. PQCRYPTO Project: Initial recommendations of long-term secure post-quantum systems (2015). https://pqcrypto.eu.org/docs/initial-recommendations.pdf
29. Shor, P.W.: Polynomial-time algorithms for prime factorization and discrete logarithms on a quantum computer. SIAM J. Comput. **26**(5), 1484–1509 (1997)

30. Silverman, J.H., Whyte, W.: Timing attacks on NTRUEncrypt via variation in the number of hash calls. In: Abe, M. (ed.) CT-RSA 2007. LNCS, vol. 4377, pp. 208–224. Springer, Heidelberg (2006). https://doi.org/10.1007/11967668_14
31. Standaert, F., Pereira, O., Yu, Y., Quisquater, J., Yung, M., Oswald, E.: Leakage resilient cryptography in practice. In: Sadeghi, A.R., Naccache, D. (eds.) Towards Hardware-Intrinsic Security-Foundations and Practice. Information Security and Cryptography, pp. 99–134. Springer, Heidelberg (2010). https://doi.org/10.1007/978-3-642-14452-3_5
32. Taha, M., Schaumont, P.: Differential power analysis of MAC-Keccak at any keylength. In: Sakiyama, K., Terada, M. (eds.) IWSEC 2013. LNCS, vol. 8231, pp. 68–82. Springer, Heidelberg (2013). https://doi.org/10.1007/978-3-642-41383-4_5
33. Zohner, M., Kasper, M., Stöttinger, M., Huss, S.A.: Side channel analysis of the SHA-3 finalists. In: DATE 2012, pp. 1012–1017. IEEE (2012)

Path Leaks of HTTPS Side-Channel
by Cookie Injection

Fuqing Chen[1], Haixin Duan[1(✉)], Xiaofeng Zheng[1],
Jian Jiang[2], and Jianjun Chen[1]

[1] Tsinghua University, Beijing, China
{cfq15,duanhx,zhengxf12,chenjj13}@tsinghua.edu.cn
[2] University of California, Berkeley, CA, USA
jiangjian@berkeley.edu

Abstract. The TLS protocol is supposed to provide confidentiality to communication channel, preventing active and passive network attacks. However, researchers have presented several side-channel attacks against TLS protected communications, due to protocol design flaws or implementation problems. We present a new side-channel attack against HTTPS (HTTP over TLS) by exploiting cookie injection. Taking advantage of cookie's weak Same Origin Policy (SOP), an attacker can inject arbitrary cookies into a victim's browser if a website is not fully protected by HTTP Strict Transport Security (HSTS), the injected cookies can then be used to infer sensitive information of encrypted traffic initiated by the victim. We show two such side-channel attacks. The first allows the attacker to identify whether the victim is visiting a known sensitive URL or not. The second is able to reveal the full path of unknown URLs visited by the victim, exploiting cookie-path matching vulnerabilities in Internet Explorer, Edge, Safari, etc. With experiments, we investigate several popular cloud storage services and demonstrate that most of them (including Google Drive and Dropbox) are vulnerable to such attacks. The issues we discovered in Internet Explorer, Edge and Safari are also acknowledged by Microsoft (MSRC Case 39133, will be fixed in future version) and Apple (Case 666783646, has been fixed). Finally, we discuss potential defense and mitigation against these attacks.

Keywords: Privacy · Side-channel attack · HTTPS
Cloud storage service · Path leaks · Cookie

1 Introduction

Cloud storage services, such as Dropbox or Amazon Cloud Drive, are widely used because of their convenience to share images or some sensitive content among friends. Anyone who knows the shared links can get the access to the private content. In order to protect the owner's privacy, cloud service providers often use a hashed-string like path to prevent attackers from enumerating the links. Additionally, most of shared services are protected by HTTPS, which is assumed

© Springer International Publishing AG, part of Springer Nature 2018
J. Fan and B. Gierlichs (Eds.): COSADE 2018, LNCS 10815, pp. 189–203, 2018.
https://doi.org/10.1007/978-3-319-89641-0_11

to prevent the traffic from passive monitoring and Man-In-The-Middle (MITM) attacks against leakage of the content.

However, HTTPS suffers from a variety of side-channel attacks. Attackers can leverage information leaked by HTTPS traffic, including timing and length of ciphertext, to recover some secret data believed to be protected by TLS. The first family of attacks, such as CRIME [13] and BREACH [14], exploit information leakage in TLS compression to uncover HTTPS secrets (e.g. session cookies and CSRF tokens). The second family of attacks use traffic analysis with statistical algorithm to recover user's browsing privacy [9,10].

In this study, we propose a new HTTPS side-channel attack which can allow MITM attackers to infer the request path of encrypted traffic by injecting carefully crafted cookies. The fundamental problem is that the notion of "origin" regarding cookies [1] is different from the standard web "origin" [3] - cookies are not separated between different schemes like HTTP and HTTPS. Therefore, an MITM attacker can inject cookies from HTTP sessions into HTTPS sessions and infer the request path of encrypted traffic, by monitoring the size of HTTPS requests. In practice, this new attack can be realized in such two forms:

1. **Known Path Identification.** Before a victim's browser visits a known HTTPS URL, an MITM attacker intentionally injects a large probe cookie whose path matches the requested path through HTTP sessions. When the victim visits the HTTPS URL, the probe cookie would also be included in an HTTPS request and the size of this HTTPS request is obviously different from other traffic. On the basis of this trick, the attacker can easily find the correlations between the TLS record and request-URL, which leads to user privacy leakage, or even some other attacks (e.g. HTTPS Bicycle [8]).
2. **Unknown Path Inference.** Moreover, we identify some popular browsers (including IE, Edge, Safari) vulnerabilities in cookie path-matching. Combined with these vulnerabilities, the attacker can even infer the unknown request path from HTTPS traffic. We analyze several famous cloud storage services and demonstrate that most of them (including Google Drive and Dropbox) are vulnerable to such attacks. The attacker can recover the private or selectively shared files stored in cloud storage previously believed to be protected by HTTPS. We reported these browser vulnerabilities to Microsoft and Apple, they confirmed our report and planned to fix them in a future version.

Our study shows that despite encryption, HTTPS side-channel attack with cookie injection poses a serious threat to user's security and privacy (e.g., the share link, thumbnail link, shopping history).

2   Background

2.1   Cookies

Cookies are associated meta-data sent from web server and stored in client browser for state management [1]. Web servers usually determine the users' identification and session status based on cookies they set before. Beside the mandatory name and value attributes, a cookie has six optional attributes: Expires and Max-Age indicating the maximum lifetime of the cookie; Domain and Path specifying its scope; Secure flag limiting it only transmitted over HTTPS connections, and HttpOnly preventing client side scripts from reading the cookie.

To store the state, the origin server sets a cookie by including a Set-Cookie header in an HTTP response. In subsequent request headers, the user agent includes all unexpired cookies whose domains and paths match the requested URL, excluding those marked as Secure from the inclusion in an HTTP request.

The SOP is an important concept in the web application security model, guarding the web content being accessed from different origins. An origin is defined as a combination of scheme, hostname and port number [3]. However, the security policy for cookies is not as stringent as the classic SOP. Cookies from different schemes (e.g., HTTP and HTTPS) are not isolated, that is, cookies from the same domain but different schemes will be stored in the same cookie jar.

2.2   Cookie Path

The Path attribute limits the scope of each cookie to a set of paths [1]. If the server omits the Path attribute, the user agent will use the "directory" of the request-URI's path component as the default value. The user agent will include the cookie in a HTTP request only if the cookie's Path attribute matches the path portion of the request-URI, where the "/" character is used as a directory separator.

Although seemingly useful for isolating cookies between different paths within a given host, the path attribute cannot be relied on for security. There is a critical disconnection between cookies set and read. Both JavaScript in browser and web servers can set the value for the Name/Domain/Path attributes, but only name-value pairs are presented to servers. Moreover, the writer can specify arbitrary value for the Path attribute, not limited by the URL of the writer's context.

2.3   Path-Match

When a browser requests a URL, it will look up its cookies storage for all matching cookies. According to RFC 6265, only cookies whose Domain and Path attributes matched with the request-URL will be included in the request Header.

Because "/" is interpreted as a directory separator, the cookie-path is a "block prefix" of request-path. That is, the path string and the URL should be in divided into blocks separated by "/" and be matched block by block, instead of character by character. For example, when a browser tries to access https://www.example.com/share/token/image.jpg and it has two cookies in storage:

```
cookie: a=1; domain=.example.com; path=/share;
cookie: b=2; domain=.example.com; path=/share/t;
```

Only the first cookie is supposed to be included, because the path of the requested URL is not the subdirectory of cookie b. So, the request header should look like:

```
GET / HTTP/1.1
Cookie: a=1
```

2.4   Cookie Injection Attack

It is a known vulnerability that cookies can be injected by HTTP response into subsequent HTTPS request, and from one domain to another related domain. The root cause is that: the integrity of cookies can't be protected well by loosely-defined SOP of cookies. The MITM attackers even temporarily on an HTTP session can inject the crafted cookies from HTTP into HTTPS and then overwrite or shadow legitimate cookies, according to [5]. In 2015, Zheng et al. [7] conducted in-depth and real-world empirical assessment of cookie injection attacks in cookie practices. Their study showed that most websites are potentially susceptible to cookie injection attacks by network attackers.

2.5   TLS Leaks Length

The TLS protocol was designed to provide privacy and data integrity between two communicating applications. However, its specification [2] has an explicit warning about traffic analysis, because the type and length of a record are not protected by encryption. Indeed the basic building block of TLS, the TLS Ciphertext record, transmits the Content type, Version and Length of the record in clear. The MITM observer could easily reconstruct the length. Many attacks against TLS exploit the issue of TLS leaking length [10, 13, 14]. This length leak is the major ingredient in establishing compression side-channel attacks. In our study, we use the information of length leaked by TLS for traffic analysis.

3   Attacks

According to the cookie specification [1], cookies lack integrity and are not separated between different schemes like HTTP and HTTPS. The active MITM attacker at unsafe networks like open wireless networks, who is able to manipulate network traffic, can inject arbitrary cookies from HTTP session into victim's browsers, and these cookies will be attached to subsequent HTTPS requests when the domains and paths of cookies match the request-URL.

Leveraging this feature of cookie, an MITM attacker can inject large crafted cookies from HTTP sessions and monitor the size of HTTPS requests. If the cookie path matches the path of an HTTPS request-URL, the size of HTTPS request will increase obviously, that enables the side-channel attacker to infer sensitive information of request-URL from encrypted traffic.

We identify two forms of HTTPS side-channel attack. (a) **Known path identification**, which allows an attacker to identify whether a victim is visiting a known HTTPS URL. (b) **Unknown path inference**, which allows an attacker to infer an unknown URL included in HTTPS request. We investigate 5 popular browsers, as shown in Table 1. The first attack works in all browsers, and the second one works in 3 out of 5 browsers.

Table 1. Assessment of browsers vulnerabilities

Browsers	Vulnerable to known path identification attack?	Vulnerable to unknown path inference attack?
Chrome	Yes	No
Firefox	Yes	No
Safari	Yes	Yes[a]
IE	Yes	Yes
Edge	Yes	Yes

[a]Safari before version 10 is vulnerable to unknown path inference attack.

3.1 Known Path Identification

Among some existing attack methods, determining the correlations between the TLS record and request-URL is a prerequisite for the attack. Guido shows how an attacker can identify the length of personal data, such as password and GPS coordinates, after gaining the correlation between login requests and TLS records by fingerprinting method [8]. Previous studies focused on complex statistical approach for web request identification within HTTPS traffic [9,10]. With the attack we propose, the correlations can be determined more effectively and accurately.

At first an attacker injects a large size of probe cookie, whose path is carefully constructed, into the victim through HTTP. When the victim requests an HTTPS URL whose path matches the probe cookie Path, this cookie would be included in the HTTPS request and makes the length of the TLS record corresponding to this request distinctly different from others. Thus, an attacker can correlate this TLS record with the request-URL.

For example, for request-URL: https://www.example.com/share/token, normal request header (without probe cookie) is as follows:

```
GET /share/token HTTP/1.1
Host: www.example.com
User−Agent: Mozilla/5.0 ...
Accept−Encoding: gzip, deflate
Cookie: Session=12345; ID=67890
```

The attacker injects the probe cookie via HTTP protocol (Fig. 1):

```
Set−Cookie: probe−cookie=aaa..a−large−cookie..aaa; domain=.example.
    com; path=/share/token
```

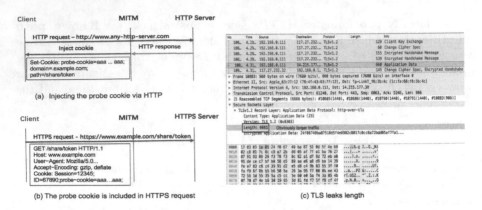

Fig. 1. Injecting a large cookie into HTTPS session.

The maximum size of one probe cookie can be set to about 4000 bytes. In practice, the attacker can inject multiple probe cookies for more noticeable traffic differences. In Sect. 3.3, we investigate the cookie size limitation on client and server side. When the victim requests the URL again, this cookie will be included in the request header and submitted to the server. The request header will be as follows:

```
GET /share/token HTTP/1.1
Host: www.example.com
User−Agent: Mozilla/5.0 ...
Accept−Encoding: gzip, deflate
Cookie: Session=12345; ID=67890; probe−cookie=aaa..a−large−cookie..aaa;
```

Thus, the attacker can correlate this large TLS record with the access to https://www.example.com/share/token.

3.2 Unknown Path Inference

3.2.1 Cookie Path-Match Based on String Prefix

We have mentioned in Sect. 2.3 that cookies should be matched based on "block prefix", separated by "/". However, after in-depth tests we find that some browsers (IE, Edge, Safari) do not strictly follow the "block prefix" rule. Instead, these browsers match cookies with URL following "string prefix" rule. For example:

```
URL: https://www.example.com/share/token_unknown/image.jpg;
cookie: id = 123; domain=.example.com; path=/share/t;
```

Since */share/t* is not a block prefix of the request-URL */share/to-ken_unknown/*, the cookie, id = 123, should not be included in the request header, according to RFC 6265 [1]. However, the above browsers incorrectly include the cookie in the request header, which enables the following side-channel attacks.

3.2.2   Inferring Path

Web servers protect user's privacy through TLS, and some sensitive information (e.g., private images link, files link, shopping history) are always included in an HTTPS page. The vulnerability of string prefix can be exploited to infer these sensitive paths. For example, an HTTPS page (https://www.example.com) includes a sensitive image, whose path is https://www.example-img.com/upload/img-unknown.jpg. The string "unknown" in the path always is a hashed string, which is unknown to others, but the string "/upload/img-" is exposed and known to the attacker. When the vulnerable browser accesses the fixed URL https://www.example.com, it also requests the sensitive image. Then the local cookie whose domain is "example-img.com" and path is a string prefix of "/upload/img-unknown.jpg" would be sent. So an attacker can take advantage of the size difference between TLS records caused by probe cookies to guess the string "unknown" byte by byte, and finally get the complete path.

Algorithm 1 shows the concrete steps. Firstly, the attacker hijacks an HTTP page and injects a hidden iframe pointing to the fixed URL https://www.example.com. Then the attacker can force the victim's browser to send repeated HTTPS requests by refreshing the iframe. So the attacker can get the maximum size of TLS record data of requests per round, and properly set the *base_cookie_length* which denotes the length of cookie being injected in the algorithm 1. The candidate char comes from an array guessArray[] consisting of printable characters.

An MITM attacker can inject multiple cookies each time, so it is straightforward to conduct a binary search on the expected request path, which can improve attack efficiency. For example, assuming that the prefix of path is "/upload/img-", and the guessed characters set is composed of a-z, the attacker can inject a batch of cookies: /upload/img-a, /upload/img-b, ... /upload/img-m. If the *packetLength* $>= 2 *$ base_cookie_length, the attacker can judge that the right character is in a-m. This method can greatly improve efficiency.

In order to force victim's browser to send repeated HTTPS requests, an attacker may use two methods:

– **Hidden iframe.** The attacker hijacks a normal HTTP page and injects a malicious JavaScript code with a hidden iframe pointing to the HTTPS page, which includes the sensitive path. When the iframe is refreshed by the malicious code, the victim's browser would send repeated HTTPS requests. Since the iframe is hidden, the victim will not be aware of the page anomaly.
– **Window.open().** After the attacker injects a malicious code into the normal HTTP page, the target HTTPS page can be opened in a new browser tab by window.open() method. Obviously, the HTTPS page is the child window of the normal HTTP page. So the malicious code injected in the HTTP page can reload the HTTPS page to force the browser to send repeated HTTPS requests. If the normal HTTP page has opened a page in new tab already, the attacker also can reuse that page to send repeated HTTPS requests. This method reduces the concealment of the attack, making it possible for the victim to perceive.

Algorithm 1. Unknown path inference.

Input: $baseURL$=https://www.example-img.com,
$\quad\quad$ $targetDomain$=".example-img.com",
$\quad\quad$ $secretPrefix$="/upload/img-",$endString$=".jpg", $base\_cookie\_length$;

Output: $guessedPath$;

1: $secretString$="", $cookieData$="";
2: $guessArray[]$=[a...z, A...Z, 0...9, %, ., !, _, -];
3: **for** $i = 0$ **to** $base\_cookie\_length$ **do**
4: $\quad$ $cookieData += \,'a'$;
5: **end for**
6: Set $Cookie\_A$: $value = cookieData, path = secretPrefix, domain = targetDomain$;
7: Inject $Cookie\_A$ to the victim browser;
8: **repeat**
9: $\quad$ $index = 0$;
10: $\quad$ **for** $index < length(guessArray[])$ **do**
11: $\quad\quad$ $guessChar = guessArray[index + +]$;
12: $\quad\quad$ $guessPath = secretPrefix + secretString + guessChar$;
13: $\quad\quad$ Set $Cookie\_B$: $value = cookieData, path = guessPath, domain = targetDomain$;
14: $\quad\quad$ Inject $Cookie\_B$ and refresh the iframe to send repeated HTTPS requests;
15: $\quad\quad$ **repeat**
16: $\quad\quad\quad$ Wait for the HTTPS requests data;
17: $\quad\quad\quad$ $packetLength = length(\text{TLS record of requests})$;
18: $\quad\quad$ **until** $packetLength >= base\_cookie\_length$
19: $\quad\quad$ Delete Cookie_B in the victim browser;
20: $\quad\quad$ **if** $packetLength >= 2 * base\_cookie\_length$ **then**
21: $\quad\quad\quad$ Guess one char successfully, $secretString += guessChar$;
22: $\quad\quad\quad$ break;
23: $\quad\quad$ **end if**
24: $\quad$ **end for**
25: **until** End($secretString$) == $endString$
26: $guessedPath = baseURL + secretPrefix + secretString$;
27: **return** $guessedPath$;

We have verified the feasibility of such attack in practice. In the experiment, when we use the hidden iframe and refresh it every 1 s, it usually takes about 10 s to guess one character. In most cases, for the common unknown path whose length is usually not more than 120, it generally takes us ten minutes to infer the unknown path successfully. Because the iframe being hidden, the constant refreshing does not affect the user's browsing of the web page. But the HTTP page which injected hidden iframe should remain open during the attack. After numerous experiments, we found that the length of probe cookie does not affect the time spent in the attack, as long as it is large enough to make a clear distinction between TLS records. We usually set the probe cookie length to about 2000 which works well.

3.2.3 Cloud Storage Leakage

The most harmful scenario applying the above attacks is to infer the private image files in cloud storage. After files (e.g. photos) are manually or automatically uploaded to the cloud, servers will generate a unique id (like a hashed string) for each file. While the file is accessed, unique id must be used as part of the request parameter or request path. Obviously, this hashed string is the victim of above attacks.

We have investigated 11 popular cloud storage services which have deployed HTTPS. As a result, 8 of them are vulnerable (see Table 2), in which thumbnail (a reduced-size version of original image) link or share link of file may be leaked.

Table 2. Assessment of cloud storage leakage

Cloud storage	Vulnareble ?
Google drive	Y
Google photos	Y
iCloud	N
Dropbox	Y
OneDrive	N
Flickr	Y
Amazon cloud drive	Y
Weiyun (Tencent)	Y
Taopan (Alibaba)	Y
BaiduPan	N
Jianguoyun (Nutstore)[a]	Y

[a]Nutstore is a Dropbox like cloud storage service, developed by a Shanghai based company in China.

Leaking Thumbnail Link

Almost all of the cloud storage services load the thumbnail image file to the main page. Baidu Cloud and iCloud require additional authentication parameters for legitimate access to files. Therefore, they are not affected by thumbnail link leakage. Except Dropbox and OneDrive, all other cloud storage services can leak thumbnail. Google Drive, Google Photos, Flickr, Amazon Cloud Drive (Fig. 2), Weiyun, Taopan and Jianguo do not verify the session when private images are accessed. That means, the attacker can get the private images directly as soon as the link leaked.

In contrast, both Dropbox and OneDrive deploy HSTS, which intruct browsers to access their service through HTTPS only [4]. They both check user session strictly; thus even if the thumbnail link of private file leaks, the attacker cannot get the private files.

Fig. 2. Thumbnail link leakage on Amazon Cloud Drive with no session validation.

Leaking Share Link

Cloud storage services usually offers file sharing service through URL link. Anyone can access the shared file through a shared link, without logging in cloud storage services.

Fig. 3. Share link leakage on Dropbox.

That means cloud storage services offering file sharing service will not check user session. According to our investigation, Google Drive, Google Photos, Dropbox, Flickr and OneDrive can load shared file link into fixed page. Since Google Drive, Google Photos, Dropbox (Fig. 3) and Flickr adopt the Hashed-Path, they are likely vulnerable to information leak attack. OneDrive shares files with the authentication based on parameters, which can mitigate the threat.

3.2.4   Browsing Privacy Leakage

Making use of the leaked URL of resource file included in the web page, the attacker can also steal a user's browsing privacy. Different from private URL path leakage in Cloud Storage, browsing privacy leakage is associated with the public URL, so there is no problem of session checking. Following are two attack scenarios.

Shopping History

After online shopping, users can see the information of historical order on their account page. The product thumbnails of the historical order may become the side-channel attacker's targets, based on which the attacker can know what goods the victim has bought (Fig. 4).

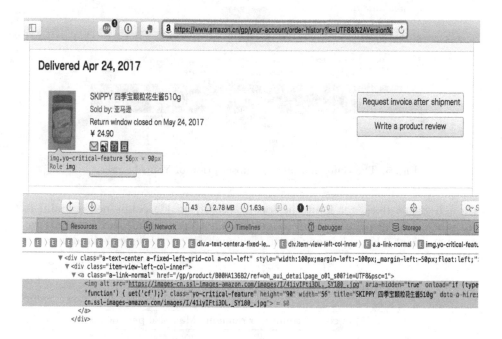

Fig. 4. The shopping history of amazon user.

Youtube Subscriptions

The subscriptions, watch history and other information of Youtube users are loaded on the web page in the form of thumbnails (Fig. 5). The side-channel attacker can also harvest private information by unknown path inference attack.

3.3   Limitation of Cookie Size

A. Browser Side

In fact, the total cookie size sent to the server is limited. We investigated respectively the browser-side and server-side cookie size limit policy. In major browsers, while single cookie size limitation is not more than 4096 bytes, the cookie count can be at least more than 50 per domain (Table 3). Theoretically, we can send a maximum of about 200 K (50 * 4096) bytes of cookie. As shown in the Table 3,

Fig. 5. The thumbnail link of subscription of Youtube user.

although Safari does not limit the locally stored cookie count per domain, it limits the total size of cookie sent to a domain not more than 8 K. Practically we construct about 4 K probe cookie size is enough for us to observe the difference of HTTPS traffic.

Table 3. The browser-side cookie limit policy

Browser	Max cookie count per domain	Max size per cookie
Chrome	180	4096
Firefox	150	4097
Safari	No limitation	4096
IE, edge	50	5117

B. Server Side

Cookie request header size is limited stringently in server side (For example, the apache limits the size of request header not more than 8 K bytes [16]).

Nevertheless, the attack targeting HTTPS requests can infer sensitive information from HTTPS requests by cookie injection. The server-side limitation of cookie request header size has little effect on this attack. In short, we can ignore the influence of browser-side and server-side cookie size limitation by precisely conducting probe cookie.

4   Possible Defenses

Side-channel attack against HTTPS by cookie injection is based on statistical HTTPS traffic analysis. Some existing techniques can help mitigate this threat.

A common tactic for mitigating such threat is to pad packets to uniform sizes. However, this approach is often inefficient. In 2009, Wright et al. proposed a novel method for thwarting statistical traffic analysis algorithms by optimally morphing one class of traffic to look like another class [12]. In 2011, Luo et al. proposed a novel browser-side system, namely HTTPOS, to prevent information leaks [11]. However, these measures are inefficient for this new class of side-channel attack against HTTPS. In this study, we have not developed any efficient approach to mitigate the known path identification by now, but we propose some mitigation measures against the unknown path inference.

Fix Vulnerability. What causes that request URL can be inferred byte by byte is that browsers don't strictly follow the accordance of path portion of the request-uri and the cookie's path attribute. Therefore, fixing this vulnerability can prevent the side-channel attack. We have reported the vulnerability to the affected browser vendors: Microsoft's IE/Edge team and Apple's Safari team. Microsoft responded that they are planning to fix this bug in a future release where they update their cookie path handling code to conform with more modern standards. Apple responded that this issue has been addressed in the newest Safari (after version 10). Actually, when we begin study this vulnerability until last year, all versions of Safari (before version 10) are always vulnerable to this attack.

URL Rules of Cloud Storage. As described in Sect. 3.2.3, some cloud storage services don't implement a strict management on file access permissions. Even if the user never shares the file, a link can directly lead to the file disclosure as long as the attackers get it. We think this is another security risk independent of vulnerabilities disclosed herein, which are worthy of improvement for the relevant manufacturers. We have reported this issue to the affected cloud storage services including our advice. But most of them may be not aware of dangers of this issue or consider the convenience of customers, they think that is working as designed (The Amazon replied it has fixed this issue).

X-Frame-Options. The X-Frame-Options header can be used to control whether a page can be placed in an iframe. In attack procedure described in Sect. 3.2, in order to achieve hidden refreshing, an attacker would be able to embed the HTTPS page A, including the sensitive URL, into the normal HTTP page as a hidden iframe. If the response header of the page A contains a security configuration X-Frame-Options, which limits this page not to be loaded as a iframe, the page A would not be rendered by the browser and the sensitive URL included in it could not be requested. Consequently, the probe cookies would not been sent to the server. Although the attacker can still create a new tab or reuse a tab to complete the refreshing work, it reduces the concealment of the attack, making it possible for the victim to perceive.

Cache. If the cache option was set in the response header corresponding to the URL, attackers could not certainly always trigger request when refreshing the page A. Therefore, a certain mitigation of the effects of attacks was made. But the differences in the implementation of browsers cache configuration make it possible for attackers to force browsers to perform network requests through some tricks. That will be what we want to complete in the next phase of this research.

5   Related Work

Our work is mainly about side-channel attacks against HTTPS. Side-channel attacks have been known for decades. A documented attack is dated back to 1943. Among related research, Shuo Chen's work [6] focused on side-channel leaks in web applications. Their meticulous research showed that surprisingly detailed sensitive user data can be reliably inferred from the web traffic of a number of high-profile, top-of-the-line web applications. There are also many studies about specific side channel attacks against HTTPS. CRIME, well known attack proposed by Rizzo and Duong [13], makes use of the size of compressed request payload as side channel, thus leak sensitive information like cookie by chosen plaintext attack. Researchers Gluck, Harris and Prado announced a variant of the CRIME exploit against HTTP compression called BREACH [14], which uncovers HTTPS secrets by attacking the inbuilt HTTP data compression used by web servers to reduce network traffic. In contrast, we utilize a different side channel, the size of TLS request, which is of diversification caused by path injection. We are also aware of several researches that are related to cookie's integrity problem. Barth's [1] and Zalewski's [15] work focused on explaining the cause of the cookie integrity problem. We've also had some research about cookie [7], and discovered some defects of cookie in practices. Cookie overwriting and Cookie shadowing lead to cookie reflection, online payment or account hijacking, or disclosure of user privacy. We focus towards cookie path in this paper, and propose security issues in some aspects.

6   Conclusions

Although the TLS protocol was designed to protect the secrecy and authenticity of a data stream, it is not always an adequate protection of the user's privacy, as the traffic information not hidden by TLS still leaks a great deal of information. The side-channel attackers can leverage information leaked by TLS traffic to recover secrets believed to be protected by TLS. We have presented a new class of side-channel attack against HTTPS. Because of the loosely-defined SOP for cookies, attackers can infer sensitive information of the request path from HTTPS request by cookie injection attacks. We proposed two forms of this attack: known path identification, which is a prerequisite for some other attacks, and unknown path inference that attackers can infer sensitive information of the request path from HTTPS request. Our work demonstrates that despite encryption, the vulnerability is realistic and serious threat to user privacy. We also investigated the challenges in mitigating such a problem. Specially, the vulnerability of cookie path matching in IE/Edge/Safari can be mitigated quickly by patching.

There are more work to be done here. The known path identification attack can help attackers to get the correlations between TLS record and request URL. We will further investigate what other attacks can take full advantage of this favorable condition.

Acknowledgments. This work is supported by CERNET Innovation Project (No. NGII20160402).

References

1. Barth, A.: HTTP state management mechanism. IETF RFC 6265 (2011). https://tools.ietf.org/html/rfc6265
2. Dierks, T., Rescorla, E.: The transport layer security (TLS) protocol version 1.2. IETF RFC 5246 (2008). https://tools.ietf.org/html/rfc5246
3. Barth, A.: The web origin concept. IETF RFC 6454 (2011). https://tools.ietf.org/html/rfc6454
4. Hodges, J., Jackson, C., Barth, A.: HTTP strict transport security (HSTS). IETF RFC 6797 (2012). https://tools.ietf.org/html/rfc6797
5. Johnston, P., Moore, R.: Multiple browser cookie injection vulnerabilities (2004). http://www.westpoint.ltd.uk/advisories/wp-04-0001.txt
6. Chen, S., Ziqing, M., Yi-Min, W., Ming, Z.: Pretty-bad-proxy: an overlooked adversary in browsers' HTTPS deployments. In: Proceedings of the 30th IEEE Symposium on Security and Privacy, pp. 347–359. IEEE Computer Society (2009). https://doi.org/10.1109/SP.2009.12
7. Zheng, X., Jiang, J., Liang, J., Duan, H., Chen, S., Wan, T., Weaver, N.: Cookies lack integrity: real-world implications. In: 24th USENIX Security Symposium, USENIX Security 2015, Washington, D.C., pp. 707–721 (2015)
8. Vranken, G.: HTTPS bicycle attack (2015). https://guidovranken.wordpress.com/2015/12/30/https-bicycle-attack/
9. Coull, S.E., Collins, M.P., Monrose, F., Reiter, M.K., Wright, C.V.: On web browsing privacy in anonymized NetFlows. In: 16th USENIX Security Symposium, pp. 339–352 (2007)
10. Danezis, G. Traffic analysis of the HTTP protocol over TLS (2008). http://www.cs.ucl.ac.uk/staff/G.Danezis/papers/TLSanon.pdf
11. Luo, X., Zhou, P., Chan, E.W.W., Lee, W., Chang, R.K.C., Perdisci, R.: HTTPOS: sealing information leaks with browser-side obfuscation of encrypted flows. In: Proceedings of the Network and Distributed Systems Symposium (NDSS), San Diego, California, USA (2011)
12. Wright, C.V., Coull, S.E., Monrose, F.: Traffic morphing: an efficient defense against statistical traffic analysis. In: Proceedings of the Network and Distributed Systems Symposium (NDSS), pp. 237–250. IEEE (2009)
13. Rizzo, J., Duong, T.: The CRIME attack. In: Ekoparty Security Conference (2012)
14. Gluck, Y., Harris, N., Prado, A.: BREACH: reviving the CRIME attack (2013). http://breachattack.com/resources/BREACH%20-%20SSL,%20gone%20in%2030%20seconds.pdf
15. Zalewski, M.: The Tangled Web: A Guide to Securing Modern Web Applications. No Starch Press, San Francisco (2012)
16. Apache: apache core features (2017). http://httpd.apache.org/docs/2.4/mod/core.html#limitrequestfieldsize

Countermeasures Against Side-Channel Attacks (2)

Protecting Triple-DES Against DPA
A Practical Application of Domain-Oriented Masking

Pascal Sasdrich[1,2] and Michael Hutter[1(✉)]

[1] Cryptography Research, 425 Market Street, 11th Floor,
San Francisco, CA 94105, USA
michael.hutter@cryptography.com
[2] Horst Görtz Institute for IT-Security,
Ruhr-Universität Bochum, Bochum, Germany
pascal.sasdrich@rub.de

Abstract. Although AES has become the predominant standard for symmetric block ciphers, T-DES is still widely used especially for electronic payment and financial solutions. In order to protect small and embedded devices against power analysis and side-channel attacks in general, appropriate countermeasures have to be considered. In this paper, we present the first practical application of the Domain-Oriented Masking (DOM) scheme for the T-DES cipher in hardware and provide practical evaluation results that confirm the security of DOM and our designs. In particular, using Test Vector Leakage Assessment (TVLA) as evaluation methodology confirms that our first- and second-order secure architectures do not exhibit detectable leakage using up to 2 billion traces. This is the first paper that presents a T-DES hardware implementation using a state of the art provable secure masking technique.

1 Introduction

Although DES as standard has been replaced with the announcement of AES in 2001, many applications still rely on T-DES especially in the financial and electronic payments sector. To this end, T-DES remains an active standard and is still implemented on many embedded devices. However, since most embedded devices are exposed to physical threats they require additional protection mechanisms and countermeasures to prevent disclosure of secret and sensitive information [15].

In recent years, Threshold Implementation (TI) [19] has been proposed as promising method to protect physical devices and hardware implementations against side-channel attacks. In particular, it has been applied to many different ciphers, including but not limited to AES [17] and PRESENT [21].

Throughout the years, many different approaches and optimizations have been proposed to improve the efficiency of first-order secure TIs, and the original concept has been extended to higher-order protections [3]. In particular,

P. Sasdrich—This work was done while the author was at Cryptography Research.

the decomposition of the protected functions into functions with smaller alge-braic degree has been applied extensively [4,12,18,21]. Unfortunately, these approaches cannot be used for DES and T-DES due to the classification of the S-boxes [4] which renders the concept of TI rather inefficient for these ciphers.

Consequently, we decided to apply recent results for so called $d + 1$ masking schemes instead of using the concept of TI. In particular, we use the results of the Domain-Oriented Masking (DOM) scheme [8] and Unified Masking Algo-rithm (UMA) [7] in order to provide protection against side-channel attacks for our designs. The applied techniques are similar to the concepts of Consolidated Masking Schemes (CMS) [22] and we would expect to obtain similar results as presented in this paper.

Contribution. In this paper, we present a first practical application of the recently proposed DOM approach and apply it to the T-DES cipher. We focus on first- and second-order protection for which DOM is as good as the later presented UMA masking technique which mainly improves the requirement for fresh entropy for higher-order secure implementations. Therefore, this is the first paper that evaluates DOM in a practical side-channel analysis investigation. We used a Field-Programmable Gate Array (FPGA) platform in our experiments and confirm robustness of this masking technique in practice. In addition, this is the first paper that presents a hardware implementation of T-DES that makes use of a state of the art masking technique that has been recently analyzed using formal verification in [5]. We finally show that our first- and second order secure implementations do not exhibit detectable leakage using up to 2 billion power traces.

We also provide optimized round-based T-DES hardware architectures that require only 64 and 192 bits of fresh entropy per clock cycle to achieve first- and second-order protection respectively. Further, we can show that the protection increases the area only by a factor of about 3 and 8 for our first- and second-order architecture respectively compared to an unprotected architecture.

Outline. This work is organized as follows: In Sect. 2, we briefly discuss the basic concept of DOM followed by implementation details and rationales in Sect. 3. Section 4 provides practical evaluation results using a FPGA-based evaluation platform and TVLA as evaluation metric. Conclusions are drawn in Sect. 5.

2   Preliminaries

Notations. In the course of this work, we will denote single-bit random variables using italic lower-case characters, multi-bit vectors by bold lower-case ones, and shared representations as upper-case characters. Further on, lowering indexes indicate single elements of a vector while raising indexes denote single elements of a shared representation. Eventually, functions are denoted using sans serif fonts and sets using calligraphic ones.

To this end, let us denote $\mathbf{x} \in \mathbb{GF}(2^m)$ as a vector of m single-bit elements $\langle x_1, \ldots, x_m \rangle$. Given the shared representation $\mathbf{X}$ of the vector $\mathbf{x}$ using Boolean masking with s shares as $(\mathbf{x}^1, \ldots, \mathbf{x}^s)$ it holds that:

$$\mathbf{x} = \bigoplus \mathbf{X} = \bigoplus_{i=1}^{s} \mathbf{x}^i = \bigoplus_{i=1}^{s} \langle x_1^i, \dots, x_m^i \rangle.$$

Related Work. In this section, we briefly discuss relevant work with respect to hardware implementations of T-DES, side-channel attacks on these designs, and integration of countermeasures. In particular, since DES and T-DES has been around for several decades and originally has been designed to provide good performance in hardware, a wealth of different implementations has been presented and proposed, e.g., in [13,16,28,29]. However, since AES has been proposed shortly after the discovery of side-channel attacks, only a small number of protected implementations has been published by academia [14,25,27] (although it is likely that many industrial solutions integrating countermeasures exist and are used in practice). However, in particular the authors of [20] have shown the impact of breaking real-world solutions that relied on insufficiently protected T-DES co-processors.

2.1 Domain-Oriented Masking

Over the last two decades, a plethora of different countermeasures has been introduced in order to prevent or protect information leakage through unintentional side channels of modern embedded devices and digital circuits. Usually, timing behavior [10], instantaneous power consumption [11], or electro-magnetic (EM) emanations [1] are considered as the most common physical side channels. To this end, a lot of research activity and scientific effort continues to develop appropriate countermeasures that prevent or protect the leakage of sensitive information and device internals. In this context, *Domain-Oriented Masking* [8] has been proposed as a Boolean masking scheme for hardware devices that use a structured approach of domains in order to provide side-channel protection with arbitrary protection order.

Basic Concept. Boolean masking follows the principle of *secret sharing* to split sensitive intermediate data $\mathbf{x}$ into a shared representation $\mathbf{X}$ of s randomized variables $\mathbf{x}^1, \dots, \mathbf{x}^s$. Depending on the number of shares, Boolean masking schemes can provide up to d-th order protection against analysis of statistical moments using $s = d + 1$ shares which have to be processed independently. However, various physical effects (e.g., glitches and parasitic capacitances) can prevent the correct behavior of the masking scheme and compromise the protection mechanism.

Rather than the concept of TI [19] that has been introduced in order to prevent side-channel information leakage through glitches on function level using $s = t \times d + 1$ shares (given that t is the algebraic degree of the shared function), DOM introduces the notion of *share domains* in order to cope with glitches in hardware circuits.

Share Domains. Based on the idea of processing each share independently, the notion of domains has been introduced by Groß et al. in [8]. In particular, each

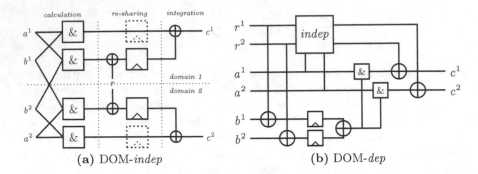

Fig. 1. First-order DOM AND gates.

individual share of a sensitive intermediate value is assigned and associated with a unique domain, i.e., $d + 1$ domains have to be defined for d-th order protection. Due to the independence of each share from other domains, security in the d-probing model [9] can be proven. However, processing of data requires to perform certain operations on the shared values. In that sense, DOM distinguishes between *intra-domain* and *inter-domain* operations depending on whether shares have to cross domain boundaries or not.

Intra-Domain Operations. Each operation that involves only shares from the same domain, e.g., all linear operations, can be considered as *intra-domain* operation. In this case, independence of the shares from other domains is given trivially making these operations inherently secure in the d-probing model.

Inter-Domain Operations. In contrast, *inter-domain* operations, as part of non-linear operations, require certain shares to cross domain boundaries. Hence, as for all Boolean masking schemes, non-linear operations are the critical part that requires particular caution during the design phase. In order to retain the security for *inter-domain* operations in the d-probing model, the DOM approach uses additional fresh entropy in order to re-mask the inter-domain operation results. In addition, additional register stages prevent the propagation of glitches.

First-Order Secure AND for Two *Independent* Inputs. The construction of a first-order secure basic AND gate allows to build arbitrary first-order protected hardware circuits. In particular, the basic AND gate, as shown in Fig. 1(a), computes the result of $\mathbf{C} = \mathbf{A} \cdot \mathbf{B}$ using two inputs $\mathbf{A}, \mathbf{B}$ in a uniform, randomly shared representation independent from each other with:

$$
\begin{aligned}
\mathbf{C} = \mathbf{A} \cdot \mathbf{B} &= (a^1 + a^2) \cdot (b^1 + b^2) \\
&= \underbrace{a^1 b^1 + (a^1 b^2 + r)}_{c^1} + \underbrace{(r + a^2 b^1) + a^2 b^2}_{c^2}.
\end{aligned}
$$

To this end, the computation process is divided into two share domains and performed in three steps: *calculation*, *re-sharing*, and *integration*.

Calculation. The multiplication stage is the first part designed to compute the required product terms of the shared inputs $\mathbf{A}, \mathbf{B}$. In particular, the calculation stages of the first-order secure 2-input AND gate provides all intra-domain products (a^1b^1, a^2b^2) and inter-domain products (a^1b^2, a^2b^1). While intra-domain products are uncritical from a security perspective, inter-domain products require special care to maintain d-th order security properties in the d-probing model that is taken in the subsequent re-sharing stage.

Re-sharing. In order to ensure statistical independence of the inter-domain products, fresh entropy is added during the re-sharing phase. The propagation of glitches and resulting side-channel leakage is prevented using additional registers to store the re-masked inter-domain products.

Integration. Eventually, the integration stage performs the integration of the inter-domain products into the domains by recombining them with the intra-domain products. Note, that the correctness still holds after the integration since the fresh random bit r has been added to both domains.

First-Order Secure AND for Two *Dependent* Inputs. In case the sharing of the inputs cannot be ensured to be *independent* (e.g., due to some glitches), the first-order secure AND gate for *dependent* inputs as shown in Fig. 1(b) has to be used. In particular, this gate extends the basic DOM-*indep* gate by re-sharing one of the inputs using fresh entropy. However, in order to still ensure correctness of the result, it is necessary to calculate according correction terms that eventually are added to the output. Note, that this gate also ensures that all flip-flops only contain freshly randomized intermediate results which also can avoid leakage due to the distance between values that are overwritten.

Higher-Order Secure 2-Input and Gate. The basic concept of the first-order secure 2-input AND gate can be easily extended and generalized for arbitrary higher-order protected 2-input AND gates. In general, this process only requires moderate modifications for each stage that we will briefly outline in the following section. Fortunately, the extension can be performed in an automated process, allowing to only provide the desired protection order while the required circuit is generated accordingly.

Calculation. As before, the calculation stage has to provide all necessary intra- and inter-domain product terms, however, with respect to $d+1$ domains (in order to achieve d-th order protection). In particular, each domain has a single intra-domain product but d inter-domain products giving in total $(d + 1)^2$ product terms (Fig. 2).

Re-sharing. Again, inter-domain products have to be re-shared with fresh entropy in order to ensure statistical independence. Further, each random bit r_i has to be unique within each domain, however, it can be re-used across

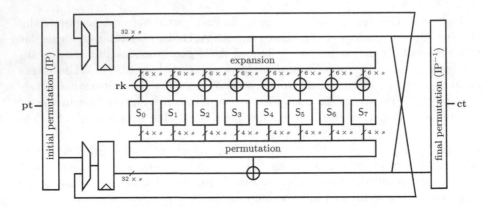

Fig. 2. Basic architecture of the protected T-DES design.

different domains (in order to ensure correctness and minimize fresh entropy requirements). In addition, each re-masked inter-domain product has to be buffered by an additional flip-flop (FF) to prevent information leakage due to the propagation of glitches.

Integration. Eventually, the integration stage reduces the number of products by integrating all inter-domain products into the domains. However, additional caution is necessary, since information leakage due to glitches should not reveal more than the intra-domain products.

3   Design Considerations

This section provides details on our protected T-DES architecture and discusses our design choices, in particular considering the implementation strategy for the S-box protection. In addition, we provide implementation results for performance and area utilization for our first-order and second-order protected architectures.

3.1   Protected Architecture of Triple-DES (T-DES)

Internally, our T-DES core implements a round-based DES architecture. Although DES is a Feistel network with 64-bit block size and only 56-bit keys (excluding 8 parity bits), T-DES artificially extends the effective key size to 112 bits using three subsequent DES calls. In general, our T-DES architecture supports both, encryption and decryption, with the standard sequence of operations, i.e., the second DES call performs an inverted operation (decryption if T-DES encryption is performed and vice versa). However, due to the Feistel structure of the DES, we can re-use the same round-based architecture for DES encryption as well as decryption, inverting the DES operation only depends on the key schedule. More precisely, since the key update function only involves simple rotation and bit-wise permutation operations, and the first and last state of the key register are

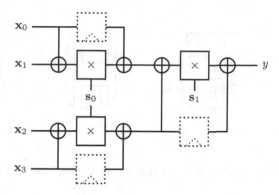

Fig. 3. Secure multiplexer.

identical, this also allows a very efficient computation of round keys in reverse order by simple rotation to the opposite direction. To this end, we also implement two additional T-DES modes which perform the same DES operation for all three calls, i.e., always encrypt during T-DES encryption and otherwise always decrypt.

Round-Based DES Architecture. We opted to implement all 8 different S-boxes of the Feistel F-function in parallel such that a single DES round is computed in one clock cycles. To this end, an unprotected DES operation could be executed in 16 clock cycles. However, since the protected AND gates introduce additional latency due to their incorporated pipeline stages, a single round of our protected architecture requires 5 clock cycles (i.e., we have 4 additional register stages) and an entire DES operation is executed in 80 clock cycles. Along with additional control overhead, e.g., to load the correct keys for each DES operation, an entire T-DES encryption and decryption requires 244 clock cycles.

Since all permutation and expansion functions of the DES cipher are linear operations, these can be masked easily using the DOM approach. However, the different S-boxes are the only non-linear operations of the DES cipher which require an implementation based on protected AND gates. In the following, we will discuss and justify our final implementation choice for the S-boxes using their internal structure for area and entropy optimization.

Key Sharing. In addition, our architecture supports key sharing. If configured, the key is shared internally in $d + 1$ shares (one for each domain) using fresh entropy provided by an internal Pseudo Random Number Generator (PRNG). Fortunately, the Data Encryption Standard (DES) key schedule can be shared easily since it only consists of linear operations. To this end, a separate key register is instantiated for each domain. Instead of adding the round key only to the first share, one key share then is added in each domain. Hence, in total this security option only requires some additional registers and XOR-gates but apart from that can be implemented with minimal overhead.

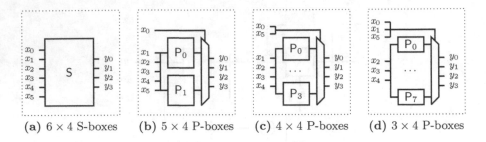

(a) 6 × 4 S-boxes   (b) 5 × 4 P-boxes   (c) 4 × 4 P-boxes   (d) 3 × 4 P-boxes

Fig. 4. Different implementation approaches for the DES 6 × 4 S-boxes.

3.2   First-Order Secure Multiplexer

In general, a single 2 : 1 multiplexer can be implemented using two XOR gates and a single DOM-*and* gate based on its Algebraic Normal Form (ANF):

$$y = x_0 + sx_0 + sx_1$$
$$= x_0 + s(x_0 + x_1)$$

In addition, a single 4 : 1 multiplexer can be represented as three cascaded multiplexers as shown in Fig. 3, hence requires three DOM-*and* gates in total.

3.3   Design Space Exploration of the S-Box Structure

In general, we decided to optimize our S-boxes for area and in particular we tried to reduce the number of DOM-*and* AND gates which simultaneously results in smaller amounts of fresh entropy that is required per cycle. On the other hand, we had only soft constraints on the resulting depth of the logic circuit and on the overall latency.

One of the most helpful observations is that each S-box structure can be decomposed in smaller blocks. In particular, each of the original 6 × 4 can be naturally decomposed into four 4 × 4 *permutations* and a multiplexer. However, similar decompositions using 5 × 4 and 3 × 4 permutations are also possible. In the following, we will discuss and explain these different options including their benefits and disadvantages regarding our global optimization goal.

In general, each of the decomposition approaches allows to share certain product terms among the smaller blocks, i.e., the permutations. To this end, we explored and evaluated the different options in order to find the best choice for decomposition and final AND gate count.

Single 6 × 4 S-Box. In a first attempt, designers might decide to implement each S-box as a single module as shown in Fig. 4(a) realizing the internals of each S-box according to their ANF. However, since all S-boxes have the maximum algebraic degree of 5, this leads to a high number of required AND gates. In particular, assuming the worst case that each product term is present in each S-box, this would result in $\binom{6}{2} = 15$ DOM-*and* gates in order to realize all possible product terms with two out of the six input bits. Similarly, additional $\binom{6}{3} = 20$ additional DOM-*and* gates would be necessary to compute all product terms with 3 input bits (by reusing the product terms with 2 inputs). Eventually, using $\binom{6}{4} = 20$ and $\binom{6}{5} = 6$ additional AND gates, all necessary product terms can be computed. In total, this approach results in 56 DOM-*and* gates for each S-box. Besides, since each DOM-*indep* gate requires $\frac{(d+1)\cdot d}{2}$ bits of fresh entropy this would for instance result in 56 bits of randomness for each S-box per round for a first-order secure implementation using only DOM-*indep* gates.

Two 5 × 4 Permutations. On closer inspection, it becomes obvious that many product terms are duplicated and could be removed by sharing and re-using previously computed product terms. To this end, an entire 6 × 4 S-box could be split into two different and independent 5 × 4 permutations P_0 and P_1 as shown in Fig. 4(b). However, both sub-modules share the same inputs $x_1, \ldots, x_5$ respectively their product terms. Then, only $\binom{5}{2} = 10$ DOM-*and* gates are necessary to realize all product terms of two inputs. Similarly, the $\binom{5}{3} = 10$ and $\binom{5}{4} = 5$ additional gates are required to compute the remaining product terms of 3 respectively 4 input bits. Eventually, this reduces the number of required DOM-*and* gates to 25, however, four additional multiplexer are required to select the correct result depending on x_0. Fortunately, each 2 : 1 multiplexer can be realized using a single AND gate raising the total number of AND required AND gates to 29 which still almost halves the AND gate count and requirements for fresh entropy.

Four 4 × 4 Permutations. Consequently, dividing the S-boxes into four smaller permutations with shared inputs is the next approach. Interestingly, this option reflects the inherent structure of the S-boxes and eventually turns out to be the best solution and choice. In particular, this approach uses $\binom{4}{2} + \binom{4}{3} = 10$ DOM-*and* gates to compute all shared product terms with two and three inputs. In addition, another 12 AND gates are necessary to realize the multiplexer stage that selects the correct result depending on x_0 and x_5 as shown in Fig. 4(c). In total, this approach requires only 22 protected AND gates to realize each 6 × 4 S-box.

Eight 3 × 4 Permutations. In theory, a decomposition into eight 3 × 4 permutations is also possible which would only require $\binom{3}{2} = 3$ protected AND gates to compute all possible combinations of product terms for the three shared inputs. However, in this approach would require twenty-eight 2 : 1 multiplexers which would become the dominant part in terms of AND gates, resulting in a final amount of 31 DOM-*and* gates. Hence, the previous solution using four 4 × 4 S-boxes turns out to be the most efficient approach in terms of minimizing the number of protected AND gates that are necessary to implement each S-box.

3.4 Source of Entropy

As a source of entropy for our evaluations, we used a PRNG that is based on the Keccak-f round function [2]. In particular, we decided to use the Keccak-f[400] permutation where only 64 bits of the state are output in each clock cycle.

To provide high entropy to our core, we re-seeded the PRNG after each cipher operation. The seed is generated from a python script that draws randomness from the underlying Windows operating system.

For first-order protection, only 64 bits of fresh randomness are required for our implementation. Each T-DES S-Box needs 22 AND gates, however, at most 8 out of the 22 gates are actually active per cycle. This reduces the required number of fresh random bits to 64 bits per cycle.

As opposed to related work which usually generated entropy from common block ciphers (AES, PRESENT, etc.), we decided to use a fast permutation function. This has the advantage that we can generate the required number of random bits in each clock cycle without any idle cycles or the need of parallel cipher computations and also without causing too much overhead in area and power. We also decided to synthesize the PRNG together with our T-DES core, which is a more practical and realistic scenario than calculating entropy a priori to the trace acquisition or sending the entropy from a measurement PC.

3.5   Design Optimizations

Depending on the use case, we can apply several optimizations to our design that allow improvements in terms of area or performance. In the following, we will discuss a small selection of possible improvements and optimizations. Note, however, that all optimizations are often highly dependent on the use case and mostly come with disadvantages in some parts. In general, reduction in area usually results in performance loss while performance improvement usually requires additional resources and area. In addition to optimization ideas, we will provide a short summary and discussion of directions for future work.

Area Reduction. So far, we opted to optimize our implementation, and in particular the S-boxes, for the total number of the AND gate count, regardless of the XOR count in the ANF. In that sense, on optimization goal could be to reduce the XOR count as well by resource sharing and increased logic depth. Along with reusing the pipeline registers of each AND gate and merging them with the state registers in order to avoid duplication, this eventually can result in a smaller but slower circuit (due to increased critical path delays and lower operation frequencies).

Performance Improvements. Throughout this work, we refrained to implement dedicated 3-input, 4-input, and 5-input secure AND gates but instead reused our basic 2-input secure AND gate in a cascaded fashion in order to compute product terms with 3 or more inputs. Certainly, this results in an increased latency due to additional register stages introduced by each AND gate. Hence, in order to reduce the latency to three or less clock cycles per round, designers could implement dedicated AND gates for three or more inputs with only a single cycle of latency but of course at higher area and resource cost. In combination with the previously mentioned optimization of merging the stage register with the pipeline registers of the AND gates, this could even allow to reduce the latency to a single cycle per round but definitely at a higher area demand.

Table 1. Performance results of our T-DES core implementations using GF28 nm.

Core[a]	AND gate	Area [kGEs]	Latency [Cycles]	Entropy [bits]	Power in mW [@100 MHz]	Max. Freq[b] [MHz]
unprotected	-	4.2	52	-	0.065	3,400
1st-order	*indep*	13.8	244	64	0.382	2,100
1st-order	*dep*	22.4	244	192	0.807	2,600
2nd-order	*indep*	26.9	244	192	0.887	2,200
2nd-order	*dep*	39.9	244	384	1.578	2,800

[a]All numbers reported do not include numbers for an entropy source/PRNG (see text for performance numbers of our used PRNG implementation).
[b]The maximum frequency of the cores was identified by multiple synthesis runs with increasing target frequency until a negative slack time was observed.

Directions for Future Work. Originally, DOM was designed to provide protection for arbitrary orders and hence can be applied in a generic way that scales efficiently. However, it might be interesting to evaluate different approaches in order to achieve higher-order protection and security against Side-Channel Analysis (SCA). In particular, designers might forgo provable security but instead pursue the notion of practical higher-order security by combining provable first-order secure implementations with additional hiding countermeasures in order to increase the random noise. For TI, it has been shown to be efficient and effective (see [23,24]). In that sense, it might be interesting to find and investigate how to combine a first-order secure DOM implementation with hiding countermeasures that will increase the noise during the acquisition phase and hamper in particular higher-order attacks that are very susceptible for noise. In the end, this approach might be more efficient and even cheaper than using dedicated higher-order DOM architectures.

3.6 Implementation Results

In this subsection, we present results of hardware implementations that we synthesized using an ASIC design flow. All designs have been implemented using Verilog and were compiled using Synopsys Design Compiler K-2015.06-SP3-1. We used a 28 nm RVT standard cell library from Global Foundry and synthesized all designs with a target frequency of 100 MHz. A two-input NAND gate in this library has a size of $0.624\,\mu m^2$.

Table 1 shows the results of our implementations. We implemented five designs: one unprotected T-DES core as a reference, and four DPA-protected cores. In particular, we designed a first-order and a second-order secure implementation using only DOM-*indep* gates. These designs include a full pipeline, i.e., we also implemented the optional registers after each intra-domain product term. We also replaced each DOM-*indep* gate by a DOM-*dep* gate (for both the first-order and the second-order secure core).

The results show that our smallest design requires 13.8 kGEs. This is about a factor of 3 times larger as compared to the unprotected core. Our 2nd-order secure designs are in general larger but still require less than 40 kGEs.

Power values have been obtained after synthesis without placing and routing the cells. They therefore serve as rough estimates. Our 1st-order secure implementation has a power consumption of about 380 μW at 100 MHz.

Note that all numbers listed in the table are without key sharing, because in many applications the key is constant and does not allow classical DPA. Masking the key schedule is optional and adds about 1 kGEs in area in the 1st-order case and about 1.8 kGEs in the 2nd-order case. Because of the low area increase, we recommend also masking the key schedule in order to also protect the cores against template attacks.

Further note that all numbers listed in the table do not include numbers for random number generation. We decided to exclude the numbers of our PRNG in order to provide plain core performance numbers (e.g., if someone wants to use an own source of entropy) and also to allow a fair comparison with related work since most works do not consider inclusion. The area requirement of our PRNG implementation, which provides the required number of random bits per cycle, depends on whether DOM-*indep* or DOM-*dep* gates are used and also depends on the targeted protection order. It needs 2.6 kGEs for 64-bit entropy, 6.3 kGEs for 192-bit entropy, and 11.9 kGEs for 384-bit entropy.

Interestingly, it also can be seen that the latency requirements of our protected cores is independent of the protection order and the type of the secure AND-gate but only depends on the logical depth, i.e., the stages of consecutive AND gates.

4   Evaluation

In this section, we describe the used measurement setup and present results of practical side-channel analysis.

The Measurement Setup. We used a custom-made FPGA platform in order to perform side-channel analysis of our T-DES cores. The platform features a Kintex 7 FPGA, a FTDI USB interface, several GIO pins, and a circuit for power measurements that includes a measurement resistor. The voltage across that resistor was measured using an 8-bit digital storage oscilloscope from Tektronix (DPO7104). The scope allows to collect power traces which are at most 200 MBytes of size. We set the sampling rate to 500 MS/s and used a bandwidth of 250 MHz. All the cores that we analyzed were running at 50 MHz. Note that lowering the target frequency of the cores is usually recommended because it avoids that signals from a previous clock cycle are ringing into the current clock cycle which may causes an unintended bivariate leakage. However, this was not a concern in our experiments as shown in the following evaluation results.

Figure 5 shows a single power trace of one of our protected T-DES cores.

Test Vector Leakage Assessment. During the evaluation process, we kept the secret key fixed and did not enable key sharing (i.e., key was not masked).

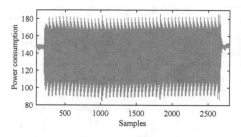

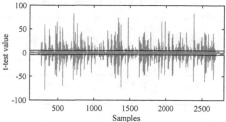

Fig. 5. Single power trace that shows all three DES operations.

Fig. 6. FvR t-test result using 10k traces when PRNG was turned off.

We provided our design with the plaintext already in its shared representation in order to avoid the detection of leakage related to the inputs. For an evaluation methodology, we applied the TVLA scheme using the *non-specific* (Fixed-vs.-Random) *t*-test according to [6, 26].

More precisely, a fixed plaintext is chosen prior to the measurement. During the evaluation, the Device Under Test (DUT) arbitrarily processes either a randomly chosen or the fixed plaintext. Certainly, this test methodology helps to examine if side-channel information leakage can be detected during the operation of the device. Given the assumption that exploitable leakage should always be detectable as well, we can conservatively assume that no exploitable leakage is present in our design if the *t*-test does not detect any differences in both sets.

In order to improve the efficiency of leakage detection, we decided to not store the traces on the hard drive. Accessing the hard drive is usually expensive in terms of measurement performance. Instead, we calculated the t-test statistics on-the-fly and used a similar approach as it was proposed by Schneider and Moradi [26]. At a sampling rate of 500 MS/s, we were able to process about 7,000 traces per second. Analyzing 100M traces therefore took us about 4 h including calculation of the first four statistical moments, which we also did on-the-fly during the time when the traces got transferred from the scope to the measurement PC.

Figure 6 shows the result of a Fixed-vs.-Random (FvR) t-test when the PRNG was turned off (and did generate zero mask values for the implemented countermeasure). For that test, we used 10,000 traces and obtained t-test sigma values of up to 80. This test was applied in order to test our measurement setup and that the device indeed leaks intermediate values when the countermeasure is disabled.

Analysis Result of the First-Order Protected Core. We evaluated the robustness of our first-order secure T-DES implementation against 1st, 2nd, and 3rd-order statistical moments. All our tests are based on the univariate setting (no sampling points have been combined in our attacks) because all shares are always processed in the same clock cycle and we expect leakage in higher statistical moments. We also focus our evaluation in this paper on cores using only DOM-*dep* gates and mark the evaluation of cores using DOM-*indep* gates for future work.

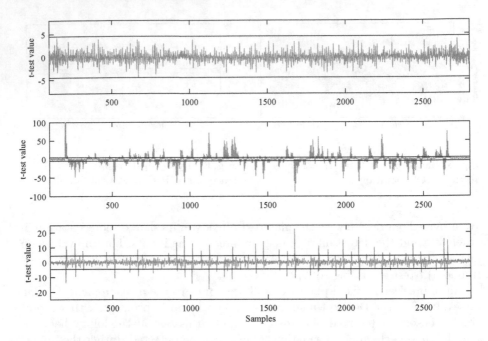

Fig. 7. 1st-order secure T-DES implementation (DOM-*dep* gates): univariate Fixed-vs.-Random t-test results using 50M traces for 1st (top), 2nd (middle), and 3rd (bottom)-order statistical moments.

Figure 7 shows the result of a Fixed-vs.-Random t-test using 50 million traces. It shows that no detectable leakage is observable when evaluating the first statistical moment (mean). However, we can clearly detect a leakage in the second-order statistical moment (variance) as expected (due to parallel processing of masked shares). We also identified leakage when considering the skewness of the sample distributions. However the t-test value is significantly lower than in the second-order case which can be explained by the higher impact of noise in higher-statistical moments.

Analysis Result of the Second-Order Protected Core. We also evaluate the robustness of our 2nd-order secure T-DES implementation. Figure 8 shows the result of a Fixed-vs.-Random t-test for all four statistical moments. We collected 2 billion traces for the analysis. As expected, we can not detect any 1st or 2nd order leakages during the cipher operation. However, we observed that the output is starting to leak after 700 million traces (around sample point 2,700). This leak needs further investigation but in general does not imply a security concern because it is the output of the cipher operation.

3rd-order leakages are detectable with the largest leak being around 40 sigma. We observe that the t-test values are in general smaller than the sigma values obtained for the 1st-order secure T-DES implementation. We also detect 4th-order leakages which are all below 10 sigma. It is worth to note that in our experiment the 4th-order leaks become significant after 200 million traces.

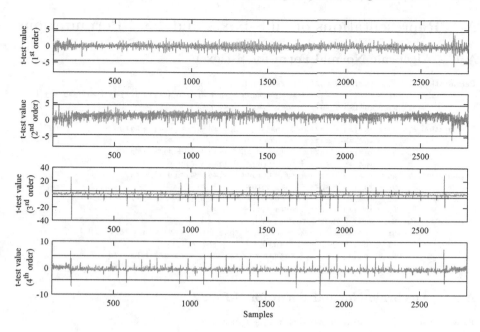

Fig. 8. 2nd-order secure **T-DES** implementation (DOM-*dep* gates): univariate Fixed-vs.-Random t-test results using 2 billion traces for the first four statistical moments.

5   Conclusion

This paper has two main contributions which we summarize here. First, we investigated the practical application of the DOM countermeasure on an FPGA platform. In the past, the efficiency of DOM was evaluated on simulated traces only and the masking technique was not yet tested using practical DPA. Our results confirm the robustness against 1st- and 2nd-order analyses using up to 2 billion power traces.

Second, the paper is the first to present a **T-DES** hardware implementation that is secure in the presence of glitches. There exist several papers describing and evaluating provable secure masking schemes like Threshold Implementations (TIs) on **AES** or **PRESENT**, for example. However, no state of the art masking technique was applied and described on **T-DES** so far.

A   Representations of all S-boxes and 4×4 Permutations

A.1   Algebraic Normal Form for S-Box 1

Permutation P_1: $y_0 = x_0x_1x_3 + x_0x_2 + x_0x_3 + x_1 + x_3$

$y_1 = x_0x_1 + x_0x_2x_3 + x_0x_2 + x_0x_3 + x_0 + x_1x_2x_3 + x_1x_2 + x_1x_3 + x_1 + x_2x_3 + 1$

$y_2 = x_0x_1x_3 + x_0x_1 + x_0x_2 + x_1x_3 + x_2 + x_3 + 1$

$y_3 = x_0x_1x_2 + x_0 + x_1x_2x_3 + x_1x_2 + x_2x_3 + x_2 + x_3 + 1$

Permutation P_2: $y_0 = x_0x_1x_3 + x_0x_2x_3 + x_0x_2 + x_0x_3 + x_0 + x_1x_3 + x_1 + x_2x_3$

$y_1 = x_0x_1x_3 + x_0x_2x_3 + x_0x_2 + x_0x_3 + x_0 + x_1 + x_2 + x_3$

$y_2 = x_0x_1x_2 + x_0x_1x_3 + x_0x_1 + x_0 + x_1x_2 + x_1 + x_2x_3 + x_2$

$y_3 = x_0x_1x_2 + x_0x_1 + x_0 + x_1x_2x_3 + x_2x_3 + x_2 + x_3$

Permutation P_3: $y_0 = x_0x_1x_2 + x_0x_1 + x_0 + x_1x_2x_3 + x_1x_2 + x_2x_3 + x_2 + x_3$

$y_1 = x_0x_1x_3 + x_0x_1 + x_0x_2 + x_0x_3 + x_1 + x_3$

$y_2 = x_0x_1x_3 + x_0x_2x_3 + x_0x_2 + x_0x_3 + x_0 + x_1x_2x_3 + x_1x_2 + x_1x_3 + x_2x_3 + 1$

$y_3 = x_0x_1x_3 + x_0x_2 + x_1x_3 + x_1 + x_2 + x_3$

Permutation P_4: $y_0 = x_0x_1 + x_0x_3 + x_0 + x_1x_3 + x_1 + x_2 + 1$

$y_1 = x_0x_1x_2 + x_0x_1x_3 + x_0x_2x_3 + x_0x_2 + x_0 + x_1x_2 + x_1 + x_2 + x_3 + 1$

$y_2 = x_0x_2 + x_0x_3 + x_1 + x_2x_3 + 1$

$y_3 = x_0x_1x_3 + x_0x_1 + x_0x_2x_3 + x_0x_2 + x_0x_3 + x_1x_2x_3 + x_2 + x_3 + 1$

A.2   Algebraic Normal Form for S-Box 2

Permutation P_1: $y_0 = x_0x_1x_3 + x_0x_2x_3 + x_0x_2 + x_1 + x_2 + 1$

$y_1 = x_0x_1x_2 + x_0x_2 + x_0 + x_1x_2 + x_1 + x_3 + 1$

$y_2 = x_0 + x_1x_3 + x_1 + x_2x_3 + x_3 + 1$

$y_3 = x_0x_1x_3 + x_0x_1 + x_0 + x_1x_3 + x_2x_3 + x_2 + 1$

Permutation P_2: $y_0 = x_0x_1 + x_0x_2 + x_1 + x_3 + 1$

$y_1 = x_0x_1x_2 + x_0x_1x_3 + x_0x_2 + x_0x_3 + x_0 + x_1x_3 + x_1 + x_2x_3 + x_3 + 1$

$y_2 = x_0x_1x_2 + x_0x_1 + x_0 + x_1 + x_2x_3 + x_2 + x_3$

$y_3 = x_0x_1x_3 + x_0x_1 + x_0 + x_1x_3 + x_2 + x_3$

Permutation P_3: $y_0 = x_0x_1x_3 + x_0x_2x_3 + x_0x_3 + x_1 + x_3$

$y_1 = x_0x_1 + x_0x_2x_3 + x_0x_3 + x_0 + x_1x_2x_3 + x_1x_3 + x_1 + x_2x_3 + x_2$

$y_2 = x_0x_1x_3 + x_0x_2x_3 + x_0 + x_1x_3 + x_1 + x_2x_3 + x_3$

$y_3 = x_0 + x_1x_3 + x_2$

Permutation P_4: $y_0 = x_0x_2x_3 + x_0x_2 + x_0 + x_1x_3 + x_1 + x_2x_3 + 1$

$y_1 = x_0x_1 + x_1x_2x_3 + x_1x_3 + x_1 + x_2 + x_3$

$y_2 = x_0x_1x_2 + x_0x_1 + x_0 + x_1 + x_2x_3 + x_2 + x_3 + 1$

$y_3 = x_0x_1x_3 + x_0x_1 + x_0x_2 + x_0x_3 + x_1x_3 + x_2 + 1$

A.3   Algebraic Normal Form for S-Box 3

Permutation P_1: $y_0 = x_0x_1 + x_0x_2 + x_1 + x_3$

$y_1 = x_0x_1x_2 + x_0x_1x_3 + x_0x_2 + x_0x_3 + x_0 + x_1x_2x_3 + x_1x_2 + x_1x_3 + x_1 + x_2x_3 + x_3 + 1$

$y_2 = x_0x_1 + x_0x_2x_3 + x_0x_2 + x_0x_3 + x_1x_2x_3 + x_1x_3 + x_2x_3 + x_2$

$y_3 = x_0x_1x_3 + x_0x_1 + x_0x_2x_3 + x_0x_2 + x_0 + x_1x_2x_3 + x_1x_2 + x_1x_3 + x_2 + x_3 + 1$

Permutation P_2: $y_0 = x_0x_1 + x_0x_2 + x_1 + x_3 + 1$

$y_1 = x_0x_1x_3 + x_0x_1 + x_0 + x_1x_3 + x_2 + x_3$

$y_2 = x_0x_2 + x_1x_2x_3 + x_1 + x_2 + x_3 + 1$

$y_3 = x_0x_1x_2 + x_0x_2 + x_0 + x_1x_2x_3 + x_1x_2 + x_1x_3 + x_1 + x_2 + x_3 + 1$

Permutation P_3: $y_0 = x_0x_2x_3 + x_0x_3 + x_0 + x_1 + x_2x_3 + x_2 + 1$

$y_1 = x_0x_1x_2 + x_0x_1x_3 + x_0x_1 + x_0 + x_1x_2 + x_2x_3 + x_3$

$y_2 = x_0x_1 + x_0x_2 + x_2 + x_3 + 1$

$y_3 = x_0x_2x_3 + x_0x_2 + x_0 + x_1 + x_2x_3 + 1$

Permutation P_4: $y_0 = x_0x_2x_3 + x_0 + x_1x_2x_3 + x_2 + x_3 + 1$

$y_1 = x_0x_1x_2 + x_0x_1 + x_0 + x_1x_2 + x_1x_3 + x_2$

$y_2 = x_0x_1x_2 + x_0x_1 + x_0x_2 + x_1x_3 + x_1 + x_2 + x_3$

$y_3 = x_0 + x_1 + x_2x_3$

A.4   Algebraic Normal Form for S-Box 4

Permutation P_1:
$$y_0 = x_0x_1x_3 + x_0x_1 + x_0x_3 + x_1 + x_2x_3 + x_2 + 1$$
$$y_1 = x_0x_1x_2 + x_0x_1 + x_0 + x_1x_2x_3 + x_2 + x_3 + 1$$
$$y_2 = x_0x_1 + x_0x_2 + x_1x_2x_3 + x_2x_3 + x_2 + x_3 + 1$$
$$y_3 = x_0x_1x_3 + x_0x_2x_3 + x_0x_2 + x_0x_3 + x_0 + x_1 + x_2x_3$$

Permutation P_2:
$$y_0 = x_0x_1x_2 + x_0x_1 + x_0 + x_1x_2x_3 + x_2 + x_3 + 1$$
$$y_1 = x_0x_1x_3 + x_0x_1 + x_0x_3 + x_1 + x_2x_3 + x_2$$
$$y_2 = x_0x_1x_3 + x_0x_2x_3 + x_0x_2 + x_0x_3 + x_0 + x_1 + x_2x_3 + 1$$
$$y_3 = x_0x_1 + x_0x_2 + x_1x_2x_3 + x_2x_3 + x_2 + x_3 + 1$$

Permutation P_3:
$$y_0 = x_0x_1 + x_0x_2 + x_1x_2x_3 + x_1x_3 + x_1 + x_3$$
$$y_1 = x_0x_1x_3 + x_0x_2x_3 + x_0x_2 + x_0x_3 + x_1x_3 + x_1 + x_2 + 1$$
$$y_2 = x_0x_1x_3 + x_0x_1 + x_0 + x_1x_3 + x_2x_3 + x_2 + x_3$$
$$y_3 = x_0x_1x_2 + x_0x_2 + x_0 + x_1x_2x_3 + x_1x_2 + x_1x_3 + x_2x_3 + 1$$

Permutation P_4:
$$y_0 = x_0x_1x_3 + x_0x_2x_3 + x_0x_2 + x_0x_3 + x_1x_3 + x_1 + x_2 + 1$$
$$y_1 = x_0x_1 + x_0x_2 + x_1x_2x_3 + x_1x_3 + x_1 + x_3 + 1$$
$$y_2 = x_0x_1x_2 + x_0x_2 + x_0 + x_1x_2x_3 + x_1x_2 + x_1x_3 + x_2x_3$$
$$y_3 = x_0x_1x_3 + x_0x_1 + x_0 + x_1x_3 + x_2x_3 + x_2 + x_3$$

A.5   Algebraic Normal Form for S-Box 5

Permutation P_1:
$$y_0 = x_0x_1x_2 + x_0x_1 + x_0x_2x_3 + x_0x_2 + x_0x_3 + x_1x_3 + x_2$$
$$y_1 = x_0x_1x_2 + x_0x_1x_3 + x_0x_1 + x_0x_2x_3 + x_0x_2 + x_0x_3 + x_0 + x_1x_2x_3 + x_1x_2 + x_1 + x_3 + 1$$
$$y_2 = x_0 + x_1x_3 + x_1 + x_2$$
$$y_3 = x_0x_1x_2 + x_0x_1x_3 + x_0x_1 + x_0 + x_1x_2 + x_1x_3 + x_3$$

Permutation P_2:
$$y_0 = x_0x_1x_3 + x_0x_1 + x_0x_2x_3 + x_0 + x_1x_2 + x_3$$
$$y_1 = x_0x_1x_3 + x_0x_1 + x_0x_2 + x_1x_3 + x_2 + x_3 + 1$$
$$y_2 = x_0x_1x_2 + x_0x_2 + x_0 + x_1x_2x_3 + x_1x_2 + x_1x_3 + x_1 + x_2x_3 + 1$$
$$y_3 = x_0x_1x_3 + x_0x_1 + x_0x_2x_3 + x_1 + x_2x_3 + x_2 + x_3 + 1$$

Permutation P_3:
$$y_0 = x_0x_1x_3 + x_0x_2 + x_1x_2x_3 + x_1 + x_2x_3 + x_3$$
$$y_1 = x_0x_1x_3 + x_0x_2x_3 + x_0 + x_1x_3 + x_2x_3 + x_3$$
$$y_2 = x_0x_1x_2 + x_0x_1 + x_0 + x_1x_2x_3 + x_1x_3 + x_1 + x_2x_3 + x_2 + 1$$
$$y_3 = x_0x_1 + x_1x_2x_3 + x_1x_2 + x_2 + x_3$$

Permutation P_4:
$$y_0 = x_0x_2x_3 + x_0 + x_1x_2x_3 + x_1x_3 + x_1 + x_3 + 1$$
$$y_1 = x_0x_2x_3 + x_0x_3 + x_0 + x_1 + x_2x_3 + x_2 + 1$$
$$y_2 = x_0x_2 + x_1x_2x_3 + x_1x_2 + x_1 + x_2x_3 + x_3$$
$$y_3 = x_0x_1x_2 + x_0x_1x_3 + x_0x_1 + x_0x_2x_3 + x_0x_2 + x_0x_3 + x_1x_2x_3 + x_2 + x_3 + 1$$

A.6   Algebraic Normal Form for S-Box 6

Permutation P_1:
$$y_0 = x_0x_1x_2 + x_0 + x_1x_2x_3 + x_1x_2 + x_1x_3 + x_2x_3 + x_2$$
$$y_1 = x_0x_1x_3 + x_0x_2x_3 + x_0x_2 + x_1 + x_2x_3$$
$$y_2 = x_0x_1x_2 + x_0x_2 + x_0 + x_1x_3 + x_1 + x_2 + x_3 + 1$$
$$y_3 = x_0x_1x_2 + x_0x_1 + x_0 + x_1x_2 + x_2x_3 + x_3 + 1$$

Permutation P_2:
$$y_0 = x_0x_1x_3 + x_0x_1 + x_0 + x_1x_3 + x_2x_3 + x_2$$
$$y_1 = x_0x_1x_3 + x_0x_1 + x_0x_2x_3 + x_0x_2 + x_0x_3 + x_1 + x_2x_3 + 1$$
$$y_2 = x_0x_1x_2 + x_0x_1x_3 + x_0x_2 + x_0 + x_1x_3 + x_1 + x_2 + x_3$$
$$y_3 = x_0x_2 + x_1x_2x_3 + x_1 + x_2x_3 + x_2 + x_3 + 1$$

Permutation P_3:
$$y_0 = x_0x_1 + x_0x_2 + x_0 + x_1x_2x_3 + x_1x_3 + x_2x_3 + x_2 + 1$$
$$y_1 = x_0x_2x_3 + x_0 + x_1 + x_2 + x_3$$
$$y_2 = x_0x_1x_3 + x_0x_1 + x_0x_2x_3 + x_0x_2 + x_0 + x_1x_3 + x_1 + x_2x_3 + x_3$$
$$y_3 = x_0x_1x_2 + x_0x_1 + x_0x_2 + x_1x_2 + x_2x_3 + x_2 + x_3 + 1$$

Permutation P_4:
$$y_0 = x_0x_1 + x_0x_2 + x_0 + x_2 + x_3$$
$$y_1 = x_0x_1x_3 + x_0x_2 + x_0x_3 + x_0 + x_1 + x_3$$
$$y_2 = x_0 + x_1x_2x_3 + x_1x_3 + x_1 + x_2 + x_3 + 1$$
$$y_3 = x_0x_1x_3 + x_0x_1 + x_0x_2x_3 + x_0x_2 + x_1x_3 + x_2 + x_3$$

A.7   Algebraic Normal Form for S-Box 7

Permutation P_1:
$$y_0 = x_0x_1x_2 + x_0x_1 + x_0 + x_1x_2 + x_2x_3 + x_2 + x_3$$
$$y_1 = x_0x_1x_3 + x_0x_1 + x_0 + x_1 + x_2 + x_3$$
$$y_2 = x_0 + x_1x_3 + x_1 + x_2x_3 + x_3 + 1$$
$$y_3 = x_0x_1x_2 + x_0 + x_1x_2x_3 + x_1x_3 + x_2x_3 + x_2$$

Permutation P_2:
$$y_0 = x_0x_1x_2 + x_0x_1x_3 + x_0x_1 + x_0 + x_1x_2 + x_1x_3 + x_2x_3 + x_2 + x_3 + 1$$
$$y_1 = x_0x_1x_2 + x_1x_2x_3 + x_1x_2 + x_1 + x_3$$
$$y_2 = x_0x_1x_2 + x_0x_1x_3 + x_0 + x_1x_3 + x_1 + x_2x_3 + 1$$
$$y_3 = x_0 + x_1x_3 + x_2 + 1$$

Permutation P_3:
$$y_0 = x_0x_1x_2 + x_0x_1 + x_0 + x_1x_2 + x_2x_3 + x_2 + x_3 + 1$$
$$y_1 = x_0x_1 + x_0x_2x_3 + x_0x_2 + x_1x_3 + x_1 + x_2x_3 + x_3$$
$$y_2 = x_0x_1x_2 + x_0 + x_1x_2x_3 + x_1x_3 + x_2x_3 + x_2$$
$$y_3 = x_0x_1x_3 + x_0x_2x_3 + x_0x_2 + x_1 + x_2 + x_3$$

Permutation P_4:
$$y_0 = x_0x_1x_3 + x_0x_3 + x_0 + x_1 + x_2 + x_3$$
$$y_1 = x_0x_1x_3 + x_1x_3 + x_1 + x_2 + x_3 + 1$$
$$y_2 = x_0 + x_1x_2x_3 + x_2 + x_3 + 1$$
$$y_3 = x_0x_1x_3 + x_0x_1 + x_0x_2x_3 + x_0x_2 + x_0 + x_1 + x_3$$

A.8   Algebraic Normal Form for S-Box 8

Permutation P_1:
$$y_0 = x_0x_1x_3 + x_0x_1 + x_0 + x_1 + x_2 + x_3 + 1$$
$$y_1 = x_0x_1 + x_0x_2 + x_0 + x_2 + x_3$$
$$y_2 = x_0x_1x_3 + x_0x_2 + x_0x_3 + x_0 + x_1x_3 + x_1 + x_2x_3 + x_3 + 1$$
$$y_3 = x_0x_1x_3 + x_0x_3 + x_0 + x_1x_2x_3 + x_1x_3 + x_1 + x_2 + 1$$

Permutation P_2:
$$y_0 = x_0x_1x_2 + x_0x_1x_3 + x_0x_1 + x_0x_2 + x_0x_3 + x_1x_2 + x_2x_3 + x_2 + x_3 + 1$$
$$y_1 = x_0x_1x_3 + x_0x_1 + x_0x_2 + x_0x_3 + x_0 + x_1x_2x_3 + x_1x_3 + x_2x_3 + x_2$$
$$y_2 = x_0x_1x_3 + x_0x_2 + x_0x_3 + x_0 + x_1x_3 + x_1 + x_2x_3 + x_3$$
$$y_3 = x_0x_1x_3 + x_0x_1 + x_0 + x_1 + x_2 + x_3$$

Permutation P_3:
$$y_0 = x_0x_1 + x_0x_2x_3 + x_0x_2 + x_1x_3 + x_1 + x_2x_3 + x_3 + 1$$
$$y_1 = x_0x_2x_3 + x_0x_3 + x_1 + x_2 + x_3 + 1$$
$$y_2 = x_0 + x_1x_2x_3 + x_1x_2 + x_2 + x_3 + 1$$
$$y_3 = x_0x_1x_3 + x_0x_1 + x_0x_2 + x_0x_3 + x_0 + x_1x_3 + x_2$$

Permutation P_4:
$$y_0 = x_0x_1x_2 + x_0x_2 + x_0 + x_1x_2x_3 + x_3$$
$$y_1 = x_0x_1 + x_0 + x_1x_2x_3 + x_1x_3 + x_2x_3 + x_2 + 1$$
$$y_2 = x_0x_2 + x_1 + x_2 + x_3$$
$$y_3 = x_0x_1 + x_0x_2x_3 + x_0x_2 + x_1x_3 + x_1 + x_2x_3 + x_3$$

References

1. Agrawal, D., Archambeault, B., Rao, J.R., Rohatgi, P.: The EM side—channel(s). In: Kaliski, B.S., Koç, K., Paar, C. (eds.) CHES 2002. LNCS, vol. 2523, pp. 29–45. Springer, Heidelberg (2003). https://doi.org/10.1007/3-540-36400-5_4

2. Bertoni, G., Daemen, J., Peeters, M., Van Assche, G.: Keccak. In: Johansson, T., Nguyen, P.Q. (eds.) EUROCRYPT 2013. LNCS, vol. 7881, pp. 313–314. Springer, Heidelberg (2013). https://doi.org/10.1007/978-3-642-38348-9_19

3. Bilgin, B., Gierlichs, B., Nikova, S., Nikov, V., Rijmen, V.: Higher-order threshold implementations. In: Sarkar, P., Iwata, T. (eds.) ASIACRYPT 2014. LNCS, vol. 8874, pp. 326–343. Springer, Heidelberg (2014). https://doi.org/10.1007/978-3-662-45608-8_18

4. Bilgin, B., Nikova, S., Nikov, V., Rijmen, V., Tokareva, N.N., Vitkup, V.: Threshold implementations of small S-boxes. Crypt. Commun. **7**(1), 3–33 (2015)

5. Faust, S., Grosso, V., Del Pozo, S.M., Paglialonga, C., Standaert, F.-X.: Composable masking schemes in the presence of physical defaults and the robust probing model. Cryptology ePrint Archive, Report 2017/711 (2017). https://eprint.iacr.org/2017/711

6. Gilbert Goodwill, B.J., Jaffe, J., Rohatgi, P.: A testing methodology for side-channel resistance validation. In: NIST Non-invasive Attack Testing Workshop (2011)
7. Groß, H., Mangard, S.: Reconciling $d + 1$ masking in hardware and software. In: Fischer, W., Homma, N. (eds.) CHES 2017. LNCS, vol. 10529, pp. 115–136. Springer, Cham (2017). https://doi.org/10.1007/978-3-319-66787-4_6
8. Groß, H., Mangard, S., Korak, T.: An efficient side-channel protected AES implementation with arbitrary protection order. In: Handschuh, H. (ed.) CT-RSA 2017. LNCS, vol. 10159, pp. 95–112. Springer, Cham (2017). https://doi.org/10.1007/978-3-319-52153-4_6
9. Ishai, Y., Sahai, A., Wagner, D.: Private circuits: securing hardware against probing attacks. In: Boneh, D. (ed.) CRYPTO 2003. LNCS, vol. 2729, pp. 463–481. Springer, Heidelberg (2003). https://doi.org/10.1007/978-3-540-45146-4_27
10. Kocher, P.C.: Timing attacks on implementations of Diffie-Hellman, RSA, DSS, and other systems. In: Koblitz, N. (ed.) CRYPTO 1996. LNCS, vol. 1109, pp. 104–113. Springer, Heidelberg (1996). https://doi.org/10.1007/3-540-68697-5_9
11. Kocher, P., Jaffe, J., Jun, B.: Differential power analysis. In: Wiener, M. (ed.) CRYPTO 1999. LNCS, vol. 1666, pp. 388–397. Springer, Heidelberg (1999). https://doi.org/10.1007/3-540-48405-1_25
12. Kutzner, S., Nguyen, P.H., Poschmann, A., Wang, H.: On 3-share threshold implementations for 4-Bit S-boxes. In: Prouff, E. (ed.) COSADE 2013. LNCS, vol. 7864, pp. 99–113. Springer, Heidelberg (2013). https://doi.org/10.1007/978-3-642-40026-1_7
13. Leitold, H., Mayerwieser, W., Payer, U., Posch, K.C., Posch, R., Wolkerstorfer, J.: A 155 Mbps triple-DES network encryptor. In: Koç, Ç.K., Paar, C. (eds.) CHES 2000. LNCS, vol. 1965, pp. 164–174. Springer, Heidelberg (2000). https://doi.org/10.1007/3-540-44499-8_12
14. Maghrebi, H., Danger, J.-L., Flament, F., Guilley, S., Sauvage, L.: Evaluation of countermeasure implementations based on Boolean masking to thwart side-channel attacks. In: International Conference on Signals, Circuits and Systems, SCS 2009, Jerba, Tunisia, 5–8 November 2009, pp. 1–6 (2009)
15. Mangard, S., Oswald, E., Popp, T.: Power Analysis Attacks - Revealing the Secrets of Smart Cards. Springer, Heidelberg (2007). https://doi.org/10.1007/978-0-387-38162-6
16. McLoone, M., McCanny, J.V.: High-performance FPGA implementation of DES using a novel method for implementing the key schedule. IEE Proc.-Circ. Devices Syst. **150**(5), 373–378 (2003)
17. Moradi, A., Poschmann, A., Ling, S., Paar, C., Wang, H.: Pushing the limits: a very compact and a threshold implementation of AES. In: Paterson, K.G. (ed.) EUROCRYPT 2011. LNCS, vol. 6632, pp. 69–88. Springer, Heidelberg (2011). https://doi.org/10.1007/978-3-642-20465-4_6
18. Nikova, S., Nikov, V., Rijmen, V.: Decomposition of permutations in a finite field. IACR Cryptology ePrint Archive 2018:103 (2018)
19. Nikova, S., Rechberger, C., Rijmen, V.: Threshold implementations against side-channel attacks and glitches. In: Ning, P., Qing, S., Li, N. (eds.) ICICS 2006. LNCS, vol. 4307, pp. 529–545. Springer, Heidelberg (2006). https://doi.org/10.1007/11935308_38
20. Oswald, D., Paar, C.: Breaking mifare DESFire MF3ICD40: power analysis and templates in the real world. In: Preneel, B., Takagi, T. (eds.) CHES 2011. LNCS, vol. 6917, pp. 207–222. Springer, Heidelberg (2011). https://doi.org/10.1007/978-3-642-23951-9_14

21. Poschmann, A., Moradi, A., Khoo, K., Lim, C.-W., Wang, H., Ling, S.: Side-channel resistant crypto for less than 2,300 GE. J. Cryptol. **24**(2), 322–345 (2011)
22. Reparaz, O., Bilgin, B., Nikova, S., Gierlichs, B., Verbauwhede, I.: Consolidating masking schemes. In: Gennaro, R., Robshaw, M. (eds.) CRYPTO 2015. LNCS, vol. 9215, pp. 764–783. Springer, Heidelberg (2015). https://doi.org/10.1007/978-3-662-47989-6_37
23. Sasdrich, P., Moradi, A., Güneysu, T.: Affine equivalence and its application to tightening threshold implementations. In: Dunkelman, O., Keliher, L. (eds.) SAC 2015. LNCS, vol. 9566, pp. 263–276. Springer, Cham (2016). https://doi.org/10.1007/978-3-319-31301-6_16
24. Sasdrich, P., Moradi, A., Güneysu, T.: Hiding higher-order side-channel leakage. In: Handschuh, H. (ed.) CT-RSA 2017. LNCS, vol. 10159, pp. 131–146. Springer, Cham (2017). https://doi.org/10.1007/978-3-319-52153-4_8
25. Sauvage, L., Guilley, S., Danger, J.-L., Mathieu, Y., Nassar, M.: Successful attack on an FPGA-based WDDL DES cryptoprocessor without place and route constraints. In: Design, Automation and Test in Europe, DATE 2009, Nice, France, 20–24 April 2009, pp. 640–645 (2009)
26. Schneider, T., Moradi, A.: Leakage assessment methodology - extended version. J. Cryptogr. Eng. **6**(2), 85–99 (2016)
27. Standaert, F.-X., Rouvroy, G., Quisquater, J.-J.: FPGA implementations of the DES and triple-des masked against power analysis attacks. In: Proceedings of the 2006 International Conference on Field Programmable Logic and Applications (FPL), Madrid, Spain, 28–30 August 2006, pp. 1–4 (2006)
28. Trimberger, S., Pang, R., Singh, A.: A 12 Gbps DES encryptor/decryptor core in an FPGA. In: Koç, Ç.K., Paar, C. (eds.) CHES 2000. LNCS, vol. 1965, pp. 156–163. Springer, Heidelberg (2000). https://doi.org/10.1007/3-540-44499-8_11
29. Wilcox, D.C., Pierson, L.G., Robertson, P.J., Witzke, E.L., Gass, K.: A DES ASIC suitable for network encryption at 10 Gbps and beyond. In: Koç, Ç.K., Paar, C. (eds.) CHES 1999. LNCS, vol. 1717, pp. 37–48. Springer, Heidelberg (1999). https://doi.org/10.1007/3-540-48059-5_5

Threshold Implementation in Software
Case Study of PRESENT

Pascal Sasdrich[✉], René Bock, and Amir Moradi

Horst Görtz Institute for IT-Security, Ruhr-Universität Bochum,
Bochum, Germany
{pascal.sasdrich,rene.bock,amir.moradi}@rub.de

Abstract. Masking is one of the predominantly deployed countermeasures in order to prevent side-channel analysis (SCA) attacks. Over the years, various masking schemes have been proposed. However, the implementation of Boolean masking schemes has proven to be difficult in particular for embedded devices due to undisclosed architecture details and device internals. In this article, we investigate the application of Threshold Implementation (TI) in terms of Boolean masking in software using the PRESENT cipher as a case study. Since TI has proven to be a proper solution in order to implement Boolean masking for hardware circuits, we apply the same concept for software implementations and compare it to classical first- and second-order Boolean masking schemes. Eventually, our practical security evaluations reveal that amongst all our considered implementation variants only the TI can provide first-order security while all others still exhibit detectable first-order leakage.

Keywords: Side-channel analysis · Boolean masking
Threshold Implementation · t-test · Micro-controller · AVR
PRESENT

1 Introduction

Among the protection schemes against side-channel analysis (SCA) attacks, it can be dared to say that *masking* is the best studied countermeasure. Many different kinds of masking schemes for both software and hardware platforms have been introduced [1,5,10,13,15,20,25,29,35,37]. Each of them comes with its own advantages (e.g., simplicity and scalability to high protection orders) and disadvantages (e.g., high area and time overheads) and some with shortcomings (see for example [19,27]). Our focus in this work is the realization of Boolean masking scheme in software implementations.

It is already known that – due to the internal architecture of micro-processors – masked implementations may still exhibit undesired exploitable leakage (see [3] as an example). It indeed becomes more problematic when details of the internal architecture of the underlying commercial micro-processor are kept secret. For instance, the way the pipeline is built, the shared bus between ALU and memory together with the fashion in that the masked program code

© Springer International Publishing AG, part of Springer Nature 2018
J. Fan and B. Gierlichs (Eds.): COSADE 2018, LNCS 10815, pp. 227–244, 2018.
https://doi.org/10.1007/978-3-319-89641-0_13

is written, can impact the leakage of the resulting implementation. As a simple example, suppose that two Boolean shares (x^1, x^2) of a secret value x are consecutively transferred through a bus, that leads to leakage depending on distance between the shares, i.e., $x^1 \oplus x^2 = x$. The attack reported in [27] follows the same principle. In this case, the implementation would exhibit first-order leakage while it is not possible to detect such a flaw by analyzing the program code without considering the details of the internal architecture.

On the other hand, Threshold Implementation has been introduced as a proper way to realize Boolean masking in hardware platforms [30]. It provides a suitable guideline on how to avoid heuristics in masked hardware (see [8,31]) that can provide provable first-order security. In short, in this paper we examine the efficiency of applying such a scheme on a software implementation. As the case study, we focus on the PRESENT cipher [7] and an Atmel AVR microcontroller. We give details of different ways to realize a masked implementation including first- and second-order classical Boolean masking and the Threshold Implementation variant. Our investigations are based on the performance figures (code size and latency) as well as security analysis. More precisely, we present the result of leakage detection over practical SCA measurements.

Outline. In Sect. 2 we deal with the essential concepts to follow the rest of the paper including Boolean masking, Threshold Implementation, and possible ways to apply Threshold Implementation on PRESENT S-box. Section 3 gives the details of different variants of the masked PRESENT implementations, and in Sect. 4 the corresponding practical SCA analyses are presented. Finally, we conclude our research in Sect. 5.

2   Concept

2.1   Notation

We denote single-bit random variables using lower-case characters while we indicate multi-bit vectors by bold ones. Further, we use subscripts for elements within a vector, bars for shared representations of random variables and superscripts for elements of a shared representation. Functions are indicated using sans serif fonts and sets are denoted by calligraphic ones.

Moreover, let us denote any vector $x \in \mathbb{GF}(2^m)$ of m single-bit elements by $\langle x_1, \ldots, x_m \rangle$. Then, the shared representation $\bar{x}$ of a vector x under Boolean masking with s shares is given as $\bar{x} = (x^1, \ldots, x^s)$, where:

$$x = \bigoplus_{i=1}^{s} \bar{x} = \bigoplus_{i=1}^{s} x^i = \bigoplus_{i=1}^{s} \langle x_1^i, \ldots, x_m^i \rangle.$$

2.2   Boolean Masking

During the last two decades, Boolean masking has become the common approach to prevent information leakage of digital devices through physical side channels such as the instantaneous power consumption or electromagnetic radiations. Since sensitive information can be extracted from those physical observations by means of statistical analysis based on statistical moments of different orders, Boolean masking uses the concept of *secret sharing* to split a sensitive variable x into s shares $x^1, \ldots, x^s$ such that $x = x^1 \oplus \ldots \oplus x^s$.

In general, Boolean masking can provide protection up to the d-th order using $s = d + 1$ shares that have to be processed independently. We should note that several physical effects, such as glitches or parasitic capacitances, can affect the security and lever the protection mechanism. Nevertheless, while linear operations can be applied independently to each share (due to the transparency of XOR over Boolean masking), all challenges of realizing a Boolean masked implementation are due to the non-linear functions (S-boxes) involved in any cryptographic primitive. To this end, masking in software is realized following two different approaches:

- The S-box is represented by a sequence of operations including a unique (or a limited number of) non-linear function, e.g., a 2-bit AND gate. Then, based on the underlying protection order d, the masked (secure) version of such a unique non-linear function is developed as a gadget. As the final step, the operations of the S-box are replaced by their secure version. This needs fresh randomness every time the secure non-linear function (the gadget) is called, and due to the sequential nature of the algorithm its timing overhead is not negligible compared to a naive unprotected implementation. The interested reader is referred to [17,18,37] for a couple of examples.
- Alternatively, the S-box is realized using a randomized look-up table S' in terms of

$$S'(x \oplus m^1 \oplus \ldots \oplus m^{s-1}) = S(x) \oplus n^1 \oplus \ldots \oplus n^{s-1}, \qquad (1)$$

with $m^1, \ldots, m^{s-1}$ considered as input masks and $n^1, \ldots, n^{s-1}$ as output masks. Depending on the S-box size and the number of shares s, it is usually impossible to precompute and store the masked S-box S' for all possible masks (known as Global Look-Up-Table [34]). Therefore, S' is frequently recomputed to avoid large memory requirements. Examples include but are not restricted to [36,38], and [41], where such a construction for AES at arbitrary order is presented while its flaw has been reported in [11].[1]

In this work, our focus is on the second approach, i.e., the pre-computed and randomized look-up table S', to which we refer as **classical Boolean masking**. In case Eq. (1) is implemented as single look-up table, the input and output masks have to fulfill certain criteria in order to realize a secure Boolean masking scheme. In particular, input and output masks cannot be the same. Otherwise, if the masked S-box input $x \oplus m^1 \oplus \ldots \oplus m^{s-1}$ is overwritten by the masked S-box output $S(x) \oplus m^1 \oplus \ldots \oplus m^{s-1}$, the leakage depends on unmasked value $x \oplus S(x)$ [27] (see [4] and [26, Chap. 9] as examples where such a flaw exists).

---

[1] Alternatively, there exist other solutions [9,14,15] which make use of the S-box construction, e.g., $GF(2^8)$ inversion of AES S-box.

Hence, in a conservative manner the output masks have to be independent of the input masks. However, since this might be impracticable particularly for higher orders, more practical approaches may use a function to derive the output masks from the input masks but have to ensure the uniformity. More precisely, if $n^{i \in \{1,\ldots,s-1\}} = f(m^i)$, it must be ensured that $n^i \oplus m^i$ is uniform over $\mathbb{GF}(2^m)$. Otherwise, the above expressed distance (between the S-box input and output) would not be uniformly masked. We should also refer to low-entropy masking schemes [5,29] which are designed to enable keeping all masked tables in memory, i.e., no recomputation and mask update is required, but at the cost of limited protection [19,24,42]. For example, the Rotating S-box Masking (RSM) construction introduced in [29] (and used in DPA contest V4.1) makes use of a reduced 8-bit mask space of 2^4 elements $\{m_0, \ldots, m_{15}\}$. This allowed the authors to precompute all masked S-boxes as $S'_i(x \oplus m_i) = S(x) \oplus m_{i+1}$. In means that the output mask is derived from the input mask as $f(m_i) = m_{i+1}$. As shown in [27], the distance between the input mask and the output mask $m_i \oplus m_{i+1}$ is not uniform, hence first-order leakage considering the distance between the S-box input and output $x \oplus S(x)$ is detectable.

2.3   Threshold Implementation

As a special case of Boolean masking using multi-party computation, Threshold Implementation (TI) has been proposed by Nikova *et al.* [30] as a provable secure first-order masking scheme for digital circuits even in the presence of glitches. In this work, we make use of its basic concept in software, which is defined by the following properties.

Correctness. In order to evaluate any function $F(x) = y$ on the shared representation $\bar{x} = (x^1, \ldots, x^s)$ with s shares, we can use corresponding component functions $f^{i \in \{1,\ldots,n\}}(\bar{x}) = y^i$ in order to evaluate F for each output share individually but have to ensure *correctness*, i.e., the result $\bar{y} = (y^1, \ldots, y^n)$ has to be the shared representation of y with $n \geq s$.

Non-completeness. Security in the sense of the first-order statistical moment is achieved using *non-complete* component functions $f^{i \in \{1,\ldots,n\}}$, i.e., each resulting share $(y^1, \ldots, y^n)$ should be independent of at least one input share.

Uniformity. The security of Boolean masking schemes is based on the *uniform* distribution of the masks. Supposing that the input of a TI function is uniformly shared, its output should also be a uniform sharing since it will be used as an input to another shared function (e.g., next cipher rounds). This means, given all possible input sharings $\mathcal{X} = \{\bar{x} | \bigoplus_{i=1}^{s} \bar{x} = x\}$, the set of all possible output sharings $\{f^1, \ldots, f^n | \bar{x} = \mathcal{X}\}$ should be *uniformly* drawn from $\mathcal{Y} = \{\bar{y} | \bigoplus_{i=1}^{n} \bar{y} = y\}$ as all possible sharings of $y = F(x)$. Otherwise, the output would be shared with masks drawn from a biased source, and the first-order security cannot be guaranteed.

2.4   Application to PRESENT Cipher

PRESENT has been designed as Substitution-Permutation Network (SPN) with 31 rounds, a 64-bit block size and either an 80-bit or 128-bit key size. Each round consists of a key addition, succeeded by a confusion phase which consists of the same 4-bit S-box that is applied to all 4-bit words of the state in parallel before the bit permutation layer[2] provides diffusion. In particular, the S-box is a non-linear, cubic, 4-bit function with truth table S : C56B90AD3EF84712. All round keys are derived from the initial key using bit-wise rotations, addition of round constants and the application of the S-box. Eventually, a final post-whitening key addition is performed after the last round.

Table 1. Non-linear function $N(m) = n$.

m	0	1	2	3	4	5	6	7	8	9	A	B	C	D	E	F
n	E	4	F	9	0	3	D	5	7	8	A	2	B	1	6	C
$m \oplus n$	E	5	D	A	4	6	B	2	F	1	0	9	7	C	8	3

Boolean Masking. Classical first-order Boolean masking uses 2 shares x^1, x^2 with $x^1 = x \oplus m$ and $x^2 = m$. Due to its small size (4-bit to 4-bit), the entire masked S-box as an 8-bit to 4-bit look-up table $S'(x \oplus m, m) = S(x) \oplus n$ can fit into even a restricted memory. Hence, the recomputation of the masked S-box when m changes is not required. In this case we need to derive the output mask n from the input mask m in such a way that the uniformity of $m \oplus n$ always holds. An example of such a function, so-called $n = N(m)$ is given in Table 1. Note that we have derived this table by a search through random bijections $m \rightarrow N(m)$.

Threshold Implementation. In several articles, the TI concept has been applied on the PRESENT S-box leading to first- and second-order uniform TI constructions. Under the TI definitions, the minimum number of required shares s depends not only on the desired level of security (order d) but also on the algebraic degree t of the underlying S-box, i.e., $s > t\,d$. Since the PRESENT S-box is a cubic bijection ($t = 3$), for first-order security ($d = 1$) at least $s > 3$ shares are required. Therefore, all the reported TI PRESENT designs have followed a decomposition fashion by representing the S-box by two quadratic bijections as S = F∘G. This allows to reduce the number of shares to 3 with the cost of adding a register between the shared functions F and G for hardware implementations.

In the first relevant article [33], the authors have followed a non-systematic way and provided F and G whose *direct sharing*[3] automatically satisfy the uniformity, i.e., a first-order secure PRESENT S-box. In other works [28,39], the authors followed the principle explained in [6] and decomposed the S-box into forms like

---

[2] A detailed description and discussion of the permutation layer can be found in the original article [7].

[3] See [30] for the definition and examples for direct sharing.

$$S = A'' \circ Q_2 \circ A' \circ Q_1 \circ A, \tag{2}$$

with A, A', and A'' being affine transformations, and Q_1 and Q_2 the identifiers of quadratic classes whose uniform sharing can be easily achieved by direct sharing. Since application of affine transformations does not change the uniformity, such a construction inherently fulfills the uniformity property.

However, since not all 4-bit S-boxes can be decomposed following the concept of Eq. (2), Kutzner et al. proposed the notion of *factorization* in order to enable 3-share decomposition for all possible 4-bit permutations [21–23]. Fortunately, the PRESENT S-box belongs to those permutations that natively allow a decomposition into quadratic terms which enables more efficient designs.

According to [6] the PRESENT S-box belongs to the class C_{266} which can be decomposed by quadratic classes[4] $(Q_{12}, Q_{12}), (Q_{294}, Q_{299}), (Q_{299}, Q_{294})$, and (Q_{299}, Q_{299}) as identifier for (Q_1, Q_2) in Eq. (2). As an example, the (Q_{299}, Q_{294}) case has been used in [28] and (Q_{12}, Q_{12}) in [39].

We selected (Q_{12}, Q_{12}) with $Q_{12} : 0123456789\text{CDEFAB}$, $A : 01\text{AB}892345\text{EFCD}67$, $A' : 0\text{B}835\text{ED}61\text{A}924\text{FC}7$, and $A'' : \text{C}98\text{D}6327\text{AFEB}0541$. However, since our goal is to realize such functions (including the component functions of the shared Q_{12}) by means of look-up tables on software, we represent the S-box as

$$S = \underbrace{A'' \circ Q_{12} \circ A}_{F} \circ \underbrace{A^{-1} \circ A' \circ A''^{-1}}_{A'''} \circ \underbrace{A'' \circ Q_{12} \circ A}_{F}. \tag{3}$$

Hence, it lets us reduce the required look-up tables to $F : \text{C}905\text{AF}8\text{D}63\text{EB}4127$ and $A''' : 8\text{FDACB}9\text{E}43160752$.

Applying direct sharing on Q_{12} would lead to a unique component function $f_{Q_{12}}(\langle a^1, b^1, c^1, d^1 \rangle, \langle a^2, b^2, c^2, d^2 \rangle) = \langle e, f, g, h \rangle$ as

$$e = a^1, \qquad\qquad f = b^1 + b^2 d^2 + c^2 d^2 + d^2 b^1 + d^2 c^1 + b^2 d^1 + c^2 d^1,$$

$$g = c^1 + b^2 d^2 + d^2 b^1 + b^2 d^1, \quad h = d^1, \tag{4}$$

with $\langle a^1, b^1, c^1, d^1 \rangle$ the 4-bit input share x^1 (respectively for input share x^2), $\langle e, f, g, h \rangle$ the 4-bit output share, and a and e the least significant bits. Hence, the three 4-bit output shares $\bar{y} = (y^1, y^2, y^3)$ provided by $y^1 = f_{Q_{12}}(x^2, x^3)$, $y^2 = f_{Q_{12}}(x^3, x^1)$ and $y^3 = f_{Q_{12}}(x^1, x^2)$ make a uniform first-order TI of Q_{12}.

In a software implementation, we can make a look-up table

$$T(x^i, x^j) = A'' \left(f_{Q_{12}} \left(A\left(x^i\right), A\left(x^j\right) \right) \right), \tag{5}$$

which is a component function of the shared function F in Eq.(3). Therefore, in addition to a 4-bit to 4-bit look-up table $A'''(.)$ it is sufficient to implement $T(.,.)$ as an 8-bit to 4-bit look-up table to fully realize the TI S-box by 6 times look-ups through $T(.,.)$ and 3 times look-ups through $A'''(.)$ (see Eq. (3)). As a reference to our construction, we below list the truth table of $T(a, b)$. Interestingly, the result is independent of the LSB of input b (see also Eq. (4) which is independent of a^2), hence we only have to store half of the table and can reduce memory requirements (Table 2).

---

[4] Excluding the quadratic class Q_{300} whose uniform sharing needs two stages.

Table 2. Truth table for $\mathsf{T}(a,b)$

a \ b	0	1	2	3	4	5	6	7	8	9	a	b	c	d	e	f
0	c	c	2	2	c	c	c	c	c	c	6	6	8	8	c	c
1	9	9	7	7	9	9	9	9	9	9	3	3	d	d	9	9
2	e	e	0	0	0	0	0	0	a	a	0	0	0	0	4	4
3	b	b	5	5	5	5	5	5	f	f	5	5	5	5	1	1
4	a	a	a	a	a	a	4	4	e	e	a	a	a	a	0	0
5	f	f	f	f	f	f	1	1	b	b	f	f	f	f	5	5
6	8	8	8	8	6	6	8	8	8	8	c	c	2	2	8	8
7	d	d	d	d	3	3	d	d	d	d	9	9	7	7	d	d
8	6	6	c	c	2	2	6	6	6	6	8	8	6	6	6	6
9	3	3	9	9	7	7	3	3	3	3	d	d	3	3	3	3
a	4	4	e	e	e	e	a	a	0	0	e	e	e	e	e	e
b	1	1	b	b	b	b	f	f	5	5	b	b	b	b	b	b
c	0	0	4	4	4	4	e	e	4	4	4	4	4	4	a	a
d	5	5	1	1	1	1	b	b	1	1	1	1	1	1	f	f
e	2	2	6	6	8	8	2	2	2	2	2	2	c	c	2	2
f	7	7	3	3	d	d	7	7	7	7	7	7	9	9	7	7

Higher-Order Boolean Masking. The above explained TI construction is a 2nd-order Boolean masking. Therefore, ignoring the non-completeness property of TI (which indeed has been defined considering hardware platforms), we can realize larger look-up tables hence reducing the latency. To this end we follow two procedures:

- As a classical 2nd-order Boolean masking we can implement a 12-bit to 12-bit look-up table which realizes the entire masked S-box. More precisely, we can build a look-up table $\mathsf{T}(x^1, x^2, x^3) = (y^1, y^2, y^3)$ with $y^1 \oplus y^2 \oplus y^3 = \mathsf{S}(x^1 \oplus x^2 \oplus x^3)$. In order to ensure the uniformity, we can build such a look-up table in such a way that it realizes the above-explained TI S-box. In the following sections, this approach is referred to as "classical 2nd-order Boolean masking".

- As an alternative, we can build a 12-bit to 12-bit look-up table $\mathsf{T}(.,.,.)$ that implements the shared function F (see Eq. (3)). Hence, by looking-up through such a table $\mathsf{T}(.,.,.)$ twice and thrice through the 4-bit to 4-bit look-up table A''', the output of the masked S-box can be computed which also guarantees the uniformity. We refer to this scheme as "classical 2nd-order Boolean masking with affine transformation".

In addition to the two above-expressed approaches, we consider two other implementation variants including (*i*) classical 1st-order Boolean masking and (*ii*) Threshold Implementation in our practical experiments presented in the next sections.

3   Implementation

In this section we introduce the target platform and describe and compare the performance figures of our implementations.

3.1   Target Platform

As the target platform, we have chosen an Atmel ATmega163 which is an 8-bit micro-controller with 16 KB programmable flash memory and 1024 B internal SRAM. It is constructed of two internal pipeline stages, provides 32 general purpose 8-bit registers, and uses an 8-bit RISC instruction set that can be programmed either using C compiler or AVR Assembler. In our experiments, we opted the micro-controller to operate at a frequency of 4 MHz. This choice has been made to obtain accurate side-channel measurements.

3.2   Pseudo-Code

Below we provide further implementation details on the realization of our considered implementation variants of Sect. 2. In particular, we want to stress that all implementations have been realized using AVR Assembler in order to maintain maximum control over the executed code and to prevent problems due to adverse compiler optimizations [3].

In general, all implementations consist of a key schedule routine and a round function that is sub-divided into key addition, substitution, and permutation layer. Since we opted to implement a key schedule without shared keys, this routine is the same for all implementation variants. Moreover, the AddRoundKey and pLayer are shared among the different variants as well and only the sLayer routine differs depending on the underlying masking scheme.

In the following, we provide pseudo-codes for all of our implementations and highlight important aspects and optimizations that have been applied.

Classical 1st-Order Boolean Masking. Algorithm 3.1 outlines our implementation of the classical Boolean masking scheme presented in Sect. 2.4 using a masked S-box look-up table S′ and a non-linear mask update function N chosen in accordance with our presented concept. During the design and implementation process, we particularly took care of the processing of intermediate values in order to avoid side-channel leakage due to the distance between two successively processed values.

In general, if a masked value $x^1 = x \oplus m$ and its mask $x^2 = m$ are processed consecutively, internal registers may be overwritten and leak through the

---

Algorithm 3.1. CLASSICAL 1ST-ORDER BOOLEAN MASKING

Input : $\bar{x} = (x \oplus m, m)$: *shared plaintext*
　　　　k : *cipher key*
Output: $\bar{y} = (y^1, y^2)$: shared ciphertext

begin
　　$rk \leftarrow KeySchedule(k)$
　　for $i \leftarrow 1$ **to** 31 **do**
　　　　$x^1 \leftarrow x^1 \oplus rk[i]$
　　　　$\bar{x} \leftarrow (\mathsf{S}'(x^1, x^2), \mathsf{N}(x^2))$
　　　　$x^1 \leftarrow \mathsf{P}(x^1)$
　　　　$x^2 \leftarrow \mathsf{P}(x^2)$
　　end
　　$y^1 \leftarrow x^1 \oplus rk[32]$
　　$y^2 \leftarrow x^2$
end

---

distance of these values, i.e., $x^1 \oplus x^2 = x$. In particular for load and store instructions of the ATmega163 an internal shadow register is involved in order to buffer the processed data which then creates a remnant of previous memory accesses [32]. Since this shadow register is not directly accessible, it can only be cleared by reading or writing a dummy value (e.g., 0). More precisely, every read and write operation has to be preceded by such a clear instruction to prevent leakage due to the distance between the consecutively accessed data. However, this holds not only for the shadow register but also for every internal register that is used for holding sensitive data.

Moreover, since the micro-controller has two internal pipeline stages [2], we have to ensure that a masked value and its corresponding mask are never processed consecutively, i.e., they never appear in the same pipeline. In particular for the substitution layer, this may occur if the two shares are loaded to perform the table look-up. In order to avoid insertion of unnecessary NOP operations, we start with loading the entire 64 bits of the first share into eight registers before we load the next 64 bits of the second share into another eight registers. Still, we process the last 8-bit chunk of the first share and the first 8-bit chunk of the second share in the same pipeline. However, since the mask is drawn uniformly from a random source, it is unrelated to the first share which is masked by another random value.

Threshold Implementation. Algorithm 3.2 presents the pseudo-code for our TI design according to Sect. 2.4, using the decomposition based on $\mathcal{Q}_{12}$ and an affine transformation A''' as described in Eq. (3). As mentioned before, this decomposition improves the efficiency by limiting the number of look-up tables that have to be stored (one 8-bit to 4-bit and one 4-bit to 4-bit).

Algorithm 3.2. THRESHOLD IMPLEMENTATION

Input : $\bar{x} = (x^1, x^2, x^3)$: *shared plaintext*
   k : *cipher key*
Output: $\bar{y} = (y^1, y^2, y^3)$: shared ciphertext

begin
   $rk \leftarrow KeySchedule(k)$

   for $i \leftarrow 1$ **to** 31 **do**
      $x^1 \leftarrow x^1 \oplus rk[i]$

      $t^3 \leftarrow \mathsf{T}(x^1, x^2)$
      $t^2 \leftarrow \mathsf{T}(x^3, x^1)$
      $t^1 \leftarrow \mathsf{T}(x^2, x^3)$

      $t^3 \leftarrow \mathsf{A}'''(t^3)$
      $t^2 \leftarrow \mathsf{A}'''(t^2)$
      $t^1 \leftarrow \mathsf{A}'''(t^1)$

      $x^3 \leftarrow \mathsf{T}(t^1, t^2)$
      $x^2 \leftarrow \mathsf{T}(t^3, t^1)$
      $x^1 \leftarrow \mathsf{T}(t^2, t^3)$

      $x^1 \leftarrow \mathsf{P}(x^1)$
      $x^2 \leftarrow \mathsf{P}(x^2)$
      $x^3 \leftarrow \mathsf{P}(x^3)$
   end

   $y^1 \leftarrow x^1 \oplus rk[32]$
   $y^2 \leftarrow x^2$
   $y^3 \leftarrow x^3$
end

Again, processing the shared values has to be done carefully in order to avoid side-channel leakage due to internal (shadow) registers and the pipeline of the micro-controller. Fortunately, compared to the classical Boolean masking – due to its *non-completeness* property – our TI design always processes only two shares at once. However, special care has to be taken for the order of processing the individual shares (for all implementation variants). For instance, starting with the addition of the round key to the first share x^1 and updating this share using the look-up table T would result in unintentional leakage since both shares x^2 and x^3 have to be loaded after x^1 has been processed. Due to this, our implementation starts with updating the third share first before the remaining shares are processed (see Algorithm 3.2).

Classical 2nd-Order Boolean Masking. This implementation, as presented in Algorithm 3.3, uses three shares (similar to the TI), but the masked S-box instead is realized by a single look-up table $\mathsf{T}(., ., .)$ as described in Sect. 2.4.

In particular the realization of a 12-bit to 12-bit look-up table on an 8-bit micro-controller is challenging. On one hand, the 12-bit look-up table will

---

Algorithm 3.3. CLASSICAL 2ND-ORDER BOOLEAN MASKING

Input : $\bar{x} = (x^1, x^2, x^3)$: *shared plaintext*
  k : *cipher key*
Output: $\bar{y} = (y^1, y^2, y^3)$: shared ciphertext

begin
  $rk \leftarrow KeySchedule(k)$
  for $i \leftarrow 1$ **to** 31 **do**
    $x^1 \leftarrow x^1 \oplus rk[i]$
    $\bar{x} \leftarrow \mathsf{T}(x^1, x^2, x^3)$
    $x^1 \leftarrow \mathsf{P}(x^1)$
    $x^2 \leftarrow \mathsf{P}(x^2)$
    $x^3 \leftarrow \mathsf{P}(x^3)$
  end
  $y^1 \leftarrow x^1 \oplus rk[32]$
  $y^2 \leftarrow x^2$
  $y^3 \leftarrow x^3$
end

---

increase the memory requirements significantly. On the other hand, 12-bit addresses can be realized easily by combining two 8-bit registers but at the cost of wasting the four most significant bits. Still, we opted for this approach in order to reduce the overhead due to additional and more complex control logic as well as to guarantee a constant-time implementation (i.e., to prevent data-dependent timings).

Classical 2nd-Order Boolean Masking with Affine Transformation. Eventually, Algorithm 3.4 extends the classical second-order Boolean masking using an affine transformation in order to realize the masked S-box. In particular, the table look-up is done twice and interleaved by applying the affine transformations (see Eq. (3)). However, this variant still has to face the same challenges as the former approach. The motivation to include this variant in our analyses is to examine whether the algebraic degree of the underlying function of the masked look-up table has any effect on observable SCA leakage. The former implementation variant is not formed following the TI principles; its look-up tables have only been extracted from a TI construction hence fulfilling the uniformity. However, this variant additionally stays with 3 shares per quadratic function.

3.3 Comparison

Table 3 provides a summary and comparison of our implementation variants in terms of code size, memory usage (SRAM), and performance (clock cycles). Since all implementations use the same key schedule routine, 256 B of the SRAM usage of all variants are due to the 32 derived round keys and only the remaining memory usage is implementation-specific.

Algorithm 3.4. CLASSICAL 2ND-ORDER BOOLEAN MASKING WITH AFFINE TRANSFORMATION

Input : $\bar{x} = (x^1, x^2, x^3)$: *shared plaintext*
$\quad\quad\quad k$: *cipher key*
Output: $\bar{y} = (y^1, y^2, y^3)$: shared ciphertext

begin
$\quad rk \leftarrow KeySchedule(k)$

$\quad$ **for** $i \leftarrow 1$ **to** 31 **do**
$\quad\quad x^1 \leftarrow x^1 \oplus rk[i]$

$\quad\quad \bar{x} \leftarrow \mathsf{T}(x^1, x^2, x^3)$

$\quad\quad x^1 \leftarrow \mathsf{A}'''(x^1)$
$\quad\quad x^2 \leftarrow \mathsf{A}'''(x^2)$
$\quad\quad x^3 \leftarrow \mathsf{A}'''(x^3)$

$\quad\quad \bar{x} \leftarrow \mathsf{T}(x^1, x^2, x^3)$

$\quad\quad x^1 \leftarrow \mathsf{P}(x^1)$
$\quad\quad x^2 \leftarrow \mathsf{P}(x^2)$
$\quad\quad x^3 \leftarrow \mathsf{P}(x^3)$

$\quad$ **end**

$\quad y^1 \leftarrow x^1 \oplus rk[32]$
$\quad y^2 \leftarrow x^2$
$\quad y^3 \leftarrow x^3$
end

The code size of each implementation comprises the key schedule and the round function including all look-up tables which are stored in the flash memory. Obviously, the classical 2nd-order Boolean masking schemes have the largest code due to the 12-bit to 12-bit look-up tables that require complex handling on an 8-bit micro-controller. Similarly, the TI design has a slightly larger code size than the classical 1st-order Boolean masking due to its more extensive substitution layer that has to handle three shares.

Considering the performance, we measured the latency in terms of clock cycles using the simulator of the Atmel Studio 6.2 environment. In order to prevent any vulnerabilities against timing attacks, we ensured data-independent and constant execution time for all of our implementations. Notably, the latency is particularly dependent on the number of shares and decomposition of the S-box. Hence, the classical 1st-order Boolean masking scheme has the smallest latency, since it operates on only two shares and the substitution layer is realized as a single table look-up. Consequently, the TI design has the highest number of clock cycles, since it uses three shares and the S-box is realized by six table look-ups interleaved with three affine transformations.

Table 3. Comparison between different implementation variants

Variant	Code	Memory	Time
	(*Bytes*)	(*Bytes*)	(*Cycles*)
Classical 1st-order Boolean masking	1 542	272	53 861
Threshold implementation	1 576	304	165 802
Classical 2nd-order Boolean masking	9 328	280	91 557
Classical 2nd-order Boolean masking with affine	9 448	280	148 012

4   Evaluation

4.1   Measurement Setup

For the SCA evaluations, by means of a digital oscilloscope we measured the voltage drop over an $1\,\Omega$ resistor placed at the GND path of the target micro-controller. During the measurements, the micro-controller was operating at a low clock frequency of $4\,\text{MHz}$ (provided internally), and the traces have been collected at a sampling rate of $125\,\text{MS/s}$. We have also made use of one of the I/O pins of the micro-controller to provide a stable and jitter-free signal to trigger the oscilloscope.

4.2   Non-specific Statistical t-Test

During the entire measurements, we kept the key constant (allowing us to forgo masking of the key schedule), and provided the input masks externally, i.e., the random m_t have been generated by a PC and in addition to the masked plain-texts x_t are sent to the micro-controller. This way we could easily examine and ensure the uniform distribution of the masks. As a metric to evaluate the existence of 1st-order leakage in our implementations, we applied the fixed versus random t-test [16,40]. In short, a fixed plaintext is selected, and prior to every measurement a coin is flipped, based on that either the fixed plaintext or a random plaintext is given to the micro-controller. Indeed, such a t-test can examine whether there is a detectable leakage in the measurements without giving any impression about its exploitability. However, the intuition is that if the leakage is exploitable, it is also detectable. Therefore, as a conservative condition, if there is no detectable leakage, no exploitable leakage exists.

4.3   Results

For each of our considered implementation variants we collected 100 000 power traces following the procedure explained in [40]. In our analyses we focused on the first cipher round as well as on a 1st-order t-test.

   Figure 1 presents the corresponding evaluation results for all four implementations. Interestingly, it can be seen that the TI design is the only variant which

240   P. Sasdrich et al.

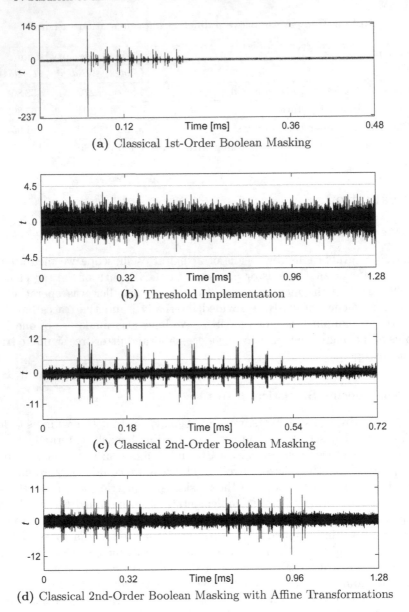

(a) Classical 1st-Order Boolean Masking

(b) Threshold Implementation

(c) Classical 2nd-Order Boolean Masking

(d) Classical 2nd-Order Boolean Masking with Affine Transformations

Fig. 1. SCA evaluation results based on 1st-order non-specific t-test using 100 000 power traces.

does not exhibit detectable leakage. In all other implementations, either with 2 shares or 3 shares, 1st-order leakage is detectable. We have localized the points in time where the t statistics exceeds the 4.5 threshold; they are exactly corresponding to the timing of the performed table look-ups.

Notably, we observe the 1st-order leakage for both variants of the classical 2nd-order Boolean masking. We should highlight that the only difference between these two implementations and the TI design is the way the look-up tables are realized. In these two variants all three shares are present at the input of the table look-ups while in the TI design at most two shares form the input of every table look-up. Our intuition is that the observed leakage is due to the unknown details of the internal architecture of the underlying micro-controller. Similar to the shadow register which we could identify to buffer data for load and store operations, further hidden architecture details of the memory bus and unit could be responsible for the detected leakage. To this end, it seems that the memory control unit exhibits non-linear leakage depending on the given address during the table look-ups. Hence, following the non-completeness principle of TI seems to be a suitable choice which avoids all three shares to appear as an address for a look-up, since it is hardly possible to get the necessary but missing details of the architecture. We should emphasize that we have just shown that if all shares appear at the address of a table look-up, there exists detectable first-order leakage. On one hand, with the current experiments we cannot comment on the exploitability of such observed leakages. On the other hand, the very high t-test statistics for the classical 1st-order Boolean masking shown in Fig. 1(a) induce the exploitability of the leakage.

5 Conclusion

In this paper, we have investigated the application of Threshold Implementations for software implementations in order to provide first-order security against side-channel analysis attacks. In this context, we have developed and implemented a classical first-order Boolean masking scheme, two second-order Boolean masking schemes and a first-order TI. In general, our findings show that the classical Boolean masking schemes (through pre-computed look-up tables) could not be implemented securely on the chosen AVR micro-controller. More precisely, only the first-order TI variant does not exhibit detectable first-order leakage using up to 100 000 power measurements.

In addition to our practical side-channel evaluation, we could efficiently realize the Threshold Implementation in terms of code size and memory requirements, eventually implementing the TI variant with 1 576 B of code and 304 B of memory which is close to the classical Boolean masking with only two shares. However, the code size and memory reduction comes at cost of increased latency results in terms of clock cycles. In particular, the TI requires about 165 k cycles whereas the first-order classical Boolean masking takes only 53 k clock cycles. All in all, this work shows that although TI has been proposed for hardware platforms, the concept can be transferred and applied for software as well in order to realize first-order secure implementations.

Acknowledgments. The work described in this paper has been supported in part by the German Federal Ministry of Education and Research BMBF (grant nr. 16KIS0602 VeriSec).

References

1. Akkar, M.-L., Giraud, C.: An implementation of DES and AES, secure against some attacks. In: Koç, Ç.K., Naccache, D., Paar, C. (eds.) CHES 2001. LNCS, vol. 2162, pp. 309–318. Springer, Heidelberg (2001). https://doi.org/10.1007/3-540-44709-1_26
2. Atmel: 8-bit AVR Microcontroller with 16K Bytes In-System Programmable Flash, Rev. 1142E-02/2003
3. Balasch, J., Gierlichs, B., Grosso, V., Reparaz, O., Standaert, F.-X.: On the cost of lazy engineering for masked software implementations. In: Joye, M., Moradi, A. (eds.) CARDIS 2014. LNCS, vol. 8968, pp. 64–81. Springer, Cham (2015). https://doi.org/10.1007/978-3-319-16763-3_5
4. Bayrak, A.G., Regazzoni, F., Novo, D., Brisk, P., Standaert, F.-X., Ienne, P.: Automatic application of power analysis countermeasures. IEEE Trans. Comput. **64**(2), 329–341 (2015)
5. Bhasin, S., Danger, J.-L., Guilley, S., Najm, Z.: A low-entropy first-degree secure provable masking scheme for resource-constrained devices. In: Proceedings of the Workshop on Embedded Systems Security, WESS 2013, Montreal, Quebec, Canada, 29 September–4 October 2013, pp. 7:1–7:10. ACM (2013)
6. Bilgin, B., Nikova, S., Nikov, V., Rijmen, V., Tokareva, N., Vitkup, V.: Threshold implementations of small S-boxes. Crypt. Commun. **7**(1), 3–33 (2015)
7. Bogdanov, A., Knudsen, L.R., Leander, G., Paar, C., Poschmann, A., Robshaw, M.J.B., Seurin, Y., Vikkelsoe, C.: PRESENT: an ultra-lightweight block cipher. In: Paillier, P., Verbauwhede, I. (eds.) CHES 2007. LNCS, vol. 4727, pp. 450–466. Springer, Heidelberg (2007). https://doi.org/10.1007/978-3-540-74735-2_31
8. Canright, D., Batina, L.: A very compact "perfectly masked" S-box for AES. In: Bellovin, S.M., Gennaro, R., Keromytis, A., Yung, M. (eds.) ACNS 2008. LNCS, vol. 5037, pp. 446–459. Springer, Heidelberg (2008). https://doi.org/10.1007/978-3-540-68914-0_27
9. Carlet, C., Goubin, L., Prouff, E., Quisquater, M., Rivain, M.: Higher-order masking schemes for S-boxes. In: Canteaut, A. (ed.) FSE 2012. LNCS, vol. 7549, pp. 366–384. Springer, Heidelberg (2012). https://doi.org/10.1007/978-3-642-34047-5_21
10. Chari, S., Jutla, C.S., Rao, J.R., Rohatgi, P.: Towards sound approaches to counteract power-analysis attacks. In: Wiener, M. (ed.) CRYPTO 1999. LNCS, vol. 1666, pp. 398–412. Springer, Heidelberg (1999). https://doi.org/10.1007/3-540-48405-1_26
11. Coron, J.-S., Prouff, E., Rivain, M.: Side channel cryptanalysis of a higher order masking scheme. In: Paillier, P., Verbauwhede, I. (eds.) CHES 2007. LNCS, vol. 4727, pp. 28–44. Springer, Heidelberg (2007). https://doi.org/10.1007/978-3-540-74735-2_3
12. Francillon, A., Rohatgi, P. (eds.): CARDIS 2013. LNCS, vol. 8419. Springer, Cham (2014). https://doi.org/10.1007/978-3-319-08302-5
13. Fumaroli, G., Martinelli, A., Prouff, E., Rivain, M.: Affine masking against higher-order side channel analysis. In: Biryukov, A., Gong, G., Stinson, D.R. (eds.) SAC 2010. LNCS, vol. 6544, pp. 262–280. Springer, Heidelberg (2011). https://doi.org/10.1007/978-3-642-19574-7_18
14. Genelle, L., Prouff, E., Quisquater, M.: Secure multiplicative masking of power functions. In: Zhou, J., Yung, M. (eds.) ACNS 2010. LNCS, vol. 6123, pp. 200–217. Springer, Heidelberg (2010). https://doi.org/10.1007/978-3-642-13708-2_13

15. Genelle, L., Prouff, E., Quisquater, M.: Thwarting higher-order side channel analysis with additive and multiplicative maskings. In: Preneel, B., Takagi, T. (eds.) CHES 2011. LNCS, vol. 6917, pp. 240–255. Springer, Heidelberg (2011). https://doi.org/10.1007/978-3-642-23951-9_16

16. Goodwill, G., Jun, B., Jaffe, J., Rohatgi, P.: A testing methodology for side channel resistance validation. In: NIST Non-invasive Attack Testing Workshop (2011)

17. Goudarzi, D., Rivain, M.: How fast can higher-order masking be in software? In: Coron, J.-S., Nielsen, J.B. (eds.) EUROCRYPT 2017. LNCS, vol. 10210, pp. 567–597. Springer, Cham (2017). https://doi.org/10.1007/978-3-319-56620-7_20

18. Grosso, V., Prouff, E., Standaert, F.-X.: Efficient masked S-boxes processing – a step forward. In: Pointcheval, D., Vergnaud, D. (eds.) AFRICACRYPT 2014. LNCS, vol. 8469, pp. 251–266. Springer, Cham (2014). https://doi.org/10.1007/978-3-319-06734-6_16

19. Grosso, V., Standaert, F.-X., Prouff, E.: Low entropy masking schemes, revisited. In: Francillon and Rohatgi [12], pp. 33–43

20. Ishai, Y., Sahai, A., Wagner, D.: Private circuits: securing hardware against probing attacks. In: Boneh, D. (ed.) CRYPTO 2003. LNCS, vol. 2729, pp. 463–481. Springer, Heidelberg (2003). https://doi.org/10.1007/978-3-540-45146-4_27

21. Kutzner, S., Nguyen, P.H., Poschmann, A.: Enabling 3-share threshold implementations for all 4-bit S-boxes. In: Lee, H.-S., Han, D.-G. (eds.) ICISC 2013. LNCS, vol. 8565, pp. 91–108. Springer, Cham (2014). https://doi.org/10.1007/978-3-319-12160-4_6

22. Kutzner, S., Nguyen, P.H., Poschmann, A., Stöttinger, M.: Minimizing S-boxes in hardware by utilizing linear transformations. In: Pointcheval, D., Vergnaud, D. (eds.) AFRICACRYPT 2014. LNCS, vol. 8469, pp. 235–250. Springer, Cham (2014). https://doi.org/10.1007/978-3-319-06734-6_15

23. Kutzner, S., Nguyen, P.H., Poschmann, A., Wang, H.: On 3-share threshold implementations for 4-bit s-boxes. In: Prouff, E. (ed.) COSADE 2013. LNCS, vol. 7864, pp. 99–113. Springer, Heidelberg (2013). https://doi.org/10.1007/978-3-642-40026-1_7

24. Kutzner, S., Poschmann, A.: On the security of RSM - presenting 5 first- and second-order attacks. In: Prouff, E. (ed.) COSADE 2014. LNCS, vol. 8622, pp. 299–312. Springer, Cham (2014). https://doi.org/10.1007/978-3-319-10175-0_20

25. Maghrebi, H., Guilley, S., Danger, J.-L.: Leakage squeezing countermeasure against high-order attacks. In: Ardagna, C.A., Zhou, J. (eds.) WISTP 2011. LNCS, vol. 6633, pp. 208–223. Springer, Heidelberg (2011). https://doi.org/10.1007/978-3-642-21040-2_14

26. Mangard, S., Oswald, E., Popp, T.: Poweranalysis Attacks - Revealing the Secrets of Smart Cards. Springer, New York (2007). https://doi.org/10.1007/978-0-387-38162-6

27. Moradi, A., Guilley, S., Heuser, A.: Detecting hidden leakages. In: Boureanu, I., Owesarski, P., Vaudenay, S. (eds.) ACNS 2014. LNCS, vol. 8479, pp. 324–342. Springer, Cham (2014). https://doi.org/10.1007/978-3-319-07536-5_20

28. Moradi, A., Wild, A.: Assessment of hiding the higher-order leakages in hardware. In: Güneysu, T., Handschuh, H. (eds.) CHES 2015. LNCS, vol. 9293, pp. 453–474. Springer, Heidelberg (2015). https://doi.org/10.1007/978-3-662-48324-4_23

29. Nassar, M., Souissi, Y., Guilley, S., Danger, J.-L.: RSM: a small and fast countermeasure for AES, secure against 1st and 2nd-order zero-offset SCAs. In: Rosenstiel, W., Thiele, L., (eds.) 2012 Design, Automation and Test in Europe Conference and Exhibition, DATE 2012, Dresden, Germany, 12–16 March 2012, pp. 1173–1178. IEEE (2012)

30. Nikova, S., Rijmen, V., Schläffer, M.: Secure hardware implementation of nonlinear functions in the presence of glitches. J. Cryptol. **24**(2), 292–321 (2011)

31. Oswald, E., Mangard, S., Pramstaller, N., Rijmen, V.: A side-channel analysis resistant description of the AES S-box. In: Gilbert, H., Handschuh, H. (eds.) FSE 2005. LNCS, vol. 3557, pp. 413–423. Springer, Heidelberg (2005). https://doi.org/10.1007/11502760_28

32. Papagiannopoulos, K., Veshchikov, N.: Mind the gap: towards secure 1st-order masking in software. In: Guilley, S. (ed.) COSADE 2017. LNCS, vol. 10348, pp. 282–297. Springer, Cham (2017). https://doi.org/10.1007/978-3-319-64647-3_17

33. Poschmann, A., Moradi, A., Khoo, K., Lim, C.-W., Wang, H., Ling, S.: Side-channel resistant crypto for less than 2,300 GE. J. Cryptol. **24**(2), 322–345 (2011)

34. Prouff, E., Rivain, M.: A generic method for secure Sbox implementation. In: Kim, S., Yung, M., Lee, H.-W. (eds.) WISA 2007. LNCS, vol. 4867, pp. 227–244. Springer, Heidelberg (2007). https://doi.org/10.1007/978-3-540-77535-5_17

35. Prouff, E., Roche, T.: Higher-order glitches free implementation of the AES using secure multi-party computation protocols. In: Preneel, B., Takagi, T. (eds.) CHES 2011. LNCS, vol. 6917, pp. 63–78. Springer, Heidelberg (2011). https://doi.org/10.1007/978-3-642-23951-9_5

36. Rivain, M., Dottax, E., Prouff, E.: Block ciphers implementations provably secure against second order side channel analysis. In: Nyberg, K. (ed.) FSE 2008. LNCS, vol. 5086, pp. 127–143. Springer, Heidelberg (2008). https://doi.org/10.1007/978-3-540-71039-4_8

37. Rivain, M., Prouff, E.: Provably secure higher-order masking of AES. In: Mangard, S., Standaert, F.-X. (eds.) CHES 2010. LNCS, vol. 6225, pp. 413–427. Springer, Heidelberg (2010). https://doi.org/10.1007/978-3-642-15031-9_28

38. Rivain, M., Prouff, E., Doget, J.: Higher-order masking and shuffling for software implementations of block ciphers. In: Clavier, C., Gaj, K. (eds.) CHES 2009. LNCS, vol. 5747, pp. 171–188. Springer, Heidelberg (2009). https://doi.org/10.1007/978-3-642-04138-9_13

39. Sasdrich, P., Moradi, A., Güneysu, T.: Affine equivalence and its application to tightening threshold implementations. In: Dunkelman, O., Keliher, L. (eds.) SAC 2015. LNCS, vol. 9566, pp. 263–276. Springer, Cham (2016). https://doi.org/10.1007/978-3-319-31301-6_16

40. Schneider, T., Moradi, A.: Leakage assessment methodology. In: Güneysu, T., Handschuh, H. (eds.) CHES 2015. LNCS, vol. 9293, pp. 495–513. Springer, Heidelberg (2015). https://doi.org/10.1007/978-3-662-48324-4_25

41. Schramm, K., Paar, C.: Higher order masking of the AES. In: Pointcheval, D. (ed.) CT-RSA 2006. LNCS, vol. 3860, pp. 208–225. Springer, Heidelberg (2006). https://doi.org/10.1007/11605805_14

42. Ye, X., Eisenbarth, T.: On the vulnerability of low entropy masking schemes. In: Francillon and Rohatgi [12], pp. 44–60

A First-Order SCA Resistant AES
Without Fresh Randomness

Felix Wegener$^{(\boxtimes)}$ and Amir Moradi

Horst Görtz Institute for IT Security, Ruhr-Universität Bochum,
Bochum, Germany
{felix.wegener,amir.moradi}@rub.de

Abstract. Since the advent of Differential Power Analysis (DPA) in the late 1990s protecting embedded devices against Side-Channel Analysis (SCA) attacks has been a major research effort. Even though many different first-order secure masking schemes are available today, when applied to the AES S-box they all require fresh random bits in every evaluation. As the quality criteria for generating random numbers on an embedded device are not well understood, an integrated Random Number Generator (RNG) can be the weak spot of any protected implementation and may invalidate an otherwise secure implementation. We present a new construction based on *Threshold Implementations* and *Changing of the Guards* to realize a first-order secure AES with zero per-round randomness. Hence, our design does not need a built-in RNG, thereby enhancing security and reducing the overhead.

1 Introduction

In 1999 Kocher *et al.* introduced the extraction of key information from the power consumption of a hardware device during cryptographic computations [22]. To break a symmetric cipher, key hypotheses are formed that categories power traces into groups and a statistical test is performed to estimate the likelihood of a correct guess. This process is known as Differential Power Analysis (DPA).

To prevent side-channel analysis (SCA) attacks extensive research in countermeasures has been undertaken [16,18,20,28,30]. A notable protection method is Threshold Implementation (TI) [25], as it grants provable security against first-order SCA attacks and can potentially be realized without additional randomness. TI demands three properties to ensure the security of an implementation: correctness, non-completeness and uniformity. While correctness simply preserves the validity of the computation, non-completeness ensures that every intermediate value is independent of secret values even in the presence of glitches. Uniformity implies that when the input is shared by the masks drawn from a uniform distribution, the output should be also represented by masks drawn from a uniform distribution. So far, all first-order protected AES implementations inject randomness in every round to achieve a uniform masking. Hence, they require to employ a random number generator on the embedded device in addition to the creation of the shared plaintext, which is considered to be done externally before being provided to the cryptographic core.

© Springer International Publishing AG, part of Springer Nature 2018
J. Fan and B. Gierlichs (Eds.): COSADE 2018, LNCS 10815, pp. 245–262, 2018.
https://doi.org/10.1007/978-3-319-89641-0_14

Related Works

S-box Structure. In 2005 Canright suggested a tower field approach to realize the $GF(2^8)$ inversion in the AES S-box by inversions and multiplications in smaller finite fields [8]. Due to its reduced size compared to a naive implementation most of the recent first-order secure AES implementations are based on this S-box design.

Threshold Implementation. Bilgin *et al.* suggested to mask all multipliers, squarers and inverters in Canright's construction separately by applying TI with two to four shares. This approach requires 16 random bits per S-box evaluation to recombine the different components in a uniform way and occupies an area of 2224 GE in the UMC 180 nm library [4].

Domain-Oriented Masking (DOM). Based on Canright's construction Groß *et al.* presented masked version of all multiplications in $GF(2^2)$ with a DOM independent multiplier to achieve first-order security. The construction consumes 2600 GE in UMC 0.18 μm and requires 18 bits of randomness per S-box call [17].

Masking with $d+1$ Shares. In [10] Cnudde *et al.* suggested to apply masking with $d + 1$ shares [28] to operations in $GF(2^2)$ to realize the AES S-box in 1872 GE in the NanGate 45 nm Open Cell Library with 54 bits of randomness per S-box call. In contrast, Ueno *et al.* kept the inversion in $GF(2^4)$ as a single primitive and applied the same masking scheme, which requires 64 bits of randomness per S-box call and can be realized in only 1389 GE in TSMC 65 nm standard cells library [31].

Changing of the Guards. Recently, Daemen [11] showed that uniformity for a bijective S-box can be easily achieved on the entire S-box layer by injecting some additional randomness, called guards, into the first S-box. In order to satisfy the uniformity of the subsequent S-boxes, he introduced a mechanism to make use of the shares of the former S-box. More precisely, the uniformity is achieved by remasking, but instead of fresh randomness part of the shared cipher state is used.

Zero per-Round Randomness. One of the several designs presented by Ghoshal and De Cnudde in [14] is a four-share AES S-box with zero fresh randomness. They considered the S-box construction of Boyar and Peralta [6] and replaced the non-linear gates with their TI variants.

Our Contribution. Obviously, our target in this paper is the same as that of the four-share design of [14], i.e., no extra randomness per S-box. First, we demonstrate a first-order leakage of that construction both in theory and with a practical evaluation. Second, we present an alternative and novel design for the AES S-box which enables us to reuse the hardware modules hence shrinking the area. Our approach, which is also a four-share TI design, is based on a bijective decomposition of the AES S-box allowing us to apply the *Changing of the Guards* method to achieve the uniformity. We would like to highlight that the application of this method is only possible in bijective constructions, and our design is the first in which the AES S-box is decomposed to bijective functions. Third, we present a trick in order to employ our four-share S-box in a two-share AES encryption design without additional randomness. In consequence, our practically-evaluated first-order secure AES implementation eliminates the necessity of generating any random bits in hardware as it only requires the externally shared plaintext and guards, but no fresh randomness. Further, our design has a comparable size to recent first-order secure implementations.

2 Preliminaries

In this section we introduce relevant definitions and our notation for the rest of the paper.

Adversary Model. To appropriately model the influence of glitches in a hardware circuit Ishai *et al.* suggested a d-probing model where the attacker may probe up to d wires corresponding to the intermediate values of the cipher [20]. As we focus on first-order security the attacker may probe only one wire. According to Duc *et al.* [12], it is commonly known that this corresponds to an attacker who only estimates the means (and no higher-order moments) on the recorded side-channel measurements.

Masking. As this paper exclusively deals with four-share implementations, we restrict our definitions to four shares for better readability. For a secret value $x \in \mathbb{F}_2^n$ we denote its Boolean sharing into four shares as $X = (a, b, c, d)$ with the property:

$$x = a \oplus b \oplus c \oplus d.$$

We write $\int(x)$ for the set of all possible Boolean sharings X of x.

Threshold Implementation. In 2006 Nikova *et al.* introduced TI as a provably secure masking scheme for hardware platforms [25]. Below, we give an introduction following our own notation.
Let $f : \mathbb{F}_2^n \to \mathbb{F}_2^m$ be a Boolean function. We write that

$$F : \mathbb{F}_2^{4n} \to \mathbb{F}_2^{4m}, \qquad F(X) = \left(F^A(X), F^B(X), F^C(X), F^D(X) \right),$$

with $F(.)$ being a first-order TI of $f(.)$ if it fulfills two properties. First, it is *correct*, i.e., the summation of all output shares reveals the unshared result of the computation $f(.)$ on x:

$$F^A(X) \oplus F^B(X) \oplus F^C(X) \oplus F^D(X) = f(x).$$

Second, it must be *non-complete*, i.e., each component function $\mathsf{F}^{A/B/C/D}(.)$ computing one output share does not depend on all input shares. As an example,

$$\mathsf{F}^A(X) = \mathsf{F}^A(b,c,d), \qquad\qquad \mathsf{F}^B(X) = \mathsf{F}^B(a,c,d),$$
$$\mathsf{F}^C(X) = \mathsf{F}^C(a,b,d), \qquad\qquad \mathsf{F}^D(X) = \mathsf{F}^D(a,b,c).$$

The latter property ensures the security in the 1-probing model even in the presence of glitches as probing one output share yields at most three input shares. In the following, we are going to use a capital letter F to denote the TI of a function f. If it is clear which shared function we are referring to, we abbreviate a, b, c, d for its input shares and A, B, C, D for its output shares.

The central theorem underlying TI guarantees that given a sharing of x drawn equiprobably from all sharings $\int(x)$, the evaluation of the TI function $\mathsf{F}(.)$ does not cause first-order leakage. As $\mathsf{f}(.)$ is not the only non-linear function used in a cipher, and its output derives other non-linear TI functions (e.g., at next cipher rounds), we are interested in achieving the equiprobability of output sharings as well. This can either be achieved by injecting randomness or maintaining the equiprobability by a clever design of the TI functions $\mathsf{F}(.)$. This leads to a third property: a TI function $\mathsf{F}(.)$ is said to be uniform, if – given a uniform input – all sharings of the output occur with equal probability:

$$\forall x \in \mathbb{F}_2^n, \ \exists c_x, \ \forall X \in \int(x), \ \forall Y \in \int(\mathsf{f}(x)); \ Pr(\mathsf{F}(X) = Y) = c_x.$$

Unfortunately, no uniform TI of the AES S-box is known. If uniformity is violated, the security proof of TI no longer holds.

Higher-Order Masking. In 2015 De Cnudde *et al.* extended the TI to higher-order of protection for AES [9] after Reparaz showed that introducing fresh randomness is always necessary to achieve multivariate higher-order security [27]. However, as our focus is zero fresh randomness we limit ourselves to first-order security.

Changing of the Guards. In [11], Daemen questioned the assumption that uniformity must be achieved in every S-box separately, and instead suggested a scheme to generate uniformity of the entire S-box layer at once. We illustrate his scheme for four shares. Let $(\mathsf{S}^A, \mathsf{S}^B, \mathsf{S}^C, \mathsf{S}^D)$ be a **non-uniform** TI of the bijective S-box $\mathsf{s}(.)$. Furthermore, let the entire non-linear layer consist of parallel executions of t times the same S-box where we denote the inputs to the i-th shared S-box as $(a_i, b_i, c_i, d_i), i \in \{1, \ldots, t\}$. Then *Changing of the Guards* with four shares is defined as

$$A_i = \mathsf{S}^A(b_i, c_i, d_i) \oplus c_{i-1} \oplus d_{i-1}, \qquad i > 0$$
$$B_i = \mathsf{S}^B(c_i, d_i, a_i) \oplus d_{i-1}, \qquad i > 0, \qquad B_0 = c_t$$
$$C_i = \mathsf{S}^C(d_i, a_i, b_i) \oplus b_{i-1}, \qquad i > 0, \qquad C_0 = d_t$$
$$D_i = \mathsf{S}^D(a_i, b_i, c_i) \oplus b_{i-1} \oplus c_{i-1}, \qquad i > 0, \qquad D_0 = b_t$$

As the only source for extra randomness, b_0, c_0, and d_0 need to be provided beforehand. All further guards are computed from the input of each previous S-box in the layer as illustrated in Fig. 1, and B_0, C_0, and D_0 provide the guards for the next S-box layer. More precisely, the relabeling of b_2, c_2 and d_2 as D_0, B_0 and C_0 is only done to fulfill the formal non-completeness requirement that output share B does not depend on input share b and so forth. This sharing of the S-box layer inherits correctness and non-completeness from the TI of $s(.)$ and in addition achieves uniformity due to the additional guards. A formal proof of uniformity for an arbitrary number of shares can be found in the original paper [11].

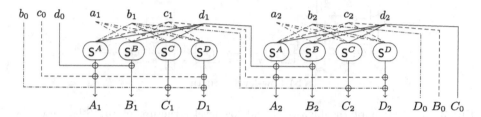

Fig. 1. Illustration of *Changing of the Guards* with four shares and two S-boxes.

3   Insecurity of a Construction of [14]

We describe the theoretical background of a flaw in the "TI design with 4 shares and no randomness" presented in [14] and demonstrate significant leakage in a practical setting.

Construction. Based on the smallest known unprotected AES S-box representation by Boyar and Peralta [6], Ghoshal and De Cnudde suggested an allegedly first-order secure implementation by representing the circuit by only 2-bit XOR and AND gates, and dividing the circuit into four stages, each of which with algebraic degree of 2, i.e., quadratic (cp. Fig. 2). They made use of a previously-known uniform four-share TI of the 2-input AND gate [25], and concluded that the uniformity of each separate gate is sufficient to achieve the uniformity of each quadratic stage, and consequently of the entire S-box.

We remind that it is not possible for any function $f : \mathbb{F}_2^n \to \mathbb{F}_2^m$, $m > n$ to be shared uniformly without introducing fresh randomness. More specifically, a sharing of $f(.)$ with d input and output shares has the form $F : \mathbb{F}_2^{n \cdot d} \to \mathbb{F}_2^{m \cdot d}$. Since $m \cdot d > n \cdot d$, this function is not surjective and therefore output shares cannot be equiprobable. Hence, stages st_1 and st_3 cannot be shared uniformly as seen in Fig. 2a. An investigation of the separate building blocks shows that the violation of uniformity does not stem from a lack of joint uniformity of all components in a stage, but even the components Q_1 and Q_3 in Fig. 2b cannot individually be shared uniformly, because of their higher output dimension. Furthermore, we verified computationally that the entire shared S-box (with 4 shares) is not a bijection over 4×8 bits, therefore it is not uniform. Hence, the requirement of equiprobable input sharing of TI is violated from stage two (st_2) on.

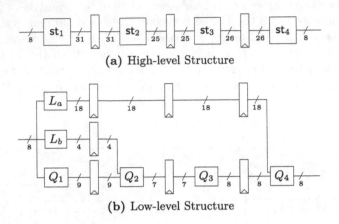

(a) High-level Structure

(b) Low-level Structure

Fig. 2. Illustration of the high-level and low-level structure of the S-box used by Ghoshal and De Cnudde [14]. L_a and L_b denote linear building blocks, while Q_1, Q_2, Q_3 and Q_4 indicate quadratic functions.

SCA Evaluation. The above-given justification makes indeed the practical results shown in [14] questionable. This may be due to the parallel use of many S-boxes which have increased the noise level and led to no detectable leakage. We re-evaluated the first-order leakage of this construction with only one instance of the S-box and observed leakage in stages two, three and four in accordance with our theoretical observations.

For all practical analyses we report in this work, we made use of the SAKURA-G board [1] (with Spartan-6 FPGA), and collected the power traces at a sampling rate of 625 MS/s using a digital oscilloscope with 350 MHz bandwidth by measuring the output of the AC amplifier embedded on the SAKURA-G. The target FPGA, on which the design is being run and measured, was operating at the clock frequency of 6 MHz. As the evaluation metric, we applied the common fixed-versus-random t-test [15] to examine the existence of detectable leakage. We further followed the procedure suggested in [29] and examined the uniformity of the random values used to initially mask the input. The result of such an evaluation on the aforementioned four-share S-box of [14] is shown in Fig. 3.

We would like to highlight that in several related works, where the Welch's t-test is applied, the probability (to reject the null hypothesis) is not calculated. Instead, by ignoring the "degree of freedom" the threshold of 4.5 based on the relation $p = 2F(-4.5, v > 1000) < 10^{-5}$ is taken, where $F(.)$ stands for the cumulative student's t distribution function and v the degree of freedom (see [29]). Since v can be different at various sample points, we estimated the probability (so-called p-value) by $p = 2F(-|t|, v)$, and similarly set the threshold to 10^{-5}.

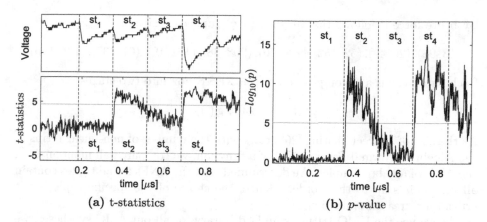

Fig. 3. Evaluation of the four-share S-box (with no extra randomness) of [14] using 10 million traces.

4 Technique

In the following we illustrate how to decompose the AES S-box into two independently-shared stages and how to reuse the same hardware for several operations without introducing leakage or requiring fresh randomness.

Decomposition. The AES S-box consists of an inversion in $GF(2^8)$ and a subsequent affine mapping $\mathsf{Aff}(.)$. As $(GF(2^8), \cdot)$ forms a cyclic group with order 255, we can alternatively represent inversion as $x^{-1} = x^{254}$. Following the idea presented in [24], we show the below observation.

Observation 1. *Let* $\mathsf{f} : GF(2^8) \to GF(2^8)$ *be a monomial* $\mathsf{f}(x) = x^k$. *Then*

– *the algebraic degree of* $\mathsf{f}(.)$ *is defined by* $w(k)$, *and*
– $\mathsf{f}(.)$ *is not a bijection for* $w(k) = 2$,

where $w(k)$ *stands for the number of '1's in the binary representation of* k, *i.e., Hamming weight.*

As the inversion is a bijection, it cannot be decomposed into quadratic monomials. In other words,

$$\nexists\, k_1, \ldots, k_n; \forall i, w(k_i) = 2, x^{254} = \left(\left(\left(x^{k_1}\right)^{\cdot}\right)^{\cdot}\right)^{k_n}.$$

Hence, we focus on decomposition into cubic monomials

$$\mathsf{f}(x) = x^p, \ \mathsf{g}(x) = x^q, \ w(p) = w(q) = 3,$$
$$x^{254} = (x^p)^q = (x^q)^p = \mathsf{g} \circ \mathsf{f}(x) = \mathsf{f} \circ \mathsf{g}(x).$$

Such a search can be reduced to

$$\forall (p, q), \ w(p) = w(q) = 3; \ p \cdot q = 254 \mod 255.$$

By brute force it follows that all such (p, q) tuples are given as[1]

$$(13, 98), (26, 49), (52, 152), (104, 76), (208, 38), (161, 19), (67, 137), (134, 196).$$

Each tuple yields a decomposition of the AES S-box into two stages

$$(f(.),\quad \mathsf{Aff} \circ \mathbf{g}(.)).$$

As the size of a direct sharing [26] grows with the number of non-linear terms in the Algebraic Normal Form (ANF) of a function, we compared all monomials in the ANF of all above tuples. We determined that the ANFs for all tuples contain all monomials up to third order. Hence, the choice of the specific tuple is not crucial for area minimization.

As we use the UMC 180 nm standard library for all our ASIC syntheses, we verified $(p, q) = (26, 49)$ as the smallest choice by synthesizing the corresponding TI circuit of all above tuples (made by direct sharing).

4.1   S-Box Construction

We construct a first-order TI of the AES S-box by separately applying direct sharing to the cubic components

$$f(x) = x^{26}, \; \mathbf{g}(x) = \mathsf{Aff}(x^{49}).$$

A naive construction that realizes the entire S-box in two cycles, would exhibit a prohibitively large area of more than 20 k GE. Hence, we follow two serialization methods, originally suggested in [23] for the PRESENT [5] S-box, to achieve an area reduction. We will refer to these methods as *serializing shares* and *serializing stages* and demonstrate the applicability to the AES S-box.

Serializing Shares. By applying direct sharing, all component functions become identical as long as we rotate the input shares in the following manner:

$$\mathsf{F}^A(X) = \mathsf{F}^*(b, c, d), \qquad \mathsf{F}^B(X) = \mathsf{F}^*(c, d, a),$$
$$\mathsf{F}^C(X) = \mathsf{F}^*(d, a, b), \qquad \mathsf{F}^D(X) = \mathsf{F}^*(a, b, c).$$

This allows us to compute all output shares with the same circuit, denoted as F^*, one after each other in a sequential manner (see Fig. 4a).

Non-completeness. Special care must be taken in such a serialized architecture to not violate the non-completeness property. From a high-level point of view the multiplexer is a combinatorial circuit and should only depend on at most $d - 1$ shares, which makes any such a serial design impossible. We overcome this challenge by

---

[1]Obviously, for each (p, q) tuple, (q, p) is also a valid tuple.

- making sure that each select signal is directly derived from a register,
- suggesting a special design that uses *Gray Code* for the select signals, and
- placing a register right after each multiplexer.

The choice of the Gray Code implies that only one select signal changes at each state transition. This guarantees the joint leakage of at most two shares at each clock cycle. As an example, considering Fig. 4b, suppose that the select signals $(s_1, s_0) = 10$ (i.e., the b input is selected). At the next state, the select signals change to $(s_1, s_0) = 11$ leading to selecting the c input. In this state transition – due to supplying the select signals directly by registers – the combinatorial logic relevant to selecting the a and d inputs stay inactive. It holds for the other transitions $a \rightarrow b$, $c \rightarrow d$, and $d \rightarrow a$. Hence, with respect to Fig. 4c, the input tuples (b, c, d), (c, d, a), (d, a, b), and (a, b, c) are sequentially selected.

Since the shared function $F^*(.)$ non-linearly combines three input shares, without having a register at its input, the circuit would potentially exhibit first-order leakage between the input transitions. By means of such a register, we reset the input of the shared function $F^*(.)$ to ZERO between each input transition. In other words, when the exemplary input tuple (b, c, d) is selected and the corresponding shared output is calculated, at the next clock cycle the input tuple (c, d, a) is selected and at the same time the input registers of $F^*(.)$ are reset. At the next clock cycle, the selected tuple is not changed and is stored by the input registers thereby evaluating the corresponding output share. This implies 8 clock cycles for the entire computation of the 4 output shares.

In contrast, both original work [23] and the recent suggestion by Gupta *et al.* [19], which applies serializing shares to GIFT by using the initial naive design seen in Fig. 4a, violate the non-completeness.

Serializing Stages. As stated, both stages f(.) and g(.) are cubic functions. Considering their ANF, we can create a function m(.) that realizes all linear, quadratic and cubic terms of both f(.) and g(.). Afterwards, by means of two linear layers which combine (i.e., XOR) the corresponding terms, the specific functions $x \rightarrow x^{26}$ and $x \rightarrow \text{Aff}(x^{49})$ can be realized.

More specifically, let $c_1(.), c_2(.)$ be two arbitrary cubic functions over the same number of bits. Each of them can be decomposed into a common non-linear layer m(.), followed by an individual linear layer $l_1(.)$ (resp. $l_2(.)$) as

$$c_1(x) = l_1 \circ m(x), \quad c_2(x) = l_2 \circ m(x).$$

A serialization of stages can be achieved by connecting the output of m(.) to both $l_1(.)$ and $l_2(.)$ and attaching either a multiplexer or registers with different enable signals to their outputs. In our case, $l_1(.)$ is the linear layer belonging to $x \rightarrow x^{26}$ and $l_2(.)$ to $x \rightarrow \text{Aff}(x^{49})$. Note that we represent the four-share version of these functions by M(.), $L_1(.)$, and $L_2(.)$.

Putting it Together. Following both serialization methods, we can now describe the S-box construction in detail (cp. Fig. 5). At the start of the S-box evaluation the non-completeness register ncR has already been set to ZERO

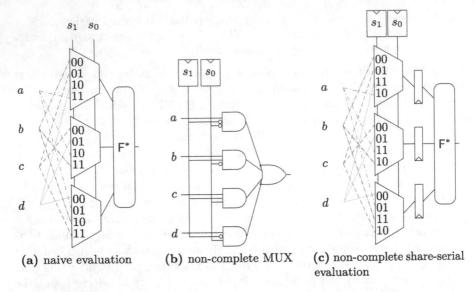

(a) naive evaluation   (b) non-complete MUX   (c) non-complete share-serial evaluation

Fig. 4. (a) A naive serialization of shares violates non-completeness. The select signals are not taken from registers and might glitch. The transition from input share $b \to c$ and $d \to a$ require both select signals to change. No register stage prevents the function $F^*(.)$ to combine all shares, (b) illustration of a multiplexer based on Gray Code with select signals are being directly supplied by registers, (c) illustration of the entire non-complete share-serial evaluation of function $F^*(.)$.

and the first multiplexer stage selects the lower inputs, i.e., (a, b, c, d). In the first cycle the non-completeness multiplexers ncM choose the shares (b, c, d) from the four-byte inputs (a, b, c, d) and the same values are written to the register gds for later use as guards. In cycle two, $L_1 \circ M$ which corresponds to $x \to x^{26}$ is evaluated, while only the register A_1 is enabled to store the result, i.e., one output share of the application of $x \to x^{26}$ before being XORed with the guards gd_d. Subsequently, at the next clock cycle the ncR register is reset, and at the same time (c, d, a) is selected by the ncM multiplexers. Analogously, it takes two cycles to write the results for shares B, C, and D of $x \to x^{26}$ to registers B_1, C_1, and D_1. After eight cycles, the secure evaluation of $x \to x^{26}$ is complete and the left-most multiplexer stage selects the upper input. Following the same procedure by resetting the ncR register and evaluating $L_2 \circ M$ the registers $A_2, \ldots, D_2$ are subsequently set to the value of the shares $x \to \mathsf{Aff}(x^{49})$ after achieving uniformity by XORing with the guards stored in gds from the previous evaluation of $x \to x^{26}$. In total, after sixteen cycles the secure evaluation of a shared AES S-box can be read from $A_2, \ldots, D_2$ while a reordering of the values in registers C_1, D_1, B_1 provides the guards for the next S-box evaluation (this corresponds to the definition given in [11]). We should highlight that all select signals controlling the multiplexers are derived by dedicated registers.

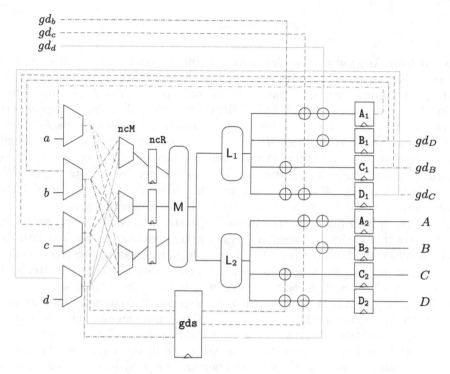

Fig. 5. Fully-Serial Design of the AES S-box. In one clock cycle three of the four input shares $a, \ldots, d$ are selected by multiplexers to be fed into registers leading to $M(., ., .)$ which realizes all cubic, quadratic and linear terms. In the first eight cycles the output of $M(., ., .)$ is processed by $L^1(.)$ to realize the first shared function and write the results to the upper registers $A_1, \ldots, D_1$. The registers feeding $M(., ., .)$ are reset after computation of each output share. In the successive eight cycles the same instance of $M(., ., .)$ is reused and its output is fed into $L_2(.)$ to realize the second shared function. In sum, after sixteen clock cycles a uniform sharing of the AES Sbox is written to the output registers.

4.2 Full AES

Based on the 8-bit version of the encryption-only design [21], we constructed a two-share AES implementation (cp. Fig. 6) with one S-box instance, a byte-wise shift register to hold the state and an unprotected key schedule.

Number of Shares. As our first-order S-box operates on four-shares, it would be natural to construct a four-share version of AES. However, sharing the entire AES state with four shares leads to a prohibitive area requirement. This motivated us to develop a heuristic that re-masks the state with itself to generate four shares from two shares. Our scheme is based on a trivial method to extend two shares (a_0, b_0) to four shares (a, b, c, d) by the introduction of two additional random bytes (r_1, r_2) via re-masking:

$$a = r_1, \quad b = r_1 \oplus a_0, \quad c = r_2, \quad d = r_2 \oplus b_0.$$

Extension. As we want to achieve zero per-round randomness, we chose a share of locally-independent state bytes as (r_1, r_2). To determine the independence of bytes, we remind that *MixColumns* is the only part of the AES round function that intermingles multiple bytes. Hence, it is the only cause of dependence between state bytes. Further, due to the diffusion properties of the AES, the combination of *ShiftRows* and *MixColumns* causes any difference to any single byte to propagate to all other bytes within only two rounds. In consequence, we can only aim at finding a heuristic to judge local independence of state bytes. We chose to look one round into the past and one round into the future to pick the state bytes that did not originate from the same *MixColumns* operation and are not used jointly in the next *MixColumns* operation. In consequence, we found that the output of the shift register (given to the S-box) can be masked with the byte at offset 2 and the byte at offset 9 (cp. Fig. 6) counted against the direction of the shift register starting from zero. This can easily be verified by iterating through all 16 states of the shift register, e.g., in the default position, byte a_0 is masked with a_8 and b_0 is masked with b_6 corresponding to columns zero, two and one in the previous round and columns zero, two and three in the next round. We have chosen two different positions in the two shares of the state to avoid undesired unmasking of any byte in the state. Needless to say that the purely heuristic nature of remasking bytes with locally-independent bytes demands for an in-depth practical evaluation (cp. Sect. 5).

Reduction. We need to securely reduce the four-share S-box output (A, B, C, D) to two shares to write it back to the state register. As the S-box already contains a final register stage for each share $A_2, \dots, D_2$ (cp. Fig. 5) we can directly reduce the four shares to two shares by XORing them without the need of an additional register stage:

$$a_{15} \Leftarrow A \oplus B, \quad b_{15} \Leftarrow C \oplus D.$$

After power-up of the circuit, only for the first AES call a 24-bit random value should be provided for the guards, and it is the only randomness required for the circuit. During the operation of the S-box, the guard register is updated, and no extra randomness will be required. The next AES calls will make use of the last value stored in the guard register corresponding to the last AES call.

5 Practical Analysis

For the practical analyses we used the same setup of the analysis presented in Sect. 3. We first investigated a single S-box of our design in a similar way that we analyzed the Ghoshal and De Cnudde construction, with a difference that we provided fresh randomness for the *guards* at the start of each computation of the S-box. The corresponding results – using 100 million traces – are shown in

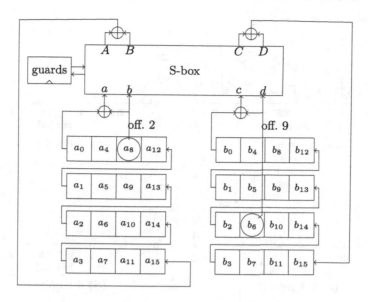

Fig. 6. Two-share state of AES operates with a four-share S-box. The guards are initially provided. The linear layer is omitted for brevity.

Fig. 7, indicating no first-order detectable leakage (p-value $< 10^{-5}$) and strong higher-order leakages.

As the next step, we implemented our two-share AES encryption design with no fresh randomness, and followed the same evaluation procedure. Since the traces are long compared to the previous experiment, we examined this design in two parts: 10 million traces covering the first encryption round, and 10 million traces for the last round. Figure 8 presents the results, where no first-order leakage is detectable.

6   Discussion

Comparison. We synthesized our design by the UMC 180 nm Standard cell library. Our S-box exhibits a two-fold to three-fold area increase compared to state-of-the-art first-order secure S-boxes. This in turn leads to an AES that occupies only several hundred to 1300 GE more than the status-quo (cp. Table 1) and does not need any fresh randomness. This comes at the cost of a greatly increased latency (eleven-fold) compared to the state-of-the-art implementations. Nevertheless, we believe the increase in area and latency to be an acceptable trade-off to be able to omit the internal generation of random bits completely. Note that all other implementations need to use either a true- or a pseudo random number generator (or a combination of them) internally, about whose area requirements we do not yet have a clear picture. In short, it is not possible to map the number of required random bits onto a meaningful area requirement of a corresponding RNG module. Hence, the reduction of required random bits

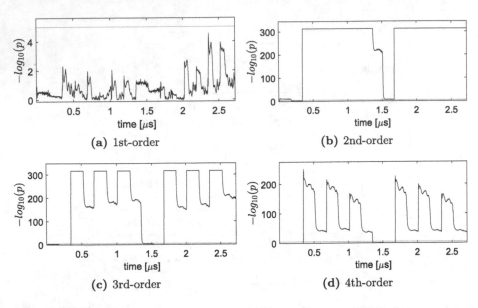

Fig. 7. Evaluation of our four-share S-box, using 100 million traces.

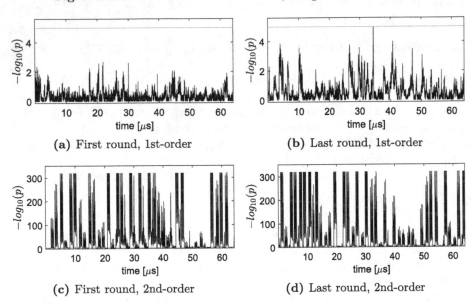

Fig. 8. Evaluation of our two-share AES encryption design with no fresh randomness, using 10 million traces.

is of paramount importance for any masking scheme. For example, there are several works in the area of masking (e.g., [2,16,18,28]) which tried to reduce the required randomness.

Table 1. Comparison of state-of-the-art first-order secure AES encryption designs with our contribution regarding latency, S-box size, total size and randomness per S-box call.

Design	Latency (cycles)	S-box size (kGE)	AES size (kGE)	Rand./S-box (bits)
Bilgin et al. [4]	246	2.2	7.2	16
Gross et al. [18]	246	2.6	6.0	18
Cnudde et al. [10]	276	1.9	6.3	54
Ueno et al. [32]	219	1.4	6.3	64
This work	2804	4.2	7.6	0

Fixing the Construction of [14]**.** As *Changing of the Guards* is only applicable to bijections, we do not see any possibilities to apply it to the design of [14] or any other design based on the Boyar-Peralta implementation [6] of the AES S-box. Hence, the only suitable countermeasure to achieve uniformity in the construction of [14] appears to be the introduction of fresh randomness in each round.

Distinction from Recent Work. Recently, Gupta et al. [19] independently introduced a TI of the light-weight block cipher GIFT [3]. They used a masking method called *combined 3-shares* to decompose the cubic 4-bit S-box of GIFT into two quadratic bijections and apply direct-sharing individually. In contrast to our work, Gupta et al. do not discuss the importance of a special multiplexer design that prevents the combination of all three shares at a time. Furthermore, they do not incorporate a register stage after the multiplexers, which again violates non-completeness. Unfortunately, they do not detect this flaw as their leakage evaluation consists of failed attacks on a certain power model instead of a more elaborate leakage detection, e.g., Welsh's t-test. Further, Božilov et al. [7] decomposed the PRINCE S-box into two quadratic functions of the same equivalence class and demonstrated a three-share TI design with serialized stages.

7   Conclusion

We introduced the first zero per-round randomness construction of a first-order secure AES S-box which mitigates the fact that generation of randomness on embedded systems remains difficult. Further, we introduced a method to extend two shares to four shares for the evaluation of an S-box using uncorrelated state bytes and without introducing any fresh randomness. We should emphasize that we cannot yet provide any proof for the security of such a combination, which led to competitive size without any requirements on fresh or internal randomness. Instead, we could just practically confirm its first-order security using an FPGA prototype while we showed elementary flaws in an earlier design that claimed to achieve the same property.

Our S-box masking methodology is universally applicable to bijective S-boxes and is the first work that achieves non-completeness in a share-serially architecture of AES, which enables a new area vs. latency trade-off.

Acknowledgments. The work described in this paper has been supported in part by the German Federal Ministry of Education and Research BMBF (grant nr. 16KIS0666 SysKit_HW).

References

1. Side-channel AttacK User Reference Architecture. http://satoh.cs.uec.ac.jp/SAKURA/index.html
2. Balasch, J., Faust, S., Gierlichs, B., Paglialonga, C., Standaert, F.-X.: Consolidating inner product masking. In: Takagi, T., Peyrin, T. (eds.) ASIACRYPT 2017, Part I. LNCS, vol. 10624, pp. 724–754. Springer, Cham (2017). https://doi.org/10.1007/978-3-319-70694-8_25
3. Banik, S., Pandey, S.K., Peyrin, T., Sasaki, Y., Sim, S.M., Todo, Y.: GIFT: a small present - towards reaching the limit of lightweight encryption. In: Fischer and Homma [13], pp. 321–345
4. Bilgin, B., Gierlichs, B., Nikova, S., Nikov, V., Rijmen, V.: Trade-offs for threshold implementations illustrated on AES. IEEE Trans. CAD Integr. Circuits Syst. **34**(7), 1188–1200 (2015)
5. Bogdanov, A., Knudsen, L.R., Leander, G., Paar, C., Poschmann, A., Robshaw, M.J.B., Seurin, Y., Vikkelsoe, C.: PRESENT: an ultra-lightweight block cipher. In: Paillier, P., Verbauwhede, I. (eds.) CHES 2007. LNCS, vol. 4727, pp. 450–466. Springer, Heidelberg (2007). https://doi.org/10.1007/978-3-540-74735-2_31
6. Boyar, J., Matthews, P., Peralta, R.: Logic minimization techniques with applications to cryptology. J. Cryptol. **26**(2), 280–312 (2013)
7. Božilov, D., Knežević, M., Nikov, V.: Threshold implementations of prince: the cost of physical security. In: NIST Lightweight Cryptography Workshop (2016). https://www.nist.gov/sites/default/files/documents/2016/10/17/bozilov-paper-lwc2016.pdf
8. Canright, D.: A very compact s-box for AES. In: Rao, J.R., Sunar, B. (eds.) CHES 2005. LNCS, vol. 3659, pp. 441–455. Springer, Heidelberg (2005). https://doi.org/10.1007/11545262_32
9. De Cnudde, T., Bilgin, B., Reparaz, O., Nikov, V., Nikova, S.: Higher-order threshold implementation of the AES s-box. In: Homma, N., Medwed, M. (eds.) CARDIS 2015. LNCS, vol. 9514, pp. 259–272. Springer, Cham (2016). https://doi.org/10.1007/978-3-319-31271-2_16
10. De Cnudde, T., Reparaz, O., Bilgin, B., Nikova, S., Nikov, V., Rijmen, V.: Masking AES with d+1 shares in hardware. In: Gierlichs, B., Poschmann, A.Y. (eds.) CHES 2016. LNCS, vol. 9813, pp. 194–212. Springer, Heidelberg (2016). https://doi.org/10.1007/978-3-662-53140-2_10
11. Daemen, J.: Changing of the guards: a simple and efficient method for achieving uniformity in threshold sharing. In: Fischer and Homma [13], pp. 137–153
12. Duc, A., Dziembowski, S., Faust, S.: Unifying leakage models: from probing attacks to noisy leakage. In: Nguyen, P.Q., Oswald, E. (eds.) EUROCRYPT 2014. LNCS, vol. 8441, pp. 423–440. Springer, Heidelberg (2014). https://doi.org/10.1007/978-3-642-55220-5_24

13. Fischer, W., Homma, N. (eds.): CHES 2017. LNCS, vol. 10529. Springer, Cham (2017). https://doi.org/10.1007/978-3-319-66787-4
14. Ghoshal, A., De Cnudde, T.: Several masked implementations of the Boyar-Peralta AES s-box. In: Patra, A., Smart, N.P. (eds.) INDOCRYPT 2017. LNCS, vol. 10698, pp. 384–402. Springer, Cham (2017). https://doi.org/10.1007/978-3-319-71667-1_20
15. Goodwill, G., Jun, B., Jaffe, J., Rohatgi, P.: A testing methodology for side channel resistance validation. In: NIST Non-invasive Attack Testing Workshop (2011). http://csrc.nist.gov/news_events/non-invasive-attack-testing-workshop/papers/08_Goodwill.pdf
16. Gross, H., Mangard, S.: Reconciling $d + 1$ masking in hardware and software. In: Fischer and Homma [13], pp. 115–136
17. Gross, H., Mangard, S., Korak, T.: Domain-oriented masking: compact masked hardware implementations with arbitrary protection order. IACR Cryptology ePrint Archive 2016:486 (2016)
18. Gross, H., Mangard, S., Korak, T.: An efficient side-channel protected AES implementation with arbitrary protection order. In: Handschuh, H. (ed.) CT-RSA 2017. LNCS, vol. 10159, pp. 95–112. Springer, Cham (2017). https://doi.org/10.1007/978-3-319-52153-4_6
19. Gupta, N., Jati, A., Chattopadhyay, A., Sanadhya, S.K., Chang, D.: Threshold implementations of gift: a trade-off analysis. Cryptology ePrint Archive, Report 2017/1040 (2017). https://eprint.iacr.org/2017/1040
20. Ishai, Y., Sahai, A., Wagner, D.: Private circuits: securing hardware against probing attacks. In: Boneh, D. (ed.) CRYPTO 2003. LNCS, vol. 2729, pp. 463–481. Springer, Heidelberg (2003). https://doi.org/10.1007/978-3-540-45146-4_27
21. Jean, J., Moradi, A., Peyrin, T., Sasdrich, P.: Bit-sliding: a generic technique for bit-serial implementations of SPN-based primitives - applications to AES, PRESENT and SKINNY. In: Fischer and Homma [13], pp. 687–707
22. Kocher, P., Jaffe, J., Jun, B.: Differential power analysis. In: Wiener, M. (ed.) CRYPTO 1999. LNCS, vol. 1666, pp. 388–397. Springer, Heidelberg (1999). https://doi.org/10.1007/3-540-48405-1_25
23. Kutzner, S., Nguyen, P.H., Poschmann, A., Wang, H.: On 3-share threshold implementations for 4-Bit s-boxes. In: Prouff, E. (ed.) COSADE 2013. LNCS, vol. 7864, pp. 99–113. Springer, Heidelberg (2013). https://doi.org/10.1007/978-3-642-40026-1_7
24. Moradi, A.: Advances in side-channel security. Habilitation thesis, Ruhr-Universität Bochum (2016)
25. Nikova, S., Rechberger, C., Rijmen, V.: Threshold implementations against side-channel attacks and glitches. In: Ning, P., Qing, S., Li, N. (eds.) ICICS 2006. LNCS, vol. 4307, pp. 529–545. Springer, Heidelberg (2006). https://doi.org/10.1007/11935308_38
26. Nikova, S., Rijmen, V., Schläffer, M.: Secure hardware implementation of nonlinear functions in the presence of glitches. J. Cryptol. **24**(2), 292–321 (2011)
27. Reparaz, O.: A note on the security of higher-order threshold implementations. IACR Cryptology ePrint Archive 2015:1 (2015)
28. Reparaz, O., Bilgin, B., Nikova, S., Gierlichs, B., Verbauwhede, I.: Consolidating masking schemes. In: Gennaro, R., Robshaw, M. (eds.) CRYPTO 2015, Part I. LNCS, vol. 9215, pp. 764–783. Springer, Heidelberg (2015). https://doi.org/10.1007/978-3-662-47989-6_37

29. Schneider, T., Moradi, A.: Leakage assessment methodology. In: Güneysu, T., Handschuh, H. (eds.) CHES 2015. LNCS, vol. 9293, pp. 495–513. Springer, Heidelberg (2015). https://doi.org/10.1007/978-3-662-48324-4_25
30. Trichina, E.: Combinational logic design for AES subbyte transformation on masked data. IACR Cryptology ePrint Archive 2003:236 (2003)
31. Ueno, R., Homma, N., Aoki, T.: A systematic design of tamper-resistant Galois-Field arithmetic circuits based on threshold implementation with (d + 1) input shares. In: 47th IEEE International Symposium on Multiple-Valued Logic, ISMVL 2017, Novi Sad, Serbia, 22–24 May 2017, pp. 136–141. IEEE Computer Society (2017)
32. Ueno, R., Homma, N., Aoki, T.: Toward more efficient DPA-resistant AES hardware architecture based on threshold implementation. In: Guilley, S. (ed.) COSADE 2017. LNCS, vol. 10348, pp. 50–64. Springer, Cham (2017). https://doi.org/10.1007/978-3-319-64647-3_4

Author Index

Printed in the United States
By Bookmasters